AF531187

ALL-AMERICAN DEER HUNTER'S GUIDE

Edited by

Jim Zumbo and Robert Elman

WINCHESTER PRESS

An Imprint of New Century Publishers, Inc.

Material in Chapters 1, 5 through 9, 11, 12, 14 through 19, 21 through 23, 25 through 27, and Appendix 1 has been expanded and revised from material in *All About Deer Hunting in America,* edited by Robert Elman, copyright © 1976 by Winchester Press. The editors thank Winchester Press for permission to use this material.

 All inquiries should be addressed to New Century Publishers, Inc., 220 Old New Brunswick Road, Piscataway, N.J. 08854.

Printing Code
11 12 13 14 15 16

Library of Congress Cataloging in Publication Data
Main entry under title:

All-American deer hunter's guide.

1. Deer hunting–United States. I. Zumbo, Jim.
II. Elman, Robert
SK301.A45 1983 799.2′77357 83-18243
ISBN 0-8329-0335-3

Contents

INTRODUCTION *by Robert Elman* v

Part I: Arms, Gear, and Methods for All-American Deer

1 Deer Rifles—And Shotguns *by David Petzal* 3
2 Optimum Optics *by Jim Zumbo* 14
3 Scouting Deer Country *by Jim Zumbo and Robert Elman* 22
4 How Not To Get Lost *by Jim Zumbo* 31
5 The Still-Hunter's Art *by Leonard M. Wright, Jr.* 38
6 The Stand-Hunter's Art *by Jim Carmichel* 48
7 The Art of The Drive *by Robert Elman* 58
8 The Case for Deer Dogs *by Tom Brakefield* 71
9 Getting Into Handgun Hunting *by Steve Ferber* 81
10 Handgun Hunting—The State of the Art *by Bob Good* 89
11 The Art of the Muzzleloading Hunter *by B. R. Hughes* 99
12 Problems and Rewards of Bowhunting *by Russell Tinsley* 108
13 The Trophy Buck *by Jim Zumbo* 118
14 Field-Dressing, Camp Care, Venison, and Buckskins *by John Madson and Jim Zumbo* 134
15 Further Notes on Field Care and Taxidermy *by Robert Elman* 144

Part II: Hunting All-American Whitetails

16 The Deer-Rich Eastern Woodlots *by L. James Bashline* 150
17 Sociable Southern Strategies *by Tom Brakefield* 162
18 Midwestern Ways *by Erwin A. Bauer* 170
19 Southwestern Rattlers and Tower-Sitters *by Byron W. Dalrymple* 180

20 Whitetails of the West *by Jim Zumbo* 192
21 All-American Whitetail Subspecies *by Leonard Lee Rue, III* 200

Part III: Hunting All-American Mule Deer

22 Hunting the Desert Mule Deer *by Sam Fadala* 212
23 High-Country Muleys *by Norman Strung* 224
24 Low-Down and Middle-Country Muleys *by Jim Zumbo* 235
25 The Great Grain-Belt Bucks *by Bert Popowski* 242
26 The West Coast's Blacktail Bonanza *by Norm Nelson* 253
27 Calling All Sitka Blacktails *by Don McKnight* 263
28 Guides and Outfitters—Do You Need Them? *by Jim Zumbo* 271

APPENDICES

1 Distribution of Whitetail Deer and Mule Deer *by Robert Elman* 277
2 Hunting America's Exotic Deer *by Craig Boddington* 280
3 Favorite Venison Recipes *by Lois Zumbo* 293
4 Deer Hunter's All-State Directory 306
5 Who's Who Among Our Authors *by Robert Elman* 328

INDEX 335

INTRODUCTION

Jim Zumbo and I have been hunting partners for several memorable years now. We've hunted together in Wyoming, Utah, Colorado, and New York. He still winces when I remind him about the time, a couple of years back, when he introduced me to a great area for muleys in Wyoming and told me I'd kick myself if I didn't pass up anything less than a 4-pointer with a good spread. It was snowing lightly the first morning as I wheezed and gasped my way up a little mountain and topped out on a flat that was about as large, level, and open as a football field. The thin cover of snow was stitched all over with deer tracks. I'd just settled myself under a stunted, leaning juniper and was regaining my breath when two does appeared, followed by a 4-point buck. The rack wasn't very wide, however—not what Jim would call a really good spread. With three days to go, the decision wasn't all that hard: What the hell, pass him up.

For what seemed like half a minute or so, I watched him through the scope, and then, tiring of the make-believe placing of shots, I stood up. The buck and both does kicked snow and rocks this way and that as they bounded down over the rim. Later that morning, when I met Jim back at the truck, I told him about it; and for the next two days he spent a lot of his time pushing deer toward me—hunting for me rather than himself, worrying that I'd go home without a deer because I'd passed one up as a result of his advice.

That's the way Jim is. He cares about a hunting partner as much as he cares about himself. He cares about the game, too—has a deep understanding, respect, and love of wildlife. Maybe that's why he's such a superb hunter.

I recall one time in Colorado when Bob Good (another superb hunter) watched through binoculars as Jim made his way up one side of a high ridge and down the other to take a bedded buck that had been spotted at a great distance. Jim took his time—more precisely, the better part of the morning—to complete that stalk, using the terrain, the vegetation, and the wind to make sure the buck wouldn't spook before the time came. The deer stood up, turned, twitched his ears, and took perhaps two nervous steps before Jim got off the shot that dropped him. Bob just smiled and said, "Well, I guess you'd have to call that a perfect stalk. It's nice to watch someone do it well." Whether it's hunting or writing about it, if anyone does it well, Jim does.

About that 4-pointer I passed up. You're wondering if I collected a record-book rack on the last day of the hunt. No. But I didn't go home without venison, either. And it didn't bother me that I never found a better buck on that trip. One of the joys I take in hunting, one of the excitements, is not knowing how things are going to turn out. Now matter how good you are, or how experienced, you can't be sure what will happen in the next instant, much less whether you're going to take the biggest buck in the county or leave him there, maybe forever unattainable, but something good to think about until the next trip.

Having passed up the 4-pointer, I killed a nice fat forked-horn buck on the last afternoon, and I took him with one shot at about 90 yards, running. For me, that deer is a splendid trophy. Postscript: Jim and I both got our deer on that trip, and so did a third friend who joined us for a couple of days; when hunter success reaches 100 percent, there's no room for complaint.

My little forkhorn brings to mind another reason why Jim and I get along as partners. We may kid around a lot, but when we're being serious, we both prefer to tell our stories straight. It would be easy to impress readers by writing that I ended the trip with a trophy too big for a den wall. Some outdoor writers do that sort of thing, perhaps figuring that it magnifies their expertise.

There are other writers—Jim among them—who have no need of that. Jim goes just the other way, admitting that he's still learning, has been learning ever since the early days when he hunted whitetails in the woods around West Point, New York, and will be learning still on the evening of the last day he ever spends in the mountains where he loves to hunt mule deer. Maybe that's what makes him a *genuine* expert. And fortunately, the same can be said of the other experts who have worked with us to put this book together. We've been very careful about selecting writers, and that care has paid off. You can trust the information you'll find here, and you can trust all the tips and advice crammed between these covers.

In a way, this book has been in the making ever since 1976, when Winchester Press published my first book on the subject, *All About Deer Hunting in America.* Like the present work, it wasn't written entirely by me. I was determined to fill it with the best information and advice from the country's best deer-hunting authorities, so I recruited 17 top men and had each of them cover a deer-hunting subject in which he was particularly expert. The book was praised by reviewers and has been selling well ever since. Eventually, however, several publishers and a couple of book clubs asked me to compile an even more comprehensive, much larger, and more lavish collection of deer-hunting wisdom—a volume that could rank as the definitive guide to all American deer hunting.

At first I declined because it was too big a job for me to take on by myself. But inevitably, I started talking to my hunting partner about the idea. What about adding a really useful chapter on scouting? That's something that a lot of hunters do incorrectly, if they do it at all. What about adding a chapter on hunting strictly for a trophy? And another on how not to get lost in strange country? And how about a full, up-to-date chapter on optical equipment, which has been improved considerably since 1976, and about which too much misleading literature has been printed? What about today's much improved handguns, handgun loads, and handgun hunting techniques?

The ideas just kept coming: When and how to arrange a guided western hunt and hire an outfitter—and when and how to do it yourself; a collection of tested venison recipes, both for camp cooking and home cooking; an appendix on hunting the exotic deer species—axis, fallow, sika, and red deer—all of which can be hunted on American preserves and some of which have become established as free-ranging wild herds: exotic deer on public land.

One of Jim's ideas struck me as especially valuable. He suggested adding a chapter on hunting whitetails in the West, a subject that has been surprisingly neglected in print despite the fact that there are plenty of Western whitetails and plenty of Western whitetail hunting. There are, after all, some important differences between Eastern and Western whitetail hunting.

We kicked that idea around and ultimately decided it would be smart not only to add the Western whitetail chapter but to add material on hunting every variety of deer *in every type of habitat.* It sounds like a tall order, but Jim Zumbo, who has degrees in forestry and wildlife biology, is a recognized authority on deer habitat and on ways to suit each hunting technique to the behavior of game within a given type of habitat.

At about that point in our discussion, I realized that Jim would be as good a writing and editing partner as he is a hunting partner. If I needed a clincher, it was the appearance of his book, *Hunting America's Mule Deer,* undoubtedly the best work of its kind. Among its splendid features is a state-by-state directory at the back of the book, an extremely useful compendium of facts, tips on the best hunting areas, special seasons, addresses, and so on for anyone who wants to hunt muleys in any state.

I called him up. "Zumbo," I said, "if you'll let me swipe your directory idea and use it in the big, all-inclusive deer book, I'm ready to start work on that book. The only thing is, I still can't do it all myself. I can leave in some of the material from the earlier book—it's good stuff by the top writers—but there's too much to add. So far, I've only solved two of the problems. I'll take your suggestion about getting Craig Boddington to add an appendix on hunting the exotic deer species. No one knows more about that than he does. And I doubt there's a more accomplished handgun hunter than Bob Good, so I'll ask him for a chapter on the state of the art today. Then I've got myself plus the other writers who've agreed to let me use their stuff and add new material to it, and I know I can count on you for a few chapters, but I need more help than that. A lot more. I mean, the object is to make this book the most comprehensive guide for any deer hunter, anywhere."

"Well," Jim said, "what exactly do you need?"

"What do I need? After all the talking we've done you ask me, what do I need? What do you think I need? I need a partner, partner."

"Uncle Bob," he said, "you've got one."

You're holding the result of that partnership in your hands. A lot has gone into this book, and I think you'll get a lot out of it. In my introduction to the 1976 deer-hunting book, I wrote that the outlook for deer hunting in most parts of the country was very good. About the only notable exception was in the Great Lakes states, where I predicted that hunter success ratios would decline, partly owing to the growing numbers of hunters and partly because of habitat loss. The success ratios did drop somewhat in those states, but the deer herds have shown signs of stabilizing or increasing under improved management. Just about everywhere else in the country, whitetails were, and are, increasing both in numbers and range. (No one could have foretold in 1976 that New Jersey would establish half a dozen special seasons or permits in addition to the standard gunning season.) In 1976, the West Coast's blacktails were abundant—too abundant for the habitat in some areas—and that's still true. The regulations seem to be liberal enough, but the blacktails simply aren't as popular among hunters as the Rocky Mountain mule deer, and blacktail habitat in some places is rather daunting to anyone or anything other than a blacktail. Up in Alaska, the Sitka blacktails were, and are, abundant, though restricted in range. Elsewhere, mule deer are generally faring well, their populations recovering in some areas where there had been a decline. The 1981 Utah buck harvest, for example, totaled 76,000, an all-time record. Available habitat is still shrinking, of course, and in a few places whitetails are competing with the mule deer, but game management has become more and more sophisticated and the predictions for the future are optimistic.

Muley hunting has changed somewhat, however. There seem to be fewer truly big bucks than in past years—or maybe the bucks with the best racks have learned to hide from hunters by staying way back in remote, rough terrain, far from the roads that now cover so much of the Western landscape. A mature buck, with 4 points on each antler, has to be more than three years old and is probably more than four if he has a good rack. Having survived several seasons, he has been scared by hunters, perhaps many times, and in all likelihood has had a few narrow escapes. He has learned to avoid the sight, smell, and sounds of the human predator. The supposedly "dumb mule deer" is a creature of the past.

At one time, New Englanders called the ruffed grouse a "fool hen," and it still goes by that name in parts of the upper Northwest where it's seldom hunted. But in the East and Midwest the grouse is now among the wariest of game birds. Increasingly heavy hunting pressure has had the same effect on mule deer. That being the case, both of the common suppositions about the change in muley hunting are undoubtedly true: First, with so many more hunters going after them, more young bucks are being killed and there really are fewer big, mature bucks surviving in many of the herds; second, those that do survive have learned to be as wary as a grouse—or a whitetail.

I don't find the latter development at all depressing. A good buck *should* be hard to take. If the sport were easy, it would be less of a sport.

A brief summary of the current situation, then, would be that deer are more abundant than ever, and game management has improved sufficiently so that the future outlook is good despite diminishing habitat, but really good mule deer bucks are now as hard to come by as good whitetail bucks. The deer hunters who succeed with some consistency now and in the future are those who, like Jim Zumbo, never stop learning no matter how experienced they are. Those, I think, are the hunters who will benefit most from this book and enjoy it most. Whether they're new to the sport or old hands, the material in this volume will give them plenty to think about, plenty to do, plenty of new ideas to try.

That's the most satisfying part of an editor's work in compiling a truly thorough, comprehensive, *all*-American guide. Jim and I will be well satisfied knowing we've helped someone somewhere—or better yet, a lot of someones in a lot of somewheres—to put venison on the table and a trophy on the wall.

Robert Elman
Shirttail Deer Camp

PART I

Arms, Gear, and Methods for All-American Deer

CHAPTER

1

DEER RIFLES—AND SHOTGUNS

by David Petzal

Anyone who has spent some time in a deer camp is aware of the following indisputable facts: The lever-action carbine is the only fit gun for a whitetail hunter. The lever-action carbine is inaccurate and underpowered, and any deer killed with one is a victim of extreme bad luck. The scoped, bolt-action rifle is as out of place in deer woods as a Grand Prix racing car in city traffic. The scoped, bolt-action rifle is the only arm powerful and accurate enough to drop deer dependably under all circumstances, Buckshot is worthless. Buckshot is deadly ... and on, and on.

The reason for these contradictory opinions seems to be that deer hunters are like the blind men describing the elephant. Each man is convinced that the part he touched is what an elephant really is like. Similarly, there are many ways to hunt deer, and the guns and cartridges that work best for each technique and each set of conditions differ considerably. That's why, as you read this book, you'll find that some of the authors disagree with certain of the opinions expressed here, or they may disagree with one another. But bear in mind that they're all experts. What you're getting here isn't the view of a single hunter but the views of many authorities. You'll just have to think hard about the opinions (as well as the out and out facts, which won't prompt much disagreement) and decide which of them will be most relevant to *your* kind of deer hunting. But before we get into the technical end of things, let's take a look at this creature we're hunting. Or rather two creatures. First we'll discuss the whitetail, then the mule deer.

Contrary to what most tyros believe, the average whitetail is neither large, nor tough, nor tenacious of life. A respectable Eastern buck will weigh 150 pounds on the hoof, and the *average* mature male probably goes 20 pounds less. Does are even smaller. Whitetails' hides are not thick, and they lack the massive layers of muscle that make their larger relatives, elk, so hard to drop. So the first concusion we can draw about whitetail arms and cartridges is that, obviously, you don't need a really powerful rifle or a tough-jacketed bullet that offers great penetration.

Indeed, the single greatest cause of lost deer—poor marksmanship aside—is probably the use of heavy bullets designed for larger game. There is, for example, a great difference between the 180- and 150-grain bullet in cartridges such as the .30-06 and .308. The heavier projectile opens up far more slowly, and is suited for game such as elk and moose. On encountering a whitetail, these bullets expand hardly at all, punch their way completely through, and expend very little of their force inside the animal, where it should be spent. A whitetail with a pencil-size hole through its lungs will die eventually, but it will run a long way before it does, and it will not leave much of a blood trail.

A thinner-jacketed 150-grain bullet, traveling at higher speed, will penetrate the hide and then expand, violently. It probably will not exit, but then it won't have to, because a deer struck in the lungs or the heart with such a bomb will do only one thing—drop.

This is one valid argument against the so-called "deer" cartridges such as the

This hunter's rifle is a Winchester Featherweight Model 70, a deservedly popular choice where much hiking or climbing is done. His efforts resulted in a fine muley buck killed high on a Montana mountain. *(Courtesy of Montana Department of Fish, Wildlife and Parks)*

.30-30, .32 Special, and .35 Remington. The first of these cartridges (the second is even less effective) pushes a 150-grain bullet at 2,400 feet per second. The .30-06, by comparison, drives a bullet of the same weight a full 500 fps faster. The slower velocity is just not sufficient to impart quick expansion to a bullet of any type, and things are made worse by the fact that many ill-informed hunters use 170-grain .30-30 loads, which move out at only 2,200 fps. The .35 Remington is a little better. Its ballistics are the same, but by virtue of its larger bullet diameter, it punches a slightly bigger hole.

So why, you ask, have so many million lever-action carbines been sold, and why do so many people still use them? The answer is twofold: First, the .30-30 was considered a red-hot high-velocity cartridge ... 70 years ago. Second, and more important, the light, short-barreled, fast-shooting guns chambered for it are wonderfully handy in the dense, brushy country where so much whitetail hunting is done. A lot of these guns were sold because they were the best there was at the time. They're still wonderfully handy, but are they still the best or is much of their attraction a matter of tradition? These guns come equipped with open iron sights that are next to worthless and, on some of them, scope mounting is a problem. Rear peep sights on these guns would be fine, except that many of the people who buy them don't bother to have such sights installed. With fine modern rifles available from the very same manufacturers, you can see why the old thutty-thutty does not get a top recommendation.

Light, Mannlicher-stocked carbines are popular in whitetail habitat, where you may get a shot at a deer at any distance from a few yards to 100 or more. In brushy woods, you don't want an extreme-velocity varmint rifle or a firearm that shoots a big, slow-moving bullet, but something in between.

Short, light, quick-handling guns are indispensable to one of the several tactics that deer hunters use—still-hunting. Still-hunters are in frequent motion, and because of this, when a deer is spotted, things happen fast. You may kick one out of a tangled thicket and have no more time to draw a bead on it than a grouse hunter swinging on a partridge. So the last thing you want is a 10-pound rifle with a 24-inch barrel and a 6× scope. Speed is of the essence.

Autoloaders have an advantage over levers or pumps because their gas-operated actions soften recoil, and that, together with the fact that you don't have to pump or lever anything, allows you to get off a quicker second shot.

At left is a custom .30-06, stocked in the Mannlicher style, employing a Springfield action and a 20-inch barrel, and mounted with a 2¾X scope. Author David Petzal won't call it an ideal whitetail rifle, but he says it comes close. At right is a custom-built .280 with a 2X-7X variable scope that has served Petzal well in muley country.

There are a number of excellent autoloaders on the market—Browning, H&R, Remington, Ruger, and Winchester all make good ones—chambered for a wide variety of appropriate cartridges, including .270, .280, .308, .30-06, and .44 Magnum. All of these will do just fine.

But what of that second piece of ordnance mentioned at the outset, the scoped, bolt-action rifle? Well, it's what many of us really prefer to use. This type of arm places a premium on precision, on driving one shot right where you want it, at short and long range alike.

The other primary style of deer hunting—sit and wait—is the province of the precision shooter. When you're moving, the odds are against your seeing a whitetail before he sees you (unless there's soft snow on the ground, or the woods are wet, or you're an exceptionally skillful stalker, or any combination of these). Very often, it makes sense to lurk, especially if the woods are full of hunters who are keeping the deer moving.

So you find a comfortable stump to lean against, making sure there's some brush near you to break up your outline, and that you have a clear field of fire. Your stand may overlook a deer trail, and your shot may be taken at only 25 yards, or it may open on an apple orchard 100 yards distant or a powerline right-of-way where venison may appear 300 yards off.

If this is your approach to the sport, what you want is an accurate bolt-action in any caliber from .243 or 6mm up through .30-06. Nothing smaller, nothing bigger. Those who use 7mm and .30 Magnums on whitetails are kidding themselves. A whitetail will drop no faster from a .300 Weatherby than from a .30-06. More important, the .300 has a 24-inch barrel, should weigh about nine pounds if it's not to tear your shoulder off, kicks more, and has far more muzzle blast than the smaller gun. For bigger game the Magnums are great, but not for whitetail.

As long as you stick to the standard calibers, the choice of cartridge is perhaps not so important as the choice of bullet. For example, if you're using a 6mm, don't use the 80-grain projectile, which is strictly for varmints and will blow up on a deer's hide. Take the trouble to read the information on the ammunition box before you buy it, and make note of the type of game for which it's intended. If you're a handloader, all of the major bullet companies supply excellent data on the construction and design of their various projectiles.

A word or two about sights: Scopes are better than iron sights in just about all circumstances, and low-powered scopes are better than high-powered ones which, for whitetail hunting, are useless in typical Eastern and Midwestern woodland situations. A whitetail hunter sitting in a Texas tower stand, however, might find a high-powered or variable scope very useful since some shots will be at long ranges and deer are sometimes tough to identify as to sex in the heavy brush.

A scope offers the following advantages over iron sights (both open and peep): It puts both the sighting device—the reticle—and the target on the same optical plane, which enables you to keep everything in focus. At dawn and twilight, it actually gathers light. And, perhaps most important, the magnification allows you to see just what you're shooting at: buck or doe, good head or mediocre.

Using a 4× scope, you can sometimes look into dense brush and pick out the outline of a deer, simply because the magnified image enables you to discern an ear or an antler. You can't do that with iron sights. And of course, for a long shot, a scope is invaluable.

Of all magnifications, the 4× is by far the most popular for general big-game hunting, but for whitetails the 1×-4× or 1.5×-5× variable can't be surpassed. When it's cranked down to its lowest power, you can see the whole world and pick up a running buck with no hesitation. When it's turned up to a higher degree of magnification, you enjoy all the benefits of a fixed-power scope.

The one drawback to these instruments, aside from an extra ounce or two of weight, is the fact that they cost more than fixed powers. So if the budget limitations are a problem, you might look at a 2½×, 2¾×, or 3× model.

As for reticles, again the choice is simple. The writers appearing in this book may not agree about some things, but there's no question that most of us prefer the Duplex reticle originated by Leupold and offered by other scope manufacturers

Dave Petzal favors these three cartridges for both whitetails and mule deer. From left, they are the .270, the .280, and the universal cartridge—.30-06. He cautions against overweight bullets in the cartridge you choose. See the text for specific recommendations.

In an area where only shotguns can be used, a hunter aims from his tree stand with a 12-gauge pump that's equipped with a slug barrel and rifle-type sights. Such sights are far better than a shotgun bead, but the author prefers a scope.

under a variety of names. This reticle consists of heavy crosshairs which taper abruptly at the center of the lens. They draw the eye to the intersection of the wires, and this enables you to pick up a target quickly and/or in poor light. The fine wires at the center allow you to shoot at distant targets without the crosshairs subtending too much.

It should be added that every deer hunter would do well to add to his gear a set of binoculars. In a subsequent chapter, Jim Zumbo will provide more detailed advice on telescopic sights, binoculars, and other optical equipment.

In some areas, rifles are forbidden for deer hunting, and you are constrained to use either rifled slugs or buckshot. If the area in question specifies buckshot only, you might think about hunting somewhere else unless you restrict your shots to 30 yards or so. Sorry about that, but experiments have shown that beyond that distance, 00 buck does not pattern consistently enough to ensure clean kills.

Happily, rifled slugs are a different matter. In a slug barrel with good sights, they are extremely accurate up to 75 yards, and occasionally you'll get an exceptional gun that will shoot them accurately at 100 yards. If you are serious about collecting a deer with rifled slugs, as opposed to just taking an optimistic walk in the woods with a shotgun, you ought to get a pump or autoloader with a slug barrel. The nice thing about this arrangement is that such a gun can be equipped with a variety of other barrels as well, and can earn its keep at a number of different pursuits.

You'll find that a 12-gauge pump gun equipped with a slug barrel and a 2× intermediate-eye-relief scope is more accurate, within its range limitations, than any whitetail would ever require. Slug barrels come equipped with open sights, which are a lot better than a plain shotgun bead, but if you can arrange to have a low-power scope mounted on your scattergun you are way ahead of the game. Some states allow you to hunt deer with a 20-gauge slug. Don't. It is at best a marginal projectile, and the 12 is far better.

Mule deer are a different story. Whereas the average shot at a whitetail is probably taken at something less than 100 yards, a great many mule deer are collected at 200. Whitetails are creatures of the dense

A deer rifle is only as good as the person who shoots it. This hunter is using the prone position to steady his firearm. Skilled hunters don't take offhand shots unless there's no other choice.

woods and thickets; muleys are, typically, residents of the forests and sage flats of the West. You may get a close shot at a muley, but the odds are just as likely that you'll get a long one.

These big-eared critters are larger than whitetails. A good mature buck will run upwards of 150 pounds, and 200-plus-pounders are not at all rare. But like whitetails, they are not made of steel, so the same remarks apply ... almost. Muleys are a little tougher because of their greater size, but not much.

For this reason a .243 or a 6mm is not a top choice for mule-deer hunting. Out at long yardages, these two numbers lack the steam you want. Perhaps nothing is "ideal" for any type of game, but where mule deer are concerned, you can't do any beter than a .270. This cartridge has it all: flat trajectory, mild recoil, and great killing power. Way out on the prairie, as the song goes, if you were to check all the rifles riding around in pickup trucks, the .270 would be among the most common.

However, there are a few other cartridges which may be as good. These are the .25-06 with the 120-grain bullet, the .280 with the 150-grainer, .284 with the same weight projectile, and the .30-06 with the 150- or 165-grain bullet. The chances are that you could shoot mule deer the rest of your life with these and never notice any real difference in effectiveness. For mule deer, by the way, the 130-grain bullet is excellent in the .270, although for hunting where there are elk, the 150-grain load has obvious advantages.

Since much of your shooting will be at long range, you'll want the most accurate rifle possible, and speed of fire will take a back seat. Here the bolt-action has no real competition. An important suggestion here: Before you use the rifle seriously, have a gunsmith tune up the trigger. For some reason, most bolt-actions have excellent adjustable trigger mechanisms which are not excellently adjusted at the factory. A good bolt-action trigger should break at three to four pounds, and break clean, with no creep or drag.

As for sights, almost nobody uses iron anymore, and just about everyone seems to like the 4× scope. It's a fine choice, though a 2×-7× variable is highly useful. But all things considered, the 4× is just about tops. Reticle choice? Again the Duplex, or one like it.

You're apt to do a lot of hiking in muley country (or, come to think of it, in certain kinds of whitetail country) so you don't want as heavy and bulky a scope as some of the higher-powered variables. In fact, a lot of us don't want to tote a mule deer rifle that weighs more than 8¼ pounds scoped, loaded, and with the sling.

Here, at least, is an area of close agreement. Jim Zumbo, co-editor of this volume, has been living and hunting in prime muley country for 20 years and, like many others, he emphatically confirms these observations about weight. His favorite rifle isn't the aforementioned .270 but a .30-06—another universally popular choice in the West. Specifically, his favorite is a pre-1964 Model 70 Winchester Featherweight .30-06 topped with a Weaver 4× scope. It's light enough that he doesn't

Well-known guide and outdoor writer Norm Strung kneels beside a good muley he took with a lung shot from a .270 at 200 yards. The buck ran about 100 yards and collapsed. Clean one-shot kills like this are what rifle selection is all about.

mind trudging and climbing with it, and it packs enough wallop to put his quarry down quickly and humanely.

Though many hunters successfully hunt muleys with a .243, 6mm, or similar caliber, you're much better off with a gun that performs well when the situation is bad. "Bad" means a big old muley buck busts through a dense spruce blowdown in Montana or scrambles through an oak-brush tangle in Colorado. In those instances, you don't have the opportunity to place the bullet precisely where you want it, as you would if the buck were standing still. Obviously, the projectile will need enough foot-pounds of energy to get the job done even if it isn't exactly on the mark. The angle of the shot might require the bullet to get through a shoulder bone, penetrate deep into the vitals, or zip through a lot of flesh to reach the chest area.

Too many hunters tend to use calibers as puny as the law allows, because of the challenge of dropping a deer with a less-than-average caliber. We all like to brag a little about our prowess. But if you need to prove yourself, you can always take up skydiving. When you're hunting deer, kill the quarry dead as fast as you can with the first shot. You can argue all night long around the campfire about how bullet placement is the prime consideration, but that argument only holds water *if* your deer is cooperative. If you hunt enough, you'll be faced with tough shots sooner or later. Your shot might be too high, too low, too far back, or whatever. That's when you want a firearm suitable to the task.

Even if most of your shots are made at less than 200 yards, now and then a buster buck will be way out there. When that happens you want to know your rifle well enough so you can make the correct judgment for bullet drop. For that reason, you should stick with one favorite deer rifle.

Being familiar with a rifle is an all-important requirement, because you never know what to expect. Mule deer are supposed to be creatures of the wide-open spaces, but you'd better be prepared for anything. Tens of thousands of Rocky Mountain mule deer are killed every year in jungles as thick as whitetail country. Don't fret about owning the flattest-shooting rifle in the land. Indeed, select one with a reasonably flat trajectory, then learn how it shoots at different yardages. That may be the most important thing you do.

Blacktail deer, which are really just a couple of subspecies of mule deer, present the same basic requirements as any other deer, but much of the country they inhabit is unbelievably dense, especially in the Western coastal forests. In some blacktail habitat, on the other hand, vegetation is fairly open.

If you're hunting in typically horrid blacktail country where visibility is measured in feet instead of yards, you'll want a firearm you can handle in dense brush. That doesn't mean a so-called "brush-buster." Most ballistics experts will tell you that a bullet plowing through brush to the target is a figment of several writers' imaginations. Despite that old myth, a slow-moving .35 or .30-30 is no better than the zippy .243 or other quickstepping rounds. So—the same advice that applies to a whitetail rifle applies to a blacktail rifle.

As for the type of action to use, settle on whatever works best for you. Don't be too obsessed with getting off a quick second shot in the heavy brush. Instead, worry about getting the *first* shot off accurately;

This buck mule deer was taken by co-editor Jim Zumbo using his .30-06 Winchester Featherweight Model 70. This rifle has become Zumbo's exclusive choice for both whitetails and muleys. The Featherweight (or a similarly light rifle) makes sense for a hunter like Zumbo, who is admittedly impatient on stand and does a lot of still-hunting—walking and climbing.

you might have only a second to identify the target, snap the gun to your shoulder, and shoot. Obviously, any firearm, no matter what kind of action it has, will let you get the first shot off cleanly if you've practiced enough to know how.

There will be situations when a running deer is partially in sight as it flashes through the vegetation. In that instance, an autoloader has an advantage because you don't need to disrupt your sight picture of the fleeting animal to chamber a second round. On the other hand, you don't want to bang away at a fleeing target just because you catch glimpses of it in the vegetation. You should shoot only when you're confident you can hit a vital area, which means you *must* pick your shots at a partially obscured deer, particularly if it's moving.

An extremely important quality of a blacktail rifle is its ability to perform under damp conditions. Rain and fog and persistent drizzle are common in the blacktail forests, requiring you to use a firearm that won't fail you at the moment of truth. If you've cared for your gun and oiled it regularly, you shouldn't have a problem.

Optics can be a big worry if your scope fogs up or if you can't keep the front and rear lenses wiped dry enough to see clearly. Scope caps help in this regard, but sometimes the necessity of removing the caps quickly can cost you a shot at a deer. The spring-loaded caps that flick away at the touch of a finger are a big asset.

Some blacktail hunters shun scopes completely and use open sights. Others use a swing-away scope mount that flips the scope down and lets them use the iron sights underneath. Still others use the high, "see-through" mounts for an instant choice of optics or iron.

Of course, much of this discussion boils down to the fact that you should use a firearm in which you feel confident and with which you're familiar. Confident—not overconfident. The 7mm Magnum, for example, is a fine choice for muleys, except that too many hunters seem to believe it can perform miracles. Well, you can't do better than the .270 or .30-06.

Choose your gun carefully, and then punch plenty of holes through paper at different ranges. Don't be satisfied with merely making a close group at 100 yards. Get to know your gun well. You'll be rewarded when you're suddenly face to face with the buck of your fantasies. When you earn that shot, you and your gun must be able to perform, but the emphasis is on you.

CHAPTER 2

OPTIMUM OPTICS

by Jim Zumbo

No deer hunter should be afield without proper optical equipment. Binoculars and a riflescope are often mandatory, and in some cases a spotting scope is a good idea, especially in the open country of the West.

There was a time when I saw little advantage in using binoculars—back when I had just a few years of hunting experience. I figured my riflescope was sufficient to glass open country for animals and to look for antlers on distant deer. But no more. A good set of binoculars is a must whenever I hunt deer. They've been invaluable, and on occasion have made the difference between a successful and unsuccessful hunt.

Buy the best binoculars you can afford. Cheap glasses can let you down when you need them most. Picture yourself glassing a heard of deer across a canyon but being unable to see antlers because your binoculars are inferior. A most frustrating experience, and one that doesn't have to happen.

Avoid buying inexpensive glasses from a mail-order catalog. You won't be able to test them, and you could be stuck if they're of poor quality. Purchase binoculars from a retail store and look them over before you buy. If possible, take them outside the store and try them. The best time to do this is in the afternoon when the light is poor. There are a number of well-known, dependable glasses that you can safely purchase without worrying about their performance. Your binoculars must give a crisp image. Otherwise they're useless.

The type of binoculars you buy depends on the primary use you have planned for them. If you hunt on foot a great deal and travel a long way through rugged deer country, you'll probably want a lightweight model. However, if you spend most of your deer hunting hours in a tree stand, a heavier model won't be a problem.

There are two basic binocular designs: the Porro prism and the roof prism. The Porro is the common one that has been around for years and will no doubt be here for many more. The typical binocular design employs two prismatic erecting telescopes that appear as one when you look through them. The prisms place the image in the normal viewing position. The Porro prism requires that the binoculars have the typical offset profile because of the interior structure. The roof prism eliminates the offset housing and creates a straight-looking design which is less bulky and weighs less. Personally, I prefer the Porro prism binoculars, as they're now available in excellent, reasonably priced models that

Binoculars are an asset in every kind of deer country, regardless of terrain and vegetation. Here, Montana hunters glass for mule deer moving down from the high plateaus. *(Courtesy of Montana Chamber of Commerce)*

aren't nearly as bulky as they used to be. some models, in fact, are very compact.

A pivoting hinge connects the twin binocular tubes so they can be adjusted to fit the eyes. Various focusing systems are currently in use. The oldest—and most impractical—is a focusing ring on each tube which requires you to turn each one until proper focus is achieved. Another system is a single wheel, between the barrels, which is turned until the tubes come into focus. A system introduced not long ago by Bushnell, called Insta-Focus, has a flat focusing lever between the tubes. Easily pressed by a finger, this lever allows for quick focus with a minimum of effort.

Binoculars are rated by two sets of figures, such as 7 × 35. The first figure refers to magnifying power, the second to the diameter of the objective lens in millimeters. The objective lens is the one farthest from the eye, while the lens in the rear, closest to the eye, is the ocular lens.

This sportsman is giving his riflescope a final check to be sure it's still properly sighted-in before hunting. A traveling hunter should always do this, because the jarring that occurs on a trip can alter the scope's adjustments.

The relative brightness factor is important to the deer hunter because it indicates light-gathering capabilities in poor light. To calculate relative brightness, let's say you have 7 × 35 binoculars. Divide the diameter of the objective lens by the power, square the result, and you get relative brightness. Thus, by dividing 35 by 7 you get 5, and 5 squared is 25. Relative brightness of 7 × 35 binoculars is 25. You get the same results with a 6 × 30 or 8 × 40 model. But take the 7 × 50. After dividing, you get 7.1, which figures out to a relative brightness of 50.4. These binoculars therefore have twice the brightness of the 7 × 35 and will perform well during the early and late hours of the day when deer are on the move. However, a 50mm objective lens is considerably bigger than a 35 mm lens, so 7 × 50 binoculars would be heavier and more bulky than the 7 × 35. In selecting binoculars, you have to weigh the advantages against the disadvantages for your kind of hunting.

For the average hunter (if there is any such thing) the good old 7 × 35 is probably the best choice. But for long-range glassing in very open Western terrain, I also have a pair of 10 × 50 binoculars.

More important than binocular design is your ability to use binoculars correctly. Too many hunters don't take the time to glass properly—or they don't glass enough—especially in whitetail country where binoculars are sometimes considered unnecessary. And even in the West, where the need for glassing is more obvious, some hunters don't seem to have the patience or concentration for it.

I recall a Texas deer hunt a few years back when I was waiting in a stand for a buck to show. Although I had my binocu-

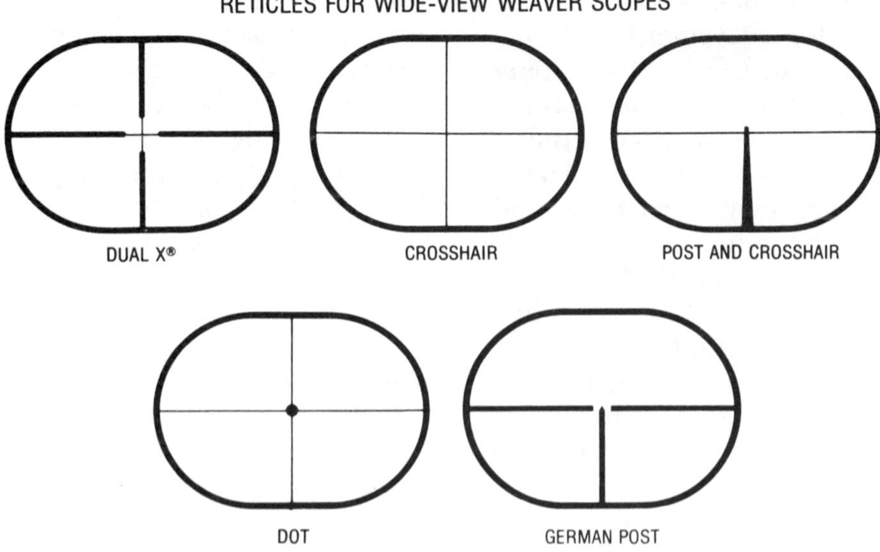

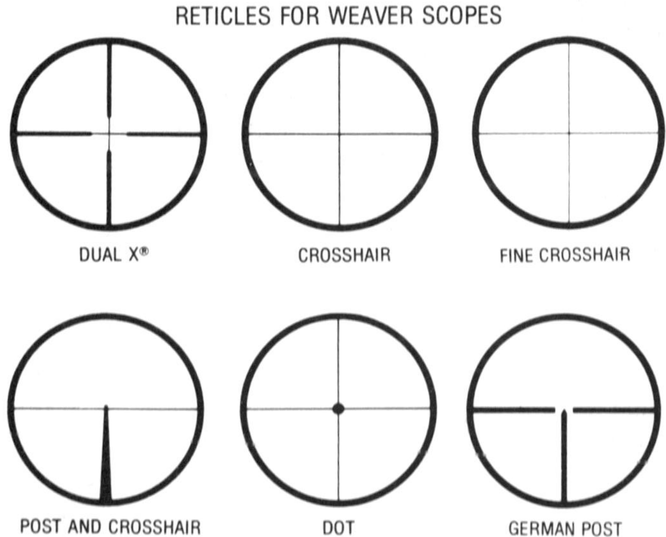

This drawing of Weaver Scope reticles shows the variety of reticle styles available today. The more popular ones are marketed by a number of manufacturers. Probably the most popular of all is the dual-thickness crosshair design, called Dual X by Weaver.

lars along, I used them half-heartedly, mostly looking for movement with my naked eyes. I failed to spot a buck slipping through some sparse brush until it was too late. The poor early-morning light didn't help. I should have used my binoculars.

There are places in Eastern hardwood forests, Southern swamps, and other thickly vegetated areas where binoculars can be an enormous asset. Once, while hunting whitetails in South Carolina, I sat in a stand while fog shrouded much of the woods. By using my binoculars intently, I managed to spot a buck and two does sneaking along the edge of a field. I killed the buck, and I'm sure I never would have spotted him without optical help. Bear in mind that binoculars, like riflescopes, gather light.

Mule deer country is often relatively open. Binoculars are a must for the serious hunter in that terrain. There is too much acreage to look over with the naked eye, and a lot of it is simply too far away. There's no such thing as too much glassing if you're in prime deer country, or even if you're in a marginal place.

No matter where you hunt, deer will be on the move just as darkness gives way to morning light. During those precious minutes, you need to be intently glassing for shapes in the poor light. As dawn progresses, glass every obvious place around you. Look *into* brush for movement or telltale colors and shapes that betray deer. When you glass the obvious spots, also look into areas that are not so obvious. Thoroughly glass the edges of cover where deer are apt to be moving. Remember that in the morning deer will be moving from feeding to bedding areas. In late afternoon they'll reverse the pattern and head from bedding to feeding areas. You can position yourself accordingly if you're familiar with the area and use the glasses to help locate animals when light is poor.

Still-hunting is my favorite technique, whether I'm pursuing whitetails or mule deer. I use glasses constantly, and more than once I've been lucky enough to spot a bedded buck. Deer are seldom motionless, whatever they're doing. A bedded deer may move its head slightly now and then; it might be chewing its cud, or twitching its tail. These little movements can be spotted by a sharp-eyed observer. Of course, you need to have a lot going for you to pick up a deer before it sees you, whether it's bedded or moving about. The wind must be right, there must be adequate screening cover to allow you to slip up unnoticed, and you must be able to walk silently.

There are times, of course, when you'll spook deer and see only flashes of them as they run off in brush. That's when you might not have time to make a quick identification with binoculars. You'll need to rely on your riflescope, another crucial optical item. A scope will allow you to make an instant decision—to tell immediately if the quarry is wearing antlers and, if so, how good they are.

There are plenty of hunters who don't use scopes, but I'm a firm believer in them, regardless of the country I'm in. My favorite deer rifle is equipped with a 4× Weaver scope with a dot reticle. Countless times it has meant the difference between venison on the table and an unfilled deer tag.

I'll come back to the subject of reticles in due course, but right here I should explain why I use the dot rather than crosshairs, dual-thickness crosshairs, or a post. After all, the dot isn't nearly as popular as it once

A spotting scope comes in handy where long-range glassing is essential. This Westerner uses it to check for mule deer on a distant slope.

was, and probably for good reason. I use it because it was one of the best available designs when I bought the scope, it worked well for me, and I'm so accustomed to it that I can shoot naturally, quickly, and accurately with it. That doesn't mean it would necessarily be the best choice for another hunter. As stated elsewhere in this book, the only right equipment is whatever works well for you.

On the other hand, that approach can be carried too far. I can hear someone out there saying, "Okay, Zumbo, I'll take you at your word. Open sights work for me." My answer: If that's so, you probably haven't given the scope a fair try—or else your deer hunting is a lot more specialized than mine. Furthermore, your scope can be installed on mounts that give you an instant choice between the optical and iron sight. More on that, too, in due course.

I recall an instance in whitetail country when a scope would have turned a friend's unsuccessful hunt into a successful one. I was hunting with a buddy, and I had killed a buck early in the morning. After dressing the buck, we left it to drive my truck closer to it for loading. On the way out of the woods we jumped a herd of whitetails. Out of instinct, I brought up my empty rifle and scoped them. I made out antlers on two deer as they moved through a hardwood forest. Both were spikes whose antlers were difficult to spot.

My buddy, who was an inexperienced hunter, threw his open-sighted rifle up to his shoulder and took a bead on the deer but didn't shoot because he couldn't tell which were bucks. The deer weren't moving rapidly, and occasionally they stopped and pranced about nervously. I constantly gave instructions to my pal, telling him which of the deer were bucks, but he wasn't able to make a positive identification as the deer kept moving. I kept pointing out the bucks, but my friend didn't shoot. I respected him for his ethics in not shooting at a questionable deer, but the fact that he had no scope meant he didn't score. It was particularly frustrating because both bucks were easily shootable a number of times.

Some hunters feel that a scope is a disadvantage in thick woods because it's tough to follow a moving deer with a scope and maintain an accurate sight picture. I disagree, perhaps because I'm familiar enough with my scope so that I can use it effectively regardless of the cover. As soon as I'm on a buck I like, I flick off the safety, lightly place my finger on the trigger, and track the moving deer. When the sight picture is right, I squeeze. This, obviously, is why every hunter should practice as much as possible with a scoped rifle.

People who are unfamiliar with scopes sometimes think these instruments are automatic deer-killers. All you need to do is look through a scope and the deer is as good as dead, they say. The truth is, it's just as easy to miss with a scope as with an open-sighted rifle. Sure, a scope gathers light, provides a single sighting plane, magnifies the quarry, and allows you to draw a much finer bead. If anything, the magnification will work against you because the sight picture inevitably wavers with your movement, your heartbeat, your unsteady hand, and this wavering will be magnified. The higher the magnification, the more wavering you get.

Scopes are classified by power, meaning magnification, and most deer hunters use powers from 4× to 9×. Variable scopes are popular, allowing the shooter to zoom from a low to high power. The 3×-9× is perhaps the most popular of the bunch. Experienced shooters commonly use the high power to probe for details on a distant buck or to look into screening brush and then back down to 3× or 4× to shoot. The lower setting reduces the waver and still gives you enough magnification for precise aiming.

The riflescope has an objective lens at the front of the tube and an ocular lens at the rear. An erecting lens between the two returns the image to normal after the objective lens brings it in upside-down. The ocular lens magnifies the image.

The reticle is the internal structure that allows the shooter to line up the target. It can be a standard crosshair pattern, or a dot, post, or combination. Some reticles allow you to estimate distances by lining up the target with a series of calibrated horizontal lines or other means. Then you can compensate for bullet drop at the range of the quarry.

On the chance that some reader, somewhere, has never used crosshairs, I'll specify here that they consist of two black lines, one horizontal and one vertical, which intersect at the center of the reticle. The intersection is, of course, the aiming point. A post is a thicker vertical line, usually tapered from a thick bottom to a thin top, which extends up to the center of the reticle. A dot is just that—a dot in the center of the reticle; as a rule, it's employed with crosshairs and simply accentuates the aiming point. A dual-thickness crosshair design is one in which the crosshairs are relatively thick from the outer edges of the reticle almost to the center and then, abruptly, taper to thin lines. The thick portions draw your eye to the center, enabling you to get your sight picture fast, and thin portions allow for precise aiming since they subtend (or cover) very little of the target. There are variations on all these themes, but there you have the essential features.

Currently, the dual-thickness crosshair design is by far the most popular, and there's no doubt that it's excellent. Regardless of reticle type, you can get a standard scope or one with a wide (rather than round) ocular lens, which gives you a wider field of view. This lets you find your target fast, and it's probably especially useful to shooters who aren't thoroughly accustomed to shooting with a scope.

Scopes come in a variety of models. Besides offering a sharp image, your scope should be waterproof. The last thing you want is a foggy scope at the moment when a big buck saunters into view. Scope caps are a wise investment.

Scopes can be mounted so they swing off to the side with a flip of the finger. Or they can be mounted high enough so you can use the iron sights beneath at will.

With swing-off mounts, you can flip the scope out of the way quickly, but you do have to go through the motion of moving it before you can use the iron sights. A moment is thus lost before the shot. Moreover, with some swing-off mounts, there's a possibility that you won't flip your scope back into perfect zero position; or at least that's a theory, and one I believe. They aren't my favorite, but I have to admit that a number of extremely experienced and successful hunters swear by them.

The see-through mounts remain stationary. They're merely high and arched to form a tunnel under the scope, through which you can use the iron sights instantly. You just tilt your head up slightly to sight through the scope or down slightly to aim with the open sights. Thus you have an instant choice. And that's something very good to have if you unexpectedly find your scope is inoperable or if you get a close shot at a deer running through brush. These mounts get my vote if you feel you need the open-sight option.

Your scope will be useless if you can't shoot accurately with it. It's of paramount importance to sight the scope so your gun shoots where you want at different yardages. Take your rifle out to a range and adjust your scope. When you arrive at your hunting area, take the time to resight just to be sure, especially if you've traveled a distance. A rifle will be bounced around, and it's possible to jar the scope so it will lose its zero. By all means, if you fly to your hunt, make *sure* you resight. The vibration on a jetliner can alter your scope's adjustment, requiring you to sight it in again.

Spotting scopes are essentially big, sturdy telescopes used to locate game in the distance. In open country, a spotting scope is a handy item, especially if you're the discriminating type and want a better look at far-off antlers. The magnification of some spotting scopes is only 15×; with others it may be as high as 65×, and many are zoom models with adjustable (variable) power. You'll need a steady hold to look through the scope at the higher magnifications. Most models have attachments for a tripod (or come with a tripod) and some have attachments that enable you to clamp the scope to the window of a vehicle.

Not many deer hunters will ever need a 65× spotting scope (though I've used one to get a good look at a buck two miles away). But a scope of somewhat lower power is a definite asset in open-terrain mule deer hunting. The one I use is a zoom model with an adjustment ring that sets magnification at any power from 16× to 36×.

Don't overlook optical equipment on your deer hunt. While it's nice to meet the challenge with a minimum of equipment, optics can make or break your hunt.

CHAPTER

3

SCOUTING DEER COUNTRY

by Jim Zumbo and Robert Elman

Scouting is an essential part of hunting that is usually done too little, too much, or incorrectly. Few hunters scout to their advantage, which is unfortunate because it can make the difference between success and failure.

The chief reason for scouting is simply to determine whether deer are in the area you're planning to hunt. That's the basic principle. Beyond that, scouting can tell you much about deer habits as well as the size of the bucks that inhabit the area. If you're a trophy hunter, your scouting might be very intense, as your objective might be to locate a particular buck. To that end, you would actually look for individual deer before the season rather than observing routine deer sign.

Scouting is often unnecessary if you're familiar with the country you're hunting and you're confident that you know the behavior patterns of your quarry. If you don't, you should scout.

Before you start, learn all you can about the quarry you intend to pursue. Perhaps the most important factor is the daily habit pattern of deer in the hunting area. Home range varies with the kind of deer you're hunting as well as the landscape. Whitetail in good habitat, for example, tend to have a rather small home range if they haven't been stirred by hunting pressure. If you know that whitetails in a chosen area travel no more than a one-mile radius, you'll have a good idea of their daily movements. Unfortuately, you can't easily find out this information. It's a matter of judging the area you're hunting as well as other factors, such as the availability of water, feed, and the number of animals using an area. The time of year makes a difference as well, since deer move a great deal more

Colorado hunter Kirt Darner, who has taken nine record-book deer, is shown as he looks over a buck rub and signs of browsing.

during the breeding time than at other periods.

If you know something about daily movement, you can utilize the information that you gathered while scouting, assuming that your scouting efforts were directed toward locating habitat-use by deer and then finding those deer when the season begins. In many cases, you aren't actually looking for deer in the woods when you scout, but for clues that indicate they're in the area.

How do you find these clues and what are they? The most obvious, whether you're looking for whitetails or mule deer, are tracks. No deer walks without leaving footprints, unless it's traveling on rock. Tracks in leaves might be all but impossible to recognize, so you'll have to look where tracks are distinct. Snow on the ground makes the quest easy, but snow doesn't fall at your convenience.

The presence of tracks isn't enough to evaluate an area. You want to determine how fresh the tracks are, guess whether they were made by a buck or doe, and figure out what the deer was doing when it made the tracks. Let's take these chores one at a time.

It's difficult to tell precisely how fresh a track is, unless snow is present, and even snow isn't always a reliable indicator.

Tracks might appear fresh even though they're several days old. As a rule, tracks with sharp edges and well-defined outlines are reasonably fresh. Bits of soil, leaves, or crumbly edges usually denote a weathered track, made some time ago. The exact time the track was made isn't very important in this instance, because the reason for scouting is basically to determine the presence of deer. When you're actually hunting with gun or bow in hand and a deer tag in your pocket, then it's another story.

The matter of guessing whether a buck or doe made a track is just that: a guess. You've probably read and heard all sorts of sure-fire ways to tell the difference. There is no reliable method. There's only one *positive* way to tell, and that's to see the animal standing in the tracks. Bucks are bigger than does on the average and make bigger tracks, but we've all seen mighty big does leave tracks that we thought were made by bucks. A really big buck, one that will dress around 180 or 200 pounds, will leave a big enough track that you can be fairly certain the maker of the prints is wearing antlers on his head. Single tracks often indicate a buck because bucks are more apt to be loners. Does tend to remain in groups, but not always.

Snow can be a big help in scouting. Most of the tracks in this picture have begun to melt away, but some of them—as well as bare spots where deer have fed through the snow—are fairly fresh.

With a bit of common sense and close observation, you can figure what deer were doing and where they were going when they made the tracks. If you see several sets of tracks meandering about aimlessly, you can generally assume a herd of deer fed in the spot. Retain that information in your memory—you've located a feeding area that might be worth checking in the early morning or late afternoon. If feeding is extensive, you might consider finding a tree to watch from or a ground blind. If the tracks are heading in a straight direction, you might have found a route that deer use to move from feeding to bedding areas or vice versa, or to watering areas. Enough tracks might make the route worthy of investigation. If you're hunting in late fall and heavy snows are falling, tracks that are headed in one direction might mean that deer are migrating to winter yards or winter ranges. If you're in whitetail country and you know where winter yards are, check them out. If you're in the West, muleys might travel 40 or 50 miles to get to winter ranges, requiring a major effort on your part to find the deer.

Another sign to look for, one not usually mentioned in articles about scouting, is a bedding site. Don't confuse beds with scrapes (which we'll discuss later). Several deer beds are an indication that you've obviously stumbled into a bedding area.

Summertime hikes with a camera may tell you whether an area is heavily frequented by deer. Keep in mind, however, that by the time the season opens the animals may have switched some of their feeding-to-bedding-area routes. *(Photo by Larry Elman)*

This doesn't mean deer will necessarily return to the area, but if they liked it once they'll like it again. A deer bed is a flattened spot, usually oval in shape. The weight of the deer's body compresses the grass and leaves, and deer often paw away brush and debris before lying down.

Droppings obviously indicate the presence of deer, but they aren't reliable. They can look fresh for days or weeks. If you find large numbers of droppings in a small area, you're probably in a feeding spot. In a place with many trails, the trail with the most droppings is probably the most heavily used. Droppings are more valuable in telling you what deer are doing and where they're going than indicating the time when the deer were in the area. Of course, moist droppings during a period of hot, dry weather will tell you the deer that left them had to be there recently. Soft droppings during cold, freezing days will do the same.

If you're observant enough, you might be able to recognize the sign of recent feeding on browse plants. The problem is

This sapling shows a typical buck rub. Some hunters put too much stock in rubs. All a rub means is that deer have been in the area and a buck has used this sapling—not that he'll come back to the same spot. On the other hand, he usually will return to a scrape because he has left scent there and expects his deposit to be visited by does.

estimating how old the sign is. Deer might have nipped the plants several months before.

The good old buck rub is a well-known sign, and one we all like to see when we're evaluating an area. Rubs are made during two periods—when bucks are trying to rid their antlers of velvet in late summer or early autumn and when they're just feeling pugnacious during the breeding season in November and December. Of the two, the most vigorous rubbing that produces the biggest scars on trees and shrubs is in late summer. A buck will stand close to a tree, scraping and polishing his antlers for several minutes to work the velvet off the beams and tines.

What this tells you is that a buck was standing there by the tree you're staring at several weeks ago, if you're scouting in the fall. He might have left the county long ago, but chances are he's still around unless he was spooked badly. He isn't apt to leave his home range.

The size of a rub often indicates the size of a buck's antlers. If you spot a tree 4 inches in diameter with a couple of feet of bark shredded off about the height of your

Here are fresh blacktail tracks in soft mud. The hunter knows they were made recently because the gouged earth is dark, the edges haven't baked hard though the day is heating up, and the flattened grass has not even begun to straighten.

Two West Coast hunters check for tracks and other sign in the kind of opening that often attracts blacktail deer. Knowing the habits of whitetails or mule deer helps greatly in scouting—and scouting, in turn, teaches the hunter a great deal about those habits. *(Courtesy of Petersen Publishing Company)*

Here's a thrilling sight that might be experienced while scouting in advance of the season. The hunter-photographer has jumped a Rocky Mountain mule deer in the State of Washington. *(Courtesy of U.S. Forest Service)*

chest, you're probably in the territory of a buck that will make you shiver with excitement when you get a look at him. That's not to say that big bucks don't pick on saplings or brush, because they often do.

Scrapes are worthy of your attention, more so than rubs, because a buck will visit the scrapes he made to see if he's attracted any does. A whitetail buck makes a scrape by pawing a roughly circular or oval spot down to mineral earth and then urinating on it. It's his way of marking his territory and telling the females that he's around and available. If you find a fresh scrape, commit it to memory and observe the surrounding woods so you can find it come hunting season. Consider spending several hours watching it.

At the outset of this chapter we said that some hunters scout too much. It's possible to spend so much time in good deer woods that you'll temporarily drive deer out. This is serious if you're scouting a day or two before the season opens. The idea is to look over an area quickly, find what you're looking for, then leave and let the deer resume their natural patterns. Of course, some deer woods are crowded because of their proximity to urban areas, and some forests might have plenty of traffic from hunters out for squirrels, grouse, or other game. If you want to spend a lot of time looking, do it a week or two before the season. If you disturb the deer then, they'll have time to get back into their regular habits before the opener.

Once you've scouted, you need to know how to put together the information you've found and come up with a plan. It's not a bad idea to make a map, or mark up a map with details of your scouting efforts. Pencil in well-used trails, scrapes, water, feed, and bedding areas, and hunt accordingly. If you locate bedding areas, find a vantage point where you can see them in the early morning. Deer will be drifting toward them after feeding all night. If you find feeding areas, observe them in late afternoon when deer will be moving toward them just before nightfall.

If the truth were known, few hunters scout at all, and some make only a token effort. That's not because they don't want to or don't know how—they simply don't have the time. Many of us are caught up in a hectic lifestyle governed by the need to earn a living.

If you can't scout and you find you're hunting an area with little or no sign, pull up stakes and try a new location, if you're confident few deer are around. Not all deer woods are alike—some places are better than others. Remain observant when you're in the woods. If you're watchful, you'll see those clues that betray deer. Those hints can help you tag one.

CHAPTER 4

HOW NOT TO GET LOST

by Jim Zumbo

The articles you've read on what to do when lost all tell you to remain calm, don't panic, and control your brain. Good advice, but it makes more sense when you're reading it from a comfortable sofa than when you're out there in the trees, convinced that you'll die there.

There are many reasons why people become lost. Some folks just have a terrible sense of direction, and would get lost in a neighbor's backyard. Others lose their bearings in heavy woods while tracking a deer, or while just roaming along where there are few landmarks. Some become lost when the weather closes in, blocking out the sun and surroundings with low clouds or fog. In many cases, hunters don't plan their return to camp wisely and are overtaken by night.

Being lost is a problem of mental control. Though you might not know where you are, you are *somewhere;* all you need do is head in the correct direction to become unlost. It's not as if you're powerless, as if you're marooned on an iceberg and subject to the whims of the wind and sea. The solution, of course, is to control your brain long enough so you can make your way out of the woods safely. Panic and hysteria are common reactions when the brain goes haywire, and therein lies the problem. Lost people do things to hurt themselves because they have no reasoning capability. I think every sportsman has waded through countless articles on how to find your way out (or, when that's impossible, how to stay put safely until you're found). Most of the advice boils down to mental control and

This long, wide Montana valley doesn't have many outstanding landmarks—at first glance. But the hunter won't get lost if he takes note of the rock formations and remembers that ridges and canyons can be backtracked. *(Courtesy of Montana Department of Fish, Wildlife and Parks)*

common sense. I'm pretty sure you've read it elsewhere, more than once.

In this chapter I'll mention standard procedures to follow if you get lost, but I'll dwell more on how to prevent getting lost in the first place—as well as how to hunt without fear of being lost in strange woodlands. This is an extremely important aspect of deer hunting. If you're constantly worried about the location of the road, or trail, or lakeshore, you won't be concentrating as you should. Hunting requires attention. A distracted hunter is a poor hunter.

Despite common-sense rules about using a map and compass correctly, there will be times when you can't use them properly if you hunt enough. For instance, a couple of years ago I was hunting in Colorado as a guest of some friends, and had never hunted the area before. I arrived at night, too late to look the country over for the next day's hunt, and no one in the party had a map. The next morning, long before sunup, I was told to hunt east along a ridge, then cross a valley and meet the rest of the hunters on another ridge for lunch. I jumped out of the Jeep in the dark, and had no idea where I was.

Sound like an invitation to a big problem? Right, but I managed to find the group at the prearranged spot, even though the area was densely forested, with few landmarks in sight. I'll admit I was uneasy at times, especially after the sun disappeared behind some clouds. Western hunting, however, often lends itself to easy orientation because ridges and canyons can usually be backtracked.

Though a map is deemed a must on every hunt in unfamiliar land, some areas have poor maps, or none are available at all. I've seen huge tracts of private land where maps were almost impossible to find. Some maps are so vague or erroneous that using them will actually help one to get lost. Nonetheless, it's important to obtain accurate maps whenever possible.

Map reading takes some skill. You won't have the simple symbols and signs to help you as in highway maps. A woods map will show swamps, creeks, contours, mountains, and a variety of other topographic features. In order to follow it correctly, you need to first decipher codes and figure

Whether in whitetail or muley country, a hunter must become skillful with compass and map unless he plans to hunt only a short way from an access road. For that matter, sportsmen have become lost while en route in their vehicles. Practice with the compass, taking sightings and directional bearings, and orienting the compass with your map. Also practice interpreting symbols on topographic maps.

how contours work. It's easy to mistake a dip for a knoll or vice versa. The best way to learn basic map reading is to read a book on the subject.

A map is no good to you if you can't use a compass correctly. If, for example, you want to get to Big Buck Mountain from the White Pine Road and you know the mountain is northeast of the road, you must know how to follow a northeast bearing with a compass. And, of course, once you reach your destination, you need to know how to get back to the White Pine Road. When hunting, you don't walk in straight lines, so you must consider variations in your route. Once you get to Big Buck Mountain, you might pick up a deer track and follow it for several hours, ending up quite a way from your original bearing. To find your way out, you must determine where you are in relation to Big Buck Mountain and take the proper course back to the road.

If you don't trust yourself with map and compass, you always have the option of selecting hunting places that are easy to find your way around in.

One of the best areas is a mountainside paralleled by a road at the bottom. You can hunt to your heart's content, and when it's time to leave you need only walk downhill to the road. If you're *really* unsure of yourself, you can pick a mountain near a well-traveled highway. The sound of cars in the distance will provide the comforting knowledge that you always know where you are in relation to the highway. Don't scoff at the idea of hunting near an Inter-

Before leaving their vehicle, these Canadian hunters are making careful plans: checking their maps, agreeing on where each man will hunt, and arranging to meet at a specified time and spot. Each man will know where the others are, how to reach them if necessary, and where to rendezvous at the appointed time. *(Courtesy of Ontario Department of Tourism and Information)*

state, either. Some big bucks live just beyond the fences that parallel these road systems.

Another possibility is to hunt on a mountain that rises next to a large lake. When you're hunting you'll probably catch glimpses of the lake every now and then, and you'll know your location. The same is possible with a stream or river below. Any of these will serve as a natural route through the forest. Be careful, though, if you hunt downstream along a small creek. It's possible to strike a fork on your way back up, and you could end up miles away in a different drainage.

A fine way to stay unlost is to get on an old logging road or well-maintained trail and follow it. In areas with plenty of hunters, you might have company, but sometimes a crowd of people in the woods works to your advantage by moving the deer around. In places where old roads are numerous, pay attention to your route. You might get off on a side road and walk in the wrong direction, not realizing your error until it's almost dark and you wonder where your car is.

Powerlines run through plenty of woodlands, and they serve as good reference routes. In the morning and late afternoon, you're apt to spot deer feeding in powerline right-of-ways. When you hunt along lines, you can either wander slowly along the edge, or you can use the right-of-way as a baseline and hunt in the woods on either side with your compass to help you find your way back. For example, if the line runs north or south, you can hunt east of it at your leisure. When it's time to return you simply use your compass to show you west and follow the bearing back out.

This hunter is looking east from the top of Crow Mountain in the Absarokas toward the Lake Plateau area of the Beartooth Primitive Area in Montana. He's getting his bearings carefully and memorizing the topography—which can look confusingly different at closer range. *(Courtesy of Montana Department of Fish, Wildlife and Parks)*

Fences can be used the same way. You can mosey along one or use it as a baseline if you want to wander around in the adjacent woods.

In the West, the landscape is often open enough so that plenty of landmarks will guide you about. There are some areas, however, where Western forests will swallow you up as quickly as in whitetail country. Along the West Coast, the thickest forests in America must be negotiated. Drainages are everywhere, and they can be confusing to keep track of.

Lots of hunters use the sun to keep oriented, but *always* carry a compass, regardless of how balmy and bright it is. A storm front can quickly blot out the sun, and you'll be turned around unless you have a reasonably good sense of direction or you're familiar with the area.

The North Star is a superb guide if you're caught out at night, but again, bad weather can hide it. I recall a Montana hunt a few years back when the North Star saved us from a night deep in the forest. By using it as a reference, we walked 6 miles out of the woods. A bit of moonlight and flashlights allowed us to walk safely.

Though you can take all sorts of precautions to stay oriented, you might find yourself "turned around" some day. Perhaps you tracked a big whitetail buck too diligently and you didn't pay attention to where you were going. When it's time to head back for the road or camp, you realize you're unsure of the way to go. You confirm your suspicions by walking around and seeing nothing familiar. If you have a map, you can attempt to pinpoint your location by checking landforms and topographic features. Without a map, your best bet is to find a high vantage point and

Lakes and ponds are excellent landmarks, and often it's possible to follow watercourses to or from them. This view is in the Beartooth Range—highest mountains in Montana—with Wounded Man Lake in the middle distance.

look for familiar landmarks. If that fails, use your compass and head in the general direction of the road. Stay on the bearing and follow a straight line. Sooner or later you should reach your destination or a road or trail. If you don't, follow the directions I alluded to in the beginning of this chapter—control your brain, and prepare for a long night in the woods. Your buddies will be looking for you soon.

Some hunters mark their exact trail by tying ribbon along the route, or by blazing trees with a knife. Both methods work, but there are reasons why you shouldn't use them. If you don't return along the route and retrieve the ribbons, they'll flutter for years and add another bit of unwanted human litter to the woods. Blazing trees will damage them, or at least make them susceptible to disease and insect attack because the protective bark layer is cut. If you must mark a route, carry a half-roll of white toilet tissue with you. Place a single square on a branch every now and then. When you return on your route, pick up the squares. If you miss a few, they'll quickly deteriorate. Be sure to use white, because colored tissue won't decay rapidly.

If there's snow on the ground, you have the advantage of backtracking—but don't always count on it. If the snow layer is slight and it's a warm day, your tracks could melt away during the course of a day's hunt. If the snow is light and powdery and the wind is blowing, your tracks could be completely drifted over when you want to turn around and head back. In the event that snow is falling while you hunt, your tracks could be filled in. In any of the above situations, you could be turned around badly because of the false security you placed in the snow's ability to help you return after hunting.

You might also find yourself in another dilemma. Suppose, as you're following your tracks out of the woods, you come upon two sets of tracks and realize another hunter is in the area. You must make a decision and follow the right set. For all you know, the other hunter wandered around in an unfamiliar area, and backtracking his prints might not get you to a road or camp before dark.

Your bootprints should help you determine which tracks are yours, but it's possible the other hunter is wearing the same brand. Also, it could be impossible to see the detail of a bootprint if the snow is powdery.

All this points out that you should be just as alert in snowy woods as you are on dry ground. Don't trust the snow to get you back. It could be your worst enemy.

If you fear the woods and are afraid to penetrate them, your chances of killing a deer will be enormously reduced. Find ways to overcome this fear. You'll improve your hunting once you do. You'll hunt with more intensity, and you'll be able to concentrate.

Learn how to read a map and compass. If available, take a course in orientation. This is a superb way to find your way in the woods. Carry a daypack with survival items. It will add to your confidence when you're out there in the boonies.

An alert hunter is the best hunter. The more comfortable you are in the woods, the more deer you'll see. And that's the bottom line.

CHAPTER

5

THE STILL-HUNTER'S ART

by Leonard M. Wright, Jr.

Frankly, I've never thought the term "still-hunting" was a particularly good name for the type of deer hunting I know and like best. It sounds far too stationary. "Slow-hunting" or "quiet-hunting" might have been far better, but it's probably too late to quibble over definitions.

What we refer to as "still-hunting" is really stop-and-go hunting. A step, a long careful look, then another step. At its fastest pace, which is permissible in wet woods or when crossing a large, unproductive opening, it may approach a slow mosey. It is only partly still, but it is all hunting.

Still-hunting, you may be surprised to learn, is as American as apple pie, installment buying, and the disposable beer can. Unlike most other kinds of hunting, it has no European heritage; it evolved in our Northeast three hundred years ago simply because it was the best way to hunt whitetail deer in that terrain.

If the nobility had settled America, an early American deer hunt would have been more like a Virginia fox hunt. Only those to the manor born were allowed to hunt deer in England or on the Continent in those days, and the exercise was a very social horses-and-hounds affair. Most early American settlers were less pretentious people who tried to claw a living out of the rocky soil, and, to them, venison was a diet staple rather than the by-product of a gala event.

Certainly, these early farmers ambushed deer at dusk near their orchards or gardens, tracked and ran them down, torchlighted them after dark, trapped them, took them any way they could. But after the crops had been harvested, the few easy deer had been skimmed off, and it was time to hang the winter's supply of meat, these early hunters had to leave the valley farm and pursue the deer up through their hillside woodlots and on into the mountains above. This was a part-time effort, not a business (the winter wood had to be sawed and split, too), so the hunter, usually alone, had to secure as much venison per hour as possible or it could be a lean winter indeed.

This type of hunter couldn't travel far and, in fact, he didn't need to. There were enough deer within a half-mile—or at most a mile—of his farm to feed his family. But without a retinue of serfs, hounds, and horses, how could he best harvest this crop? Playing the deer's own game, on the deer's terms and in the deer's own backyard—which is what still-hunting is all about—turned out to be the answer.

Successful still-hunting doesn't take years of experience if the hunter moves slowly, remains constantly alert, and knows what to do. Here, Lorry Hogue of Vernal, Utah, displays a buck she took while still-hunting. A common Western technique is to stand-hunt in the morning and late afternoon, using the hours between to still-hunt just below the ridgelines where muley bucks travel and bed. *(Photo by Danny Zumbo)*

Admittedly, this is not a trophy-hunting technique when performed by the average week-end hunter although it has certainly accounted for its share of the deer heads you see on walls. It is mainly a practical way to take an average buck with an occasional rack thrown in as a surprise bonus for the patient hunter. However, skill is rewarded and error punished to a very high degree in this type of hunting. A novice may blunder onto a big buck at dawn on opening day, but over the years, a skilled practitioner will outproduce him ten to one.

The inexperienced and the casual are inclined to go wrong in a great many ways—equipping themselves improperly, moving too fast, hunting the wrong places or hunting the right ones at the wrong times, misinterpreting what they see, and so on. Fortunately, most of us learn from our mistakes, and class is in session whenever a smart hunter is in the woods.

First, there is the matter of equipment. Fortunately, the gear needed for this type of deer hunting is pleasantly undemanding and most farmers or country-dwellers probably have most items or reasonable facsimiles already at hand. Look through your own inventory of outdoor clothes and see how much of the following you can lay your hands on.

Starting at the bottom and working up brings us first to the all-important matter of footwear. For whitetail hunting in the East, I hold that boots should be at least 10 inches high—12 inches in chronically watery habitat— and utterly waterproof.

Some say their leather boots keep their feet absolutely dry, but I've never been lucky enough to own such a pair. The same goes for pacs. I no longer take chances. I struggle along in a pair of lace-up rubber boots that reach just above my calves. Not the most comfortable footwear, but I'm not going to cover much mileage and the added insurance against any leakage plays a vital part in some of my hunts.

Admittedly, however, what I've just said requires some qualification. In recent years, great improvements have been made both in boots and in waterproofing preparation. If you're luckier (or richer) than I am and you do own a pair of truly waterproof leather boots or pacs, by all means wear them—as long as they're durable, comfortable, and high enough to reach above your calves. Also bear in mind that conditions are quite different in considerable portions of the Midwest and West, particularly in relatively dry habitat. In such regions you may well need a pair of comfortable leather hiking boots, and they don't have to be quite so high unless you're worried about thorns or rattlers. For that matter, there are regions where still-hunters often wear snake-proof boots, which are seldom comfortable but can be mentally comforting. Whatever footwear is right for your region, you'll almost certainly need soles that provide positive traction, so buy them with care.

This alert whitetail was routed from his bed by a still-hunter. A crucial aspect of this technique is to spot game quickly, then fire a well-placed bullet before the quarry spooks. *(Courtesy of Missouri Department of Conservation)*

A heavy pair of socks (or two light pairs) are all that's necessary for warmth. You'll be moving around just enough to avoid cold feet and will have no need to bundle up your toes excessively as long as your socks are made of wool. Synthetic or cotton socks may look thick and comfy, but they don't do much for you when they get damp, and feet are sure to sweat some inside rubber boots. So much so that I usually carry a spare pair of wools for a comfort change halfway through the day.

In cold weather, I like wool pants, too. Medium-weight will do if worn over a pair of long johns. You might need those heavy, feltlike blanket-pants if you're going on stand for an hour or more in late November, but I've rarely felt the need for them while still-hunting.

Still-hunting demands a keen eye for deer sign. Here a hunter stops to inspect a buck rub that's unusually high on a white cedar. Where the sign is promising, you may want to spend hours silently combing a small bit of cover, watching and listening more than moving. *(Photo by Norm Nelson)*

My midriff and upper body seem happier in wool, too. A light wool sweater, with or without sleeves, makes a fine undershirt. Over this I wear a light wool shirt topped off with a heavy wool shirt, and this is sufficient for most days. Where regulations require you to wear a certain amount of safety-orange, you can wear an orange hat and/or vest, or an orange wool shirt. When the mercury starts out below zero and looks as if it will stay there all day, I substitute a down jacket with an orange overvest for the heavy wool shirt.

Warm hands are crucial, and on the bitterest days I wear fleece-lined mittens. I can slip off the right one quickly enough when I need to shoot. If you wish, you can buy shooting mittens with Velcro-closure finger slits so you don't need to pull one off to shoot. My hat is orange, has a visor against the sun, and fold-down earflaps. And that about covers it—or me.

I do carry a few accessories, though—extra cartridges, yellow shooting glasses, a light pocketknife with a sharp 3-inch blade in case this is my lucky day, a 6-foot piece of light nylon rope for the same reason, and some sort of sandwich or quick-energy candy bar. If more trinkets mean more fun to you, carry them. A small compass and topo maps will be needed if you're in strange territory (which you shouldn't be if you're still-hunting the best way possible).

To many hunters in many regions, "a day's deer hunting" means a couple of hours in the morning, then back to camp or home for a leisurely lunch and a nap, followed by a couple more mid- or late-afternoon hours. Of course, this may help to explain success ratios as low as 10 percent in some areas that have lots of deer. But if you're an all-day hiker and hunter, one other piece of equipment can serve you well—a light backpack of the sort known appropriately as a day-pack. It doesn't have to be very roomy to hold a drag rope, extra cartridges, sandwiches, a vacuum bottle of coffee or soup or whatever, toilet tissue because roughing it has reasonable limits, and all the gadgets you'll ever need.

And, oh yes, you'll need a gun, too, won't you? Any rifle-and-sight combination that will allow you to kill a deer surely and quickly at, say, 125 yards is perfectly adequate for most whitetail hunting, but you'll want something with more range for mule deer. The .270, .308, and .30-06 are among calibers that are both practical and recommendable in the East; the .270 and .30-06 are recommendable just about anywhere. Dave Petzal's chapter on armament goes into more detail, so I won't.

Naturally, I have a personal preference and good reasons to back it up. I carry a .30-06. Overkill, many say, but I rarely have to use a second shot. This one is a very light sporterized Mauser that weighs little more than a good .22. On top of this is mounted a 3× scope with a post reticle. This is plenty of magnification for up to 150 yards and the post is easier to pick up in the dark woods than fine crosshairs. A dot reticle or dual-thickness crosshairs would also work well in my woods. For insurance, I have an open peep sight set just below this in case snow, fog, or rain fouls up my scope or in case I have to take a shot at a jumped deer.

The ultimate challenge—and reward—for the still-hunter is to walk up on a bedded buck and take him before he can detect danger and escape. This prime buck, surprised in his bed, displays the swollen neck that signifies the peak of the rut. *(Courtesy of Illinois Department of Conservation)*

This latter contingency I have avoided all but a couple of times in my life. I am against chance shots at running deer in thick woods. A wild shot can clear the nearby woods for an hour or two. But, even worse, a gut- or rump-shot deer may die a mile or two (and three posted boundaries) away, and this is surely a mug's game. Admittedly, I do have a friend who can kill a running deer nine times out of ten. He has four Purple Hearts, slept with his rifle for four years, and by the way he shoots I'm not sure he still doesn't take the thing to bed with him. Frankly, I can't shoot that well myself.

Anyway, now that you're fully equipped, where do you hunt? Any hilly or rolling country with semi-open woods will do. Hardwoods, or mainly hardwood forests, are best in the East and Midwest. In much of the West you might be still-hunting amid pinyon-juniper thickets, conifers, aspens, scrub oak, chaparral, and the like. If you can't see 50 yards you're probably better off driving deer to standers or jump-shooting deer with buckshot (where legal) or rifled slugs. On the other hand, if you can see more than 150 yards the woods are probably too thin for good still-hunting. Most hardwood stands fall between these two densities and this is where the still-hunter reigns supreme. Look at the best deer country in your area and, unless you live in the Southwest or in open country, you'll be surprised how much prime hunting territory falls into this category.

If the chosen section of woods is overrun with hunters, you may do better standing (and probably shivering) at a likely place and letting the others push the deer to you. But if you're the only hunter on a 100- to 400-acre tract, you'll usually see a lot more deer by actively searching them out. Stand-hunters and drivers will argue, but it's true.

Even if you're alone, don't confuse this with the wilderness hunting you've read about in books. The deer will be smart and wise to the ways of man and will have set up feeding and traveling patterns to cash in on man's crops with a minimum of contact. If you know the feeding areas, the bedding areas, the best-used trails, you're way ahead of the game. And if you know the woods like the back of your hand, you won't waste time glassing stumps or blowdowns. For these reasons, you'll be many times more effective still-hunting an area you know really well. If you're invited to shoot new territory, try to walk it and know it before the season starts if at all possible. Familiarity breeds venison, which is why this book contains a chapter on scouting.

Early and late in the day are prime times—early has the edge—but since still-hunting is a percentage game, it's worth our while to hunt as much of the day as possible. It pays to be well into the woods and away from houses or roads by the time legal shooting starts. Here's where my yellow shooting glasses pay off. They help me see in very dim light and they protect my eyes from twigs I would never see at that time of day. They'll do the same on the way out at dusk, too.

Once into prime hunting territory, it's usually best to hunt on a level course, or cross-hill, for the first hour or two. Deer drift up from the valley floor where they have been night-feeding until daybreak. As the morning wears on, however, it pays to work diagonally higher up the slopes to catch up with deer that may have slipped by you earlier in the day. Reverse the process as dusk approaches.

Those are only general rules. Weather should influence your tactics as much as time of day. When it's stormy, deer may stay just above a valley floor all day and not go back up to their usual bedding areas. And in very cold weather—the best, but least comfortable, still-hunting weather—deer have to move around and feed during much of the day to stay warm. Again, knowing your acreage and the habits of the deer that inhabit it are priceless advantages.

Now that you've arrived at the right place at the right time, you can finally get down to the hunting itself. The two most important questions here are: How fast (or slowly) should you move? And how can you see deer before they see you?

There are no pat answers because your tactics should change with conditions. But there are some basics that apply to all conditions. First, move much more slowly than you think you have to. And second, try to move upwind or, if you have to zigzag back and forth, try to approach the choicest spots upwind. The chief reason for this approach is that deer can't hear you nearly as well when the wind blows from them to you.

I'll now stick my neck way out and say that I don't believe our scent is the governing factor here. I'm convinced that for every deer that hightails it because he has picked up your odor, there are ten that have departed because they've picked up the noise created by your big flat feet.

When the woods are wet, you can move at a fair, steady pace. Dead leaves are then quiet, and since the forest floor is bare of snow you can even avoid stepping on twigs. But don't let twig-dodging keep you from looking ahead and around. And be sure to look farther ahead than you usually do. In fact, this is a basic rule for still-hunting under all conditions.

We all tend to look at, or focus on, the trees, landmarks, or clearings that are easily visible. This habit must be broken, because it just won't do for still-hunting. Strain to examine the outer limits that you can't really see properly. That's where the deer will be, and every few steps will open up a whole new world of these outer limits. Any place you can see clearly and easily has been vacated minutes before by any deer that were there. Count on it.

Fresh snow underfoot is the next easiest condition. Dead leaves won't make noise, and deer will stand out better against the white background, but go slowly. You can't see twigs or small branches, and when you step on them they'll sound like rifle shots to both you and the deer. There's a great temptation to follow a seemingly fresh set of tracks under these conditions, but I've found it rarely pays off. Half-hour-old tracks can look brand new, but the deer may be over a half-mile away by that time and traveling faster than you. It may be worth a try some days, but I think the percentages are better if you stick with your original plan. In any event, test each step before you put full weight on that foot when there's snow on the ground or, better still, resort to the tactics, coming up next, for hunting in dry woods.

Bone-dry leaves provide the toughest condition a still-hunter faces and the most common one. You need all the help you can get on days like this, and here are some tips to cut down on that fatal crunch-

crunch. Try to walk under evergreens just back from the hardwoods wherever conditions permit. This is a good tactic at all times since you're harder to see under that poorer light, but there's an even more compelling reason on dry days. Pine and hemlock needles are quiet underfoot even when leaves sound like saltines. You can step noiselessly on roots, rocks, and logs, too. You'll find the most rocks below ledges and exposed roots on steep slopes where erosion has bared them. Edges of hemlock swamps are excellent too, because these shallow-rooted trees often send out large, exposed roots many feet from their trunks.

Look for these same noise-reducers when there's crusty snow, too, because this situation is about as bad as dry leaves. But there's one ace in the hole that lets you beat both conditions when the chips are down and all else fails—*being properly equipped.*

Those waterproof boots I mentioned earlier are my secret weapon here. No matter how dry the leaves or crunchy the snow, I can walk up small creeks and trickles and through the soppy parts of hemlock swamps without making a sound, and in perfect comfort with this footwear. Meanwhile, any deer that so much as moves a foot within a couple of hundred yards makes enough noise to give himself away.

When you can't find shallow water to hide your sounds, there's still hope even under the worst conditions. Walk just above a major rise or ledge as you cut cross-contour. Deer may hear you and freeze, but the sound comes to them indirectly and they can't locate your exact position. Pussyfoot down to a lookout point every 200 feet or so during your traverse and spend several minutes glassing the flat below. Take your time. The deer will probably be frozen, as I've said, and they're hard to pick out, but don't move on until you're absolutely certain there are none in sight. There's a special satisfaction in catching even a doe with her guard down when you're hunting like this. It means you've executed the maneuver perfectly and you can take pride in counting a *coup* the way Indian warriors some-

Still-hunting techniques may have evolved in the Eastern woodlots, but they are at least as effective in the West. This fine muley was collected by still-hunting through a pinyon-juniper thicket. Aspen stands are also promising places to sneak around on the lookout for deer, and fresh snow helps because it lets you walk quietly and observe clear sign, then combine still-hunting with tracking to follow interesting prints. *(Photo by Russell Tinsley)*

times used to hit their enemies with a lancelike stick rather than killing and scalping them.

Not only does still-hunting give you the greatest joys of accomplishment, I'm convinced it allows the greatest flexibility, too. So far I've talked only of hunting solo, which is the most satisfying of all to me personally. But two or several hunters can still-hunt a woods simultaneously if there's enough elbow room. If they travel roughly parallel to each other a few hundred yards apart, they may even increase their chances by pushing the wariest, unseen deer toward each other.

This happened not so long ago on a still-hunt through a hemlock swamp with Bob Elman and another friend, named Duke. I heard something moving but couldn't see it. I waited, pretty sure the animal was headed toward Bob. Then Bob saw it but didn't shoot because he couldn't make out antlers. Both of us began moving again, ever so slowly—in effect, driving that deer while simultaneously still-hunting. It turned out to be a spike buck, and Duke felled it with a quick shot as it ambled out of the hemlocks.

After the best of the morning is over, cooperating still-hunters can assemble at a prearranged place and set up informal drives through dense bed-down territory with one or two of them acting as standers. Then they can still-hunt downhill separately in late afternoon and take stationary positions near feeding areas during those last productive minutes of shooting light. With a good knowledge of the territory, an understanding of the habits of the local deer herd plus a little imagination, a group of knowledgeable still-hunters can make good and productive use of all the legal shooting hours.

Then, too, there's a humbling element about still-hunting that I find not exactly unpleasing. The more you hunt this way, the more you come to respect deer as far better woodsmen than you'll ever be. Even under the best conditions, most deer will drift out ahead of you without your ever seeing or hearing them. And it will be a rare day when you scope more deer than you see tails bounding of out of sight.

But, as I've said, this is percentage hunting. Remember, bucks make mistakes, too. And sometimes vagaries of air or natural advantages of terrain can play into your hands.

Above all, don't let an occasional lucky success go to your head and lead you into sloppy habits. The better you know your territory, the more you use your head, the more you stare out beyond where you can really see, the slower and quieter you can make your way through the woods—the more venison steaks you'll enjoy.

CHAPTER

6

THE STAND-HUNTER'S ART

by Jim Carmichel

As a former Tennessee farm lad, I suppose I'm a product of what's known as the Protestant work ethnic—that being the philosophy that nothing comes easy and those who are most successful in life are those who work hardest.

I didn't realize the impact this background was having on my mode of operation—and deer hunting in particular—until one crisp day a few years back when I crashed through a final ring of brush and topped out on a high mesa in northeastern New Mexico's high plains. A few moments later there was another crashing in the dry brush and a hunting companion, a fellow of upbringing similar to mine, came into the clearing and plopped down on the log where I was sitting. For a while we panted in silence, asking ourselves why we had struggled up the steepest hill in the territory while the rest of our hunting party circled the gentle landscape below.

Finally, when we'd both gotten our wind back, my friend said, "I can't understand it. I do this every time I go deer hunting. Something in the back of my mind keeps telling me that if I work harder, push farther, and climb higher I'll be rewarded with a nice buck. But you know what? It never has worked out that way for me."

"I know exactly what you mean," I answered, "but from now on I'm going to start using my head instead of my feet."

That was my "conversion" to stand-hunting, and in the ensuing years I've managed to take more deer, walk less miles, suffer fewer sore muscles, and have more fun deer hunting than I would ever have guessed in earlier times.

By popular definition, "stand-hunting"

is taking a fixed position in a tree or relatively concealed spot on the ground and waiting for a deer to come by. This is not to be confused with still-hunting, which is the art of making a cautious stop-and-go circuit through deer country. "Stalking," by comparison, is a fairly steady gait.

The art and technique of stand-hunting is widely misunderstood and just as often misapplied. It is most especially misunderstood by overeager hunters who don't feel they've truly gotten their license-money's worth until they've bounded over every inch of the hunting territory. This, quite frankly, was me in my younger days. Likewise, I also tended to share the opinion that stand-hunters were just too lazy or uninterested to go after deer in proper fashion. It always seemed to me that the odds were against the stand-hunter. After all, I reasoned, there were few deer to start with, they were scattered over a wide area, and the chances of seeing one while waiting in any particular spot were extremely remote.

Actually, almost the exact opposite is true. There are more deer in most areas than the average moving hunter will ever realize; they are not scattered over a wide area but, rather, tend to concentrate in certain pockets; and the chances that a given deer will pass by a certain spot every day are almost as good as the chances that you regularly pass a given spot on your way to work each day!

"Ah," you say, "but there's the rub. How do you know that magic spot where a deer will pass?"

That, dear deer hunter, is precisely the art of stand-hunting. When done correctly, it's not only an art but a science—the science of understanding deer habits, knowing when they move, where they move, and why they move. In recent years the more successful stand-hunters have also taken into consideration the added dimension of hunter movements. But more about this later. First let's examine the stand.

A deer stand can be anything from a stump to a cozy box on top of a tower. It should conceal the hunter but at the same time allow him clear vision over the surrounding area and permit safe and accurate shooting. This latter should never be forgotten or underestimated. Probably the worst example of this I've ever seen was a stand I once tried to use on the edge of a swamp in Africa. I was hunting the sitatunga, a little swamp-dwelling antelope that spends most of its time hidden in reeds and bulrushes and seldom ventures out into an open area. When it does, the range is often several hundred yards. Usually the only way to spot these shy creatures is from a perch in a high tree. Accordingly, my guide rigged a perch so high in a tree that it was necessary to hold on with both hands to keep from falling out! Holding and aiming a rifle was out of the question.

The same thing sometimes happens to deer hunters who spend great time and effort in climbing a tree or mounting a perch only to find that their position prevents them from making a well-aimed shot.

Every year we read about hunters who break an arm or leg by falling out of a tree. For those who cannot climb as agilely as a squirrel or perch on a limb as lightly as a bird, the portable tree stand or "self-climbing" platform can be, literally, a lifesaver. Several types are available, and regardless of differences in design they're all in-

Wildlife photographer and noted deer authority Lennie Rue draws a bead from a portable tree stand. He's hunting in New Jersey during the shotgun season, when a tree stand is especially valuable because deer are apt to come close without seeing or scenting the hunter; and with a shotgun, close range is essential.

tended to perch you up there efficiently and safely.

I personally perfer a stand that is up in a tree or at least elevated enough to give a wide view. I'm of the opinion that deer have more difficulty picking up a hunter's scent if he is somewhat elevated, although I know some experienced hunters who are of a different mind.

Surprisingly, perhaps, the stand does not need to be especially well camouflaged or for that mater, camouflaged at all. Once in Europe and again in South Carolina, I hunted from a stand that was nothing more than a simple 4 × 4-foot plywood box on top of a 12-foot metal tower. Naturally, if you erect such a stand on the first day of deer season there is about as much chance of a buck stopping by as there is of holding the Southern Baptist Convention at the Vatican. The trick is to establish your blind well ahead of the hunting season so that the deer in the area will become accustomed to the structure and accept it as a normal, harmless part of their environment. Three months ahead of the season opening is none too soon.

Also, don't set up some sort of eyesore contraption that will offend the landowner, state or federal authorities (if you hunt on public land) and other hunters. And, of course, check the local and state regulations. Such a structure is legal in most regions, but you can't take that for granted. The building of a permanent structure, in particular, is prohibited on some lands. Finally, to prevent off-season vandalism or the unauthorized use of your blind, it should be concealed so as to hide it from other people throughout the year.

An effective ground-level stand can be made by piling up slash from logging operations or whatever natural growth may be at hand. Remember, though, if you cut brush during the summer the green leaves will dry and fall off and leave a pretty sorry-looking blind. So plan ahead and "think winter." Oak is a good choice for blind material because the dead leaves hold pretty fast, and of course evergreens will stay dense. I advise making several openings for spotting and shooting rather than just looking over the top of a brush blind. If you have to stand up and shoot over the top of a blind, your movement will spook a buck before you can get a shot off. It may be a great thrill to pull off a shot at a bounding buck, but the averages are all in favor of the hunter who has a standing or slowly moving target.

This Texas whitetail hunter uses a well-hidden platform stand in a tree that gives him a clear view of the densely brushy habitat. The tree isn't high, but the foliage helps conceal him without obstructing his view. *(Photo by Russell Tinsley)*

A little while back I said that a stand can be just about anyting, including a stump. In fact, there are parts of the country where deer hunters refer to themselves as "stump-sitters." It bears repetition here that a stand, to be good, doesn't always have to be a man-made platform or artificial blind. Often the best blind is provided by the terrain or vegetation near a deer run, crossing, or other choice location. In other words, an excellent stand may simply consist of a position that gives you a good view where deer traffic can be expected, and at the same time either hides you or breaks up your outline sufficiently so that a buck won't spot you before you spot him. You also want to be as careful as conditions permit so that your scent won't spook him, and I'll go into that in a moment.

The point I'm making here is that an effective blind may be a blow-down, a little shrubbery thicket, the crotch of a sufficiently large tree, even a rock outcropping or cliff. Bob Elman tells me that for three

The late Larry Koller, one of this country's most proficient hunting authors, proves that a stand on the ground can be effective—provided the hunter is concealed or has his outline broken by vegetation. The stand must also allow good visibility and be located with the breeze favoring the hunter—not wafting his scent straight at the deer.

Here's how a hunter gets up a tree with a typical portable stand. His feet are secured to the stand proper with straps, while he uses a "climber" accessory to pull himself up. Both the accessory and the stand press against the tree to ease the ascent. *(Courtesy of Baker Manufacturing Company)*

years in a row he had a 30- to 40-yard shot at a browsing whitetail from atop a 6-foot boulder on a beech ridge in the Catskills. The boulder overlooks a heavily used deer trail between daytime bedding grounds and some abandoned orchards where the whitetails love to feed at night. The prevailing early-morning breeze flows up the ridge toward him, so it doesn't carry his scent to the game. From his boulder he can look down on any passing deer, but they seldom look up at him.

Properly locating a deer stand is far more complex than just strolling out in the woods and setting up shop in a likely looking spot. This is where careful preseason scouting pays big dividends. As you scout an area, you'll find that the local herd tends to follow well-used trails. During a buck's daily activity he will feed, water, and bed down according to a regular schedule. More important, from the hunter's standpoint, is the fact that the buck will tend to follow a specific route as he attends to these daily activities. The preseason scouter who discovers these routes will be able to take up a stand where he knows there is regular deer traffic.

If you intend to hunt from a natural stand such as downed timber, slash piles, etc., you are flexible enough to adapt to prevailing wind conditions on any given day. However, if you intend to establish a permanent blind, you'll be smart to take into account annual prevailing wind conditions and locate yourself accordingly.

To us humans, the scenting of other animals over a distance of several hundred yards is only an abstraction. We believe it because we've been told it's true but we still tend to regard it as a rather ghostly supposition. But to a deer, a hunter's scent is as real as seeing or touching him and just as good a cause for running the other way. You wouldn't stand up, wave your arms, and shout at a deer, and neither should you get located where he is sure to catch your scent.

If you scout an area during the last few days before the season opens, be on the lookout for deer rubs and scrapes. When the velvet on a buck's antlers dries, he rubs it off on slender trees. This tears the bark and some of the limbs off and is usually easy to spot. Areas that show lots of rub sign are natural areas to look for bucks and are good places for stand-hunting. "Scrapes," or "kicks," are even better. These are spots where a buck cleans the ground and leaves his scent to attract females. A rubbed sapling merely indicates that a buck has been there and probably will return to the same general area, but certainly not that he'll come back to the very same spot. He will, however, return to a scrape. He will visit his scrapes periodically to see if he has "caught" any does. Don't locate your stand right on top of these "baited" spots but only close enough to have a reasonably clear view.

One of the smartest things a deer hunter can do is to get into the hunting area a few days before the season opens—the last couple of days are no good because of too much human activity—and study deer movements from dawn until dark. This experience quite often completely changes the hunter's perspective and makes him far more effective in his technique.

I know individuals who confessed utter amazement at the number of deer they saw just by sitting still in one place for the day. And, too, it can be a delightfully pleasant day. Take your camera along. One of the things you'll be most impressed by is the relatively high activity at first and last light of day. On an average, you'll see at least as many deer during the first and last half-

Having taken a stand near the intersection of two active deer trails, this hunter now has the drop on a whitetail. Notice how he has used a tree to break up the outline of his body. *(Courtesy of Tennessee Game & Fish Commission)*

hours of the day as the rest of the day in total. The value of this observation is that from then on you'll be at your stand before daylight.

Another lesson worth learning is that bucks tend to be considerably more wary than does of suspicious-looking situations. Some years back, when I was testing the relative effect on deer of different types and colors of camouflage hunting gear, I noted that so long as I remained perfectly still and more or less blended with the background, does would come amazingly close without showing alarm or even concern. Once, within three hours, I had no less than eleven does browse by within 50 yards, even though I was completely visible from the soles of my boots to the top of my cap. But at no time during a three-day period did a buck come within sight! I'm convinced they spotted me from a distance and decided that all was not as it should be. However, bucks will come close if the hunter is well hidden in a stand. This is why successful stand-hunting calls for a fair degree of thought and preparation.

Such thought and preparation can include a few fancy touches that increase your chances of connecting. So far we've been talking about the science of hunting from a stand—proven facts and techinques that get results. But the real experts go a step farther and apply the art of stand-hunting.

If you hunt in an area where there are few other hunters, you will undoubtedly be most successful by playing the odds and using a stand near established and known deer-traffic areas. But with more and more hunters taking to the fields and forests every season, the day has all but passed when you can reasonably assume you're the only person in the woods with a gun.

Most hunters dislike this competition, but a smart stand-hunter can make good use of the other hunters. The presence of a few hunters in an area does not seem to seriously affect a deer's daily regime. However, when a lot of hunters are in an area, the animals will alter their habits drastically. Consider a case in point:

Let's say a local herd of deer is in the habit of feeding in a low meadow during the predawn hours and then, just at sunup, they normally circle clockwise around a low hill, move into a valley between two higher hills, and disperse into their favorite bedding areas on the lower slopes.

But on the opening morning of deer season, dozens of hunters move into the area and disturb the normal routine. Even though the deer's usual habits have been aborted, they will follow a more or less predictable pattern. The smart hunter knows this and will take advantage of the situation while his less astute fellow hunters are wondering where all the deer went.

First of all, keep in mind that deer are creatures of habit. If a buck likes to bed down during the day at a certain spot, he is not likely to give up that spot simply because his normal route is blocked. Instead, he will get there by the back door. If hunting pressure is really intense, he may decide to leave the area altogether, but in either case he will follow a route that is familiar.

The observant preseason scouter will have made note of little-used game trails which generally lead to the same location as the more heavily used trails.

These are escape routes, used throughout the year whenever dogs, lumbermen, hikers, campers, etc., disrupt the daily habits of the deer. During the hunting season, these routes frequently become the principally used deer highways. Thus the abovementioned deer, which normally move clockwise around a low hill, may suddenly find that they must go over the hill or possibly circle it in the opposite direction in order to reach their customary bedding area.

Usually deer will have several such routes, but it's a good bet they will select the one that heads them into the wind on that particular day. So the smart hunter who knows the various possible routes can take a stand on the path most likely to be used that day.

In fact, a clever hunter can sometimes even determine which way the deer will travel before they know themselves. If there is a road or popular camping site near the hunting area, it's a good guess that a high percentage of the hunters will be entering the woods from that direction. This means the deer will be driven in the opposite direction.

By taking this into consideration, plus investigating the possible routes the retreating deer will take, you can be at your stand, ready and waiting, when that big buck comes by.

CHAPTER

7

THE ART OF THE DRIVE

by Robert Elman

I've heard some hunters talk about driving deer the way primly pure-minded fly-rodders talk about fishing with nightcrawlers. Neither of these spiritually enlightened types is inclined to dwell much on anything so banal as success—that is, fish caught or venison in the freezer. On the other hand, I'll readily concede the virtues of still-hunting (its challenge, its requisite skill, and, under certain conditions, its effectiveness) as claimed by Len Wright elsewhere in this book. I've spent enough days in the woods with Len so that I can attest to his knowledge of the game. I'll also concede the advantages of stand-hunting described in the preceding chapter by Jim Carmichel, who notes that a lot more deer are taken that way than by still-hunting. Jim is a nationally respected expert, and anyway the truth of his remark is obvious.

Although both of these gentlemen are superb fly fishermen (and I can't say whether they look askance at angleworms) I do know they're not snobbish in the deer woods and they have taken their share of driven deer. They would agree that there is no such thing as a best hunting method. It all depends on time and place and situation.

Without doubt, driving accounts for more deer per hunting hour than the other methods. However, it requires teamwork by at least two hunters, sometimes two dozen or two score, so it doesn't necessarily take more deer per man. I'll state only that under certain conditions driving is the method of choice.

Let's say, for instance, that you want to hunt very thick cover where the brush won't give you many chances to see a deer at 40 yards, much less at 80 or 100. There are few or no spots here that combine the three requisites for a really good stand: signs of deer traffic within range; a wide, deep arc of visibility for the hunter; and a way to avoid being seen, heard, or winded by his game before he can get a shot.

Just to make it a classic situation, and one calling for a particular kind of drive, let's also say you're in a place where you can't use a rifle. In New Jersey, to cite the usual example, for the sake of safety in woods rimmed by heavily populated areas the pre-1975 law called for buckshot or nothing. Slugs have been permitted since opening day of 1975, but still no rifles; hence no shots at long range. Still-hunting is apt to be chancy here. (And by the way, some of my muzzleloading Jersey friends have been relying more than they used to on driving. Seems they discovered driving is not only effective but "authentic," having been used by Jersey hunters before New Jersey was a state.)

Maybe the visibility will do at a couple of shots along the edges, but the wind is wrong or a farmhouse is too close or there's some other disadvantage. So you decide against a stand. As for still-hunting through these thickets, the weather has been so dry that every step sounds like popping corn, only louder. During the first or last half-hour of shooting light, you might get stubborn and take a stand, but now it's midmorning and the deer aren't moving unless something pushes them.

They're invisible but you know they're in there. You've seen tracks, droppings, buck rubs, even scrapes. You've seen the ends of twigs nipped where they've browsed. One recent evening, perhaps, you've even seen a good buck bound across a road at one edge. There you have a situation that calls for a drive—a big, noisy drive.

I recall reading a description by an eminent expert—I think it was the late Warren Page—of a situation like that. Most of my

This whitetail buck was moved past a hunter during a small, quiet drive. The deer isn't running full-out, but moving slowly enough to provide a careful shot for a stander; and during the early stage of the drive he might also have presented a safe shot to one of the drivers. *(Courtesy of Illinois Department of Conservation)*

deer hunting had been with a rifle, and I thought he was exaggerating the density of the cover he'd encountered as well as the carnival atmosphere of a drive. That's what I thought—until I was introduced to the "pineys" of lower New Jersey, where there are stretches best worked by the Old World Technique involving beaters. Once I joined 17 other men to push several deer out of an extended thicket, and I'm told that some hunting clubs would have called that a small drive.

Half of us were standers. We spread out along an old dirt road on the downwind end of the woods. At one extreme of the line, three men moved forward a bit, along the edge of a fallow field, and three more at the other extreme moved forward up a wide powerline right-of-way that intersected the road where the rest of us waited. In other words, we didn't form a straight line but a rough U, because pushed deer will often sneak out to the sides, especially toward the end of a drive.

The other half of our team—nine more men—moved through the woods, beginning at a prearranged time, from the upwind end. When you're serving as a driver, that's the one time in deer hunting when you may want the wind at your back. You want the deer to scent you, because that will move them toward the standers.

Those nine drivers went through the woods at a moderate pace (no faster pace was possible in the thicker parts of the woods) but they made a hellish racket, hooting and calling. Artificial noisemakers aren't legal everywhere, but they are in New Jersey. One man had an aluminum skillet he banged against the butt of his shotgun, and another had a loud dog whistle. When they were about 200 yards from us, they spread out to the sides for safety's sake, but three deer they'd been pushing came straight on. I should add that this drive had a captain, as every drive should, and—again for safety—his word was law. As another standard precaution, no stander budged from his assigned position, regardless of temptations.

The noise, the crowd, and the thickness of the cover reminded me of the club hunts with dogs in parts of the South, though that's distinctly different from a conventional drive. (If you haven't hunted deer with dogs, be sure to read Tom Brakefield's chapter on the subject.) This particular New Jersey drive was noisier than a Southern hunt with dogs. It wasn't what you'd call stylish, but I couldn't argue with the results even though I much prefer

Here's what's often seen by drivers and standers in whitetail woods. Initially, the spooked deer holds its tail high, like a white flag, perhaps to alert other deer. But the tail will drop and the animal will soon revert to a trot or walk unless spooked again. Driven deer don't often run at full speed but tend to slip along through dense vegetation, so the hunter must be alert. *(Courtesy of Michigan Department of Natural Resources)* the other traditional driving method—the small, quiet drive.

With either strategy, drivers and standers take turns so that the hunt is fair to all if at least two drives are staged. Not that a driver never gets a shot. If the area being covered is big enough so that a driver can safely shoot during the early stages of the push, he may very well nail a deer. As a matter of fact, doubling back and trying to sneak out between the drivers is a frequent trick of deer, particularly mature (which means smart) bucks. And not only bucks. On a West Virginia grouse hunt, of all things, I was once almost knocked down by a doe when I unwittingly pushed her up a ridge into a very steep, thick tangle that she didn't like the looks of. She panicked, wheeled, came straight back at me, and bounded out right over my head.

To counter this backtracking habit of deer, the most effective drives employ what my friends and I call "backstops"—a few hunters who follow the drivers, straggling a good distance behind them to intercept game that insists on heading the

wrong way. This is most important in hunting whitetails, but it's also good insurance when driving mule deer through some thicket or canyon. And perhaps it's most important not on the big, noisy drives but on the small, quiet type that I prefer.

Now let's examine that more restrained style of driving. The first point to make is that it's much more effective than the noisy stampede if rifles can be used, if the woods aren't quite so dense, and if there are openings or stretches of clear or open terrain such as fields as the terminus of the drive.

A fast, noisy invasion by the hordes of Genghis Khan will spook more deer into doubling back or sneaking out to the sides, and will panic many into a flat-out, straight-ahead run. Even with buckshot, I have reservations about shooting at a fast-running deer. Most of my venison has been collected by squeezing off careful rifle shots at deer that were pausing uncertainly, walking, or trotting. That's how deer generally move when they're just being driven from their browsing or bedding areas—when all they detect is a distant, unwelcome intrusion from which they can cautiously edge away, often in so leisurely a manner that they go right on browsing as they move unsuspectingly toward the standers.

There are classic situations that call for this kind of drive, too. One season, in the Pennsylvania Gamelands, I discovered a piece of habitat that's perfect for a small drive and has to be one of the country's game-richest pockets of land open to public hunting. In my whitetailing experience, it is surpassed only by a privately owned principality known as the Y.O. Ranch in Texas.

It's a narrow, very boggy, thickly brushed island no more than a quarter of a mile long and only a few yards from the shore of a big, deep lake. One end is just flat, open bog, so the whole quarter-mile doesn't have to be driven. On one side of the island, the lake keeps the deer from sneaking off to evade hunters. On the other side, between the island and high, dry ground, there's a thin stretch of swamp that can't be crossed by hunters without hip boots or waders. Beyond the swamp is a rise of woods, open enough to shoot through.

Beginning half an hour before sunrise on opening day, the adjacent timber is suddenly festooned with orange-clad riflemen, popping out everywhere like desert blossoms after a rain. Not wishing to invade the privacy of these gentlemen, many of the deer head for brushy thickets on the highest, farthest ridges. That's what they're supposed to do, as all of us have read in scores of books and articles. But many more are turned back by the scent, sound, and sight of all those gun-toting blobs of orange. They must look elsewhere for refuge. The deer, after all, make the rules and, when frustrated, feel free to break the rules. The swamp is a barrier to the hunters but not to the deer, and you wouldn't believe how many whitetails must crowd back onto that island. Except for my own group, I haven't yet seen any smart deer-stalkers using a canoe to get onto the island from the lake side or donning waders to reach it through the swamp.

During the first hour or so of legal shooting time, the best bet is to stay off the island and take a high stand on the ridge overlooking the swamp. Deer have been browsing down there, and they'll be moving up to drier, normally undisturbed bedding thickets. If the ground is wet or snow-blanketed, there's nothing to prevent still-hunting along the landward edge of the swamp for a little while after that first hour or so. Some of the spooked deer are now returning, and a hunter can keep pretty much out of sight as he moves along that edge. However, there's the possibility that a buck will hear or wind anyone moving and will shy away, so a better idea is to switch from the traditional stand, high on the ridge, to a lowland stand in a tree or one of the blowdowns near the game trails entering the swamp. A buck can be intercepted there as he retreats toward the island.

By midmorning, however, plenty of deer have safely made it to the island and aren't planning to leave before dusk. Now it's time for two or three men to drive that island's brushy portion from one end to the other, while three men wait on the landward side, above the swamp, and one or two more stand guard on a shoreline bluff at the far end. The standers must be in position before the drivers even begin their approach to the island, of course, or the deer may skulk their way out. Whether the drivers reach the island from the swamp side, wearing waders, or by boat or canoe from the lake side, once they've arrived the deer can avoid them only by passing the standers. The island is narrow enough to require just two or three drivers, and though it's brushy there are openings. One of the drivers may well get a shot if everyone moves slowly and quietly. And if no bucks provide shots on the island, they'll be targets for the standers as they make their way up out of the shoreside swamp and through the open woods.

On opening day, I found that ideal spot accidentally, while still-hunting with my favorite female partner (who was later to become my wife). We bumped a pair of does, failed to wait long enough to see if a buck was trailing them—and when he finally arrived our noisy walking sent him crashing and splashing back into the island's concealing brush before either of us could get a scope on him. The next day I was alone, equipped with hip boots, and determined to hunt the island itself. However, while in the swamp water I managed to step into a beaver hole. I lost my balance and my eyeglasses (which, as it happened, did not float), filled my boots with enough water to lower the swamp level, washed my hat, and got out of the woods just as my clothing was freezing stiff enough to make me creak like the Tin Woodsman. (Outdoor writers aren't supposed to confess all these blunders, but whom are we kidding?)

On the same day, two members of my party took stands near there. One of them missed a spike buck running out of the swamp, and the other, cramped by cold, was a trifle too slow to get his scope on an 8-pointer sneaking back in. I had to go home that night, but before I left I suggested the kind of drive I've just described. A couple of days later one of my friends phoned to acknowledge my cleverness (if not my agility around beaver holes) and offer me a roast from the venison he'd harvested.

There are many other kinds of habitat pockets almost as nicely suited to a small, quiet drive. Generally speaking, I'd say such a drive ought to cover no larger an area than a square mile—usually much less—or it will be spread too thin to be effective. Depending on the terrain, the

Some hunters don't seem to realize that driving is an excellent way to collect a mule deer. These two bucks are watchful and nervous, but not spooked. They're feeding their way through a small opening, although they've detected a suspicious presence nearby. Muleys usually run uphill when alarmed, often crossing ridges via saddles or notches, and they can be coaxed toward standers at strategic points. *(Courtesy of U.S. Fish and Wildlife Service)*

cover, and the number of participants you can round up, the ideal operation usually involves half a dozen to a dozen men.

With half of them standing and half of them driving, they can comb such promising spots as woodlots ending in open terrain, crossings between browse and bedding ridges, timber or brush cut by powerline rights-of-way or old logging and farm roads, swamps, notches, and saddles, or brushy gullies where standers can be ready on the rims and at one end.

I've heard about dead-end canyons where quiet drivers can corner a mule deer without the aid of standers. Having hunted muleys in Colorado, Wyoming, Utah, and Texas, I still haven't seen a canyon where deer couldn't sneak back or top out while the hunters were pushing through scrub and rubble that might keep them from spotting the game. A drive without standers isn't a true drive but a still-hunt, and should be conducted accordingly. It is, however, a team effort, and for efficiency and safety, ought to be captained like an Eastern whitetail drive and ought to follow at least a rough prearranged pattern. It does work well in some canyons, and it works perhaps even better on big wooded flats where the drivers just keep moving the deer about for one another.

These mule deer are fair game for drivers as they ascend a slope that provides a safe backstop for a shot. The snow cover makes deer easier to spot, so the standers will also have a good chance, but at the same time the snow makes the standers more visible to the deer. The standers should therefore remain still and conceal themselves as well as possible. *(Courtesy of Montana Chamber of Commerce)*

Since quiet drives of moderate size are also productive in some of the Western mountains and bottomland prairie thickets, I don't understand why many hunters seem to forget that muleys can be driven like whitetails. Drives work well in wooded basins, the thickets around streams, and the open-bordered groves of mixed shelter and browse such as aspen and oak or conifers. As I've mentioned in other writings, where ridges or draws (or both) cut through such cover as cedar and piney woods, you have another good variation on the theme. I've seen muleys as well as whitetails herded slowly out of the cover, up onto more open ridges or down into the draws to streams where a rifleman can often get a good clear shot.

Mule deer normally try to escape by running uphill—not always, but often enough so that you must assume this behavior to plan a workable strategy.

Obviously, if spooked deer run uphill, the drivers should start low and work to the standers, who stay high. That's a good idea, but the country sometimes won't allow such a plan. Then too, just enough deer will try to escape by contouring along on sidehills and outflanking standers so that you need to consider other options.

Mule deer often bed high on sidehills, usually within 200 yards of the ridgetop. That's another problem to overcome—while standers are getting into position, bucks may spook prematurely near the tops of ridges.

Since mule-deer country varies enormously, the strategy must be designed to fit the area. Muleys can inhabit high-country forests, pinyon-juniper stands, greasewood thickets, aspen forests, oak brush, and a variety of other vegetative types. Visibility and terrain vary in each regime.

Jim Zumbo introduced me to a very effective kind of Western drive involving two or three hunters in strategic stands, with just one or two hunters to get deer to their feet and moving about. It doesn't take many drivers to spook muleys and head them toward the standers.

"Strategic" stands are places where deer are most apt to run. A favorite escape route is a saddle high in a ridge, or low dip or notch. The stander should be located so he or she can see as much of the saddle as possible.

Muleys are often considered dumb when compared to whitetails. Don't believe it. A mature muley buck will double back on drivers, stand still, or lie bedded when drivers walk near, then sneak out past standers. Drivers should be alert for moving deer, especially if the cover is thick and a deer can remain partially hidden.

Once you've determined a strategy, send the standers to their positions long before the drivers begin. Deer often move out as soon as the drivers start moving. Wise bucks might flee at the first hint of disturbance, running full out. If standers aren't watching, deer can vacate the area before the game plan begins to be executed.

It's amazing what muleys will do when they're alarmed. Big bucks may stand motionless and let drivers walk close, or they may dash out of cover and dive into a rugged canyon. Drivers should walk irregular courses, stopping now and then to confuse deer that might try to sit tight. Although it's true that mule deer often run uphill to escape, when they top out they

These seven Tennessee hunters have scored 100 percent by driving thick, tangled cover. Many parts of the South are well suited to such drives, with or without dogs (depending on regulations and local conditions). Hunting clubs commonly stage well-organized drives, with hunters taking the same proven stands year after year. Knowing the country well gives them a decided advantage. *(Courtesy of Tennessee Game and Fish Commission)*

have no choice but to run downhill again. It's therefore a good idea to place a stander a quarter- or half-mile away from where you expect deer to top out. A vantage point in a side canyon or on an adjacent hillside opposite the drive area is often good enough to intercept an escapee.

Many experienced outfitters ride horseback through timber and push deer to standers waiting high on rimrock ledges. Because the outfitters know their territory so well, they place standers in superb spots, and run bucks out the same way almost every time.

Deer hunting isn't exclusively a man's sport—nor should it be. These ladies conducted a two-person drive, walking parallel routes along a ridgetop. When one of them spooked a whitetail buck, it angled off and ran in front of the other one.

In much mule-deer country, patches of timber are surrounded by open sagebrush or other low vegetation. These spots are perfect for a drive. One man can move through the trees while another watches. Every deer that breaks from the vegetation can be seen by the stander.

In the vast pinyon-juniper forests of the Southwest, hunters often have success by putting on a drive similar to those used in whitetail country. Standers sit near openings, old roads, or other places that provide some visibility, and wait for drivers to push deer through clearings. As in whitetail country, the quarry may appear as a flash, offering only a partial target in the trees.

East or West, for whitetails or mule deer, there's another ideal setup for a drive, particularly on dry, crackly mornings when still-hunting is too noisy or when the wind keeps shifting and there's no really good spot for a lone hunter to take a stand. I'm referring to any reasonably open deer-crossing between feeding areas and bedding grounds. Before daybreak, standers selected by the captain sweep around onto the high bedding grounds—heading in from the flanks and the far side to avoid prematurely pushing deer up ahead of them. Then they move down somewhat and settle themselves at the forest edge where they can see into the crossing. At a prearranged time, when the standers should be in position, the drivers begin still-hunting up from the nocturnal browsing area onto the crossing.

On the basis of my own experience, I'd say it's wisest not to walk straight out over the crossing, directly toward the higher woods. The standers are waiting at the fringes of those woods, hidden or with their outlines broken by brush, rocks, and timber. They're hoping to get shots at deer in the relatively open crossing. The drivers move along this crossing, obliquely toward the standers. The expectation is that game will be sighted before the drivers are opposite the standers. Members of either group may then be presented with shots that won't endanger anyone. And deer that are pushed laterally along a crossing will tend to flank out toward higher woods—toward the standers.

I've been describing an early-morning drive, of course. If your party keeps hunting through midday, the areas to be driven are usually the high ridges rather than the crossings, but standers at the crossings will have a chance at game driven off those ridges. And late in the day, the morning procedure is simply reversed to intercept deer coming down from bedding to browsing areas.

A point should be made here regarding the emphasis I've put on openings, cuts, borders, crossings, and the like. By no means is it always mandatory that standers be positioned along some kind of clearing. Often, particularly in hilly or mountainous regions, you won't find a field or orchard or wide open road or even a strategically located clearing, but you will find patches of woods that narrow to a neck—between hills, bluffs, watercourses, or perhaps sheer cliffs if you're lucky. Standers positioned above a neck, on each side, will often get a clear view down into it in spite of woods or brush. And a quiet drive can herd the bucks into that neck. In a narrow patch of woods, even a two-man drive may work: one man waits above while the other quietly hunts through the timber, prodding deer far ahead of him toward the neck.

Two men can also work a ridgeline quite well. One of them stays on the crest while the other moves along slowly and quietly a couple of hundred yards below. Or two men can flank a deer trail so that either of them is likely to spook a buck out across the other man's front. A trio is more efficient on a miniature trail drive, though. The third man stays more or less on the deer run. Regardless of whether a buck moving ahead of him turns out to the right or left, a hunter may intercept him. Still another variation—one I've observed in the West—is pebble-tossing, sometimes with the aid of a slingshot. Suppose a brush ravine is to be driven, and there are only two men to do it. They move along the two rims, tossing stones down into the scrub so that what a buck hears is noise down where he is. That's likely to prod him out of the shielding cover, up one side of the ravine or the other. In the Big Bend country, a friend and I once "rocked" a buck out of a coulee onto a bald flat that way.

Deer driving is a fairly simple art whose suitability and probable success depend on local terrain and cover, recent hunting pressure, the weather, the feeding and bedding habits of the deer (and the hunters if they're more inclined to sleep late and eat big than to climb early and shiver long)—and perhaps a few other variable factors that don't come to mind until they actually help or hinder the whole business.

For anyone who feels in need of advice, mine is to set up a size and style of drive suited to the immediate situation, a safe and never whimsically altered plan for both drivers and standers; use flankers almost always and backstops when possible, and have a thorough knowledge of local deer haunts and habits as well as advantageous features of topography and vegetation. At my deer camp I've heard people speak of acquiring "deer-driving sense." What they meant was horse sense.

CHAPTER 8

THE CASE FOR DEER DOGS

by Tom Brakefield

I was damp and cold, and after more than an hour motionless on the deer stand my teeth were beginning to chatter like castanets. I'd forgotten how cold southern Alabama can get during the January monsoon season. Then I heard the dogs baying for the first time. Were they getting closer or had the wind just shifted so that it was funneling the sound my way more efficiently? No, definitely getting closer now. I tensed as the dogs drew still nearer. Apparently they were coming directly toward me. I rolled my eyes from side to side, straining to take in as much territory as possible because I realized that the deer would probably be some 300 to 400 yards ahead of the dogs and not necessarily directly in front of them.

I clamped my jaws shut to stop the chattering which had graduated from the castanet class to the pneumatic drill category. I flexed my muscles, wondering if I could get them to work right after the long numbing period of stillness. Sharp needles pierced the soles of each foot but my backsides were an unfeeling block of granite.

Then the dogs veered off and their baying muted as they headed away from me. However, I continued to strain my eyes as I looked at, and tried to look through, the terrifically thick cover all around me. Just because the dogs were moving away didn't mean I was out of the ball game. They could be on a loop of deer scent while the deer, especially if he was a wily old-timer with a trophy rack, could be skulking back my way. That kind of sustained excitement is one of the bonuses of this greatly misunderstood way of hunting deer. Finally, after 15 minutes, I sighed and stretched, feeling like Rip van Winkle unwrapping from his 20 years in the sack. The deer had headed the other way, or if he had come by my stand I hadn't seen him. Either way, he was long gone by now.

That evening while I luxuriated under a hot shower I pondered about how misunderstood, throughout most of the country, hunting deer with dogs is. This is really quite surprising when you consider that the practice goes back to Colonial times in the South, that it is now unknown (in varying versions) in other parts of North America, and that it was a favored European method for centuries before the Colonists brought it to this country.

Hunters in various parts of eastern Canada regularly use dogs to trail wounded deer and moose. This is a wise and humane custom since it drastically reduces the amount of lost game. Even when a blood trail is present, it's occasionally possible for a wounded deer to elude a hunter—and any true sportsman is repelled by the thought of game dying slowly and being wasted. With dogs to do the trailing when the shot fails to bring a quick kill, this is unlikely. Dogs have also been used, at various times, in both Canada and Europe to flush out and course big game. This, too, is quite sporting when done

In most states it's illegal to have a free-running dog in the deer woods, and it's true that loose dogs do cause significant deer losses in some regions, especially in winter when the deer are yarded and can't move quickly through deep snow. In some areas, however, it's legal to drive deer with well controlled dogs or—as in this case—to use a dog for tracking a wounded deer. The hunters would have had difficulty in locating this buck (and indeed, might have lost it) without the assistance of the dog.

properly and under appropriate circumstances. The uninitiated may have visions of a panic-stricken, exhausted deer stumbling past a hunter's stand just ahead of a pack of wild-eyed, bloody-fanged dogs, but it just doesn't work that way.

The real hotbed area for hunting deer with dogs lies in the Southeastern United States. Take a look at a map of that region. If you draw a line east-west across the states of Georgia, Alabama, and Mississippi, running somewhere between Montgomery and Tuscaloosa, Alabama, you will have the northern boundary of this area, which is fantastically rich (in both deer and thick cover). Another, much shorter, east-west line across the waist of Florida so that only the northern or panhandle section of that state is included, marks the southern limit of the dog-hunting area. Dogs are used elsewhere, especially in various pockets of the general area surrounding this region, but this is far and away the primary area where the sport is still practiced regularly.

There are several reasons why it makes good sense to use dogs to run deer here. The Northern sportsman, used to hunting in thinner cover with much denser hordes of fellow hunters at his elbow, usually conjures up that nightmare picture I mentioned: a ravenous pack of dogs snapping at the very heels of the deer and finally running the poor exhausted creature to

Walking the edge of a densely wooded tract in the Southeast, these standers are being led to their assigned stations by a huntmaster. After they're positioned, the dogs will be started. *(Photo by Tom Brakefield)*

earth. The picture is reinforced by the unarguable fact that dogs can, if allowed to run loose and revert to a feral state, wreak enormous havoc on a deer herd over a period of time—especially when the deer are overcrowded, winter-weakened, or otherwise particularly vulnerable. But this is a far cry from the controlled use of dogs (and the right kind of dogs, as we shall see in a moment) to run deer in the South.

One of the reasons why dogs are used in this region is the cover. It's so thick, even in the winter, in this sub-tropical area that a Wisconsin or Pennsylvania deer hunter would be astonished. While it's true that a canny old whitetail buck can ghost his way unseen across a field with only the barest of cover, in this jungle of hanging vines and creepers (many studded with ultra-sharp heavy-duty prickers) and densely foliaged pines, a deer can often pass within 20 feet of a hunter unseen. In fact, another hunter, clad in orange, is usually spotted only at the last moment in these thickets. Still-hunting or driving in the conventional way is not only ineffective but out of the question in some of these tangles.

And there simply aren't enough hunters out, relative to the amount of deer, ground area, and cover, to stir things up enough like the massed infantry maneuvers that now pass for opening day in most of the "big" Eastern and Midwestern deer states. Without the dogs, the deer simply would not move around or be seen and harvested at anything like an adequate rate.

Even with the dogs it's doubtful that the deer are adequately harvested in many areas of this marvelously deer-rich region. Consider this: Alabama now has a herd of something over a million deer, or about 20 per square mile statewide, including downtown Birmingham, Montgomery, and Mobile. In recent years the season has stretched for a long three months and the limit has been no more than one buck per day! Probably two-thirds of this immense herd is shoehorned into the lower half of the state where the dogs are used to run deer. Florida has some 650,000 deer, Mississippi has about a million, and Georgia has more than 750,000, so these states aren't exactly slouches in the deer department, either. In fact, it's quite plain that all of these states compare with or even outstrip many of the better-publicized deer states of the East, Midwest, and West—in both herd density and total herd size.

If you have never hunted this thinly populated and thickly covered area, take my word for it that flushing out and killing deer without dogs would be extremely difficult, to say the least. In fact, to dispel the notion that with dogs the deer don't have a chance, hunter-success ratios hover around 20 to 30 percent in these states despite the tremendous deer densities, favorable hunter-to-deer ratios, and long seasons. Not exactly like potting fish in a barrel.

The preferred type of deer dog would surprise most hunters not familiar with this brand of hunting. They would probably visualize packs of hound dogs, no doubt led by bloodhounds. Nothing could be farther from reality! Deer dogs come in all shapes, shades, and sizes. All are mixed-breeds, usually with a touch (but only a touch) of hound in their checkered backgrounds. Actually, a good deer dog is one that is just about worthless for anything else. You don't want the dog to be too cold-nosed or he'll spend excessive time trying

The hunter in this picture is only 20 feet from the photographer, yet he's difficult to see. Imagine a deer slipping furtively through the same cover and it's easy to understand why dogs are a virtual necessity for effective driving in some parts of the South. *(Photo by Tom Brakefield)*

Hunting with dogs is a productive method, as shown by this group of Southern hunters. The weather often remains hot during the season, and these club members are skinning their deer immediately after the hunt to cool the meat quickly. *(Photo by Tom Brakefield)*

to unravel a single deer trail that is hours old instead of moving on until he encounters a fresh trail. Nor do you want a fast dog. If he's too fast, he'll push a deer too hard and run him right out of the country with none of the standers getting a shot in the process. You don't want him to be too energetic or persistent or he may spend too much time on a trail that's less than smoking-hot. The idea is to stir things up.

There's really no training involved. If a dog will run anything, he'll run a deer, and all that's necessary to break a new dog in is to let him run in a pack with some older, experienced deer dogs. What the knowledgeable hunters want is a dog that will range out 200 or 300 yards in front of the drivers and dog handlers until he strikes a hot trail. Then he should work the trail slowly enough so that the deer will dawdle along some 300 to 500 yards in front of the dogs and keep looping through the same territory (where all the standers are positioned), never even leaving his home ground. One of the best deer dogs I've ever seen was a combination of basset hound and several other breeds. He was slow and had, at best, a so-so nose. He never ran a deer out of the country.

The dogs hardly ever catch up with a deer. If one of them does, there's either something wrong with that deer or the hunters will never run that dog again for deer. The idea is to maneuver the deer past as many hunters as possible, not to run the deer down. If the dog is speedy enough and aggressive enough to do that, he's not welcome in a Southern deer camp.

In a classic Southern deer-with-dogs hunt, there are usually two races a day, the morning run going out at around nine o'clock and lasting for two or maybe two and a half hours, and the afternoon run starting about three o'clock and lasting the same length of time. In this type of hunting, being out at daybreak has no particular advantage; in fact, there are some positive disadvantages in stationing standers that early. Each race usually involves six to eight dogs with a driver for every pair of dogs. The drivers help move them in the right general direction, toward the line of standers, and the drivers themselves make as much noise as possible to help the dogs stir things up. If the ratio is much less than one driver per two dogs, it's often hard to round up the pack after a race is over. The favored ploy is to set standers up in either a big horseshoe-shaped arc or a rough S-curve. The drivers then move the dogs into the openings of the S-curve or around the edge of the horseshoe. These two formations offer an opportunity for the maximum number of people to spot game and get shots. Even so, in this jungle of cover, it's very easy for a canny whitetail to slip right by a stander, sometimes passing within 20 or 30 feet.

Many sportsmen hunt together year after year on these drives, especially if they belong to one of the hunting clubs which are so prevalent in the South. The layouts of certain drives become "classics" because they produce, and are used every year. The stands become well known and, in fact, may be numbered. To ensure fairness in assigning stands, numbered tags are often drawn by the hunters from a hat and this chance assignment determines which stands they'll occupy. Then no one can gripe about favoritism, nor do hunters get into any arguments about who is going to hunt where because they want to occupy the same stand.

Most dog hunts are run by a huntmaster who is in absolute charge. If a club is involved, this person is generally elected for a period of a year and serves as an officer of the club. He decides which areas will be hunted when, which dogs and how many will be used, and who the drivers will be. He is responsible for the drawing of the stand numbers and for the positioning of the standers. He also resolves any disputes that may come up about the hunt or the game. In a word, he's boss, and all agree that his word is (for that day or that season, anyway) the final one. After seeing a number of arguments that sometimes occur in Eastern or Midwestern deer camps, some so silly that even the people involved feel pretty sheepish a few hours later, I think this approach might be more widely applied. The huntmaster also sets any fines or other penalties that may be called for by infractions of the rules during a hunt.

This kind of country and this kind of

These Canadian hunters keep dogs on hand to track and locate any wounded deer. Most of the deer in this photo, taken at French River, Ontario, were killed quickly with well-placed shots, so there was no need to track them. But the dogs were available in case trailing was necessary, thus providing an excellent conservation tool to curtail the loss of crippled game. *(Courtesy of Ontario Department of Tourism and Information)*

hunting call for buckshot. Although high-powered rifles and slugs are legal in these areas and are often used in the northern portions of the same states, the thick cover and the nature of the hunt demand use of buckshot here. A rifle would be dangerous to the drivers and the other standers, and there's no possibility of long shots, anyway.

The 12-gauge gun is far and away the favorite for this type of hunting though the 16 does still have a limited number of advocates. Very few 20's are used in this type of hunting except for youngsters or some novice women hunters. The auto-loader and the pump-action both have their advocates, with the autoloader getting the nod about two times out of three. Very few doubles, of either side-by-side or over-and-under persuasion, turn up for this type of gunning.

Three sizes of buckshot are in common use and all have their advocates. The 00 ("Double Ought") size is the largest at .33 caliber, with 12 pellets to the standard 2¾-inch 12-gauge shell. The 0, or "Single Ought," runs .32 caliber for each ball and the "No. 1 Buck" is smallest at .30 caliber and 16 to the 12-gauge shell. No. 1 Buck is probably the most popular because of the feeling that the three or four additional pellets increase your chances in heavy cover.

Buckshot can be surprisingly effective at the near ranges. The first deer I ever took was killed cleanly and quickly with a single pellet at about 40 yards. The deer was threading its way through a thick clump of brush, but, as is so often the case here, I had to settle for that shot or none. However, buckshot should be limited to 75-yard shots—and preferably to 50- to 60-yard ranges, if possible.

It's a good idea for standers never to be stationed closer than 100 yards from each other, farther apart if possible. However, I must admit that often this informal rule is honored more in the breach than the execution. Sometimes there are too many hunters for the number of ideally located stands on a good drive. Then the hunters may be placed within 75 or even 50 yards of each other. This is not quite so dangerous as it may sound. All details of these hunts, including the location of the stands, are generally plotted on a topographical map, and all hunters walk in together, each dropping off at his prescribed stand. Thus, each hunter knows exactly where the other hunters are. And one of the ironclad rules in this type of hunting is: *No stander moves from his stand until the race is officially declared over.* To break this rule is generally to draw a severe penalty and much criticism. In this thick cover, it doesn't pay to go waltzing through a bunch of hunters unless you're dressed in orange and singing "America the Beautiful" at the top of your lungs!

It's important for the stander to remain absolutely still and quiet during the race. Many standers find a comfortable seat for the long and often cramped wait. This lowers a hunter's silhouette and further reduces any danger of being hit. Though I grew up in this country and killed my first deer here, I have no personal knowledge of any deer-hunting accidents occurring. In this sport as in any other, there must have been accidents over a period of many decades, but most of the hunting has become so ritualized and is so safety-conscious that a remarkable safety record has been established.

Though I would not like to limit my deer hunting solely to this method (just as I wouldn't like to limit it completely to *any* single method), the technique does offer its own particular satisfactions. The unmoving and attentive stand hunter can often see interesting and unusual wildlife sights. I have had squirrels crawl over my boot while I was waiting, and once I saw a rare sight, a gray fox skulking by some 40 yards away. I was too interested in him and what he was doing to shoot at him.

The sound of the dogs keeps you asking yourself if they're moving your way, and that tends to keep the adrenalin flowing. Also, even if the dogs aren't moving your way with the particular deer they're coursing at the moment, the very fact that they're out there stirring things up always means you have a chance of seeing a savvy old whitetail buck go slinking by.

There are few professional guides or hunting operators in this part of the country. If you'd like to set up a hunt of this type, I suggest writing to the fish and game commission of the state you're interested in and ask for a list of hunting clubs or other possible contacts to help you make arrangements. Sometimes you can even set up a simple hunt with a game warden or field biologist attached to the department if you're an agreeable chap with a sincere interest in learning more about this sport and this part of the country. Hunters here, like hunters the world over, know no barriers of age, social station, or economic status. A good sport and camp companion is always welcome and often it may be possible to trade hunts with someone: You hunt as his guest one year and he visits you the next year. An added bonus is that the deer season in this area often stretches into January, so a hunter from another region doesn't have to pass up his own local season in order to feel his nerves tingle when he hears the dogs and asks himself, "Are they heading this way?"

CHAPTER

9

GETTING INTO HANDGUN HUNTING

by Steve Ferber

Missing a shot—or worse, wounding a deer with a handgun and not recovering the animal—is the most sobering situation the handgun hunter can experience. In the unhappy instant following the gun's report and the observation of the bullet's effect, he stands there wishing, perhaps, that the shot had been attempted with a rifle. The higher risk of missing or only wounding big game by hunting with a handgun rather than a long gun is the chief argument against the sport. It's just plain harder to bring down a deer with a pistol than with a rifle. We all know that.

But not harder because bullets fired from handguns aren't potent medicine. They are. An improperly placed bullet—fired from any gun—won't stop your buck, and one placed properly will. You have to accept your own limitations with a handgun, and adhere to them, in the same way you would with your rifle. These built-in limitations involve the attitude of the target and distance of the target from the shooter. You might attempt a shot on a running buck from 200 yards with a rifle under certain reasonable circumstances, but you should not try that same shot with a pistol. You might, however, try a running shot with a handgun at lesser yardage and under favorable conditions.

These conditions can be considered quickly, at the time the target presents itself, by keeping in mind a word common in golf parlance—par. Being able to shoot "par" in golf is quite an accomplishment, and is not the rule. But the application of position, attitude, and range in handgun shooting, and the careful weighing of those factors before the decision to shoot is made, should be the rule.

Let's consider position first. Our best

competition shooters spend hours a day, almost every day, practicing. They practice sight alignment and trigger squeeze, and it's not uncommon for the serious target shooter to burn up several hundred rounds of ammo during each session. All their shooting is done from a standing position, using one hand to hold the gun at arm's length, while usually keeping both eyes open. The maximum range is 50 meters (international) or 50 yards (conventional). From that distance, a good many of them can hit a target the size of a pack of cigarettes four out of five times. It takes enormous effort and expertise to shoot that well under those controlled conditions. You, as a handgun hunter, don't have to train that way to become just as good a shot in the field. One-handed, unsupported shooting would work against you. The answer is the two-handed, supported hold. Always find a shooting rest; lean your hands or arms against something!

In the field, it's easy. If you're shooting from a tree stand, for instance, you have branches at your disposal—or even the trunk. On the ground there might be tree trunks, blowdowns, fenceposts, dirt piles, or whatever; any one of these can become a perfect shooting rest.

Two things separate handgun champions from second-place winners: consistently good sight alignment and a steady hold. And without a steady hold, good sight alignment is difficult to achieve. Again, you don't have to worry as much about a "steady" hold in the field; under most conditions, it's automatic when you use a support. Absolute zero movement is not only attainable, it's the rule. The thing that takes practice is good sight alignment, and there just isn't room for error. With open sights, if the front blade is out of alignment with the rear sight by only a small fraction of an inch, the point of impact downrange moves drastically. Because handguns have such a short sight radius (the distance between front and rear sights) compared to a typical hunting rifle, sighting errors are increased.

Without the benefit of a solid support, such as a tree trunk, and if the terrain won't let you lie prone for your shot, the sitting position is best. Draw up your knees and lean slightly forward, placing your arms at a point just forward of the elbows on the knees, and place the palm of your

Constant and consistent practice is recommended to learn the capabilities of your hunting handgun—while improving your own capabilities. This hunter uses a good rest to check the way his shots group at a known distance. It's also important to practice at estimated rather than known yardages, because fast range judgment is needed in the deer woods.

non-shooting hand under your shooting hand. Experiment a little until you're comfortable; experiment further until you've achieved a very steady hold.

An iron-sighted handgun should have a rear sight that's adjustable for elevation and windage. Adjust it until you're hitting center when you're aiming center.

Sight-in an open-sighted handgun for 50 or 75 yards, and know, too, where the point of impact is at 25 and 100 yards. In my judgment, unless you're really a fine marksman, no deer shot should be attempted with an open-sighted handgun beyond 75 yards, regardless of what caliber you're using. But virtually any average hunter, who knows his gun and loads and who practiced beforehand, can make consistent kills at distances up to 75 yards under the right conditions.

The front blade must be aligned perfectly in the center of the rear notch when you make your shot. And you *squeeze* a handgun trigger, you don't pull it as you do with a shotgun. Practice will enable you to squeeze without disrupting your sight alignment.

Target shooters concentrate on their front sight. That is, their focus is made there, not on the target, not on the rear sight. Rear sight and target are a blur, but by focusing in this way, perfect sight alignment is achieved, as well as a very good sight picture (the relationship of rear sight, front sight, and target). Misalign the front sight by 1/100th of an inch using a Colt .45 ACP, and the point of impact will move 3 inches at 50 yards. But achieve perfect sight alignment, and move the gun (which changes the sight picture) a full inch, and the point of impact will only move an inch. The gun shoots where it's aimed.

But competitive shooters not only know their target is stationary, they also know their aiming point, the bull, always measures the same. Hunters have a completely different situation, depending on which way the deer is facing, whether he's level with the ground or pointing up- or downhill, or if he's stationary, walking, or running. So first you get your sight picture. Focus on the game, through the sights, and when you're satisfied with the target—neck, heart, or chest—slip your focus back to your front sight to achieve perfect alignment and squeeze off the shot.

The only way to prepare yourself for a hunting situation with a handgun is by practicing at the range. And I don't mean by shooting tin cans—very little is learned about you and your gun that way.

Set up bull's-eye-type targets at 25, 50, and 75 yards, and another at 100. Sit at the bench or portable table, or on the ground as described earlier, and squeeze off your shots two-handed, first at 25 yards. Adjust your rear sight for windage when you begin to shoot good groups consistently. Then shoot at the 50-yard target, and the 75-yard target. Know the trajectory of the load you're using at these yardages and adjust your rear sight's vertical setting so you're hitting center-bull at 75 yards. Know where it's hitting at 50 and 25 yards after the sights are set for 75. Then take some shots at the 100-yard target. Know how much the bullet drops so you'll know where to aim should you fail to clean-kill your buck with the first shot at 60 yards—and he wheels and runs.

Practice standing, using a two-handed hold. Face the target dead-on, extend both arms completely, lean back slightly, and squeeze off the shot. Compared to sitting and using the knees as a rest, or supporting your hands against a fencepost, an unsupported two-handed hold is difficult. If you're not in a good position when the deer presents itself, and can't get into a steady position soon enough, don't shoot. But you'll probably be able to hit a chest-size target from 25 yards that way in short order.

Now let's consider the target's attitude. If you see a flash of white tail or a deer running through chokecherry vines with all four feet to the wind, or any other "snap-shot" situation, unless you're an expert you shouldn't try to make the shot. That sort of thing is hard enough with a rifle or shotgun and is usually out of the question with a pistol—particularly in the East where there's generally a lot of thick cover.

But if the attitude of the animal suits you—if the deer doesn't know you're around and is just walking or browsing or standing—get into position and think about taking him. Always try for a chest shot between 50 and 75 yards. Consider a shoulder shot between 25 and 50. The important thing, after the shot, is to cock the hammer immediately for a possible second shot. It's far easier and faster, incidentally, to prepare for a second shot with a revolver than with a bolt-action rifle—you only need to move one thumb.

What about running shots? In many Western situations, particularly with mule deer in open terrain, certain moving-target shots are reasonable. Remember this. From a solid sitting position, as many as six good handgun shots can be made in 15 seconds. If you are so positioned when a muley begins hopping down—or up—a mountain slope, and you know it will take him at least 30 seconds to reach cover, and he's only 60 or 70 yards away from you to begin with, and you know that the lead necessary to make a good shot isn't much, and you had become a good shot before the hunt began—you'll take him.

You've noticed that I keep stressing yet another factor: short range. The .357, .41, and .44 Magnum and the Long Colt .45 handgun trajectories are not flat. Some guns, like the Thompson/Center single-shot in .30 Herrett caliber do shoot fairly flat but, as a rule, range is a critical factor in handgun shooting. And don't think you're getting extra range by using a .44 Magnum instead of a .357 Magnum. What you're getting is more punch. So if you can't shoot the heavier-recoiling Magnums as well as you do the .357, for instance, don't take one along. In his chapter on handguns for hunting, Bob Good offers excellent advice about calibers. Study his suggestions concerning cartridges in light of your own shooting ability. Also remember that at long range, critical sight alignment is much harder and just shouldn't be attempted by the handgunning sportsman of average skill. Fairly exact range is easier to calculate in the East than in the West. The more open the area, the closer things look; it's that simple. But when fences, trees, and other objects dot an area between the gun muzzle and the target, 50 or 150 yards is easier to judge accurately.

Case in point. Some years ago I was on a mule deer hunt at the Mescalero Apache reservation in New Mexico, an area incorporating 460,000 acres of prime muley country. My Apache guide took me to a place called Morgan Canyon, at an elevation of about 7,500 feet. We began walking the rim of the canyon, and later, when we

The two-handed hold is absolutely necessary in handgun hunting, and the hands should be rested on a support if at all possible. But there can be occasions, especially in open terrain, when no support presents itself. Through trial-and-error experimentation, some hunters develop unusual shooting aids for those occasions. This gunner wears a bandana, tied in a long loop, for use as an improvised "hasty sling." Resting one elbow on his knee, he thrusts his hands through the loop and pushes against the bandana to keep it taut. *(Courtesy of Montana Chamber of Commerce)*

In addition to the challenges and requisite rewards of handgun hunting, the use of a sidearm has a practical advantage when the hunter has to climb—or after the kill when he drags his deer out. With the gun holstered he has both hands free, whereas a shoulder arm can get in the way even when slung over the shoulder. This hunter uses a cross-draw holster that holds the gun securely in a quickly accessible position. *(Photo by Bob Good)*

dropped down into it, we spotted a good buck and a spike browsing on the edge of a hill about 300 yards away.

The wind was directly in our faces. The guide sat down, drawing his binoculars from their case, and sat there watching the action while I began my stalk. Ten minutes later, both bucks were still there; they hadn't been alarmed and were now, I estimated, just 80 yards from me. Deciding not to push my luck, I sat down and got into a solid two-handed knee hold. I was shooting a 7-inch-barreled .357 Magnum Colt Python, with iron sights, and loaded with the 146-grain Speer hollow-point jacketed bullet in front of 18 grains of Winchester 296 Ball powder—a hot, very effective load. (Incidentally, Magnum primers are a must with that first-rate powder.)

I squeezed off a perfect shot, holding on the right shoulder of the bigger buck. It was a quartering shot. The bullet struck several inches low, throwing bark from a blowdown immediately in front of my target. But I knew I had made a perfect shot so when he wheeled and began to run I simply aimed higher for the second shot and dropped him.

We paced off the distance and I was surprised to learn that my original range estimate had been short by a full 75 yards, which caused the first shot to hit low. The buck didn't look that far away. He had been standing on a rise on the other side of an arroyo, and I had stalked him for over 100 yards. He just looked closer than he actually was. My guide was likewise surprised when he paced off 147 long steps to the blowdown. It turned out to be the longest deer shot I had ever made with an open-sighted handgun—or even attempted. The bullet passed through the left rump and quartered clear through the rib cage and stopped, perfectly mushroomed, under the skin. With a handgun, then, knowing the animal's range can be as critical as good sight alignment.

What about scope sights on a handgun? Until you've had plenty of practice, it takes considerably longer to find your target in a telescope than through open sights, and if additional shots are needed, and the deer's cover is nearby, there's a fair chance you'll never pick him up in your scope before he disappears. Of course, aside from the advantge of seeing better with a scope, the other obvious advantage of using one is the fact that you needn't worry about sight alignment. If you've sighted-in your handgun properly, the bullet will hit at the point where your crosshairs are positioned on the game animal. Handgun scopes have been enormously improved in recent years, and have become deservedly popular. Again, see Bob Good's chapter on the current state of the handgunning art before deciding on a scope for your gun.

Regardless of the caliber and sighting equipment you use, I urge you to handload your cartridges. The .45 Long Colt, properly loaded, is an adequate deer cartridge. A friend of mine loads 11 grains of Unique behind Speer's 225-grain bullet in that caliber, shoots it in the Colt Frontier Model revolver, and gets about 1,150 feet per second—a proof load plus. A safer load (in a modern gun) would be 9 grains of the same powder, working up, possibly, to 10 grains. Though we're talking about the very old .45 Long Colt cartridge, those particular loads are definitely Magnum-types.

Unique powder has been a first-rate

pistol powder for generations, the choice of many Magnum handgun shooters. But two problems with it have always been incomplete burning and lack of bulk in most cartridge cases. One of the best Magnum pistol powders I've found is Winchester 196, a Ball powder that not only burns extremely well in Magnum loads but also fills the cartridge case, either eliminating air space entirely or guaranteeing a minimum of air space between powder and bullet. As I said earlier, this Ball powder requires Magnum primers for good ignition. Having mentioned powders for handloading, I should add that plenty of good bullets are available from a number of manufacturers. For deer hunting, you want appropriately heavy bullets. For .44 Magnum deer loads, a variety of good .249-diameter bullets are available in weights from 200 to 240 grains.

Which gun to use? For most deer-hunting situations, a revolver or single-shot is best because of safety and ease of handling, as well as accuracy. Don't hunt deer with a Magnum having a barrel length of less than 6 inches. A 6-inch, or longer, barrel allows for a good sight radius. Even more important, shorter-barreled guns will not offer optimum velocity.

Revolvers by Ruger, Smith & Wesson, Colt, Dan Wesson—and a few other manufacturers—are first-rate from the standpoint of both strength and accuracy. The single-shot Thompson/Center gun is a strong and accurate pistol, available with interchangeable barrels that handle several excellent hunting (and silhouette) cartridges.

You can certainly hand-pick conditions where a single-shot like the Thompson/Center will be more than fine, but for general deer hunting, when there's no way to know what kind of shot will be offered, I think the revolver is the best bet for the average shooter. Using a fine single-shot pistol, like using a fine single-shot rifle, adds a very special dimension to the hunting experience, but the one-shot hunt is not for everyone.

CHAPTER 10

HANDGUN HUNTING—THE STATE OF THE ART

by Bob Good

Since I'm a full-time professional in the hunting and fishing business, I have had the opportunity for many years to hunt big game each year in several states and a few foreign countries. Deer are still my favorite big game and by hunting in several states each year, some of which have multiple licenses, I have been lucky enough to harvest more deer than many hunters will ever encounter in a lifetime.

Once you've made the decision to try handgunning for deer, as I did some years ago, you're faced with a number of alternatives. Let's take cartridges for a starter.

When I was a neophyte handgun hunter, I thought the .357 Magnum was the ultimate deer cartridge, and the 30-inch mule deer that resides over my fireplace mantel is testimony to the fact that the .357 will indeed take deer, and big deer. That old buck would have pushed 300 pounds on the hoof. But it was the stalk that killed that buck, not the cartridge. After two hours on my belly, I put a 158-grain .357 Magnum through his neck with my Colt Python, at point-blank range, so close I could have done it with a .22. I've taken over a dozen bucks with that Python, but I also lost four well-hit deer, and some of the bucks I did recover I tracked a good way. One memorable heart-shot buck took me two hours to find.

I've examined the internal organs of nearly a thousand big-game animals, and when you study that many wound channels you begin to understand what it takes to put an animal down for keeps in all kinds of situations, and the .357 Magnum just doesn't provide it.

Shocking power is inadequate beyond 30 yards and tissue disruption is almost nonexistent. Break a neck and any animal goes down with a thud. But hit a deer through the vitals forward of its diaphragm and you need two elements to make a good deer cartridge. First, you must have good disruption of tissue, dispensing shock and rupturing as many blood vessels as possible. Second, entry and exit holes should be substantial enough to provide a good blood trail.

These are not my thoughts alone. Larry Kelly of Mag-Na-Port Arms has taken big game world-wide with handguns. J.D. Jones of SSK Industries has the distinction of having several handgun cartridges such as the .357 JDJ carry his initials. His field experiences on big game are extensive. Both of these men are handgun hunters par exellence, and they are adamant that the .357 Magnum is marginal for deer. Bob Milek, perhaps the most experienced handgun hunter among the gun writers of the 1980s, has written many times of the limited adequacy of the .357 Magnum for deer-sized game.

After spending an hour finding a buck I had lung-shot with a .357 Magnum, I vowed to do something different before the next season. That something was a Model 57 Smith & Wesson with an 8⅜-inch barrel in .41 Magnum. That year, five shots put five deer down in their tracks. Shocking power was evident from the reaction of the animals, and internal tissue damage, while not excessive, was impressive and quickly fatal. Exit holes were prominent, but no trailing was necessary

Here are three handguns that have the kind of accuracy Bob Good recommends for hunting. From top: a customized Thompson/Center Contender with a .375 JDJ barrel, Pachmayr grips, Leupold EER scope, and SSK mount; the .41 Magnum Smith & Wesson Model 57 with Herrett custom walnut grips, 8⅜-inch barrel, and fluorescent yellow front-sight insert; and the .357 Magnum Colt Python with custom tigerwood grips and 6-inch barrel.

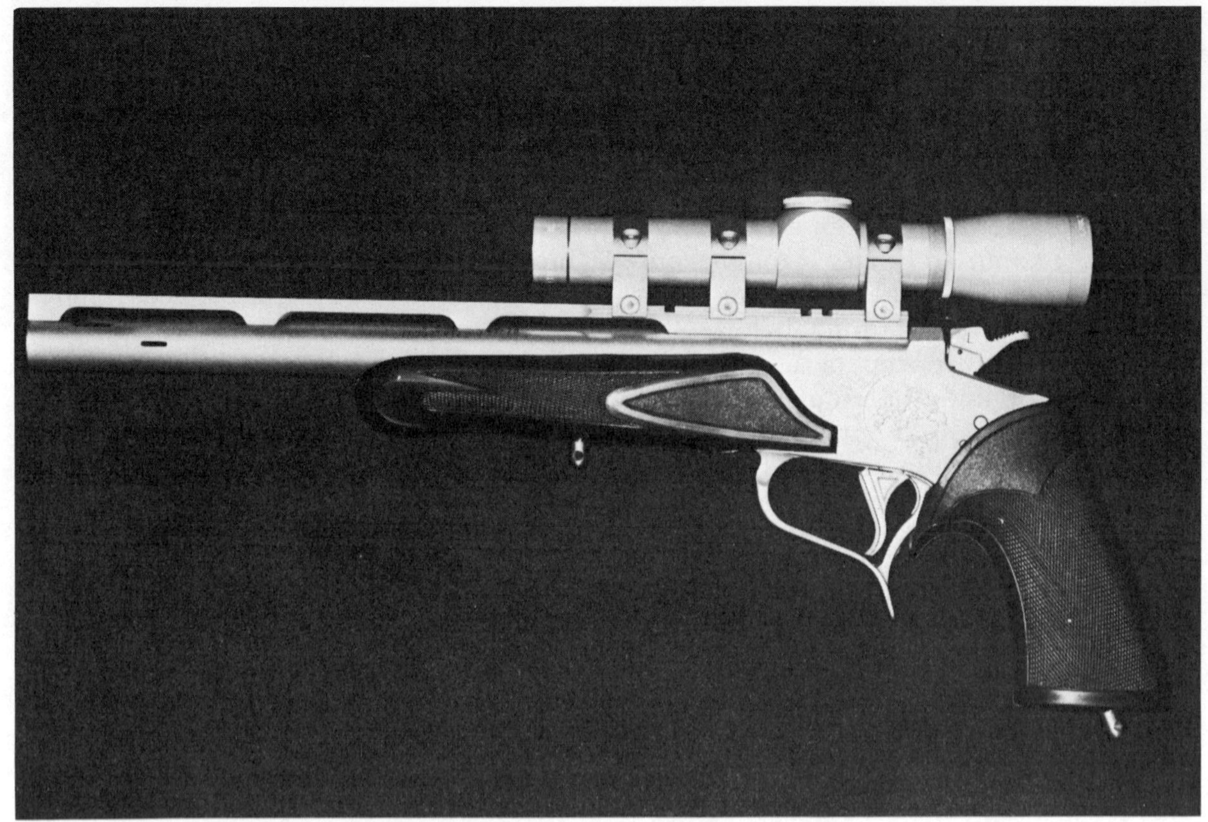

This pistolscope is secured by a three-ring bridge mount made by SSK Industries. It's installed on a Mag-Na-Ported .375 JDJ barrel in a hard-chromed Tompson Contender frame.

that year. The next season's results were similar. One running buck did keep going for 60 yards, but there was no problem tracking him through the cedars. He was spraying bright crimson on either side of the trail.

What about the .44 Magnums? Quite simply, they're deer killers. Those big, heavy bullets break bones, disrupt tissue, and knock deer off their feet. In one instance, a deer was lying down facing me at about 70 yards when struck full in the chest by my Ruger Redhawk. The deer rose completely off the ground, landing erect but quite dead in an adjoining cedar bush, reverse of the normal process, the hand-cast bullet having traveled the entire length of the spinal column. Ballistically, the charts tell us that the .44 Magnum is superior to the .41 Magnum in impact energy at reasonable deer-shooting ranges. But from a practical standpoint, based on field observation, the effectiveness of the .41 and .44 are quite similar on deer. While I have never found the .44 Magnum to be difficult to shoot, some people do. If you're recoil-conscious, I'd suggest a hard look at the .41 Magnum. It's my favorite deer cartridge in a revolver.

When Thompson/Center brought out the single-shot Contender with the interchangeable barrels, I don't believe the company had any concept of the evolution and revolution it would bring about in the world of handgun hunting. The popularity of big-game hunting with handguns has soared since the advent of the Thompson Contender, and it's more than a coincidence. A silhouette shooter hearing the clang of lead on a 200-meter steel ram punched with a T/C Contender has to say to himself, "Now that could just as easily have been a whitetail."

With the birth of the production-line single-shots, such as the T/C and Remington's XP100, came the cartridge-design experimenters. Single-shot pistols are better suited than revolvers to the high pressures involved in experimentation. Not only were they capable of handling the internal pressures of wildcat loads, they readily absorbed pressure from what had previously been the realm of rifle chambers only—the .30-30, the .35 Remington, and the hefty .45-70.

Steve Herrett and gun writer Bob Milek teamed up on a pair of successful wildcats, the .30 Herrett and the .357 Herrett. Both cartridges have accounted for numbers of deer, but it took J.D. Jones of Bloomingdale, Ohio, to really wring the performance out of the single-shot at reasonable pressure. By far the favorite cartridge among serious deer hunters is the .375 JDJ, a powerhouse of a handgun cartridge that pushes a 220-grain Hornady flat-nose bullet out of the muzzle at over 2,100 feet per second. Check that against your deer-rifle ballistics!

This is an enjoyable cartridge to load, simple to make from virgin .444 Marlin brass, and devastating on deer. On a Texas hunts, six handgunners bagged 11 bucks with that little gem—with about the same number of shots. I'd match those statistics against the popular rifle cartidges any time.

For those handgunners who are a little more conscious of recoil, the 6.5 JDJ is a fine wildcat. Its 120-grain spitzers zip along at a very impressive 2,300 feet per second, with minute-of-angle accuracy in most custom barrels. Its apparent recoil is almost non-existent, which makes it an ideal cartridge for beginning handgun hunters. When my son Robert was twelve, he neatly dispatched a standing doe in her tracks with one well-placed round that broke both front shoulders. Since then, I've witnessed several other instant kills on deer out to 200 yards and more with the 6.5 JDJ. Its light recoil and superb accuracy also make it an ideal varmint cartridge, adding a lot of versatility if you want to use the same handgun the year round.

So what handgun cartridge do I recommend for deer-sized game? I can only suggest that you use the largest caliber with the heaviest recoil you can shoot comfortably and accurately, within the range limits you have drawn for yourself.

Because of the rapidly rising interest in handgunning in the late 1970s and '80s, cartridge innovations are hitting the field in a steady flow, but no matter how good their ballistics look on paper, only several seasons of actual use in the field will determine whether a new cartridge kills deer swiftly and predictably every time it is put in the right place, whether that deer be standing, walking, feeding, or running flat out.

If you elect to go with a revolver, your cartridge choices are limited by comparison to single-shots. Because of the multiple chambers in a cylinder, revolvers are limited in the amount of internal pressure we can subject them to, compared to single-shots. This narrows the choice of revolver cartridges available to the deer hunter to the .357 Magnum, .357 Maximum, .41 Magnum, .44 Special, .44 Magnum, and .45 Long Colt.

Choose a .357 Magnum only if you are willing to severely limit your range and pass up deer that have their adrenalin flowing, unless you are in an area where tracking is easy.

The .357 Maximum is a relatively new cartridge. On paper, it promises to stretch the .357 Magnum potential out a few more yards, but will it have the intangible extra that produces venison every time? Ask me after another few seasons.

The .41 Magnum is a winner, and so is the .44 Magnum. The .45 Long Colt can be handloaded to be effective, as can the .44 Special, but hot loads should be used in new revolvers of late manufacture only.

As to manufacturer, my advice is to remember the old adage, "You get what you pay for." Since the chamber holding the cartridge is not integral with the revolver's barrel, but must be aligned each time as the cylinder rotates, a number of engineering problems must be solved, and there must be precise machining of each part involved in cylinder rotation and alignment. If the cylinder is "out-of-time" or the chambers were not machined in exact alignment, the bullet will leap into the barrel upon firing, only to be shaved or malformed by contact with the barrel throat, with resulting inaccuracy. There is no inexpensive way to solve this.

My advice is to stick to a reputable manufacturer such as Colt, Smith & Wesson, Dan Wesson, or Ruger. Even individual revolvers of theirs will occasionally leave the plant with problems, but I have always found these manufacturers to be quick to respond to any problems with their products. Their reputations are important to them.

For specific recommendations, my list would read like this. In a .357 Magnum, the Colt Python is recognized as perhaps the finest revolver ever made. In a .41 Magnum, I'm partial to the Model 57 Smith & Wesson, but I have a friend who uses the Ruger Blackhawk very effectively and it has never given him any problems, even after thousands of rounds have gone through it. The Model 29 (#629 in stainless finish) Smith & Wesson is a favorite of many .44 Magnum shooters, but my personal off-the-shelf choice is the Ruger Super Blackhawk.

If you don't mind carrying a few extra ounces and are willing to spend a few dollars for some custom trigger work and spring modifications, the Ruger Redhawk in .44 Magnum will be a reliable deer-hunting companion for years. Mag-Na-Port can tune this heavy stainless-steel revolver; smooth up the trigger; chop, vent, and crown the barrel; and replace the factory sights with a high-visibility hunting sight for a reasonable sum.

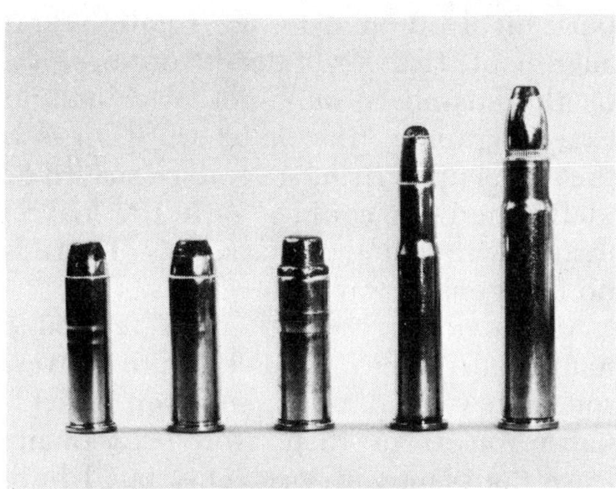

Here's a quintet of popular handgun cartridges for deer: From left: .357 Magnum, .41 Magnum, .44 Magnum, .30=30, and .375 JDJ. Stressing the need for sufficient power in handgun hunting, Bob Good feels that the lightest acceptable cartridge is the .357, and he considers that one barely adequate, preferring the heftier numbers.

In bolt-action or break-open single-shots, the list of cartridges is impressive and growing. Personally, I will never have a need for any deer handgun cartridge in a single-shot other than my .375 JDJ. It kills deer swiftly and humanely whether standing or running flat out (if I do my part). So will the .358 JDJ. The .30, .300, and .357 Herrett are effective, as is the 7mm B.R. In a lighter cartridge, the 6.5 JDJ is okay as long as you avoid quartering shots that might angle off of bone structure.

The Dan Wesson .44 Magnum has a good reputation for above-average accuracy, but I have not used one personally except for limited periods on the range.

As to barrel lengths, choose whichever length gives you a good crisp sight picture, especially the front sight. The usual rule of thumb is that the longer barrels with their longer sighting plane are easier to shoot accurately. My 8⅜-inch barrel on my Model 57 has always served me well, but the 5½-inch custom barrel on my Redhawk has also performed well and is much more convenient to carry. For starters, I'd say compromise on a 6- to 8⅜-inch barrel in a revolver. The balance is wrong on the longer ones, and the sighting plane can cause difficulties on the shorter ones.

The .375 JDJ is an excellent deerslayer. Some hunters avoid using wildcat cartridges, but this one, built on the .444 Marlin cartridge, is easy for the handloader to put together. One pass through the sizing die (left) reduces the neck of the .444 Marlin brass to the .375 diameter and produces the desired 25° shoulder. The bullet shown is the 220-grain flat-nose Hornady. To the right stands a completed round, next to the bullet-seating die.

As to brand, I'd have to say go with the winner. The Thompson Contender dominates the market. It's well made, well designed, and backed by a good company to deal with. Since the barrels are interchangeable, you can build a whole battery of calibers as your desires and your pocketbook may allow.

I'd probably start with a 14-inch bull barrel in .41 Magnum. This will allow you to buy ammunition off the shelf and gives you muzzle velocities approaching 1,500 feet per second with 200-grain bullets. If you roll your own loads, you might purchase another 14-inch bull barrel in 6.5 JDJ. By then you'll be hooked, and a 12-inch barrel in .375 JDJ will handle all your deer-hunting needs for life.

What about automatics? Availability of Magnum-class autos is currenty limited. Automatics that can digest Magnum loads have just not proved reliable to date, and until they do a single-shot or revolver is a much better choice for the deer hunter.

Whether you buy a revolver or single-shot, there are three things you should consider doing before you ever fire the first round. First, replace the grips. Most standard grips are a disaster. They are built to feel comfortable in an average-size hand, but I've never met the handgunner who had this mysterious product of statistical marketing—the average-size hand. To perform properly, a handgun must fit perfectly, almost as an extension of yourself. Very few shooters can get that feeling with production-line grips. If you're handy, you can build yourself a set. Otherwise, companies like Herrett's will produce excellent grips for you from a drawing of your hand.

The synthetic grip material used by Pachmayr is almost a necessity on any handgun that approaches .44 Magnum recoil and above. These grips "give" on impact, absorbing a good portion of the inertia and adding a great deal of comfort.

The next thing I personally would do is ship my handgun off to Mag-Na-Port of Mt. Clemens, Michigan, for venting. Putting these ports on the barrel reduces muzzle lift considerably, allowing a smooth second shot with a revolver, and a better retention of sight picture with a single-shot. Mag-Na-Porting also reduces the degree to which the grips tend to twist in the hand with each shot from a Magnum handgun, adding to the comfort of extended practice.

The third recommendation is a quite personal one, made because manufacturers are so concerned with product liability that many handguns leave the factory with the trigger pull set anywhere from 4 to 7 pounds. It's very difficult to maintain accuracy with a trigger pull that hard. I suggest you find a good gunsmith and have your handgun worked over to smooth the trigger release and reduce the pull to around a clean, crisp three pounds. You'll be much happier with your score on the range and in the field. Make sure your gunsmith knows you will be using your handgun for deer hunting with Magnum loads. Lightening the hammer spring excessively can cause misfires; no great problem on the range, but it will usually result in a lost opportunity in the field.

Next, purchase a good pair of ear protectors. The muzzle blast of a Magnum handgun is devastating. Visiting with the old-timers at the range is like attending a meeting of the deaf. For a few random shots you'll fire while hunting, ear protectors are probably not necessary, but for sustained shooting in the confines of a range they are absolutely mandatory.

Leupold, Bushnell, and Weaver all produce reliable handgun scopes, and innovative touches like illuminated reticles and center dots are becoming popular. Typical deer hunters usually are most comfortable with 2× magnification, but most serious shooters move to 4×.

Rifle scopes are designed to be in focus when the shooter's eye is up close. Handgunners need optics that are in focus at arm's length. Most scopes designed for pistoleros carry the designation EER, the abbreviation for extended eye relief, or LER for long eye relief. If you experience structural failure with a handgun scope from one of the reputable manufacturers I've named, just package it and send it along with a letter of explanation. Service is usually swift and courteous. Buy handgun *hunting* scopes, not those designed for silhouette use. Silhouette scopes have extended turrets for ease in changing reticle settings on the range, but they are excess baggage for the hunter.

I think electronic aiming devices will play a substantial role in the future. By the early '80s, shooters using Aimpoint sights were dominating some national handgun matches, but the reliability of these sighting devices under extended use in the field was questionable. That will change. The market is there, and manufacturers will rise to the need.

Scopes are only as reliable as the mounts that hold them to the handgun. Mounts are subjected to the same G-force as the scope, and I've seen mount screws sheared off after a volley from a Magnum handgun. The B-Square Company makes modestly priced mounts that are adequate for most handgun calibers, but for strength and field reliability I feel a mount using a three-ring assembly instead of two is necessary. SSK Industries produces the best I've seen. They aren't cheap, but if your whole deer season hinges on one shot then their price is cheap, especially when their reliability is forever.

The typical two-ring scope mount works on a rifle because the directional forces applied to the scope during recoil are generally along the same plane as the scope, although slightly upward. A handgun tends to rise rather violently in the micro-second as the bullet leaves the barrel. These upward directional forces applied against the normal two-ring support system will put stress on the light steel tube which encourages it to flex, raising havoc with internal optics and reticles. The three-ring system distributes this stress. I have put thousands of rounds out of the muzzle of my hunting handguns, and have never experienced scope failure or a mount malfunction with the three-ring system.

Obviously, you'll want a good holster. For revolvers, I'm torn between the comfort of a shoulder holster and the swift accessibility of a forward-tilt cross-draw. Hunting holsters are not concealment rigs

Veteran handgun hunter Bob Good is shown with a fine Texas whitetail and the scoped Thompson Contender pistol that killed it. A 220-grain Hornady bullet from the gun's .375 JDJ barrel dropped the heavy buck in his tracks. This kind of clean-kill efficiency is essential in dense brush where a wounded deer might easily be lost.

so there is a great deal more flexibility in their design. Alessi Brothers of New York turn out a very efficient standard production swivel holster for hunting handguns. Thad Rybka in Arkansas is one of the top producers of custom shoulder rigs and cross-draw designs for hunters.

Some hunters prefer a sling. Michaels of Oregon produces a number of variations, all good. But I still prefer to tuck my handgun away in a good, well-designed holster.

No discourse on handgunning for deer would be complete without mentioning the use of scents that camouflage human odor. I've tried them all, I think. I find I need only one, and for ease of handling, the two-bottle system and scent created by bowhunter and chemist Tex Isbell is the one. It's marketed as Skunk Screen or Skunk Coverscent. Used liberally on a cotton patch pinned to your hat, it will bring tears to your eyes and deer to your blind. As best I can tell, it totally disguises human scent. It also will destroy family relationships if you forget and bring it into the house.

Concerning the difference in techniques between hunting deer with a handgun and a rifle, I haven't found any. I know that statement will raise a few eyebrows, but the longer I hunt with a handgun, the more I realize the rules are the same: Only shoot at ranges you know that you, your equipment, and your cartridges can handle; always use a rest (and to the creative mind, something is always available); get as close as you can to the quarry, then 10 steps closer; show your quarry the respect it deserves by never exceeding your limitations or those of your cartridge. For a handgunner, the restrictions are no different, just tougher. Hunting with a handgun will make you a better student of deer habits and habitat, a better stalker, and a more disciplined hunter.

CHAPTER

11

THE ART OF THE MUZZLELOADING HUNTER

by B. R. Hughes

Dawn came slowly to the heavily forested ridge bordering La Pile Creek in southeastern Arkansas that misty, cold December morning. The hunter sat with his back against a large pine tree, watching a game trail at the base of the ridge. Despite his blaze-orange down jacket, warm pants, and insulated boots, there was no denying he was cold.

A flight of mallards, apparently heading for nearby Open Brake, caught the hunter's eye, and when he lowered his gaze to the trail, there, perhaps 65 yards away, where nothing had been visible a few seconds previously, stood a 6-point whitetail buck, cautiously slipping along.

Carefully, slowly, the sportsman raised his rifle, centered the blade of his front sight in the V of the rear on the shoulder of the buck, and gently—ever so gently—squeezed the trigger. At the report, the deer broke into a stumbling run and disappeared down the trail. The hunter approached the spot where the deer had been standing at the time of the shot, and noted with satisfaction a spray of blood. No more than 50 yards away he found the body of the buck. The slug had hit the deer through the lungs, and all he had to do now was field-dress the whitetail and drag it out.

This scene, or one very similar to it, took place numerous times in many different locales last season. There was one factor, however, that makes this particular hunter the exception to the rank and file: his rifle was a muzzleloader.

According to figures released by the National Shooting Sports Foundation, muzzleloading is one of the fastest-growing of the many shooting activities. Practically every state has a special

Wildlife photographer Leonard Lee Rue, wearing buckskins and a coonskin hat, kneels beside a whitetail buck he harvested the old-fashioned way—with a flintlock rifle. For many black-powder enthusiasts, the appeal of a muzzleloading hunt lies not only in its challenge but in recapturing the aura of a romantic, adventurous, bygone era. *(Photo by Irene Vandermolen)*

muzzleloader season, and deer harvests with black-powder firearms are growing steadily. To cope with the rising numbers of muzzleloading hunters, quotas or restrictions have been introduced in several states.

Why should a person use such a gun? A difficult question to answer, but part of it is probably related to a desire to return to a simpler era. Many seek some release from their everyday worries, and if a person derives enjoyment from shooting front-loaders like those in daily use perhaps 150 years ago, it's a wholesome pastime. Then there are those who maintain that using a high-powered rifle with a telescopic sight makes taking game too easy. Most such sportsmen are veteran outdoorsmen looking for a new challenge.

Those who imagine that the modern deer hunter who uses a front-loader is working under a tremendous handicap are in for a tremendous surprise when they test their first good muzzleloader. I have always felt that the average quality percussion rifle with open sights is about as accurate out to approximately 100 yards as the typical modern lever-action .30-30. Moreover, good cap-and-ball rifles are extremely reliable, provided they're given some care and consideration.

If a man has in mind collecting deer-size game with a muzzleloader, then I suggest that nothing smaller than a .50-caliber be selected. This is not to say that thousands of deer have not been collected with .36s and .45s, but the same could be said of the .22 Long Rifle. When it comes to optimum calibers, I personally feel that either the .54 or .58 is a much more reliable arm than any smaller bore. Most states set a minimum caliber for black-powder deer hunting, so check the game laws before you buy.

Mark it well: A heavily loaded .54 or .58 will provide more punch at modest ranges than will the .45-70 factory load. Thus, the man who states that black powder should not be used for big game simply does not understand the potential of a full load of FFG black powder in a large-bore front-loader. It has been my experience that a good .54-caliber rifle, for example, loaded with a patched .535 round ball weighing approximately 220 grains, and backed with 110 grains of FFG powder, will develop more "knock-down" effect out to about 75 yards than will, for example, a

200-grain slug from the .35 Remington cartridge. The paper ballistics show more than 1,400 foot-pounds of energy at the muzzle, and this is not truly indicative of its actual power.

When round balls are used for hunting, some consideration must be given to the patch lubricant. While many shooters use saliva for match shooting, this is not at all a sage idea for hunting, because the rifle will be loaded in the morning and perhaps not fired until late in the afternoon, if indeed at all. It doesn't take long for the saliva to dry out, and you are then in reality shooting an unlubricated patch. While such a load may shoot well enough, this is almost a sure-fire way to rust and ruin your chamber. There are excellent commercial lubricants on the market, and, for what it's worth, my favorite is Thompson/Center's Maxi-Lube. Many shooters swear by Crisco or Vaseline, and as long as you're shooting in relatively warm weather, these two substances certainly do a very good job.

Many experienced shooters feel that a front-loader is much more effective on medium to large game if a Minie ball is used instead of a round, patched ball. A Minie is a hollow-based conical slug which loads easily and expands to fill the bore when the powder ignites. I will readily concede that were I to go deer hunting with a front-loading rifle with a bore smaller than .50-caliber, I would certainly use a Minie. A typical .45-caliber Minie ball will weigh 265 grains, and 60 grains of FFFG black powder will drive the slug at approximately 1,425 fps at the muzzle. This translates to about 1,200 foot-pounds of energy. Otherwise, I prefer a patched round ball for deer, primarily because I have obtained somewhat superior accuracy with this projectile.

While Minie balls are most popular, the solid-based Maxi-Ball made by Thompson/Center appeals to many deer hunters. If you're confused as to what type to shoot, try them out on the range. If you're like most muzzleloading hunters, you'll quickly develop an affinity for one particular type.

Occasionally I read where some misguided soul has suggested loading two patched balls atop a normal powder charge in an effort to improve the potency

Bill Hughes likes to hunt deer with a half-stocked plains rifle, and these guns are, indeed, among the most popular muzzleloaders for hunting. Although some hunters use .45-caliber muzzleloaders, Hughes feels that .50 is the smallest acceptable bore size for the black-powder deer hunter.

of a muzzleloader. In my opinion this is a dangerous practice and one that I cannot recommend under any circumstance. When the old-timers needed more power, they went to a bigger bore. This is still a good rule. If your .45- or .50-caliber rifle isn't adequate, go to either a .54 or a .58.

Were I choosing a muzzleloading rifle strictly for deer and larger game, there is no question in my mind that the .54 is the ideal caliber. This was a favorite bore size of the Mountain Men, and their predilection for this caliber was no idle whim.

The man looking for his first front-loading rifle is very likely to purchase a gun that looks flashy and costs perhaps $100 less than some of the "name" brands on today's market. Generally this is a mistake. There are a number of half-stock plains rifles on the market that are reasonably priced, and without consulting the loan officer at your bank it is possible to purchase a front-loader that will prove accurate, safe, and long-lived. I have a decided preference for the percussion rifle, and I think that beginners who purchase flintlocks often regret their selection. (However, a state may restrict muzzleloading hunters to the use of flintlocks only—as Pennsylvania does—so check the laws

The rifle and load to be used for deer should be checked out on a target before hunting. Bear in mind that you're testing the load and equipment, not your shooting skill, so you should use a benchrest or comparably steady support. With no bench available, this shooter makes good use of sandbags atop his car.

where you'll be doing most of your deer hunting). First-class muzzleloading marksmen can shoot flinters about as well as percussion rifles, but there aren't many first-class marksmen of any type, much less front-loaders. Moreover, to obtain comparable value in a flintlock, you should be prepared to spend more than you would for a percussion model.

The better-made Civil War replicas are good values. These rifles, which generally come in .58-caliber, make dandy hunting arms. Tops in this class is the 1861 Enfield replica imported by Jana, Inc. The Remington M 1863 Zouave rifled caplock musket is one of the most popular of its kind, and is especially popular in mule deer country. Navy Arms markets these reproduction models.

With no hesitancy at all, I can safely say that the number-one buy currently available for the man interested in a front-loading hunting rifle is Thompson/Center's .54 Renegade, a well-made, accurate rifle.

It is certainly not necessary to spend

Hunter Raymond Rhodes poses with a fine Southwestern whitetail and the rifle he used to get it. The gun is a .58 Texas Carbine, and he loaded it with a Minie ball. *(Photo by Hal Swiggett)*

$400 or so for a decent muzzleloader. As a matter of fact, a few of the $400 rifles that I have examined show signs of sloppy workmanship. This is not to say that there are no expensive muzzleloaders worth their price; one has only to examine the artistry of a John Bivins, for example, to realize that here is an $800 investment that is sure to increase in value as the years go by. Unfortunately, however, paying a big price is no guarantee of quality.

Let's suppose you've selected your front-loading rifle. The first problem that will confront you is deciding upon a load. For target shooting I prefer charges running around one grain of powder "per caliber." For example, in a .45 I generally use about 45 grains of powder. For hunting, however, heavier charges are needed. (*Note:* Civil War replicas should not be used with charges exceeding approximately 65 grains of powder.) With the heavier-barreled plains rifles a good hunting load would be 2 grains of powder per caliber. In a .54 this would translate out to 108 grains, which makes a dandy load.

When it comes to a selection of powder, the rule of thumb is to use FFFG powder in calibers up to and including .50, and FFG powder in calibers larger than .50. This works very well in practice, and there is no good reason not to follow this simple guide.

A great many muzzleloading enthusiasts now use Pyrodex instead of black powder. Pyrodex is a relatively new development, and a genuinely revolutionary one. It owes its existence solely to Dan Pawlak, an ingenious pyrotechnics engineer. Before he proved them wrong, experts said there was no way to produce an effective substitute for black powder—something with all of its advantages and none of its disadvantages. Well, Pyrodex is just as effective, safer to use, and not subject to all the red tape and regulations applied to black powder. It has become the most popular propellant for muzzleloading hunters. Naturally, it comes with loading directions. Number 2F Pyrodex can be used in most of the same loads as FFG black powder, and No. 3F substitutes for FFFG. The Pyrodex powders are simply loaded on an equal-volume basis.

Should you follow my lead and stick pretty much to the patched round ball for hunting, give some attention to the selection of a good patch material. Unfortunately, old tee shirts, bath towels, etc., do not lend themselves to this use. Pillow ticking is good, as is blue denim, only be sure to wash your material several times to get rid of the sizing before using it. A properly lubed patched ball should require some effort to push it down the barrel, but not extreme force. It should go down with one firm sustained push. Ideally, the barrel should be swabbed after every shot. If this practice is not followed, the barrel will foul, and considerable effort will be required to seat the ball. Some shooters believe in fouling the barrel before loading for hunting, but if you sight-in your rifle with a clean bore, wiping it after every shot, there is no reason why the barrel should be fouled. Any oil in the barrel, however, should be wiped out before loading. The bore should be clean and dry.

One make of percussion cap is probably as good as another, but you should by all means use the same size and brand for hunting as you used to sight-in your rifle.

When it comes to sights, I have seen

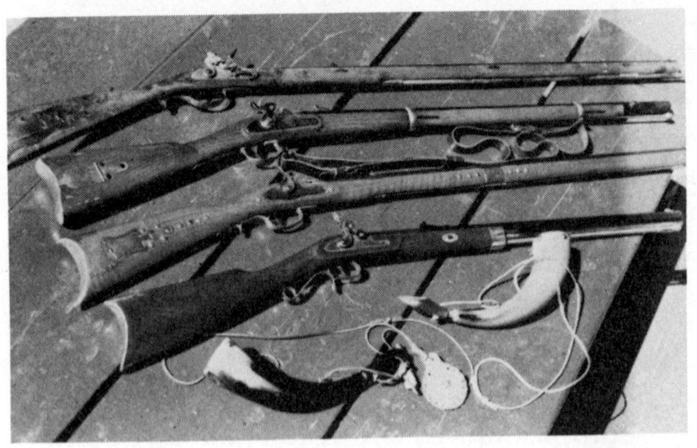

Here are four muzzleloaders typical of those used to hunt both whitetails and mule deer. From top: a .45 Hopkins & Allen flintlock; .58 Navy Arms Zouave; Dan Gardner's .45 rifle, which he built from a Dixie Arms kit; and .50-caliber Navy Arms Hawken. All but the one at top are, of course, caplocks.

virtually everything used on a muzzleloader, including telescopic sights, peep sights, and open rear types. Any good sights will bring home the venison. Many find the use of a scope on a front-loader distasteful, since the Mountain Men didn't use them. The Mountain Men didn't melt the lead for their bullets over a gas burner or in an electric pot, either. The biggest disadvantage of a telescopic sight on a front-loader that I have found is that the rear lens will get scratched and smudged from the bits of percussion cap that fly around every time such a gun is touched off. This is not true, however, with underhammer models or the Harrington & Richardson break-action Huntsman. If your eyes are a bit old or tired, you might well consider the use of a scope with one of these rifles. After all, you owe a greater obligation to the game to place your shot well than you owe to tradition. On the other hand, scopes may not be legal for the "primitive weapons" seasons that are held in some states, so once again you have to check the laws where you plan to hunt.

Personally, I prefer the old-fashioned open rear sight with a blade front. Since the trajectory of a muzzleloader cannot be considered flat by any standard—except perhaps by comparison with an arrow or a thrown rock—the maximum effective range of the typical front-loader is no more than 125 yards or so. Which is not to say that game has not and will not be taken cleanly at more extreme yardage with a muzzleloader. Iron sights do very well at modest range, and the man using a front-loader should make every effort to get as close as possible to this target before pulling the trigger. I seriously doubt if there is ever any sporting occasion when a shot should be taken at a deer with a muzzleloader at a distance exceeding 150 yards or so. Remember the .54 round ball we mentioned earlier that was kicking up more than 1,400 foot-pounds of energy at the muzzle? Well, by the time that ball has reached 100 yards, it is developing only about 540 foot-pounds of energy. Not an impressive figure. If you plan to do some long-range shooting at game animals with your front-loader, then I would suggest the use of a Minie ball instead of a patched round ball.

In the wide-open mule deer country of the West, the muzzleloading hunter has to employ special strategies to get close to deer. Being expert at shooting these primitive arms is only part of the sport. To score consistently the hunter must know mule deer and their habits, because closeness to the quarry is the basic rule. It's tempting to try a shot that is too long for the capabilities of the muzzleloading rifle, but the ethical hunter waits until the right opportunity arrives.

It's been said before, but it's worth saying again: Never, never shoot anything but black powder or Pyrodex in a muzzleloader! It should also be remembered that a front-loader must be cleaned regularly. My rule is that if I shoot on a given day, the gun must be cleaned the same day. The best procedure is to use boiling water, allow the barrel to dry, then swab out the barrel, first with dry patches, then with a lightly oiled patch. Before loading it again, a dry patch should be run down the barrel.

When hunting, I like to place a fresh load in the rifle at the beginning of each day. Snap a couple or three caps on the nipple before loading to make sure there is no oil in this area. How do I unload my gun from the previous day's hunt? Simply by firing it into a clay bank or other safe backstop. Then I clean it before going to bed. The next morning I push a dry patch down the barrel and load it. Won't the explosion of the charge frighten the deer in the area? I seriously doubt it, as the

Dan Gardner, a hunting partner of co-editor Jim Zumbo, practices prior to a hunt in south-central Utah. He's using a .50-caliber percussion rifle. This is the most popular bore size for black-powder deer hunting in the West.

sound of the gun is little different from thunder, which the game hears on a regular basis.

If you cannot stand the thought of discharging a gun in game country unnecessarily, and if it's legal in your state to leave the charge in at the close of the day's hunting, uncap your rifle and securely tie a piece of plastic around the end of the muzzle; then place a piece of this plastic material over the nipple and fully lower the hammer on it. Stand the rifle, muzzle end down, propped so that it cannot be knocked over, and the load should function properly the next day. If you stand the rifle muzzle up, there is an excellent chance that grease or oil may foul things up. After the hunt, clean your gun thoroughly, and it should last you a lifetime.

Many states now have special seasons for muzzleloaders, just as they do for bowhunters. Personally, I feel no handicap in hunting with a muzzleloader during the regular season. After all, there is no special duck season for those of us who hunt with a muzzeloader, nor is there a special squirrel season, quail season, etc. Why should there be a special deer season?

But I have to admit that not all muzzleloading hunters agree about this. Many of them prefer a season of their own, when the primitive, wilderness atmosphere of black-powder hunting won't be shattered by the sounds of modern shooting or the throngs of conventionally armed hunters. A big part of our muzzleloading sport is the romance of a century gone. Equipped with possibles bags and homemade accessories, we enjoy the historic hunting mode. So I do understand why some of my muzzleloading friends dislike crowded woods or the crack of high-powered rifles.

The man carrying a big-bore quality percussion rifle doesn't have to take a back seat to any nimrod, provided he can get into comfortable range with that frontloader and make his first shot count! If this makes you feel just a bit like Kit Carson, well, that's not a bad bonus, is it?

CHAPTER 12

PROBLEMS AND REWARDS OF BOWHUNTING

by Russell Tinsley

Archery is enjoying phonomenal growth. Every state reports yearly increases in the number of bowhunters. Manufacturers of bowhunting equipment, or "tackle" as it's commonly called, are constantly introducing innovative gear, and sales are heavy. But getting equipped doesn't automatically qualify anyone for the title of bowhunter. Some of the newcomers give the sport a brief fling, become discouraged, and quit. Determination is the primary key that separates those-that-do from those-that-don't.

Make no mistake, it is a demanding, challenging sport. You earn every deer you down with an arrow. In hunting deer with bow and arrow, there are many things that can go wrong—and something usually does! It can be frustrating and exasperating at times. Rewarding, too, even if bowhunting success can't always be measured in terms of filling the freezer. As the famed archer Fred Bear has said, bowhunting emphasizes the chase rather than the kill.

I am no purist. Much of my hunting is done with firearms and that, too, is great sport. I like bowhunting not only for the challenge, but also because it extends my hunting time, thanks to special seasons for bowhunters only.

Because of increased hunting pressure, you might see a future trend toward making a hunter select either the bow season or the regular season but not both, yet in most states as of now, you can participate in an early archery season and, if you fail to get your deer, you can then hunt with a firearm during the regular season. In a few states, if a hunter is skilled (and lucky, perhaps) he can take a deer during the bow season and another one during the firearms season. Some states—New Jersey, for example—open two bow seasons, one early and one late, giving archers a double chance. Laws vary widely from state to state, so you must get a copy of your state's hunting regulations and determine precisely what you can or cannot do.

Some areas where firearms hunting is prohibited are opened to the bowhunter. That's another bonus. Because of the limitations of his weapon, the archer is less of a threat in densely populated areas or near domestic livestock. I've personally found that the bowhunter stands a much better chance of gaining access to private property than does the gun hunter, and more whitetails are taken on private than on public lands.

Knowing that deer traffic is the key to picking a stand—especially when the game must come within range of a bow—Russell Tinsley examines a heavily used game trail. Although most hunters today buy compound bows, a large number prefer the more traditional recurve bows like the one in this picture, and quite a few even prefer the challenge of using the old-style longbow. Note that Tinsley and his recurve are both camouflage-wrapped, and he uses a bow silencer to deaden the bowstring's twang because the sound can make a deer bound before the arrow reaches its mark. *(Photo by Russell Tinsley)*

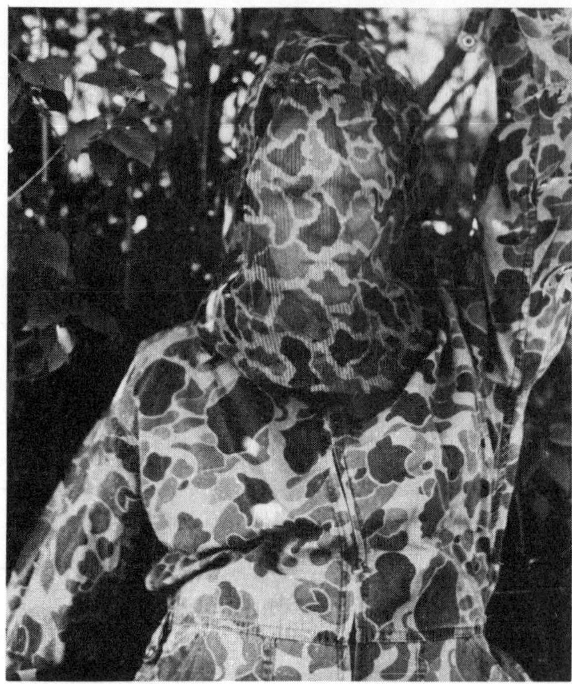

In bowhunting for deer, camouflage is usually vital—and it must be complete. A barefaced hunter can be spotted by deer if the stand is on the ground rather than in a tree. Here, Ellen Elman demonstrates two approaches to facial camouflage; one is burnt cork or camo greasepaint, and the other a camo headnet.

Do these "pros" offset the "cons?" It depends on the individual. With bowhunting you definitely pay a price for success. The task of killing a deer with an arrow is tough enough to keep the nationwide success ratio far below that of firearms hunters.

Consider what's involved. Your quarry must be close—plenty close. Each archer has his personal limitations and he must recognize them and not take shots based more on hope than skill. To do so only results in crippled game. My own maximum range is 30 yards, and I prefer the deer to be even closer than that, less than 20 yards if possible. The closer your target, the less margin for error.

You must also know your quarry and its behavior. All things considered, a mule deer is less spooky and nervous than its whitetail cousin. This is particularly true of younger deer (an old muley buck is crafty as hell!). The whitetail deer's nervous system is wound tigher than a watchspring. Just getting one within bow-and-arrow range is no guarantee of success, although that, in itself, is a formidable challenge.

There is no weakness in the deer's defense system. You, the hunter, must negate its senses of smell, sight, and hearing. If you are furtive and patiently quiet, you can stalk and shoot a mule deer, but when you're after the more widespread whitetail, pragmatic judgment also demands that you try to ambush an unsuspecting deer from a stand, preferably an elevated or tree stand rather than one at ground level. Up like this, the hunter is above the deer's normal line of sight. He can sit quietly to avoid any telltale commotion, and if there are capricious wind currents the human scent will be swirled off the ground rather than along it. Human odor is one danger signal that no deer ignores.

Yet if you are hunting an area where climbing trees is not permitted, (maybe lands owned by a timber company) you'll have to hunt from a ground-level stand and make do. Deer are killed from such stands. It only makes the task a bit more difficult. Why? That's a natural question for anyone not familiar with bowhunting. The range limitation of the weapon has virtually everything to do with it.

When a deer is at close range, the scent factor always is a problem. It is disconcerting to have a deer come your way and then, if the breeze inexplicably shifts, the critter vanishes much quicker than it appeared on the scene. To help offset this problem the hunter uses scents, to maybe confuse the deer just long enough so an archer has time to get off an arrow. There are many commercial scents with pungent odors of such variety as apples and cedar. My favorite is pure skunk musk. No, to answer the obvious inquiry, you don't put it on your clothing. Personally, I simply uncap a bottle of the malodorous liquid and place it slightly downwind from my stand. The familiar skunk smell is one of the few scents I know that will overpower human odor.

All right, by paying careful attention to the prevailing breeze and using scents wisely, you're able to watch as a deer comes within range. Now you must get your bow up, draw and release the arrow—without the deer being aware of your presence. Otherwise the critter will spook and run or simply sidestep the arrow. That brings us to the sound factor. Accidentally brush your bow against an overhanging limb and the almost imperceptible noise will make the deer suspicious. The chances of your connecting with an arrow are suddenly much reduced.

The successful bowhunter pays careful attention to every detail, no matter how insignificant it might seem. He is well camouflaged, even to putting a mesh headnet on or streaking his face with grease paint—anything to diffuse his outline and make it more difficult for a deer to detect his presence. He is constantly aware of wind direction. When he gets on his stand he looks closely for any obstruction that might get in his way as he brings his bow into shooting position. He has adequate equipment and has become proficient in its use. His broadhead is honed to razor sharpness, for he realizes that an arrow kills by hemorrhage rather than shock and he wants cutting edges that will result in massive bleeding. He knows to aim at a specific spot rather than at a general part of the animal, pinpointing his arrow into vital organs.

If everything is just right up to this crucial point, the hunter still may be dismayed to see his arrow miss its mark, perhaps thrown off by a jerky release or because the deer leaps aside a split second before the projectile arrives— "jumping the string," as it is called. Sound travels faster than an arrow; thus the deer may hear the twang of the bowstring and react before the arrow arrives. There are attachments to quiet the string, but they are far from perfect. This, then, is another reason for getting a deer as close as possible. There is less chance that it can react before the arrow gets there.

All this well-planned strategy is meaningless, of course, unless the bowhunter is in an area inhabited by deer and has positioned his stand so that he has a reasonable chance of one wandering by within bow range. This means being intimately familiar with your hunting territory. Spend much time in the woods, both prior to and during the season, to determine where the animals are likely to be found and their travel routes to and from feeding and bedding areas. There is no shortcut to success. Preparation requires dedication and hard work.

Still not discouraged? If so, then perhaps you are a candidate to join the bowhunting ranks, willing to spend the time and effort to learn how to shoot proficiently, then outwit a deer under the most demanding ground rules. It won't be easy. Learning to shoot the bow and arrow requires mastering some basic fundamentals and repetitious practice. The more you shoot, the better you get. Shooting a shotgun or rifle is more easily learned.

Getting started correctly cannot be stressed enough. Avoid bad habits and you're on the road to eventual success. It's also important to buy quality equipment of the right type. The bow, either the traditional recurve or the compound with its pulleys and cables, should have at least a 45-pound pull, even heavier if you can handle it. Check your game laws for any minimum-weight restrictions, and remember this: the more power, the more velocity and penetration you get with an arrow. And as for that arrow, buy the best you can afford. Aluminum, with its more precise manufacturing quality, is my first choice, followed by fiberglass. Cheap wood arrows simply do not have the accuracy and durability of these two products. It makes no sense to go to the expense of a deer-hunting trip, practice and plan, only to blow your chance of killing a deer by false economy; save pennies on a cheap arrow that you can't shoot accurately. And the weight of the arrows must be matched to the weight of the bow. Balanced equipment is vital to accuracy and consistency. Becoming consistently proficient with a weapon as imprecise as the bow is difficult enough without trying to overcome bad habits. Seek advice from a pro or at least an experienced bowhunter.

Take advantage of every available aid, from camouflage to scents and bow silencers. The bowhunter who is adequately prepared is confident, and confidence sometimes draws that faint line between success and failure.

If you're a gun hunter you must undergo some personal rehabilitation. Admit it or not, a far-shooting, repeating rifle tends to become a subconscious crutch for our limitations. In the open West, for example, mule-deer kills at 300 yards plus are not uncommon. Even if a whitetail buck is spooked from dense undergrowth and the hunter swings on the fleeing animal and misses, he can promptly jack in a fresh round and try again. The bowhunter seldom enjoys the luxury of a second chance. Bowhunting demands the ultimate blend of shooting and hunting skill. Of course, the bow, like the rifle, is merely

This hunter is practicing with a compound bow. The compound design has won enormous popularity among big-game archers because its unique pulley system produces the necessary arrow velocity with a draw that can be mastered by a man or woman of average strength. As the archer begins to pull the bowstring back, there is the usual resistance, or weight of draw, but it eases off considerably before the string reaches full-draw position. This not only lightens the pull itself but makes it easier to maintain a steady hold while aiming. *(Photo by Russell Tinsley)*

Whereas a bullet kills game by means of shock and massive tissue displacement, an arrow must do so by hemorrhage. A razor-sharp broadhead is therefore needed, and it must be kept sharp enough to shave hair. *(Photo by Russell Tinsley)*

This is the ideal bowhunter's shot—the theoretical, if all too rare, result of hunting skill, patience, and a bit of luck. What makes this situation all the more exciting is that the buck may still get away. If there's the slightest sound, he'll bound before the arrow reaches him. *(Photo by Russell Tinsley)*

a tool, nothing more. It is only the means to an end and not the exalted end itself. Nonetheless, there is a certain personal satisfaction to bowhunting that is difficult to describe. You need only to experience it to fully understand what I mean.

Take my case as an example. I've killed numerous deer, both muleys and white-tails. Shooting a run-of-the-mill buck with a rifle no longer holds great excitement for me. But a trophy-size buck—well, that's a different story. That "big one" is what keeps a rifle in my hands during the season. I turned to bowhunting because I was searching for something different, another challenge. It also gave me the opportunity to take advantage of the special seasons, which in some states are quite liberal. But the bow has made me a bit more humble. With a rifle, a buck has to be a pretty impressive specimen before I'll pull the trigger, with a bow I'm not as selective. In fact, you might say I am totally liberated. Let a forkhorn buck or maybe a doe—any shootable and legal deer—blunder within range and the critter better start taking evasive action in a hurry. I can't speak for other bowhunters, but for me every deer I bring home is a trophy.

When armed with bow and arrows, just watching a doe meandering down a trail, drawing closer and closer, speeds my heartbeat. Perhaps it is the slow-motion way the drama unfolds, adding to the suspense and anticipation. Or maybe I'm watching around a stand, and I turn my attention in one direction, and then when I glance back, there stands a deer, almost as if it had appeared by magic. The critter is close, real close. A very dramatic happening.

A couple of seasons back I was sitting in a low fork of an oak tree among a cluster of oaks that had produced a bumper crop of acorns. The landowner told me he'd seen an 8-point buck coming to this spot almost every late afternoon to feed. He suggested which tree I should climb into and wait.

"He'll be along," the rancher assured me. "Just be patient."

Soon after I got settled comfortably, two deer, a spike buck and a doe, arrived on the scene, and they ambled nearby, nibbling at fallen acorns. It wasn't long before another spike buck showed up, almost a twin to the first. The gathering was beginning to look like a family reunion.

I sat motionless, almost afraid to breathe, determined not to slap at the buzzing mosquitos tormenting my face, fearing that the slightest distraction would frighten the deer and their alarm perhaps would spook the 8-pointer if he was somewhere in the vicinity. One spike was feeding almost directly beneath me, not 10 feet away. Normally a buck that close would be flirting with disaster. But I was confident the bigger buck eventually would be mine. *Patience,* I cautioned myself.

As I waited and hoped, I recalled something that had happened the prior season and I wondered, with some trepidation, if history would repeat itself.

Jerry Wenmohs and I were hidden in a blind he had built near some oaks. The ground blind was well arranged, with ample room inside to maneuver, and openings through which to get off a shot no matter from which direction a deer might approach. Here on his father's ranch, Jerry had told me, he'd seen several bucks visiting the area to forage on acorns.

It wasn't long before one indeed, did, arrive and it was a handsome 8-pointer that any bowman would have been proud to claim. The buck paused at an oak tree

Here's one that didn't get away. Tinsley examines the antlers of an excellent 8-point whitetail he killed cleanly with a broadhead. *(Photo by Russell Tinsley)*

maybe 60 yards from our stand. He picked up what acorns had dropped, then lifted his head, stuck his antlers among the low-hanging branches, and shook his head vigorously, knocking more mast to the ground.

Jerry wanted me to take a crack at him, but I said the range was too far, too much of a gamble. The buck probably would wander closer and I would get a much better opportunity.

This might be called the classic image of a bowhunter. The archer pictured is a traditionalist, using a longbow. Perched in a tree stand and wearing camouflage, he hasn't given himself away by sight, scent, or sound. With his bow at full draw, he now takes aim at a deer that has come well within range.

The whitetail deer is totally unpredictable, and things seldom work out exactly as you plan. This buck fed briefly, 10 minutes or less at the same tree, then turned and nonchalantly walked away, in the opposite direction. Just like that, he was gone. Very frustrating, but I didn't regret not taking a shot. At that range—for me, anyway—too many things could go wrong.

Well, back to live action. As things turned out on this shirtsleeves October afternoon, the anticipated 8-point buck never showed. What happened, I don't know. Maybe he had a suspicion that danger lurked in the oak grove. The two spike bucks eventually got their fill and wandered away. By nightfall my nerves were shot. Yet it had been a fascinating experience, merely sitting and watching the deer. When a person observes the nervous animals this way, up close, it is amazing how much he learns.

So the bow, with its obvious limitations, has made me a better hunter. I've trained myself to be more observant of sign such as tracks, scrapes, and droppings. It is a matter of selective focus rather than taking in the whole picture. You begin to see things you've overlooked or ignored before. As for me, even if I fail to get a deer during the early season, the actual hunting is time well spent, for I am scouting areas I later will hunt with my rifle.

Bowhunting to me has been sort of a graduate course in deer behavior. I have killed less but enjoyed it more. I have been fortunate to collect a few deer with arrows, and each adventure is permanently imprinted in my memory. That's the way it is when you accept the challenge of the bow and arrow.

CHAPTER

13

THE TROPHY BUCK

by Jim Zumbo

Every serious hunter dreams of a trophy buck, the kind all of us imagine when we're sitting on stand, looking intently for a glimpse of a deer, or when we're still-hunting in a Northern swamp, hoping, always hoping, that the big one, the *really* big one will show up.

It's impossible to define a trophy buck, because a trophy means something different to everyone. Indeed, the first buck a hunter kills is considered a trophy and will long be cherished. My first whitetail, a yearling forkhorn, will always be a trophy to me. His little antlers are on the wall next to a 10-pointer, and I hold him in high esteem because he's special.

Traditionally, however, the word "trophy" is bestowed on outstanding animals that are mature, large, or above certain standards. If a deer's antlers exceed an accepted minimum, it ranks in the record books. The most popular record-keeping system—Boone and Crockett—recognizes both size and conformation. Only exceptional bucks make the presitgious book. This chapter will deal with B&C bucks, but let's briefly discuss the good, mature bucks that are considered trophies by the average hunter and undoubtedly hung on the wall of the den or the family room even though they might fall far short of qualifying for the B&C records.

In many parts of the country, an 8-point whitetail buck is king. Many hunters never kill one in a lifetime of hunting, though a few others may take one every year or so. Whitetails often grow racks with more points, but the 8-pointer is the standard that everyone strives for. A 10- or 12-point buck inspires awe in the neighborhood. A whitetail buck on good feed and having good genetics can produce an 8-point rack

Kirt Darner poses with the head of one of the bucks that have made him a legendary Western hunter. He has placed nine in the record book. Obviously, his consistent success results chiefly from his outstanding hunting skills, experience, marksmanship, and ability to judge trophies on the hoof—quickly and often at a considerable distance. But he emphasizes that it takes much time and patience. Darner's kind of success comes only to those who can arrange their lives in a way that lets them spend a great deal of time out where the deer are, scouting and hunting.

quickly, some as early as 2½ years of age. The older the buck, the more massive and larger his antlers, until eventually he is killed or declines with old age.

The mule deer grows a configuration different from the whitetail's. The later has tines growing off each main beam, while the mule deer commonly has a double fork on each antler. The typical muley has a 4-point rack, which means each antler has four tines (not counting the eyeguard, or brow tine). All the points on a whitetail's rack are counted, including the eyeguard. Although four tines per side typify a mature mule deer buck, muleys with more or fewer points are common. Nowadays a mule deer is described as a 3×4, 3×5, etc., which designates the number of tines on each antler. Sounds like something you'd buy in a lumber yard.

A hunter who works at the sport and is patient and enthusiastic has a reasonably good chance of tagging a good 8-point whitetail or 4-point muley. (Easteners include both sides in their count; the "Western count" traditionally takes only one side into account, so a 4-point muley has 8 tines.)

Practically any good deer area will have bucks that are mature, with antlers to be proud of. Most so-called "trophy" hunters go a step further and look for *superior* bucks. Not just any 8-point will do. This kind of hunter wants one bigger than anything he has at home. In order to get it, the hunter must be capable of looking at a mature buck and letting it go by if it's not quite big enough. This is something few hunters can do.

Obviously, anyone who can allow a mature deer to pass by must know what he or she is looking for. In order to be discriminating, you need to have years of experience, and you must have the utmost confidence that you can locate a bigger buck than the one you're letting go.

With experience, a hunter learns how to quickly judge a deer. Most deer won't give you much time to size them up. A glimpse of a fleeting deer and lurching antlers might be the only look you'll get.

Recently, while hunting mule deer in Utah, I promised myself I'd shoot only a 30-inch buck (meaning a 30-inch spread between antlers). During the first three days, I passed up several bucks, including two beauties that didn't have quite the spread I was looking for. On the fourth day I jumped a big buck out of thicket below me. He bounded swiftly along in 15-foot leaps, and all I saw were four points on each side and high, wide tines. The height of his rack impressed me so much I lost sight of my original plan to take one with a wide spread. Even at that, I assumed this buck was plenty wide, perhaps because I was overwhelmed by the height. Without hesitation, I fired and put him down. He was a fine buck, but he had only a 27-inch spread. Had I been *truly* trophy hunting I would have waited and sized him up a bit longer, or let him go by since I wasn't sure.

If you want a buck for the record book, your work is cut out for you. Whether you want a whitetail, muley, or blacktail, you'll be facing incredible odds. Of the hundreds of thousands of deer killed each year, a dozen or so make the book.

Where do you start? The best place is to buy a copy of the book, *Records of North American Big Game,* published by the

An ordinary spike buck can be a memorable trophy if taken under the right circumstances but, by the more usual definition, a trophy buck wears antlers so impressive that they inherently demand a wall mount. Nothing you're likely to see will top this example. It's the Number 2 non-typical mule deer listed in the Boone and Crockett Club's *Records of North American Big Game.* Taken in 1943 by Alton Hunsacker in Box Elder Country, Utah, it scored 330⅛ points.

Boone and Crockett Club. You can order it from bookstores. Carefully look over the lists and determine where the biggest bucks consistently come from. Be advised, however, that data from the book can be misleading unless you know how to interpret them and are aware of some facts. For example, the southern part of the Province of Saskatchewan has produced more record-class whitetails than any other province or state. Obviously, this is the place to hunt a record buck, but don't try it unless you're a resident of Saskatchewan. Nonresidents cannot hunt in the southern deer-rich region, and there are no prospects that the regulation will ever be changed.

There's a widespread notion that trophy whitetails are much rarer than they used to be. That's not true—and records continue to be broken. This conservation officer is holding the antlers of the world's record non-typical whitetail. The deer was what the record keepers call a "pick-up"—not killed by a known hunter but found dead in the woods. Game biologists believe the animal probably died of old age. Discovered in 1982 in Missouri, it made headlines by outscoring all previous non-typical trophies. And somewhere, sooner or later, a hunter may take a whitetail that outscores this one.

Another example. You'll see from the records that a good number of trophy mule deer were killed in New Mexico's Jicarilla Apache Indian Reservation. If you look closely, however, you'll find that those deer were killed several years ago, most of them when the reservation started letting hunters onto the property in the late 1950s.

When using the B&C book, check the dates when the deer were killed as well as the locations. Each listing has the general area of the kill. Most listings are counties, but some are more specific.

With regard to being specific, perhaps I should have mentioned that Saskatchewan is at the top in both the typical and non-typical listings for whitetails. To qualify for the B&C book's typical whitetail or mule deer listing, you must take a trophy deer with a huge rack but one that's considered normal for the species—symmetrical or nearly so. The two sides generally have the same number of tines (though one side may have an extra one or two). When you're scoring a deer in the typical category, if one side has an extra tine that's an inch long or more, it's subtracted from the score.

Symmetry of antlers is governed by genetics and by diet (particularly mineral intake). Some regions are noted for bucks with non-typical antlers that sprout a great many tines—seldom the same number on each side—jutting in all directions. Some of them have so many spiny-looking protrusions that they're known as "cactus horns." The Boone and Crockett records maintain listings of non-typical bucks in a separate category. However, if you take a big buck with an extra couple of points on one side, don't expect it to qualify for a non-typical record. A buck like that is merely classified as a typical deer with an extra couple of points *detracting* from its score. Glance at the listings and you'll see that a record non-typical buck has to be *really* non-typical—has to have a great many extra tines, usually on both sides. The Boone and Crockett scoring charts accompanying this chapter will show you what to look for and how to score a buck in either the typical or non-typical category.

Here are the top states for North America's trophy deer as recognized by the Boone and Crockett Club:

In the typical category, 456 whitetails are listed. Saskatchewan leads with 57 deer, followed by these states and provinces: Texas, 47; Minnesota, 38; Wisconsin, 34; Nebraska, 25; Alberta, 21; Missouri, 21; Montana, 19; Iowa, 17; Manitoba, 17; Ohio, 17; South Dakota, 15; Arkansas, 13; Illinois, 12; New York, 12; Kansas, 10; North Dakota, 10; and Pennsylvania, 10. Nineteen other states, Canadian provinces, and Mexico had less than 10 each.

In the non-typical category, 313 whitetails are listed. Saskatchewan leads with 38 deer, followed by these states and provinces: Wisconsin, 34; Minnesota, 26; Montana, 17; Nebraska, 17; Ohio, 15; Alberta, 14; Texas, 14; Washington, 14; and South Dakota, 11. Twenty-six other states and Canadian provinces had less than 10 each.

Among typical Coues whitetail deer, there are 133 heads in the book. Of these, 107 came from Arizona, 23 from Mexico, and 3 from New Mexico. Among non-typical Coues whitetail deer, 17 heads are listed, with 15 from Arizona and two from Mexico.

The book shows 318 typical mule deer. Colorado is by far the leader with 137 deer. Here are the other top states: New Mexico, 38; Idaho, 33; Utah, 29; Wyoming, 25; Arizona, 18; and Montana, 10. Seven other states and provinces had less than 10 each.

In the non-typical category, 254 mule deer are in the book. Again Colorado is far in front with 68 deer. Other top states and provinces are: Idaho, 36; Arizona, 29; Utah, 22; Montana, 15; Wyoming, 15; New Mexico, 13; and Saskatchewan, 10. Nine other states and provinces had less than 10 each.

Blacktails are listed only in a typical category, with 309 deer in the book. California produced 136, Oregon had 89, Washington had 72, and British Columbia had 12.

During the long history of Boone and Crockett, the minimum standards for entry into the book have been changed and are higher now than they once were. Because of the nature of the scoring system, non-typical antlers have higher scoring standards than typical racks. Here are the current minimum standards: typical whitetail, 170 points; non-typical whitetail, 195; typical Coues, 110; non-typical Coues, 120; blacktail, 130; typical mule deer, 195; non-typical mule deer, 240.

Size and massiveness are not the only criteria in the Boone and Crockett scoring systems. Symmetry is important in the typical categories, since differences between left and right antler are penalized—subtracted from the score. In addition, measure as many mounted heads as you can in order to get an idea how various racks score.

Knowing the trophy-rich locales listed in the record book is only a starting point. Plenty of other hunters have read the book and will offer you competition. You need to focus your attention on potential places that can produce a record, and then proceed with the task at hand; trying for one, year after year. Unless you are exceedingly lucky, you will be embarking on a trail that is apt to be unsuccessful. The odds against taking a B&C buck are awesome.

There are some individuals who have not only taken one record-book buck, but several. Kirt Darner of Montrose, Colorado, is an example. Darner has put eight mule deer in the book. He is a forester by profession and spends a great deal of time in the woods, much of it in prime deer country where record-class muleys are known to live. Darner hunts hard, usually all season, and knows what he's looking for. He has the ability to instantly judge a big buck and make a snap decision as to whether or not it's a book candidate. Darner has dedicated his hunting life to trophy mule deer, and he is in the woods all year long, talking to people, looking at new country, locating big bucks. He is a true trophy hunter, and probably will never be equalled for having the most deer in the record book.

Most of us don't have the time to scout deer country the way Kirt Darner does, but that doesn't mean we can't give it a good try. First let's look at the trophy buck to see what we're up against.

A buck that can grow record-class antlers is an old buck as deer go. He will be anywhere from four to seven years or more of age, which compares to a 10- or 12-year-old dog or a 15- to 20-year-old horse. The deer, of course, hasn't the comforts of a dog or horse. People are shooting at him, and he isn't being hand-fed or cared for by a veterinarian when he's ill. Besides hunters who want to tie a tag on his antler, cougars, coyotes, dogs, and various insects and diseases try their best to do him in. And if he survives all that, he rustles feed through ice and snow during severe winters and he takes his chances with speeding autos when he chases does around during the breeding season in November and December.

It is something close to a miracle when a deer reaches the old age of four or five years. In addition to longevity, a trophy-class buck must have good feed to grow big antlers, and his family tree must have the genes capable of producing a massive rack. If you told an experienced Texas hunter that you were going to hunt a Boone and Crockett whitetail in the Hill Country, you'd get a good Texas laugh. But if you intended to try for one in South Texas, you'd be taken seriously. Some regions simply produce big racks while others won't.

Age is the most important factor for the hunter to worry about. With age comes experience. That old buck with the monster rack will be the slyest, sneakiest, wariest buck in the woods. He's a superbuck, whether he slinks around in the back forty of an Ohio woodlot or grazes up in the rimrock of a Rocky Mountain peak.

You will need to discipline yourself and make deer hunting something more than a casual sport if you want this superbuck. You'll need to rearrange your lifestyle. If you aren't in good physical condition, you might need to tone up some muscles, though it's true that monster whitetails often live in urban areas where brains are more important in taking him than brawn. Mule deer are another story, but with muleys a horse can do a lot of the work for you.

Another mandatory requirement is the necessity of spending all the time you can in good deer woods where a trophy might be lurking. Plan your vacation time, weekends, every moment you can, to find your big buck. And when you're in his world, hunt a little earlier each day and a little later each afternoon. Walk an extra mile or two, and don't hesitate about shivering in the tree stand for another hour or more.

Remember, you're in his land. To get him you need to be good—darned good—and if you get him, count yourself one of the rare few. You will have earned him.

The world's record typical whitetail scored 206⅛ points. It was killed in Burnett County, Wisconsin, by James Jordan back in 1914. A modern hunter may yet break this record, though the massiveness of the antlers is unique. *(Courtesy of Boone and Crockett Club)*

The world's record typical mule deer was killed in Dolores County, Colorado, by Doug Burris, Jr., in 1972. It scored 225⅝ points. The inside spread of those antlers is 30⅞ inches, and they're more than 5 inches around at the smallest place between the burr and first point. *(Photo by William H. Nesbitt, courtesy of Boone and Crockett Club)*

OFFICIAL SCORING SYSTEM FOR NORTH AMERICAN BIG GAME TROPHIES

Records of North American Big Game — BOONE AND CROCKETT CLUB — 205 South Patrick Street, Alexandria, Virginia 22314

Minimum Score:
whitetail 170
Coues' 110

TYPICAL
WHITETAIL AND COUES' DEER

Kind of Deer ____________

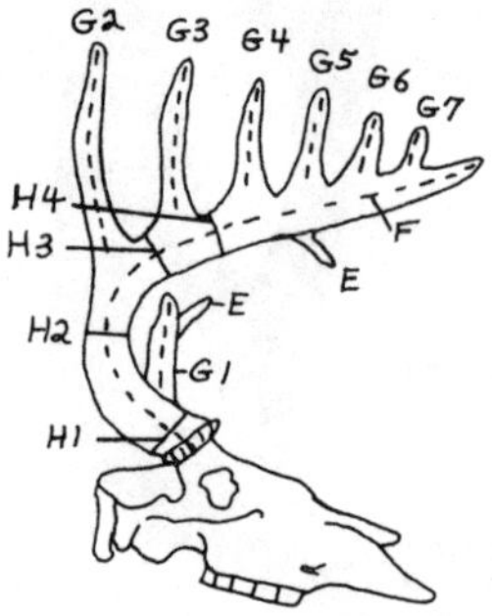

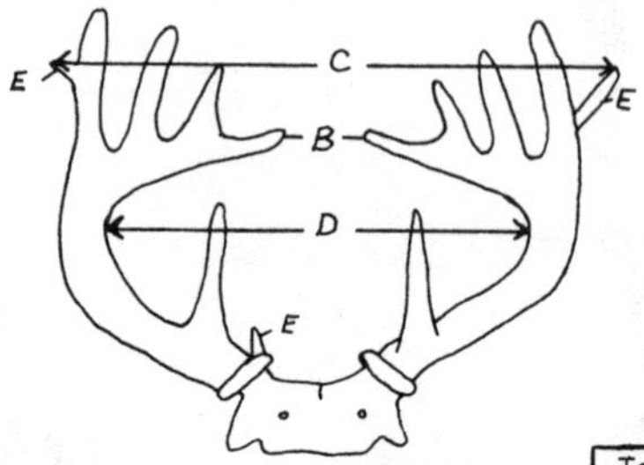

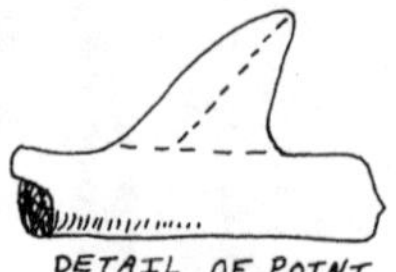

DETAIL OF POINT MEASUREMENT

Abnormal Points	
Right	Left
Total to E	

SEE OTHER SIDE FOR INSTRUCTIONS			Column 1	Column 2	Column 3	Column 4
A. Number of Points on Each Antler	R.	L.	Spread Credit	Right Antler	Left Antler	Difference
B. Tip to Tip Spread						
C. Greatest Spread						
D. Inside Spread of Main Beams		Credit may equal but not exceed length of longer antler				
IF Spread exceeds longer antler, enter difference.						
E. Total of Lengths of all Abnormal Points						
F. Length of Main Beam						
G-1. Length of First Point, if present						
G-2. Length of Second Point						
G-3. Length of Third Point						
G-4. Length of Fourth Point, if present						
G-5. Length of Fifth Point, if present						
G-6. Length of Sixth Point, if present						
G-7. Length of Seventh Point, if present						
H-1. Circumference at Smallest Place Between Burr and First Point						
H-2. Circumference at Smallest Place Between First and Second Points						
H-3. Circumference at Smallest Place Between Second and Third Points						
H-4 Circumference at Smallest Place between Third and Fourth Points (see back if G-4 is missing)						
TOTALS						

ADD	Column 1		Exact locality where killed
	Column 2		Date killed By whom killed
	Column 3		Present owner
	Total		Address
SUBTRACT Column 4			Guide's Name and Address
FINAL SCORE			Remarks: (Mention any abnormalities or unique qualities)

Here's the official scoring chart for typical whitetail and Coues deer.
(Courtesy of Boone and Crockett Club)

I certify that I have measured the above trophy on ______________________ 19______
at (address) ______________________ City ______________________ State ________
and that these measurements and data are, to the best of my knowledge and belief, made in accordance with the instructions given.

Witness: ______________________ Signature: ______________________
OFFICIAL MEASURER

INSTRUCTIONS FOR MEASURING WHITETAIL AND COUES' DEER

All measurements must be made with a ¼-inch flexible steel tape to the nearest one-eighth of an inch. Wherever it is necessary to change direction of measurement, mark a control point and swing tape at this point. Enter fractional figures in eighths, without reduction. Official measurements cannot be taken for at least sixty days after the animal was killed.

A. Number of Points on Each Antler. To be counted a point, a projection must be at least one inch long and its length must exceed the width of its base. All points are measured from tip of point to nearest edge of beam as illustrated. Beam tip is counted as a point but not measured as a point.

B. Tip to Tip Spread is measured between tips of main beams.

C. Greatest Spread is measured between perpendiculars at a right angle to the center line of the skull at widest part whether across main beams or points.

D. Inside Spread of Main Beams is measured at a right angle to the center line of the skull at widest point between main beams. Enter this measurement again in Spread Credit column if it is less than or equal to the length of longer antler; if longer, enter longer antler length for Spread Credit.

E. Total of lengths of all Abnormal Points. Abnormal points are those nontypical in location (points originating from points or from sides or bottom of main beam) or extra points beyond the normal pattern of up to eight normal points, including beam tip, per antler. Measure in usual manner and enter in appropriate blanks.

F. Length of Main Beam is measured from lowest outside edge of burr over outer curve to the most distant point of what is, or appears to be, the main beam. The point of beginning is that point on the burr where the center line along the outer curve of the beam intersects the burr, then following generally the line of the illustration.

G-1-2-3-4-5-6-7. Length of Normal Points. Normal points project from the top of the main beam. They are measured from nearest edge of main beam over outer curve to tip. Lay the tape along the outer curve of the beam so that the top edge of the tape coincides with the top edge of the beam on both sides of the point to determine baseline for point measurements. Record point lengths in appropriate blanks.

H-1-2-3-4. Circumferences are taken as detailed for each measurement. If brow point is missing, take H-1 and H-2 at smallest place between burr and G-2. If G-4 is missing, take H-4 halfway between G-3 and tip of main beam.

* * * * * * * * * * * *

FAIR CHASE STATEMENT FOR ALL HUNTER-TAKEN TROPHIES

To make use of the following methods shall be deemed as UNFAIR CHASE and unsportsmanlike, and any trophy obtained by use of such means is disqualified from entry for Awards.

I. Spotting or herding game from the air, followed by landing in its vicinity for pursuit;
II. Herding or pursuing game with motor-powered vehicles;
III. Use of electronic communications for attracting, locating or observing game, or guiding the hunter to such game;
IV. Hunting game confined by artificial barriers, including escape-proof fencing; or hunting game transplanted solely for the purpose of commercial shooting.

****

I certify that the trophy scored on this chart was not taken in UNFAIR CHASE as defined above by the Boone and Crockett Club. I further certify that it was taken in full compliance with local game laws of the state, province, or territory.

Date______________________ Signature of Hunter______________________
(Have signature notarized by a Notary Public)

OFFICIAL SCORING SYSTEM FOR NORTH AMERICAN BIG GAME TROPHIES

Records of North American Big Game

BOONE AND CROCKETT CLUB

205 South Patrick Street
Alexandria, Virginia 22314

Minimum Score:
whitetail 195
Coues' 120

NON-TYPICAL
WHITETAIL AND COUES' DEER

Kind of Deer____________

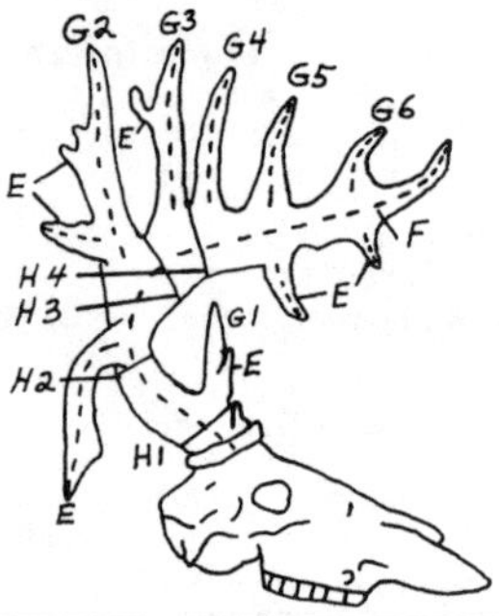

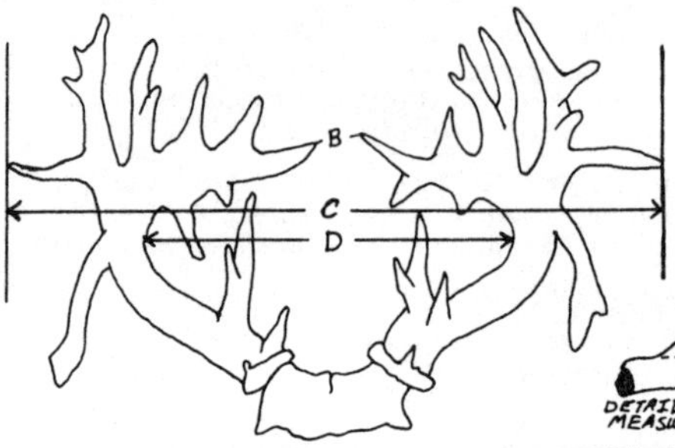

Abnormal Points	
Right	Left
Total to E	

SEE OTHER SIDE FOR INSTRUCTIONS			Column 1	Column 2	Column 3	Column 4
A. Number of Points on Each Antler	R.	L.	Spread Credit	Right Antler	Left Antler	Difference
B. Tip to Tip Spread						
C. Greatest Spread						
D. Inside Spread of Main Beams		Credit may equal but not exceed length of longer antler				
IF Spread exceeds longer antler, enter difference.						
E. Total of Lengths of Abnormal Points						
F. Length of Main Beam						
G-1. Length of First Point, if present						
G-2. Length of Second Point						
G-3. Length of Third Point						
G-4. Length of Fourth Point, if present						
G-5. Length of Fifth Point, if present						
G-6. Length of Sixth Point, if present						
G-7. Length of Seventh Point, if present						
H-1. Circumference at Smallest Place Between Burr and First Point						
H-2. Circumference at Smallest Place Between First and Second Points						
H-3. Circumference at Smallest Place Between Second and Third Points						
H-4. Circumference at Smallest Place Between Third and Fourth Points						
TOTALS						

ADD	Column 1		Exact locality where killed
	Column 2		Date killed By whom killed
	Column 3		Present owner
Total			Address
SUBTRACT Column 4			
Result			Guide's Name and Address
Add line E Total			Remarks: (Mention any abnormalities or unique qualities)
FINAL SCORE			

Here's the official scoring chart for non-typical whitetail and Coues deer.
(Courtesy of Boone and Crockett Club)

I certify that I have measured the above trophy on ______________________ 19______
at (address) ______________________ City ______________ State________
and that these measurements and data are, to the best of my knowledge and belief, made in accordance with the instructions given.

Witness: ______________________ Signature: ______________________
OFFICIAL MEASURER

INSTRUCTIONS FOR MEASURING NON-TYPICAL WHITETAIL AND COUES' DEER

All measurements must be made with a ¼-inch flexible steel tape to the nearest one-eighth of an inch. Wherever it is necessary to change direction of measurement, mark a control point and swing tape at this point. Enter fractional figures in eighths, without reduction. Official measurements cannot be taken for at least sixty days after the animal was killed.

A. Number of Points on Each Antler. To be counted a point, a projection must be at least one inch long and its length must exceed the width of its base. All points are measured from tip of point to nearest edge of beam as illustrated. Beam tip is counted as a point but not measured as a point.

B. Tip to Tip Spread is measured between tips of main beams.

C. Greatest Spread is measured between perpendiculars at a right angle to the center line of the skull at widest part whether across main beams or points.

D. Inside Spread of Main Beams is measured at a right angle to the center line of the skull at widest point between main beams. Enter this measurement again in Spread Credit column if it is less than or equal to the length of longer antler; if longer, enter longer antler length for Spread Credit.

E. Total of Lengths of all Abnormal Points. Abnormal points are those nontypical in location (points originating from points or from sides or bottom of main beam) or extra points beyond the normal pattern of up to eight normal points, including beam tip, per antler. Measure in usual manner and enter in appropriate blanks.

F. Length of Main Beam is measured from lowest outside edge of burr over outer curve to the most distant point of what is, or appears to be, the main beam. The point of beginning is that point on the burr where the center line along the outer curve of the beam intersects the burr, then following generally the line of the illustration.

G-1-2-3-4-5-6-7. Length of Normal Points. Normal points project from the top of the main beam. They are measured from nearest edge of main beam over outer curve to tip. Lay the tape along the outer curve of the beam so that the top edge of the tape coincides with the beam on both sides of the point to determine baseline for point measurement. Record point lengths in appropriate blanks.

H-1-2-3-4. Circumferences are taken as detailed for each measurement. If brow point is missing, take H-1 and H-2 at smallest place between burr and G-2. If G-4 is missing, take H-4 halfway between G-3 and tip of main beam.

* * * * * * * * * * * *

FAIR CHASE STATEMENT FOR ALL HUNTER-TAKEN TROPHIES

To make use of the following methods shall be deemed as UNFAIR CHASE and unsportsmanlike, and any trophy obtained by use of such means is disqualified from entry for Awards.

I. Spotting or herding game from the air, followed by landing in its vicinity for pursuit;

II. Herding or pursuing game with motor-powered vehicles;

III. Use of electronic communications for attracting, locating or observing game, or guiding the hunter to such game;

IV. Hunting game confined by artificial barriers, including escape-proof fencing; or hunting game transplanted solely for the purpose of commercial shooting.

****

I certify that the trophy scored on this chart was not taken in UNFAIR CHASE as defined above by the Boone and Crockett Club. I further certify that it was taken in full compliance with local game laws of the state, province, or territory.

Date______________________Signature of Hunter______________________
(Have signature notarized by a Notary Public)

OFFICIAL SCORING SYSTEM FOR NORTH AMERICAN BIG GAME TROPHIES

Records of North American Big Game | BOONE AND CROCKETT CLUB | 205 South Patrick Street, Alexandria, Virginia 22314

Minimum Score:
mule 195
blacktail 130

TYPICAL
MULE AND BLACKTAIL DEER

Kind of Deer ________

DETAIL OF POINT MEASUREMENT

Abnormal Points	
Right	Left
Total to E	

SEE OTHER SIDE FOR INSTRUCTIONS			Column 1	Column 2	Column 3	Column 4
A. Number of points on Each Antler	R.	L.	Spread Credit	Right Antler	Left Antler	Difference
B. Tip to Tip Spread						
C. Greatest Spread						
D. Inside Spread of Main Beams		Credit may equal but not exceed length of longer antler				
IF Spread exceeds longer antler, enter difference						
E. Total of Lengths of Abnormal Points						
F. Length of Main Beam						
G-1. Length of First Point, if present						
G-2. Length of Second Point						
G-3. Length of Third Point, if present						
G-4. Length of Fourth Point, if present						
H-1. Circumference at Smallest Place Between Burr and First Point						
H-2. Circumference at Smallest Place Between First and Second Points						
H-3. Circumference at Smallest Place Between Main Beam and Third Point						
H-4. Circumference at Smallest Place Between Second and Fourth Points						
TOTALS						

ADD	Column 1		Exact locality where killed
	Column 2		Date killed By whom killed
	Column 3		Present owner
TOTAL			Address
SUBTRACT Column 4			Guide's Name and Address
FINAL SCORE			Remarks: (Mention any abnormalities or unique qualities)

Here's the official scoring chart for typical mule and blacktail deer.
(Courtesy of Boone and Crockett Club)

I certify that I have measured the above trophy on ______________________ 19______
at (address) ______________________________ City ______________ State ________
and that these measurements and data are, to the best of my knowledge and belief, made in accordance with the instructions given.

Witness: ______________________________ Signature: ______________________
OFFICIAL MEASURER

INSTRUCTIONS FOR MEASURING MULE AND BLACKTAIL DEER

All measurements must be made with a ¼-inch flexible steel tape to the nearest one-eighth of an inch. Wherever it is necessary to change direction of measurement, mark a control point and swing tape at this point. Enter fractional figures in eighths, without reduction. Official measurements cannot be taken for at least sixty days after the animal was killed.

A. Number of Points on Each Antler. To be counted a point, a projection must be at least one inch long and its length must exceed the width of its base. All points are measured from tip of point to nearest edge of beam as illustrated. Beam tip is counted as a point but not measured as a point.

B. Tip to Tip Spread is measured between tips of main beams.

C. Greatest Spread is measured between perpendiculars at a right angle to the center line of the skull at widest part whether across main beams or points.

D. Inside Spread of Main Beams is measured at a right angle to the center line of the skull at widest point between main beams. Enter this measurement again in Spread Credit column if it is less than or equal to the length of longer antler; if longer, enter longer antler length for Spread Credit.

E. Total Lengths of all Abnormal Points. Abnormal points are those nontypical in location such as points originating from a point (exception: G-3 originates from G-2 in perfectly normal fashion) or from sides or bottom of main beam or any points beyond the normal pattern of five (including beam tip) per antler. Measure each abnormal point in usual manner and enter in appropriate blanks.

F. Length of Main Beam is measured from lowest outside edge of burr over outer curve to the tip of the main beam. The point of beginning is that point on the burr where the center line along the outer curve of the beam intersects the burr, then following generally the line of the illustration.

G-1-2-3-4. Length of Normal Points. Normal points are the brow and the upper and lower forks as shown in the illustration. They are measured from nearest edge of beam over outer curve to tip. Lay the tape along the outer curve of the beam so that the top edge of the tape coincides with the top edge of the beam on both sides of the point to determine baseline for point measurement. Record point lengths in appropriate blanks.

H-1-2-3-4. Circumferences are taken as detailed for each measurement. If brow point is missing, take H-1 and H-2 at smallest place between burr and G-2. If G-3 is missing, take H-3 halfway between the base and tip of second point. If G-4 is missing, take H-4 halfway between the second point and tip of main beam.

* * * * * * * * * * * *

FAIR CHASE STATEMENT FOR ALL HUNTER-TAKEN TROPHIES

To make use of the following methods shall be deemed as UNFAIR CHASE and unsportsmanlike, and any trophy obtained by use of such means is disqualified from entry for Awards.

I. Spotting or herding game from the air, followed by landing in its vicinity for pursuit;
II. Herding or pursuing game with motor-powered vehicles;
III. Use of electronic communications for attracting, locating or observing game, or guiding the hunter to such game;
IV. Hunting game confined by artificial barriers, including escape-proof fencing; or hunting game transplanted solely for the purpose of commercial shooting.

****

I certify that the trophy scored on this chart was not taken in UNFAIR CHASE as defined above by the Boone and Crockett Club. I further certify that it was taken in full compliance with local game laws of the state, province, or territory.

Date______________________ Signature of Hunter______________________________
(Have signature notarized by a Notary Public)

OFFICIAL SCORING SYSTEM FOR NORTH AMERICAN BIG GAME TROPHIES

Records of North American Big Game | BOONE AND CROCKETT CLUB | 205 South Patrick Street, Alexandria, Virginia 22314

Minimum Score: 240

NON-TYPICAL MULE DEER

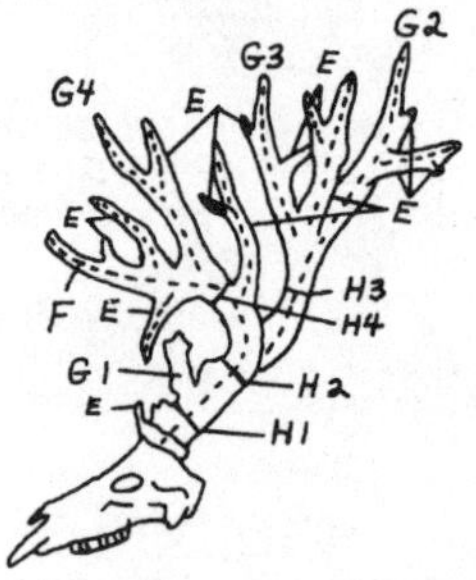

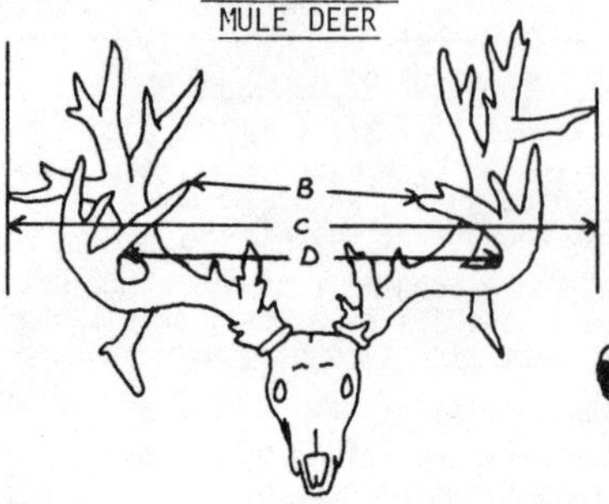

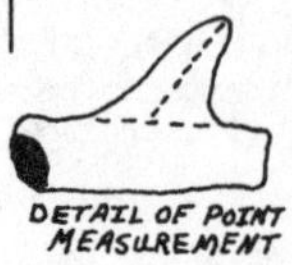

G4 G3 E G2 E E E E F E H3 H4 G1 H2 E H1 B C D

DETAIL OF POINT MEASUREMENT

Abnormal Points Right	Left
Total to E	

SEE OTHER SIDE FOR INSTRUCTIONS			Column 1	Column 2	Column 3	Column 4
A. Number of Points on Each Antler	R.	L.	Spread Credit	Right Antler	Left Antler	Difference
B. Tip to Tip Spread						
C. Greatest Spread						
D. Inside Spread of Main Beams		Credit may equal but not exceed length of longer antler				
IF Spread exceeds longer antler, enter difference						
E. Total of Lengths of Abnormal Points						
F. Length of Main Beams						
G-1. Length of First Point, if present						
G-2. Length of Second Point						
G-3. Length of Third Point, if present						
G-4. Length of Fourth Point, if present						
H-1. Circumference at Smallest Place Between Burr and First Point						
H-2. Circumference at Smallest Place Between First and Second Points						
H-3. Circumference at Smallest Place Between Main Beam and Third Point						
H-4. Circumference at Smallest Place Between Second and Fourth Points						
TOTALS						

ADD	Column 1		Exact locality where killed
	Column 2		Date killed By whom killed
	Column 3		Present Owner
	TOTAL		Address
SUBTRACT Column 4			
Result			Guide's Name and Address
Add Line E Total			Remarks: (Mention any abnormalities or unique qualities)
FINAL SCORE			

Here's the official scoring chart for non-typical mule deer. Non-typical blacktails would be listed with other mule deer, because blacktails don't tend to grow very impressive non-typical antlers and they don't merit placement in a class of their own. *(Courtesy of Boone and Crockett Club)*

I certify that I have measured the above trophy on ______________________ 19________
at (address) ______________________________ City ______________ State________
and that these measurements and data are, to the best of my knowledge and belief, made in accordance with the instructions given.

Witness: ______________________________ Signature: ______________________
OFFICIAL MEASURER

INSTRUCTIONS FOR MEASURING NON-TYPICAL MULE DEER

All measurements must be made with a ¼-inch flexible steel tape to the nearest one-eighth of an inch. Wherever it is necessary to change direction of measurement, mark a control point and swing tape at this point. Enter fractional figures in eighths, without reduction. Official measurements cannot be taken for at least sixty days after the animal was killed.

A. Number of Points on Each Antler. To be counted a point, a projection must be at least one inch long and its length must exceed the width of its base. All points are measured from tip of point to nearest edge of beam as illustrated. Beam tip is counted as a point but not measured as a point.

B. Tip to Tip Spread is measured between tips of main beams.

C. Greatest Spread is measured between perpendiculars at a right angle to the center line of the skull at widest part whether across main beams or points.

D. Inside Spread of Main Beams is measured at a right angle to the center line of the skull at widest point between main beams. Enter this measurement again in Spread Credit column if it is less than or equal to the length of longer antler; if longer, enter longer antler length for Spread Credit.

E. Total of Lengths of all Abnormal Points. Abnormal points are those nontypical in location or points beyond the normal pattern of five (including beam tip) per antler. Mark the points that are normal, as defined below. All other points are considered abnormal and are entered in appropriate blanks, after measurement in usual manner.

F. Length of Main Beam is measured from lowest outside edge of burr over outer curve to the tip of the main beam. The point of beginning is that point on the burr where the center line along the outer curve of the beam intersects the burr, then following generally the line of the illustration.

G-1-2-3-4. Length of Normal Points. Normal points are the brow and the upper and lower forks, as shown in the illustration. They are measured from nearest edge of beam over outer curve to tip. Lay the tape along the outer curve of the beam so that the top edge of the tape coincides with the top edge of the beam on both sides of the point to determine baseline for point measurement. Record point lengths in appropriate blanks.

H-1-2-3-4. Circumferences are taken as detailed for each measurement. If brow point is missing, take H-1 and H-2 at smallest place between burr and G-2. If G-3 is missing, take H-3 halfway between the base and tip of second point. If G-4 is missing, take H-4 halfway between the second point and tip of main beam.

* * * * * * * * * * * * *

FAIR CHASE STATEMENT FOR ALL HUNTER-TAKEN TROPHIES

To make use of the following methods shall be deemed as UNFAIR CHASE and unsportsmanlike and any trophy obtained by use of such means is disqualified from entry for Awards.

I. Spotting or herding game from the air, followed by landing in its vicinity for pursuit;
II. Herding or pursuing game with motor-powered vehicles;
III. Use of electronic communications for attracting, locating or observing game, or guiding the hunter to such game;
IV. Hunting game confined by artificial barriers, including escape-proof fencing; or hunting game transplanted solely for the purpose of commercial shooting.

****

I certify that the trophy scored on this chart was not taken in UNFAIR CHASE as defined above by the Boone and Crockett Club. I further certify that it was taken in full compliance with local game laws of the state, province, or territory.

Date__________ Signature of Hunter______________________________
(Have signature notarized by a Notary Public)

CHAPTER

14

FIELD-DRESSING, CAMP CARE, VENISON, AND BUCKSKINS

by John Madson and Jim Zumbo

FIELD-DRESSING AND HAULING

When your deer is down, never approach it closely until you are sure it's dead. There are reliable reports of hunters being attacked by wounded bucks and finally killing the animals with belt knives. One hunter straightened the head of his prize and laid his rifle across the antlers before taking a photograph. He backed up, focused his camera, and looked up just in time to see the deer leap to his feet and disappear into the brush, rifle still hung from his antlers. (And Bob Elman, who has a habit of admitting things an outdoor writer isn't supposed to admit, tells us that once, in his innocent youth, he was almost knocked off his feet by a not-so-dead buck.)

Many deer hunters use "sticking knives" whether the deer requires further bleeding or not. If the animal has been hit in the head, neck, or spinal cord, bleeding may be necessary. But if the wound is in the lungs or heart and the deer has run for any distance, it may be almost "bled out" before you reach it. In any case, bleeding generally occurs without your even thinking about it, because prompt and proper field dressing will eliminate all the blood in the cavity. Intentional bleeding seldom does much more than drain local blood from the vicinity of the knife cut. If you're planning on caping your deer for a mount, *don't* bleed it. The knife cuts could destroy an otherwise good cape or at least cause problems for your taxidermist.

If you believe there's a need to bleed your deer, plunge your knife to the hilt at the junction of neck and chest, tilt the blade toward the backbone, and withdraw it with a slight slicing effect. This should sever the carotid arteries where they join midway between the shoulders. When blood drainage has stopped, the next job is to remove the viscera as quickly and cleanly as possible.

Place the deer on its back on a slight slope or over a log or rock with the head uphill so that blood will drain to the hind parts. With a very sharp knife—and keeping a whetstone handy—make your first cut along the centerline of the belly from the point of the breastbone back to the pelvic bridge below the tail. Make this cut through the abdominal wall with the knife's cutting edge up, inserting the first two fingers into the incision to guide the blade from beneath, and being infinitely careful not to cut the paunch or intestines. This done, cut around the anus and free it, tie it off with string, and draw it up into the body cavity. This should also include a doe's reproductive organs. A buck's genitalia can be easily removed while making the belly cut, but be sure of your hunting regulations. The law may require leaving the buck's scrotum in place.

Cut the diaphragm between chest and abdomen, reach far up into the chest cavity, and sever the windpipe and esophagus. Some hunters split the chest to do this, freeing the ribs at their cartilage junctions with the breastbone. Other hunters, especially in cool weather, may never split the chest or remove its contents until they reach home.

The rectal area can also be removed by splitting the cartilaginous aitchbone of the deer's pelvis with a heavy knife or a belt ax, but be careful of this pelvic cut. If you're sloppy about it, you can ruin some prime "round."

If you want to save the heart and liver, cut these organs away and lift them from the cavity—before rolling the entrails out on the ground—so they don't get dirty. Turn the heart upside down for a moment to allow the blood to drain out. If you pack the organs in a plastic bag, remember to cool them as soon as possible. A plastic bag will retain heat and hasten spoilage.

After cutting out all anchoring membranes, the entire mass of viscera can be rolled out of the deer's carcass. Prop open the chest and abdomen with short sticks to facilitate rapid cooling. Many hunters never wash out a deer's body cavity, but prefer to wipe it out with clean rags or paper towels and permit a protective blood glaze to form.

But if the viscera has been cut while cleaning the deer, or if the deer was shot in the abdominal area, wash the body cavity throughly with clean water and flush out all blood and debris.

During the entire field-dressing process, do not allow meat to come in contact with hair, especially if the deer is a buck. Hair can taint the meat. Some hunters advocate immediate removal of the metatarsal glands on the hind legs. If this is done, wash your hands and knife before getting on with the job. Removal of these glands is not necessary, however, if the deer is handled property and care is taken to avoid rubbing the glands. The deer may be left unskinned. A deer carcass will cool readily with the hide attached, although larger game animals with heavier hides or thick coats may sour rapidly if skinning is delayed.

But if you're hunting in blazing hot weather, for instance during an August hunt in California when the air temperature can climb above 100°, it's a good idea to skin the deer as soon as possible and hang it in the shade if you can't get it out of the woods right away. Obviously, you'll need to take extra care transporting the skinned carcass to keep it free of dirt and debris. Dragging out a skinned deer is not known to enhance the quality of the venison.

With the deer hog-dressed, it's ready to move to camp. If you're in good condition, in open country, and if the deer isn't large, you may choose to drape it over your shoulders in storybook fashion. But in any kind of poor light, timber, or brushland, this is a pretty fair way of getting shot at. Few things are more dangerous than carrying a deer through hunting country, and it becomes work of the heaviest sort, for a freshly killed deer is as limp and boneless as a hundred-weight of gelatin.

If you do carry a deer out on your shoulders, festoon the carcass with generous amounts of bright orange ribbon. An extra hunter-orange vest tied over it will improve your chances of not being mistaken for a deer.

There are commercial devices for hauling deer, but most hunters prefer to drag them. This is easiest and best on snow, for dragging a deer over dry ground can bruise and soil the meat. But it may be the only choice. In such a case, try tying the forelegs together and lashing the head to these legs with the muzzle pointing forward. The drag line is lashed to the forefeet, making a streamlined bundle that slips easily over most surfaces.

If you're in mule-deer country and tag your deer in the hinterlands, your only choice might be to cut the carcass in quarters, tie one or two to a pack frame, haul them out on your back, and return for another load. If you don't have a pack frame, you can carry one or more quarters over your shoulder. Some hunters carry an empty rucksack, bone their meat on the spot, and take it out in boneless chunks. It's surprising how much worthless weight in bones you can leave behind for coyotes and magpies.

The niftiest way to haul a deer out, other than dropping the animal next to an old wood road and driving your vehicle up next to it, is to toss the carcass over a horse and let the bronc do the work. Unfortunately, this luxury is possible only if you own a horse, are hunting with someone who does, or hire a guide to do the horsework.

The most miserable two-man way of hauling a deer is by tying the feet over a long pole and carrying it with the carcass dangling and swinging freely. This can almost split a man to his wishbone when walking over rough ground. If you have a partner, bend the deer's forefeet around the back of its head, tie them in place, and lash a 4-foot pole to the antlers. With a man at each end of the short pole, the carcass can be easily dragged.

The hunter at left is about to pull the whitetail buck around into a position with its head uphill before the man at right begins eviscerating it. Most experienced hunters agree that field dressing goes better when the animal is on a slight slope, with its head higher than its hindquarters. This also bleeds the body cavity efficiently, as the blood will drain to the hind parts.

CAMP CARE

The secret of sweet venison is to cool the meat as quickly as possible, and to keep it as cool as you can until it is processed. If you plan to remain in camp for some time after the deer is shot, and if the law permits, it may be wise to skin and quarter the deer. The hide is split along the backs of the hind legs to the anus, pulled from the haunches and off the back, and worked off the thin meated sides by pulling with one hand while hammering the taut hide away from the flesh with the butt of your fist. "Fisting" a hide is not difficult, and once the peeling has begun it may hardly be necessary to use your knife again until you come to the forelegs. If you plan to have the head mounted as a trophy, do not split the skin on the underside of the neck. Cut around the base of the neck—perhaps even extending this cut around the foreshoulders and lower chest—and cut up the back of the neck to between the ears. Remove the head by cutting across the "Adam's apple" to the atlas joint—the only joint on the neck that has no interlocking bones.

Some hunters make the first cut from the breastbone back to the pelvic bridge, as advocated by John Madson. Others, like this man, begin at the pelvic bridge or scrotum and work forward. Either way is all right if you use a sharp knife, keeping the cutting edge facing up and slitting the belly skin from underneath, with infinite care not to cut into the paunch or intestines.

When the deer is field-butchered, the quarters can be wrapped in muslin or cheesecloth to prevent magpies or Canada jays from attacking the meat as it hangs high in the tree. Commercial game bags made of such materials are available in sporting-goods stores. If the entire deer is to hang in camp for a few days, some hunters coat the exposed portions of meat with blood from the body cavity to form a "rind" or glaze that dries hard and seals the flesh from blowflies. On areas of heavy muscle that tend to stay moist and don't glaze, a coating of black pepper can be applied, and blowflies should avoid it, but don't count on it. The pesky critters will often find a place to attack the meat. If you wrap the deer in cheesecloth or other material, be sure the entire carcass is covered, particularly the head. Flies will enter the body cavity by crawling into the nostrils and ears. If you find unhatched fly eggs on the carcass, scrape them off immediately and the meat will be fine. Once you

Some hunters insist on cutting the metatarsal musk glands from the inner surface of the hock joints, as this man is doing, before field dressing a buck. It isn't necessary, as long as you're careful not to rub or cut the glands while dressing out the deer. You merely want to avoid getting any glandular secretion on the meat. If you feel safer cutting the glands away, go ahead, but wash your hands and knife before proceeding with field dressing.

spot eggs, however, carefully check the rest of the meat. There are probably more. If the eggs have hatched and you find maggots, cut away the affected meat, and immediately begin butchering the carcass or have someone do it for you.

Internal animal heat damages fresh deer meat quicker than external weather heat. Use spreader sticks to prop open the body cavity, and elevate the carcass by hanging it from a tree so that it cools uniformly. If left on the ground, the meat in contact with the earth may cool so slowly that it spoils, and this spoilage may spread to other areas. During the day in warm weather make every effort to keep the carcass in shade, hung in a place where air circulates freely around it.

If possible, start your trip home in early morning. After being in the chill night air, the carcass will be cool and in the best condition to travel. There's no longer much danger of ruining a deer by strapping it to a front fender next to the hot car engine; modern cars aren't made that way. But if you carry the carcass in a car trunk or in the back of a station wagon, be sure there are no gasoline cans or contaminants nearby. In cool weather the best place to carry the deer is on a cartop carrier where air can circulate evenly around it, or on a "duckboard" in the back of a pickup truck.

When you get your deer home, make sure you hang it high enough off the ground so neighborhood dogs can't work it over. A single dog can make quick work of a hindquarter. You might need to be concerned about human thieves as well. More than one deer has been carted off in the night. If you aren't the trusting sort, store your deer inside, in a cool place, or take it to a locker plant.

VENISON VIANDS

Prime deer meat, properly and promptly cared for, is delicious. People in the backcountry know this, and venison is one of their staples. Then why will a city housewife condemn the "sour, gamey taste" of deer meat?

An old woodsman may choose his deer as carefully as the housewife buys a lamb roast. He doesn't want a trophy, but a fat young buck or, where it's legal, a plump young doe. He shoots it near home, hog-dresses it in as little as 10 minutes, and has the deer cooled, skinned, and aging in the woodshed while a novice hunter is still stoning his knife. Result: properly handled venison, sweet and prime, and fresh liver and speckled gravy simmering on the range.

Assuming that the deer was in prime condition in the first place, the venison will be no better than the treatment it receives in the interval between the bullet and butcher. No later processing can repair the damage done to venison in the early stages of cleaning and handling.

Once your deer is home, the meat will be best if aged before final butchering, packaging, and freezing. Many hunters allow the carcass to hang in a cool place or a walk-in refrigerator for about a week or 10 days. They leave the hide on to keep the meat from drying and turning dark. Butchering the deer is not a difficult job if you have the basic tools and a clean place to work. The butchering guides for calves and lambs—available from county extension agents—can also be used for deer. Most hunters, however, prefer to turn their deer over to commercial lockers for processing and freezing.

The great majority of these hunters have their deer processed into conventional chops, steaks, roasts, and burger. But a few people convert almost every scrap of deer meat to "chipped" venison, sausage, or other specialties.

If you're hunting a long distance from home and don't want to go through the bother and expense of hauling or shipping your fresh venison, you can take it to a locker plant in any large town and trade it for deer sausage, pepperoni, salami, or whatever. You won't have to wait, but you'll be getting someone else's deer meat in the trade. Processors make big patches of sausages and such, package them in small quantities, freeze them, and trade them for fresh meat.

Even though you trade, you must pay for the meat you select. Game regulations prohibit the outright sale of wild game, but it can be traded, with allowances made for extra pork or beef suet added to venison sausage. For example, if you bring 70 pounds of boned deer meat to a processor, he'll let you buy 70 pounds of already processed sausage as well as an extra 10 percent, or seven more pounds, because of the suet added. If your deer isn't boned, you'll be charged extra. Processors will accept deer in any form, even unskinned, but you'll pay extra. Naturally, they will not accept spoiled or tainted meat. Most plants will pack your frozen sausage or whatever in insulated cartons. You can take it home in your vehicle or ship it as luggage if you're flying.

BUCKSKINS

It takes a heap of hunting to make a man a coat.

An average deerskin is good for about three or four pairs of gloves, but it takes at least three medium-size hides for a really good short jacket and as many as five if you want a real "Hickok tuxedo" that drips with tradition and 10-inch fringe.

If deer must remain in camp for some time before butchering, they should be hung well off the ground for cooling. Some hunters hang their bucks by the antlers, which is fast and easy. Others cut through the hind legs, run a gambrel pole through the slits above the joints, and hang the deer head-down, as in this picture. Most hunters agree that the head-down position makes skinning easier. In cold weather, the skin can stay on for a while, but prompt skinning is best in hot weather. *(Photo by Norm Nelson)*

Unless a buck is unusually heavy, one man should have little trouble hanging it up off the ground from a tree limb. A drag rope is secured to the antlers, draped over the limb, and—after pulling the deer up—anchored to the ground or tree. Two ropes may make the job easier, and there are commercial rope-and-pulley devices to make it easier still.

In any case, your deerskin is worth investing some extra effort and money in. Buckskin is a remarkable leather, soft and immensely durable. But it does have drawbacks. When wet, it sops up water like a sponge and swiftly sags and stretches. As the old Indian said: "Dry buckskin pants good for one man. Get 'um wet, good for two men." And according to one frontiersman, buckskin moccasins "will wet through two days before it rains."

Historian Bernard De Voto wrote that many early Mountain Men preferred woolen trousers and hooded woolen capotes when they could get them, partly for the frontier snob appeal of such clothing but mostly because wet buckskin is clammy and stretchy, and dry duckskin is hot in warm weather. But by the time the fur brigades convened at the June "rondyvoo," they'd all be in buckskin again. The wool wore out; buckskin goes on forever.

Since the demise of ponyskin as a jacket leather, our softest and toughest leather is buckskin, which also makes up into fine vests, gloves, bags, and slippers. If you have strong arms and a stronger stomach, you can tan your own buckskin. Don't try to leave the hair on, for deer hair is hollow and brittle, easily broken, and won't wear well. But tanning is a smelly, tedious chore that you probably won't cotton to, and you'd be far better off sending your deerskins to a tanner.

Rub the skin side of your fresh deerhide with fine salt and spread it hairside down on a clean, dry surface. Brine will form. In a couple of days the hide should be folded, skin to skin, to keep it from becoming hard and dry.

Big tanneries seldom accept single skins. It's best to just send the deerskin to a taxidermist or someone specializing in trophy skins. He will probably mark it for identification, store it with other skins, and hold it until he has a lot large enough to send to a tannery. However, there are a few commercial houses that specialize in buckskin and may tan your deerskin and make it up into any item you wish.

It will cost, but it's worth it. You'll own an item that's comfortable, durable, and uniquely personal. And when asked where you bought that handsome jacket you can snort: "Bought it? Man, I don't buy my clothes, I shoot 'em!"

CHAPTER

15

FURTHER NOTES ON FIELD CARE AND TAXIDERMY

by Robert Elman

Differences of opinion add much to the fascination of deer hunting, and in a book like this there are bound to be minor disagreements between some of the authors. Now I seldom disagree with John Madson because I'm in awe of his knowledge, but I'd like to add some qualification to his advice that bleeding may be necessary if a deer has been hit in the head, neck, or spinal cord. True, a head-shot animal may need draining by severing the carotid arteries or jugular. But I'll go out on a limb here, with the opinion that in other cases—even when the shot is to the neck or spinal cord—bleeding is rarely necessary because the bullet wound initiates at least a little drainage, and this drainage vastly increases and continues as you field-dress the game.

Some years ago I killed a good-size Texas mule deer with a neck shot. I was hunting with a guide, and he insisted that dressing it out was part of his job. In situations like that, I can be as slow about opening my knife as some people are about opening a wallet at a business lunch. I wondered if he'd bleed the animal. He didn't, and I wouldn't have, either, if he'd let me dress that deer. The lack of bleeding did not make the gutting job messier than it would otherwise have been, and the meat was delicious. There was a time when most hunters carried a sheath knife with a 6-inch blade. One of its uses was as a sticking knife. Nowadays more and more hunters carry a shorter (and therefore handier) sheath knife or a folding model such as I favor. If bleeding isn't necessary, neither is a 6-inch blade.

John also mentions the importance of preventing deer hair from getting on the meat. I agree, of course, but I think hair-

The guide in this photo is pointing out good bullet placement (the hunter had made a quartering shot from the rear, and the bullet penetrated from the right rear of the rib cage forward through the lung area for a one-shot kill). However, if he moved his pointing hand forward a bit on the carcass, he'd be indicating where the hide should be caped for trophy mounting. The caping cut should circle the body behind the shoulders to leave plenty of skin. For detailed instructions, see the text.

less meat is the ideal rather than the rule. Maybe I'm incurably sloppy, but I've never been able to dress and skin a deer without getting a little hair on the meat. I pick off what I notice, and before freezing the butchered cuts I blot away any more that I can find. Still, a few hairs invariably escape me, and they haven't yet soured a piece of my venison. I've asked several hunting acquaintances about their experiences in the matter. It turns out they're as sloppy as I am. However, that hair business may be more important in the warmer hunting regions.

I ought to add here that John and I are in complete agreement that it isn't necessary to cut away the knobby musk glands from the inner surface of a buck's hock joints, even if the animal is at the peak of the rut. Another Texas guide I once hunted with—a superb hunter and all-around outdoorsman—thought I was out of my mind because I didn't want to bother slicing those glands off a whitetail I'd shot. It was a case of his learning a "rule" during boyhood and ever afterward believing it as gospel. If those glands aren't rubbed or cut while the deer is being dressed out, they won't taint the meat.

Before leaving the subject of myths that are hard to debunk, let me mention a more peculiar one. In a couple of regions where I hunted quite some time ago, the local sportsmen insisted that when a deer was to be kept in camp for a while it absolutely had to be hung upside down. Supposedly it would cool and age better that way. Well, I can't see why that should be so. In fact, if drainage hasn't quite stopped, an upside-down chest cavity must act as a catch basin, which doesn't seem at all desirable. You don't need to spread the hind legs wide and hang the deer by them to keep the carcass cool; just keep the body cavity open wide, as John suggests, with spreader sticks. Besides, it's much easier to hang a deer by its antlers. The one really good argument for hanging a deer upside down is that most of us find the skinning job easier with the deer in that position. Of course, if your deer doesn't have much of a rack, you may have difficulty hanging him by the antlers. And if you plan to have the

Co-editor Bob Elman took this fine desert mule deer in south-central Texas. A good shoulder mount was facilitated by generous caping, by taking care not to slit or split the skin on the underside of the neck, and by a liberal salting of the cape's flesh side. The weather was hot, and there was no available freezer that could accommodate the head, so it was rushed to a taxidermist as quickly as possible.

head mounted, one thing you should *not* do is run a rope around the neck. This can rub off hair and leave a very unsightly rope mark.

In connection with taxidermy, I'd like to add a few details about this business of "caping," to use the traditional big-game hunter's expression. As John Madson says, the right way (that is, the neat and easy way) to remove the head is to cut through the neck at the atlas joint—also known as the axial joint. If you do this, you won't need an ax or saw because you'll be able to remove the head simply by grasping it at the bases of the antlers and twisting it off. But this point is way at the top of the neck (the first vertebra under the skull) and you don't want any cuts in the hide there; you have to take extreme care about parting the skin from the flesh and leaving enough skin for a generous wall mount. John's advice merits emphasis here: *Do not split the skin on the underside of the neck.* It also merits further elucidation:

Use a sharp, reasonably short knife. Holding it with the cutting edge up, use the point to slit the skin from the top of the withers straight up the back of the neck to the midpoint between the ears. Now, back at the withers, at the rear end of this cut, circle the body with another cut—down behind the shoulders and across the legs at the bottom of the brisket. The *bottom.* That will leave plenty of hide. You can then peel the skin forward, up to the ears and jaws, exposing the point where you want to cut through the neck. Finally, rub salt liberally into the flesh exposed under the head, and also into the flesh side of the cape—the hide you've left attached to the head. If you're going to have a taxidermist do the mounting, that's all there is to it except to freeze the head as soon as possible and keep it frozen until it goes to the taxidermist.

Many sportsmen like to do their own taxidermy, not just to save money (and mounting has become increasingly expensive) but because it's an enjoyable hobby. A good home-mounted job will give you quite a sense of artistic accomplishment, and it isn't terribly difficult nor does it require very expensive or hard-to-find tools and materials. You can, in fact, buy do-it-yourself kits that include instructions as well as a plaque, a "form" over which the skin will be fitted, and the other needed materials.

Of course, nothing is more depresing than to botch a fine trophy, and if you do spoil it the chances are that the damage can't be completely undone even by a professional taxidermist. It's therefore an excellent idea not to make your first mounting attempt on a trophy that means a lot to you. Start by mounting a "learning" head—your next spike buck, for instance. It doesn't even have to be a deer. Any kind of game will help you learn the principles and techniques. Use a rabbit if you want to, or a coyote or a bobcat or anything you please. If you think this hobby might interest you, your first step must be to get a good book on the subject and follow its instructions carefully. I can recommend Waddy F. McFall's book, *Taxidermy Step by Step* (Winchester Press, 1975).

A deer that really deserves mounting is apt to be large in body as well as antlers, and any hunter has a natural curiosity about the weight of his trophy buck. Usually, in fact, a hunter is eager to know the weight of any deer he's taken, even a plump young spike or forkhorn. However, it's not likely that you'll be able to weigh it before you get it out to a checkpoint, much less before you dress it out, so you'll have to be satisfied with a sensibly estimated live weight based on the weight of the hog-dressed carcass. I've heard a lot of arithmetical formulas, some of them pretty complicated, but you just don't need any algebraic brainteasers to arrive at a close estimate. I'll leave you with this last tip, which will make it easy for you to judge the weight of any deer you take: Forget the formulas and just remember the simple, imperfect but accurate enough rule that a deer's live weight is 25 percent more than its weight after you've field-dressed it.

PART II

Hunting All-American Whitetails

CHAPTER

16

THE DEER-RICH EASTERN WOODLOTS

by L. James Bashline

From Maine to Georgia, the Appalachian Mountains are considered "Eastern" deer country. The adjacent geography that extends to the east and west of this range for 200 miles in some cases is different in character, but for hunting purposes it is still the same general type of real estate. Combination stands of conifers and hardwoods are the typical Eastern deer woods, and this is the main reason whitetails are so abundant there. Before man and his need for lumber reduced the nearly solid stands of huge pine and hemlock to a mere shadow of what they once were, whitetail deer were not nearly so plentiful in the East.

The towering pines prevented much undergrowth from taking root, and deer food was extremely meager. By 1910, practically all of the native pine and hemlock were gone. Vast areas were left in an almost barren condition. Surprisingly, little pine regenerated. Instead, dormant seeds of hardwood species and woody shrubs began to cover the Eastern hills, and with a bit of help from artificial stocking and enlightened legislation, the whitetail deer began to fill the void. The black cherry, maple, ash, sassafras, black birch, and other succulent shoots were exactly to the deer's liking, and the rest is history.

An annual harvest of 150,000 deer is not unusual for Pennsylvania these days. New York State's harvest is even higher—160,000—and small states like New Jersey and Vermont post 20,000 or more each year. The Maine harvest sometimes reaches 40,000. Indeed, the whitetail deer is in no danger of being eliminated in the East. The problem is keeping the population in check rather than increasing the output of venison.

Logged clearings, slash patches, and the like—including plenty of low second growth—are frequented by deer in the Appalachian woods. Jim Bashline is shown in Maine, during a successful day of combined stand- and still-hunting—a classic Eastern technique. Driving also works very well in this habitat. *(Photo by L. James Bashline)*

With all these deer available, it would seem that hunting them must be a snap. Yet the success ratio of Eastern hunters is not close to that enjoyed by Westerners. Admittedly, the hunting pressure is greater in the East and there are probably more hunters afield, say, in Pennsylvania than in several Rocky Mountain states put together on any deer-hunting day. But does that fully explain the rather low success statistics? The ratio most hunters are concerned with is their own ratio. How many seasons do they connect? The other guy can take care of himself. How can I attain a better batting average?

All successful hunters I have known are quick to point out that they never underestimate the craftiness of the whitetail deer. Many well-traveled big-game chasers who have sampled the best the world has to offer consider the whitetail the most elusive of trophies. Not just an ordinary deer with antlers mind you, but an honest-to-goodness trophy buck. Anyone who has hunted deer for more than a few seasons knows that putting your tag on a less than magnificent spike buck or even a baldy can be full of frustration. Magnify that times ten for a whitetail that would make a respectable wall-hanger.

This eastern whitetail is looking straight into the camera but doesn't know what he's seeing. He hasn't scented or heard the hunter, who is concealed in a well-chosen stand. At the click of the shutter, the deer shied back and bounded into the woods, but didn't go far before he slowed to a walk. Still-hunting can also be productive in a situation like this, with fresh, silencing snow on the ground and in woods sufficiently open for the hunter to spot deer moving at some distance. *(Courtesy of Pennsylvania Game News)*

Eastern whitetails are smart. They have to be. Living in proximity to man has made them that way. And even in deep-woods habitat, deer that seldom see a human being spook at the smell of man. A one-on-one situation in Maine's cedar swamps can be the toughest sort of hunt imaginable. Just as difficult is the small-woodlot deer that lives in Hunterdon County, New Jersey. That deer sees humans almost every day of his life. He has learned to feed mostly at night and when pursued can make a veritable army of hunters look extremely foolish. He knows all of the byways of his relatively small bailiwick and takes advantage of every available bit of cover.

In most Eastern states, with the exception of Connecticut and Massachusetts, there is a considerable amount of public land for deer hunters to operate on. Maps, available from the respective conservation agencies in most states, illustrate just where the public land is. In spite of increased pressure from militant protectionists, many large landowners will permit hunters to enter their acreage for deer hunting. They should be asked for permission to hunt, however. Eastern hunters depend heavily on private land

His flag is up, and he'll be gone in an instant, but Jim Bashline easily could have shot this buck instead of photographing him before he disappeared. The deer was jumped by the still-hunting technique at the edge of a crossing. This would be a good spot for a stand-hunter—or for a stander during a drive. *(Photo by L. James Bashline)*

Sometimes a drive can result in a concentration of deer where woodland cover ends and the animals hesitate to cross a field, clearing, stream, or back road in daylight. Co-editor Bob Elman once counted 60 whitetails at the edge of a rolling Pennsylvania field—concentrated there by a big, noisy group of drivers perhaps a quarter-mile behind them. These deer were photographed in central New Jersey, a state whose herds (and hunting opportunities) have increased dramatically. *(Courtesy of New Jersey Division of Fish, Game, and Wildlife)*

and, while I hate to be "preachy," hunters must be more respectful of private land in the future. The right to hunt is not a God-given favor just because a hunting license has been purchased. A good relationship with private landowners must be maintained.

In the small woodlots, three basic methods of hunting prove successful. The first is the watch-and-wait method. This is simply the old stump-sitter style that requires you to watch a popular trail or keep a steady eye on known feeding areas, such as an orchard or clearing edge. The basic requirement for the hunter in this case is to stay put and avoid all unnecessary movements and sounds. A stump hunter who coughs, sneezes, crackles potato-chip bags, and otherwise converses with himself won't do well on this sort of hunt. He'd best take part in an organized drive which allows him to be more active.

The organized drive can be conducted in big woods areas, too, but it's most effective in the small patch situation where drivers and standers can be employed in an encircling way. The hunters who employ such driving methods should select a leader who knows the area well and allow him autonomy in deciding who is to do

At a sportsmen's meeting sponsored by the Pennsylvania Game Commission, Jim Bashline examines a magnificent non-typical whitetail trophy. Heavily antlered, multi-tined bucks continue to be harvested in the Eastern woodlots and at the edges of the fields and orchards. *(Photo by James Bashline)*

what. For a group of strangers to attempt a deer drive in unfamiliar territory is like hiring a bunch of Eskimos to serve as tour guides in Manhattan.

The standers should be posted at obvious vantage points where they can command a reasonable patch of viewing area. The drivers should be deployed to travel routes that will roust the deer out of their resting places. A drive should be well planned so each member of the party knows exactly where every other member of the group is located and from which way the drivers will approach. Conspicuous blaze-orange clothing should be worn by all. Standers and drivers must always follow the game plan and assemble at the designated spot when the drive is over. An organized drive is not the kind of hunt for the free-spirit sort. Nothing is more disgusting to a group of veteran drivers than to have one of the standers wander off on his own because he got a hunch that things were more promising at some other location. Many valuable hours of hunting time are taken up by looking for the supposedly lost hunter.

The free spirit who would be unwelcome in a driving group has the third option of hunting techniques and that is the still-hunt or plain old "pussyfooting." For those hunters in good physical condition and who have developed a good set of deer-spotting eyes, this is perhaps the most satisfying deer hunting available. It is best done when the ground is wet or there is a good tracking snow and in an area where few hunters are upsetting the deer from their daily routine. Still-hunting is difficult to manage when there are a lot of license-holders charging about. A stump hunter has a much better chance at the deer that the still-hunter will be tracking. The still-hunter becomes the driver for the guy who is simply waiting them out.

There are all sorts of variations on the three hunting methods listed. Which one is best? The truth is, all of them are best under certain conditions. Let's take a closer look. There is really no such thing as typical Eastern deer cover. The elusive whitetail can be found in open woods, barren fields, cedar thickets, and hemlock swamps. The terrain can be steep and rocky, gently rolling, or flat as a table top. The method used is determined by the geography.

In thick cover such as scrub oak or conifer tangles laced with windfalls and uprooted stumps, the drive is the most productive method if your group has the area to itself. Interlocking limbs and low foliage prevent long shots and good visibility. These factors make the drive most effective if everyone follows the plan. The drivers should be spaced in such a way that each one will cover an area deer are expected to pass through. A group of five watchers and three drivers can make several half-mile drives per day and never leave a 500-acre plot. Frequently, the deer will never leave such a patch of cover.

In open fields and woods that are reasonably clear of understory, the stump hunter has the best chance. Deer in such areas can see the hunter approaching (although they'll probably smell or hear him first) and the organized drive usually turns up nothing. The sit-and-watch technique is also the best way to operate on the first day of the season in areas that have a reasonably heavy concentration of hunters. A lot of the first-dayers will sit on watch for a while, but cold feet and a

Naturalist, photographer, writer, and editor George Harrison rests after dragging a fine buck back to a Pennsylvania deer camp. Many of these camps are heated by woodstoves or fireplaces and are comfortable, well equipped, and situated in excellent deer habitat. *(Photo by L. James Bashline)*

general nervous anticipation will put most of them on the march within an hour or two. The patient stump hunter who sits out a good stand on opening day in reasonably good deer country will almost always see deer. He may not see the buck of his dreams but the odds are good that some venison will pass his squatting place. In back-in woods situations or during the later part of the deer season when fewer hunters are afield, the still-hunter's chances become better.

The traditional New England method of taking a track on fresh snow and walking it down can be practiced everywhere that whitetails exist. It can be the toughest sort of hunt imaginable or it can end in 15 minutes. The skill of the tracker is all-important. Veteran deer trackers learned long ago that the second a wise buck knows someone is hot on his trail, the evasive action begins. Steady plodding may bring a glimpse of the buck and you may even collect the trophy but by the time you do,

you could be so far into the "boonies" that dragging the venison home or to the nearest road becomes a major undertaking.

A far better trick is to weave a series of long, lazy S's that occasionally intersect the track. As the hunter cuts the deer's prints, he may spot an ear flicking or a leg stamping and drop the buck in short order. Keen eyes are needed for still-hunting, especially for pussyfooting through thick cover on bare ground. With no visible tracks, the still-hunter looks for fresh sign in the form of droppings or a freshly cut twig that tells him deer are in the immediate vicinity. A short, fast-handling rifle is important to the woods-walker. A deer may suddenly materialize at close range and the shot must be taken in an instant or not at all.

The impressive 8- and 10-point bucks with wide spreads and long tines are the dream of every whitetail hunter. To grow a trophy rack, a buck must be over 3½ years old and manage to find a reasonably well-balanced diet. Some parts of the East regularly produce larger than average bucks but practically anywhere east of the Mississippi can harbor a real trophy. The big bucks are where you find them. Maine traditionally turns up heavy bucks each year—some of them weighing 300 pounds. Some heavy-antlered bucks come from the flat farm country of Ohio. Even Pennsylvania and New York with their huge populations of slightly underfed deer annually record some smashers. I have seen deep-chested bucks in the tidal marshes of Maryland. The hunter who manages to collect a prime, well-antlered whitetail has reason to be proud. Sheer numbers of smaller deer work against him. Some luck, maybe a lot of it, is involved but it isn't all a matter of chance.

In the foreground lies a fine 8-point buck. The successful hunter approaching the deer is Jim Zumbo, pictured during one of the well-spent days of his youth when he habitually cruised the Eastern woodlots. His old Catskill haunts still yield many fine deer each season.

I lived for 31 years in what is perhaps one of the best deer regions of the United States, north-central Pennsylvania. As a boy and later as a young adult, I spent a lot of time hunting deer there and observing the styles of other hunters. As in all deer-hunting areas, there were some catch-as-catch-can hunters who occasionally killed a deer. There were a few better deer stalkers who usually killed a buck. Then there were a small handful of deer experts who always got a buck and often placed their tag on a head that was worth mounting.

One of these "lucky" ones was an ex-farmer named Howard Snyder who for several years worked for a gas company. Howard usually arranged his working hours so he could be on shift during the dark hours and out hunting during the day, an ideal arrangement for a hunter. He owned a lever-action .300 Savage that carried a battered 2½× scope. He hunted everything with that rifle, including turkey and squirrels. I know, since I used to load his ammo for him. Each year with that lever-action he nearly always downed a turkey and killed a truckload of squirrels.

I hunted with Howard on two or three occasions only, since he didn't really enjoy hunting with anyone. It wasn't that he was unsociable, he just preferred doing things his way. His style of stalking didn't jell with a companion, and while the buddy system suits most hunters, it didn't suit Howard.

On one occasion when I talked him into letting me go along on a squirrel hunt on an oak-covered ridge, I was astounded to discover that I was soon 400 yards ahead of him. We had begun walking slowly through the woods, watching the tree tops for the telltale flop of a tail. I thought I had been moving slowly, but Howard was practically creeping. Every second step (I stopped and watched him coming through the woods), he'd stop dead-still and move his head slowly searching the entire landscape from top to bottom. Once he raised his rifle carefully and shot the head off a squirrel with a reduced load from that favorite .300. Not an ideal squirrel gun in my eyes but it certainly was effective.

From later conversations with Howard and others who know about his prowess as a deer hunter, I found out that he hunted whitetails in exactly the same way. He loved the quiet snowy or, even better, rainy days when he could be relatively sure that few other hunters would be out. His notion of whitetail hunting was to do a lot of looking and move very slowly. If a movement was spotted or if he observed a patch of brown hair that seemed out of place, he would stop and wait until he ascertained what the something was or until it moved. Great patience is required for such a technique, but it works.

With a few exceptions, deer hunting in the East does not require long-range shooting. A short, easy-to-handle rifle or shotgun (some areas require the use of shotgun slugs or buckshot) with a low-powered scope or aperture sight is what's needed. The shots are usually less than 100 yards, and 50-foot shots are not at all uncommon. Large calibers that shoot ponderous projectiles and are usually classified as "brush" guns are okay if you want to stick to tradition. I prefer a bullet that moves relatively fast (above 2,700 fps) and opens up quickly. A soft-pointed bullet that opens up fast and delivers the shock inside the animal instead of passing on through seems to work out best.

I may be a bit old-fashioned in my choice of guns for whitetails but two better calibers were never designed than the old .250-3000 and the .257 Roberts. They both shoot 100-grain bullets with ample velocity and, with a chest hit, put whitetails down instantly. There's no way I'll be caught knocking the old .30-30 or .32 Special or the venerable .30-06 in 150-grain loadings. As a matter of fact, I've killed more than a dozen whitetails with the relatively modern .308 with 150-grain soft-points. But the hot .25 calibers always caught my fancy.

You may have guessed by now that I don't take much stock in "brush-busting." Even though great reputations have been made by cartridges that are supposed to shoot through three laurel bushes, six oak trees, and an acre of assorted debris before knocking a whitetail sunny side up—I just don't buy it. A stick the size of a lead pencil will deflect any slug ever made and if the path isn't clear to the deer, you just ain't gonna hit him! Pick the opening and touch it off.

I wrote a magazine article some years ago in which I took the premise that hunting whitetails could be compared with the modern shibboleth that says "football is a game of inches." Whitetail hunting is a game of seconds. There is the second when you determine that the mysterioius shape ahead of you is a deer's ear. There is the second when you decide that those are antlers on the deer's head. There is the second when you decide you will attempt to shoot, and then, that micro-second that is the very best, the ultimate time, to press the trigger. Woods hunting for whitetails is exactly that: a game of important seconds. The opportunity comes fast and it's over just as quickly. The end result is, ideally, an instant kill or a clean miss.

Scoring on a whitetail in the eastern United States can be as easy as picking the morning paper out of the mail box or as difficult as finding an Arab sheik on welfare. Patience, a watchful eye, and good woodsmanship separate the lucky hunters from the license buyers. Nothing (including reading this book) can compare with experience. Go deer hunting every chance you get—even without a gun, during the off-season. If you can learn to pick out that flick of an ear with heavy foliage on the trees, you'll have a running start on tagging yourself some venison when the season opens.

CHAPTER 17

SOCIABLE SOUTHERN STRATEGIES

by Tom Brakefield

Deer season in each part of the country is a special time, one with special memories and traditions. Nowhere is this more true than in the Southeast, where I grew up and where I brought in my first venison. I had been on a stand, huddled against the cold, for several hours. Out of the corner of my eye I spotted just a hint of movement. Then another and another. Silently and miraculously four gray ghosts materialized out of the damp, soggy underbrush and began daintily moving my way. At first I thought they must be goats and had broken out of some farmer's pen. Just a lad, I made the common mistake of most novices and looked for deer (after all, they were "big" game, weren't they?) to be chest-high rather than beltbuckle-high. Most adult whitetail bucks stand somewhere between 36 and 39 inches at the shoulder.

Finally I made up my mind that these were, indeed, the long-coveted deer I had come after. As they worked their way closer to me, I made out two does and two bucks. One of the bucks was a little spike but the other was right respectable, with antlers that probably had an 18-inch spread to them.

Closer and closer they drifted and I slowly began to raise the huge old muzzle-heavy 12-gauge that seemed heavier than I was, inching it up toward the proper line of sight. I was scared stiff and my tensed muscles were shaking like Jell-O in a high wind. The big buck drifted farther away from me as he edged around the other side of a particularly thick patch of cover. But the little fellow moved closer and, just as he was about to be hidden by a particularly dense patch of undergrowth, I let fly with the No. 00 buckshot. Down he went and the brush and creepers shook as he thrashed his last. I stood there mesmerized for a moment, then I moved forward to see if my prize was actually still there. Wonder of wonders, he was, and I'll never forget the feeling of accomplishment that little spike buck gave me and the good-natured ribbing that I proudly took back at the clubhouse that evening. The warm glow of fellowship and good food during that hunt have remained with me ever afterward. Good hunts never end, not so long as we remember them, and that one typified the warmth and good times of a traditional Southern deer hunt.

Actually, the Southeast is a very large region, and deer hunting of several different types is available. Throughout any large part of the country the sport can vary considerably, depending upon terrain, traditions, densities of both hunters and game, and a number of other factors. When most hunters visualize traditional Southern hunting, they think of hunting with dogs in the lowland belt stretching across the southern portions of Georgia, Alabama, and Mississippi. This is strictly buckshot hunting, 12-gauge preferred, and the details are covered in another chapter. But there are other, equally interesting aspects to Southern hunting.

There are parts of the South where buckshot is the rule, but in the rugged wooded parts of western North Carolina, as well as Virginia and Kentucky, rifles are favored and the old .30-30 has at last begun to give ground to such eminently practical calibers as the .308. The deer in this photo stands in a clearing amid rather open Carolina woods where a .308 would be a good choice. *(Courtesy of North Carolina Wildlife Resources Commission)*

Most of it is done through hunting clubs or other groups that lease prime acreage on one- to three-year contracts. This type of leased hunting is also very common in Texas, parts of Florida, and other Southern states, and it has begun to show up more and more in other states. It costs a bit of money but it gives the landowner some incentive to manage his land with the game's best interest in mind and it assures the sportsman of a place to hunt.

A hunt I made once in southern Alabama pretty well typifies this type of deer shooting. I stayed in a rustic old cabin that had been patched and spruced up a bit to double as a clubhouse for the small club that rented the hunting rights to the land in that area. This club had 32 members, a bit smaller than many; on the particular weekend that I hunted with them, about 40 hunters were there, including guests. We were all sleeping in Spartan but comfortable dormitory-style double bunks and it seemed that, warmed by the glow of a fire in the outsized fieldstone fireplace and a substantial bourbon-and-branchwater, I had hardly put my drink down when someone was shaking me the next morning and advising me to "Come and git it"!

Deer season can be a monsoon season in parts of the Southern backcountry where autumn rains tend to be plentiful. Here, a 4-wheel-drive vehicle winches another 4WD out of a backroad washout in farmland where hunting is excellent. Winches and 4-wheel-drive are as valuable here as in the West. *(Photo by Tom Brakefield)*

Now there are breakfasts and there are *breakfasts.* In these Deep South deer camps, eating and good fellowship rate right up on par with the hunting itself. Two fellows were bellied up to the two stoves in the kitchen, one cooking eggs three different ways and the other frying bacon, thick slabs of country ham, and huge patties of tart country sausage. Still another fellow was making up big hoe cakes (outsized biscuits so named because in antebellum times the slaves took them to the fields to eat for lunch and heated them, and the meat they placed inside, on their hoe blades over an open fire).

The hunters were yawning and stirring and gulping scalding coffee that was strong enough to put starch into a predawn backbone. The heady kitchen aromas were enough to make the hunt worthwhile. I put away six eggs and a goodly sampling of all three meats, topped off with grits, soft and fluffy white, swimming in puddles of real butter.

After the meal we drew lots for our stand assignments (assuring fair treatment for all) and departed in 4WD vehicles for the day's drive area. Most of the vehicles had heavy-duty winches. During the late part of deer season in this area, the rains come with a vengeance. I once saw it rain 19 days running. The land is really a gummy clay and the roads become slick and bottomless during the rains. Just walking in the soupy bog that had been the clubhouse front yard was a major chore.

With all due respect to solitary hunters, the traditional Southern hunting clubs turn the pursuit of deer into a jolly social affair. At this Southern camp, hunters join their wives for a leisurely lunch between morning and afternoon hunts. That big cauldron holds steaming Mulligan stew made with plenty of venison. *(Photo by Tom Brakefield)*

Often I thought the glop would actually suck off my tightly laced 8-inch hunting boots.

You have to experience this clay mud, called "gumbo" hereabouts, to believe it. As you drive along and stir it up, air is trapped within it and it snaps-crackles-and-pops with almost deafening loudness. Ahead of us, as we drove to the hunt area, I could see a big pickup begin to bind up. Mud was packing so tightly to the wheels that it was binding them in the wheel wells and, although the gunk never got to the point of stopping the truck cold, it often can happen. When this goo dries out, it has a Rockwell rating of something over 60C in hardness and you can easily injure your foot by trying to kick chunks of it off the bumpers or wheels.

The roads become so bad because this is flat, piney-woods country with generally poor drainage and you have to stick to the gouged-out super-slick ruts that pass for roads rather than driving to the side on the edges of the grassy fields where the traction is considerably better. The local landowner who leases the hunting rights raises cattle and soybeans, as do most other farmers in this area, and if the hunters drive off the roads their vehicles quickly chew up valuable cropland or grass for cattle forage. Good hunter-landowner relations are an absolute must (as they are in any type of hunting anywhere) so one of the club's basic rules, enforced by severe fines when necessary, is to never leave the road with a vehicle.

The club's two parcels of leased hunting land run 2,000 and 1,200 acres. The club is financed by annual dues, chipped in by the members at the first of each year, plus any fines that are levied and collected for rule infractions.

The hunters learn their leased area minutely. Eventually they come to know every wrinkle and hollow in the sizable acreages about as intimately as the deer do. Aerial photo maps and topo maps are posted in the clubhouse and records are kept of kill sites and dates as well as drive dates and exact stand sites. Thus, over a period of time, rather exact data are available to help hunters plan better hunts or adjust stand locations as needed. There is more to this type of hunting than just releasing some dogs and hoping that a deer runs by.

This low, flat, marshy land that comprises roughly the southern 40 or 50 percent of Alabama, Georgia, and Mississippi is the "dog-hunting belt" of the South. Immediately to the north is another zone, roughly 100 to 250 miles deep, depending upon the spot, where the low coastal plain begins to hump up into the more rolling piedmont area. Here smaller mixed-crop farms are more in evidence. The cover isn't quite as thick and more of the land has been cleared, though large wooded acreages owned by paper companies can still be found. Drainage is better, so access by ordinary vehicles is much more feasible during the rainy season.

In this area, clubs with leased hunting rights are somewhat less common, and the individual or informal group is more commonly seen. Though buckshot, slugs, and centerfire rifles are all legal in most of this area, the slug is probably the most commonly used ammunition. Ranges can be a bit long for buckshot, and often the cover isn't quite heavy enough to warrant its use. Yet this area is still reasonably flat and, for this part of the country, relatively densely populated. Much of the best hunting is in rather civilized areas around the edges of the small to medium farms. Thus, the common use of the 12-gauge rifled slug. However, there is great variety in Southeastern hunting conditions, and rifles are used effectively in many spots.

Still farther north, beginning in the top portions of these three states and moving into Tennessee and Kentucky, the piedmont continues to build up into some respectable ridges and hills—mountains by Eastern standards. Some are pretty steep and rough, and reminiscent of deer stalking in the Adirondacks or the Catskills or the mountains of Pennsylvania.

Large valleys and lowland farming areas are dotted all through this higher, rougher zone but, to one degree or another, hill

The club members in attendance draw for the morning's stand assignments, and then the huntmaster discusses the plan, explaining every detail of the drive. After that, he leads them out and stations them. Here, an Alabama huntmaster (the man facing right) tells a member this is where he's to drop out of line and take his stand. All members will be positioned before the drive starts. *(Photo by Tom Brakefield)*

hunting is generally the most commonly encountered hunting. Many visitors are amazed, in fact, at just how rugged and wild the northern portions of Alabama and Georgia are in certain spots, not to mention eastern Tennessee, western North Carolina, and various areas throughout Kentucky and Virginia. Here the rifle is king, with modern calibers edging out the old reliable "thutty-thutty" carbines.

The .308 has found much favor here, and many hunters want a flat-shooting rifle of the .270 persuasion that they can also use on mule deer and pronghorn out West. Also, there can be an occasional long shot here on a powerline right-of-way or across from one hill to another. Scopes are seen on the vast majority of rifles, even the .30-30s and other rainbow-arced lever-actions.

The vast majority of younger hunters coming up in this area do not place a lot of credibility on the brush-busting capabilities of these older, low-velocity and big-caliber slugs. They may help penetrate brush a tad better in certain very specialized circumstances (such as hitting a twig immediately in front of the deer and then hitting him because the bullet ricocheted at a somewhat less acute angle) but apparently the greater number of hunters opt for the flatter-shooting cartridges, believing that they gain more than they give up by doing so. I am certainly in agreement.

Southern deer hunting is rich in tradition and history, and the hunting is good. Most sportsmen from other regions are astonished when they learn the size of the deer herds here and the length of the seasons and generosity of the bag limits. Even in parts of the North, deer herds occasionally require thinning because of reduced habitat. In stipulated portions of some Southern states, antlerless deer are legal game, or several days of the regular season are open for antlerless deer on a state-wide basis. True, a number of states in other parts of the country employ the same approach, but if you care more about good venison than about a rack on your wall you'll do well to inquire about the does in a state like Alabama. As for bucks, the limit there is mentioned in another chapter and it's worth repeating here. The limit is one. Not one per season—one per day! One per day for three months, because that's how long the season lasts, and the deer are most definitely not being overharvested.

Florida coastal whitetails tend to be relatively small, though they often have handsome racks. This one, photographed in a lush, grassy environment, is obviously in fine condition. Some of Florida's deer country is less hospitable to the hunter, for it can bristle with palmetto thickets and it has hot, hard-to-traverse swamps. ***(Courtesy of Florida Game and Fresh Water Fish Commission)***

This Virginia whitetail, pictured during a drive, is loping across a fairly open wooded flat. He's moving at fair speed but offers a close, fully exposed broadside target that should mean a one-shot kill.

More out-of-state hunters should trek south for a deer-hunting vacation, and this can usually be arranged after the home deer season is over. Also, though the weather can be a bit brisk (especially when you remain motionless for several hours on a stand) it is warm indeed when compared with the chilling temperatures in the North—a welcome break in the winter cold for Northern visitors. Southern hospitality still reigns supreme, and even though professional hunting guides and outfitters are rare in this region, a stranger can usually make a connection by calling or writing the state fish and game commissions for leads.

The authorities can often give you the names of hunting clubs and information as to how to contact their officers or the names of some of the small towns in the midst of the richest deer-hunting areas. It's then a simple matter to contact the local chambers of commerce or mayors of these towns with requests that they put you in touch with someone who might be able to help you set up a hunt. Some farmers or ranchers would be happy to work with you for a modest fee, and many hunting clubs, if they sense you're a good guy and ardent deer hunter, will be glad to welcome you as a guest for a long weekend of hunting just so they can swap tall tales and deer lore with another hunter from a different region. Often, exchange hunts—whereby a Southern hunter visits you the following year—can be arranged, and this is a good way to form new friendships as well as expand your hunting horizons.

CHAPTER

18

MIDWESTERN WAYS

by Erwin A. Bauer

During the late 1960s, my old friend Lew Baker established a record that would be difficult, perhaps impossible, to match anymore. Early in the mornings of four consecutive opening days, he bagged extremely good bucks. Except that Lew missed a hard shot during a blinding snow squall, he might have made it five in a row. But what, it's fair to ask, is so extraordinary about that?

To begin, Lew was hunting in Ohio, a state where the deer herd is not large and where (on the average) only two hunters in every 10 bag any kind of deer at all. Some years, success is considerably lower than that. Therefore the odds of getting a fine buck on four first days in a row are about like pitching no-hitters in both ends of a big league baseball doubleheader.

What is even more remarkable is that my friend didn't use any deep, dark, or illegal techniques to score. He hunted on unposted land open to the public and took his chances along with the multitudes of other eager sportsmen in the state. It's true that Lew was a very experienced outdoorsman, and that is always a great factor in any gunner's favor. His secret (if it can be called that) was just to plan ahead and to hunt the way everyone should proceed under the circumstances. It is also the best formula for hunting whitetails almost anywhere in the Midwest—that belt stretching from Ohio westward to Missouri and from the Ohio River northward to Minnesota. Throw in Kentucky for good measure since it is more similar to the Midwest geographically than it is to the South.

This is a region of mixed habitats. The Southern part is either entirely agricultural or partly so, begin punctuated by hardwood forests, second-growth hillsides,

Hunters check for fresh sign in a leaf-strewn clearing between a farm and a hardwood forest, where deer may have been feeding on a variety of items, ranging from maple sprouts, beech twigs, or acorns to corn or apples. This typifies much agricultural land in the Midwest as well as the East.

and strips of bottomland brush or timber along many waterways. The farther north you travel into the Midwest, the more the farming lands evaporate into Northern evergreen forests. Taken on the average, the portions that might be called ideal deer cover are neither as lush nor as dense as whitetail country in the Southeast, nor as open generally as the muley country of the Western mountains.

But an interesting evolution has taken place in many parts of the Midwest. Here the once woodland whitetail has somewhat adapted to farmland living—at least to thriving and growing heavy along the fringes of cultivation. All at once during the past few decades, cornfed venison has become available from cornfed bucks that grow much bigger than their cousins of the spruce and balsam swamps. Now suddenly there is deer hunting where none existed before. And true or not, a good many hunters are convinced that living off the fat of the land has also made the grainfield whitetails a lot wiser. Maybe they have to be to cope—to survive—in a more open environment within sight of silos and cattle compounds.

Now back to Lew Baker. The first thing Lew did was to locate and know local deer intimately. The next thing, the clincher, was to hunt them by the best, most deadly (and legal) method possible in that area.

For at least a week and usually longer before opening day, Lew went scouting. The day the season begins, he correctly reasoned, is much too late to start looking for whitetails unless you simply enjoy being baffled and outwitted. So consider, as Lew did, the following vital points.

Whitetails go largely unmolested during most of the year, but their quiet daily

This old-timer is sweating with exertion after dragging an unusually big buck—big even for Minnesota. Note that the wide, high rack has five long, thick tines jutting from each main beam. *(Photo by Norm Nelson)*

Here you see a fine 8-point buck in thick, head-high second growth. This is excellent deer habitat, and it abounds in parts of the Midwest, including some areas that were formerly deer-poor because of mature forests or the opposite— excessive clear-cut timbering. *(Courtesy of Michigan Department of Conservation)*

routines are suddenly disrupted early on opening day when the hunters hit the woods. The bulk of the kill is made on opening day, and the number of deer taken declines rapidly thereafter as each day of the season passes.

Deer behavior changes abruptly from normal to abnormal, and finding the animals becomes increasingly difficult. Old bucks become especially unpredictable and elusive. They actually seem to vanish from the earth. So the hunter with the best chance of success is the one waiting in the best possible position at daybreak on opening day. And only preseason scouting can locate the right place. Hunting groups that make big drives often benefit from the preseason scouting, too.

Assume that you are an enthusiastic deer hunter and have set aside a week or so of your annual vacation time for deer hunting. A survey in several Midwestern states revealed that the average deer hunter spent 3½ days in the woods, although he may have intended to spend a week or more. More significantly, most of those surveyed hunted on the first 3½ days of the season.

Instead of scheduling vacation time to begin with opening day as most men do, why not go early and spend several days scouting before the other hunters hit the heavy cover? That way, you get the jump on them as well as on the deer.

Preseason scouting has a fascination all its own. You're not under any great pressure, and buck fever isn't a factor. So you'll probably be a better observer, and you'll learn more about whitetails than you would if you were carrying a firearm. When you're reconnoitering on foot, you can also brush up on your woodmanship—trying to walk more quietly, for instance.

In some states it is perfectly legal to combine some form of hunting with preseason scouting before the firearms deer season. For example, the archery deer season may immediately precede the firearms season. In such circumstances you could be bowhunting while you look for a deer to take with your rifle later on. Elsewhere the season on such species as ruffed grouse and snowshoe hares may be open, and that also provides an opportunity to double up. But because of the shooting involved in upland gunning and the concentration it requires, it isn't as helpful as bowhunting. You won't spot deer so often if you're blasting noisily away at birds.

In some regions that are crisscrossed by many roads, a lot of scouting can be done by car. In rough country, a 4WD vehicle is a great help. It is wise to get a county map, available in almost every county courthouse, or if you're hunting in a national forest, a forest map available at regional headquarters and most ranger stations. Large-scale topo sheets may also be very helpful.

Sighting the animals themselves is obviously the best possible evidence. But in some areas, especially when the weather is very mild, deer may not move about much until after dark. So you may have to rely on tracks and other testimony.

Fresh tracks are a good indication that deer are in the area. Keep an eye out for fresh pellets, pawings in the earth, and rubs on saplings and trees. Rubs are easy to spot. They are made just before and during the rut by bucks that are scraping the velvet off their antlers. That rubbing often peels off the bark, leaving a bare spot that is noticeable from a distance. You'll often find the ground pawed up nearby.

Another preseason scouting method is to drive about at night and use a spotlight to locate deer. Their eyes show up clearly when the artificial light hits them, and you can often see antlers, too. Never carry both a spotlight *and any kind of firearm* in your car at the same time at night. Having both during darkness is usually considered to be good evidence of deer jacking—illegal everywhere. Whenever I have gone out at night with a spotlight, I've always informed the local game warden or forest ranger beforehand about what I was going to do, so that there could be no mistake.

Small areas are best scouted by simply hiking across them, perhaps once from north to south and then from east to west. Two or more hunters hiking on parallel paths can inspect an area even more thoroughly. Although the hikers should certainly take note of actual sightings, a man afoot usually must depend heavily on the fresh sign he finds along his route.

There are many places in the Midwest and southern Canada where a canoe float trip or a slow cruise around the edge of a lake can reveal a great deal. Tracks on sandy or muddy beaches are easy to spot. Preseason scouting for whitetails is productive because going afield early can make you a better, more confident hunter. You're more likely to succeed when you have confidence and are familiar with your surroundings. It's a simple matter of psychology.

If you know where the deer are on opening morning, you are sure of yourself, so you're much more likely to hunt skillfully and shoot well.

And if all the camp chores are done and you've enjoyed a good night's sleep, you're even more likely to do your best. Going out on a hard day's hunt relaxed and refreshed means more than most hunters realize. Any hunter needs every small advantage he can muster when the whitetail buck is the game.

Yet scouting alone will not put a Midwest buck in the freezer or a trophy rack on the wall. You still have to apply the scouting information properly. An extremely important survey conducted by John Cartier, of *Outdoor Life,* suggested how to do exactly that.

Cartier contacted the fish and game departments of all states to find out how deer are killed across the country. As anyone might guess, techniques vary greatly from region to region and are dictated by the geography, by the vegetation types which are common, by the number and species of deer. But hunting pressure is extremely important, too, and at least in the Midwest may be the most important consideration of all.

Consider these figures compiled by Cartier. In the Midwestern states only 11 percent of the deer killed are taken by still-hunting and 7.5 percent by stalking. Driving accounts for 28.8 percent of all whitetails harvested. The most significant statistic is that over half (53.5 percent) of all deer are taken from stands. Digging a little deeper, we can safely assume that still-hunting and stalking percentages are as high as they are because they work better in the evergreen forests of the North. At the same time, the percentage for standing success would be greater if only the most heavily populated states—the agricultural belt (where hunting is most concentrated in isolated spots)—had been censused.

A Michigan buck, temporarily socializing with a doe and fawn, peers out of a brush-and-sapling thicket. This kind of cover is often interspersed with big coniferous stands. It's this second growth that will attract the deer, but in such cover you may not get a clear shot except at close range, so it's probably wise to pick a good stand and wait for deer to come to you. *(Courtesy of Michigan Department of Conservation)*

Cartier learned that an incredible 95 percent of all deer shot in Missouri were taken by hunters waiting on stand.

We have already pointed out that the great, sudden invasion of deer habitat by hunters on opening morning creates a general confusion among hunters and hunted alike. Initially deer will try to escape the crunch by following old familiar runways, along which the really wise deer hunter (like Lew Baker) will be waiting at dawn's first light. Even after that first barrage, a patient, well-concealed stander has the best possible advantage because the army of hunters will keep the deer circulating. There's a good chance that eventually one will move within good gunshot range of the stander, even if he isn't in the best possible position.

Let's face some other facts. Most deer hunters in the woods today are relatively inexperienced and in no way a match for whitetails, which have keenly developed senses. An old buck's eyesight is remarkable. Therefore an inexperienced hunter's best bet, bar none, is to find a hidden spot

This deer probably qualifies as a resident of the lower Midwest. The picture was taken in the Land Between the Lakes—the TVA recreation area between Kentucky Lake and Lake Barkley in western Kentucky and Tennessee. The area supports a wide variety of wildlife, including whitetail deerlike this one and fallow deer.

and to stay motionless there. That way he will be most inconspicuous to alert, nervous deer. In much of the Midwest any hunter's chances of scoring are in direct proportion to how well he blends into his background and how many other hunters are milling about in that area.

Of course, considerable skill is involved in standing, a subject considered in more detail elsewhere in this book. Let's just list a few basics here. The stander should select a comfortable spot because that way he can better remain entirely motionless for long periods. He should have a good field of fire all around and not have his vision badly obscured by foliage or the terrain. It is always a considerable advantage to be above the deer, as in a tree blind, but some states have regulations governing the use and building of such structures. In Minnesota, for instance, there is a limit on height. Be sure to check thoroughly the limitations or laws wherever you plan to hunt.

One more crucial item remains. You've picked your stand properly and a big buck is on the way. He may be strolling closer, cautiously making a few short steps at a time, while buck fever unsteadies your posture. Or he may be pounding pell-mell head on. Either way, you have to put him down to stay.

Missed shots at vanishing whitetails are as common as wool shirts during the deer season. If shirttails actually were cut off every time somebody blew a shot at a buck, America's shirtmakers wouldn't be able to keep up with the demand.

No statistics exist to prove it, but I'm sure that the number of shots fired for each animal taken is greater with whitetail bucks than it is with any other big-game animal. That claim is certainly true in my own experience, and every other veteran big-game hunter with whom I discussed the matter says the same thing. Why are so many whitetails missed, and what can you do to improve your score?

First, let's consider the quarry. The mature whitetail buck is an extraordinary animal. A buck that has survived several hunting seasons as well as brutal winters has been honed sharp by danger and hardship. He is not the fastest animal on four feet, but I believe he can reach his top speed more quickly than any other animal of similar size.

The whitetail's vision, excellent hearing, and superb scenting ability have been thoroughly described in hunting literature, and the whitetail takes full advantage of the environment in which he lives. the forests of mixed hardwood and evergreen, the swamps and second-growth thickets, the laurel and honeysuckle tangles are perfect for the deer, but not for the deer hunter. When you consider typical Midwest habitat and the whitetail's ability to race through it at high speed or seemingly vanish in the cover, you know you are hunting an animal that was made to be missed.

Most deer hunters add to their troubles because they only dust off the old shooting iron once a year. Misses are to be expected if you don't shoot much, but even very experienced marksmen miss whitetails. Few men can honestly say that they always connect. In his excellent book *The Hunting Rifle,* Jack O'Connor admits that he has missed more deer in the brush than anywhere else.

Too many deer hunters do not use the best firearm for the purpose. There are two types of deer rifle—one for short-range use in brush or forest, the other for shooting in open or hilly country. The long-range rifle is used mostly for hunting mule deer out West. The ideal brush rifle for whitetails should be light, should be fast to operate, and should have a short barrel.

It's obvious that the whitetail hunter must be able to get on target fast, not unlike a scattergunner swinging on a flushed bird. With whitetails, you seldom have time to squeeze off a shot at a stationary target from a rest. When spotted, two out of three bucks are already in motion, and the third soon will be.

Although there's no question about the superiority of a bolt-action for certain uses, lever-action, pump-action, and semiautomatic rifles are popular for whitetail hunting because they are faster to use than a bolt-action rifle. In the brush, a second or sometimes even a third shot can be very useful, but you must get them off before the deer vanishes.

The rifle you select may well depend on your preference regarding a combination of caliber and action—lever, pump, or auto—as well as the design, weight, handling qualities, price, and various features available among the many hunting models.

In a number of Midwestern (and Eastern) states, deer hunters are required by law to use smoothbores and rifled slugs instead of rifles because bullets carry too far for use in densely populated areas. When used at close ranges in brush, the 12-gauge shotgun slug is extremely effective. It is practical to mount a peep sight or a scope on most shotguns. for many years I used a pump shotgun with a 20-inch barrel, designed especially for rifled slugs. On it is mounted a 2½× Weaver scope. The gun has accounted for lots of deer.

Using the best possible gun will not guarantee venison in the freezer. The hunter must know how to shoot it accurately and quickly, and that takes a lot of practice. The hunter must also learn to aim at a particular part of the deer—not the whole deer. The best aiming point is the heart-lung area just behind the front legs. A hit anywhere in that area will eventually drop any deer if it does not do so instantaneously. If the animal is not standing or running broadside, the shot should still be aimed to reach the forepart of the rib cage by quartering into it from the rear or driving forward between the hams.

Today the future of Midwestern whitetail deer and deer hunting appears fairly bright. The herds seem to be stabilized and are well managed by game biologists. The numbers of hunters—hunting pressure—can be regulated carefully. Without question the threat to a great sport is coming from uncontrolled sprawl and development—the destruction of habitat—far out across the beautiful Midwestern landscape. Unsound forestry management, which the Forest Service seems to endorse in too many woodlands, could also greatly diminish deer herds.

Over most of the Midwest, the prosperity of deer offers an unfailing index of the quality of life in general. If we lose the deer, and the sport they provide, we may have lost far more than delicious venison dinners.

CHAPTER

19

SOUTHWESTERN RATTLERS AND TOWER-SITTERS

by Byron W. Dalrymple

When one speaks of hunting whitetail deer in the Southwest, the term means chiefly Texas. The other states involved are Oklahoma, New Mexico, and Arizona, but Texas has most of the deer. This largest of the contiguous states is an enormous expanse of country, just over 267,000 square miles, and it has a phenomenal whitetail herd.

It is estimated, in fact, that at least one-fifth of all the whitetails in the nation are in Lone Star country, a state population of more than 3 million head. The harvest in good years surpasses 350,000, an astonishing number.

To anyone east of the Mississippi, some of the hunting habitat would seem strange, indeed. I remember with wry amusement my introduction to what is locally called the Brush Country in southern Texas. This is the region beginning roughly one tier of counties south of San Antonio, and fanning out on the west toward Eagle Pass, southeastward toward George West, and running south to the Mexican border, with a hub at Laredo.

The Brush Country counties contain the largest whitetails in Texas. Like the majority of Texas whitetails, these are the subspecies *texanus,* but something about the habitat turns out deer much larger than elsewhere in the state.

At any rate, my first visit to the region, over 30 years ago, was not for deer (the season was over) but for javelina. When I saw the gently rolling, arid terrain, an endless sweep of dense thornbush and cactus, with few large trees except here and there a clump of ancient mesquites, I thought it the most barren hunk of real estate I had ever looked at. During the javelina hunt, I was startled witless when I jumped an enormous whitetail buck from a thicket. The time was January and the bucks still had their antlers.

I'd not given a thought to deer. It seemed an impossible country for them. Before the hunt wound up, however, I had seen several more and I was already making plans to go deer hunting there. Not long afterward we moved permanently to Texas and I have hunted the brush many times. I have hunted deer in many states, but the largest whitetails I have ever seen and shot have been there.

The whitetail deer has proved to be one of the best colonizers of all our big-game animals. It has adapted to an amazing variety of terrain. Nowhere is this more vividly illustrated than in the Southwest. You can hunt in the piney woods of East Texas in areas reminiscent of southern Georgia or northern Florida. In portions of eastern Oklahoma, you literally hunt in the Ozarks, the tail end of those mountains. Elsewhere in Oklahoma there are big, fat deer keeping their private lives supremely private in farm-country woodlots. On the western fringe of the Texas Brush Country—for example, in the Devil's River region of Val Verde County—there are rugged, low mountains that look for all the world like the domain of desert mule deer, but actually teem with whitetails of husky dimensions. In the Texas Hill Country, in the south-central part of the state, the hunting is among live oaks, Spanish oaks, and Ashe juniper, in most scenic settings, with brushy, steep canyons through which flow small crystal streams. In southwestern New Mexico and southeastern Arizona the prime whitetail country is up in the grass and oak zone of the mountain ranges at about 6,000 feet. Thus, one of the unique features of Southwestern whitetail hunting is that you can take your pick of a wide variety of hunting country.

It will be useful to prospective hunters first to get a clear picture of where the deer are in the Southwest. In Oklahoma, whitetails are found in all 77 counties but the preponderance of the herd is in the east. The southeastern counties rate highest, but east-central and northeast also rate high. Westward, in general, the heaviest concentrations follow the large river courses and their tributaries—the Cimarron, North and South Canadian, Washita.

Oklahoma is fortunate in having numerous tracts owned by the state, where hunting is fair to good. There are also two large blocks of the Ouachita National Forest in the southeast, plus scattered expanses of national grasslands in the west. The McAllister Military Depot has some of the best hunting, by permit, in the state.

In Texas, whitetails range throughout the state. There are excellent opportunities in the eastern and northern counties, in the Panhandle, and even in parts of the lower desert-mountain country of far-West Texas. But the heaviest whitetail concentration is on the Edwards Plateau, which takes in most of the south-central area of the state and spreads westward along and north of the Rio Grande. Within this broad region, the so-called Hill Country encompassing the counties west and northwest of San Antonio has the most deer, possibly the heaviest whitetail concentration on the continent.

The average size of these deer varies from county to county. They are relatively small, by no means as large as those to the south, in the Brush Country. There the deer are numerous, but less so than in the Hill Country. The two areas cover the best whitetail hunting in the state.

Far to the west, across the Pecos River in Brewster and Presidio counties, there is a very small, handsome whitetail often mistaken for the Arizona whitetail or Coues deer. It is the subspecies *carminis,* the Carmen Mountains whitetail. It dwells, in sparse population, in the high portions of small mountain ranges in the Big Bend region. This sprightly deer, which I have had opportunity to hunt and collect several times, lives in the pinyon oak, and madrona cover, usually from an elevation of 5,000 feet up to the top of the mountains that rise from the desert floor. The larger Texas *(texanus)* whitetails are found in modest numbers in the foothills.

It is not finding the deer but finding a place to hunt that poses problems in Texas. There is very little public land—some national forest tracts north of Houston, some national grasslands in the Panhandle, a scattering of timber-company lands in the east that allow hunting, and a very modest amount of on state-owned game-management units, with hunting regulated by drawings. Otherwise, Texas deer hunting is strictly for fees. There are three chief arrangements: day hunting at so much per day, most of it on small ranches in the Hill Country; lease hunting, common throughout the state, wherein an individual or group will lease hunting rights on a specified acreage for a season or for several years; and package hunts, on which a rancher furnishes guide and transport for a hunt of a specified length. On some of these, meals and lodging are also available, at stipulated prices. A few package-hunt ranches offer guaranteed hunts—no deer, no pay.

Thus, unless you own land or have a friend who does, you generally have to pay to hunt deer in Texas. Although all types of hunting are getting more and more expensive, there are advantages to the fee system. On a well-run day hunt, only a given number of hunters is assigned to any pasture. On a lease, no one is there but the lessees. On a package hunt, the success rate is usually 100 percent and there is no crowding; usually only a single party in any one pasture at a given time.

The usual procedure for finding a place to hunt in Texas is to contact chambers of commerce in the area where you wish to go. Many landowners who need hunters are listed with the chambers of commerce. Or you might place a preseason ad in a local daily or weekly, stating how many hunters you have and what type of hunt you want. A few large ranches, such as the well-known Y.O. Ranch near Mountain Home and Dolan Creek Ranch on Devil's River, advertise nationally in outdoor magazines. These and others like them offer package hunts.

Getting a lease or a package or day hunt nowadays in the Brush Country is chancy. Leases are long, with dozens of takers in line. The Hill Country, in general, offers the best opportunity for visitors. So far as the little Carmen Mountains deer are concerned, all are on huge ranches, and this is basically desert muley country. The season is brief and the ranches are mostly booked full with mule deer hunters. It's every man for himself in lining up a hunt. In fact, it's pretty much that way throughout Texas, yet success is so high that it's worthwhile to

This magnificent 10-point buck disproves the notion that Texas whitetails are invariably found in dense, head-high brush. The deer was rattled to a stand in relatively open woods by the famous hunter and hunting-equipment manufacturer, Murry Burnham. *(Photo by Murry Burnham)*

Here's where it all begins. This is a whitetail fawn, lying still in a concealed spot where its mother left it. The doe is probably hiding about 100 yards away. She returns only for brief periods to suckle her young, because her presence might attract predators. Fawns can walk within half an hour after birth, but they remain motionless if an intruder approaches, and they are nearly odorless for about the first month of life.

A typical Eastern whitetail, this buck looks bigger than he really is; he probably stands only a trifle over three feet high at the shoulder, though he may consume 12 pounds of browse per day. Antler development doesn't reveal age once a buck matures, but the deer shown here is probably wearing his third set. *(Photo by Richard Simms, Tennessee Wildlife Resources Agency)*

Stephanie Boyle, Associate Editor of *Outdoor Life,* poses happily with a 10-point whitetail buck she took in South Carolina.

Pictured in very early autumn, these two Virginia whitetails are still in velvet, but their antlers are fully grown. The bristly-haired velvet membrane, which carries a blood supply to nourish developing antlers, will soon dry and begin to peel away.

Jim Zumbo approaches a whitetail buck he killed in a typical Northeastern woodlot. Although still-hunting is Zumbo's favorite method, it can be too noisy when the fallen hardwood leaves are crackling-dry. He waylaid this deer from a well chosen stand.

In this scene, a thin cover of new snow makes for good tracking. However, if the snow has already begun to melt, prints can be deceiving. The whitetail buck shown here was coaxed out into a clearing by several hunters making a quiet drive. The deer never became sufficiently alarmed to run. *(Photo by Richard Simms, Tennessee Wildlife Resources Agency)*

Hunting from a tree stand can be recommended in all kinds of whitetail country, but such a stand is especially valuable where regulations prohibit the use of rifles. This hunter is watching for a New Jersey deer during that state's shotgun season. On his elevated perch he won't be seen or scented, so game is likely to approach well within shotgun range—or bow range, for that matter. *(Photo by Rick Methot)*

Owing to the very short effective range of arrows, stealth and concealment are essential to bowhunting. Camouflage clothing is standard. Some archers also wear camo gloves and headnets. Others daub their faces and hands with camouflage greasepaint, as in this picture.

Late in the season, when the weather has turned wintry, a couple of hours on stand can be a trying experience. This hunter is about to leave his chosen post to still-hunt through thickets where deer often take shelter during snowfalls. His quarry may be either whitetail or mule deer, as he's on a self-guided hunt in a Western national forest that holds both species.

ferret out a place, and with a little persistence it can be done.

There is not much whitetail hunting in New Mexico. A scattering of Texas whitetails is found in the Lincoln National Forest in south-central-southern New Mexico, a few west of Raton, and a very few (possibly another subspecies) in the sandhills and brushy draws of several eastern counties. In the extreme southwest, mainly in the Animas and Peloncillo Mountains, there is a fair population of the handsome and sporty Coues, or Arizona, whitetail. The total New Mexico whitetail population is probably no more than 10,000.

Most of the Coues deer—about 15,000—are found in southern Arizona. Although this small whitetail subspecies ranges in suitable terrain across most of the southern half of the state, and is the only whitetail in Arizona, the preponderance of the population is in the various mountain ranges of the Southeast. Some of the better ranges include the Santa Ritas, Catalinas, Huachucas, Grahams, Galiuros, Santa Teresas, Tumacacoris, and Chiricahuas. An average annual whitetail kill in Arizona runs about 3,000, possibly a fifth or less of the state's total deer harvest. The others, of course, are mule deer. In both Arizona and New Mexico there is no problem finding places to hunt. There are vast acreages of national forest and other public lands.

Most Southwestern deer hunting is done by the standard methods of still-hunting or stand-hunting. Deer drives, except for a casual small attempt here and there to push deer out of a cedar brake, are all but unknown. There are, however, some unique methods used in Texas that apparently originated there and that are not very common elsewhere in the country. One is the tower or high blind. Nonresidents have spoken of these as "high sits" (a term derived from the German), although I've never heard a Texan use the term. In fact, in the Hill Country where hundreds of gunners hunt this way, everyone knows that when you speak of a deer blind you don't mean one on the ground but one high above.

On many ranches these so-called towers take the form of small buildings on stilts. My first deer hunting in Texas, as I recall with some amusement because I could hardly believe it, was done from one of these permanent installations. I was dropped off at dawn by my host and told I'd be picked up at nine-thirty. I climbed a ladder, pushed up a trap door, entered a snug little room about 6 × 6. There were sliding windows on three sides, a comfortable chair, a bottle of water, and a roll of toilet paper. There was even a small sand bag for a rest to be placed on the window sill. Shooting avenues had been cleared in the cedar and live oak so crossing deer could be seen.

The basic idea, of course, is that deer seldom look up, and the hunter has an excellent view plus comfort. Many ranchers use these permanent stands, which also keep visiting hunters from walking and possibly endangering one another. Some have a rule that you stay in your stand until picked up—except, of course, to gut a kill.

Down in the Brush Country, towers of this sort are usually not as plush. Some are rather rickety open boxes attached to a tall upright of telephone-pole size. Hundreds of portable tower stands are also in use,

You'd be grinning, too, if you'd taken this Texas whitetail buck. Such a deer is a rare trophy, and considering the massive beams of its magnificent antlers it's no surprise that the animal was killed in the Brush Country—a region comprised of just a few counties stretching from below San Antonio to the border. Almost all of the record-book Texas whitetails have come from this region. *(Photo by Byron W. Dalrymple)*

and building them is a big business in Texas. Most of these have a steel tripod frame, atop which is affixed a swivel seat with a circular footrest. Some are topped with small enclosed or partially enclosed blinds. If you enjoy this kind of hunting, such stands are extremely productive in the dense cactus and thornbush. From ground level you can't see into it, and most of it is high enough so deer don't show above it. A high view gives the hunter a chance to see deer moving at close range or distantly.

The man at left is Byron Dalrymple, and he's holding a pair of antlers to rattle up a rutting, bellicose buck. It's surprising how close bucks can be lured by rattling, even from an exposed position like this, if the hunters stay still and quiet except for the rattling. Also note that Texans are ingenious when it comes to mobility and tower hunting. In this case the tower is a platform mounted atop a hunting car. From such a vantage point the hunters can spot deer in clumps of low cover far out in the open terrain.

Most interesting and dramatic of Texas hunting methods is rattling antlers during the rut. Although rattling has been used in other places across the country, it supposedly originated in the dense brush of the border country in Texas, and most of it is still done in Texas. For those who have never seen it, the results are all but unbelievable.

While producing a film some years ago, I had a cameraman partner who was from Michigan. He had heard of rattling but I could tell he really didn't put much stock in it. Just after dawn on the first morning, I parked my 4WD, got my rattling "horns," and beckoned him to follow me. With movie camera mounted on a gunstock, he did so. We walked quietly into the cover for possibly 100 yards. There was a small opening here. I backed up into a cedar thicket, he got set behind me, and I began rattling.

At the first clash of the antlers there was a clatter of stones. A big 10-pointer barreled into the opening. Eyes wild, nostrils flared, he came tearing straight at us. He slid to a stop not 10 feet away, staring, confused. Then he whirled and ran. I tickled the antlers together and darned if he didn't wheel and come back. Meanwhile I realized I wasn't hearing the whir of the camera. I looked around. The camerman was sitting with eyes wide, staring. In his amazement he had forgotten to run this superb footage!

Rattling is effective only during the rut, but that may be a period of a month or more. It is a simple routine. To fix up a set of rattling antlers, saw them individually from the skull. I like an 8-point set, including brow tines, which I saw off. I leave the burl on the base of each antler, but if they bother your hands, cut them off, too. Smooth down the saw cuts with a file. If the antler points are especially sharp, trim and file them so they won't hurt your hands. Drill a hole in each antler base if you've cut off the burls, so you can tie a thong between them and sling the set over your shoulder for carrying.

The best rattling time is a still, crisp dawn. Select a stand where you can see out well but keep hidden. I try to pick a spot where I can sit, and have a tough bush within reach and also a rough-barked tree of fair size like a live oak, plus a patch of gravel or small rocks. I begin by bringing the antlers smartly together, tines intermeshing, followed with a sharp crack produced by rattling them loudly together. Then another rattle, and follow up by raking and whacking the dry bush, then raking the points of one antler down the tree bark and finally scraping the points in gravel. Then one more rattle. The entire effect sounds like two bucks fighting, breaking twigs, raking trees, and sliding in rock or gravel.

After a brief pause, go through it again or vary it. Some bucks come on the run, ready to fight. Some sneak in as if hoping to run off with a doe that is watching two bucks fight. Young bucks act ridiculously naive at times. Watch a spike buck and if he turns and stares away from you, look where he looks. Probably a big buck is coming and the spike isn't anxious to tangle with him. If you've had no action after you've been on a stand for 20 to 30 minutes, the next tactic is usually to move on. However, if the place looks good, don't hesitate to stay longer.

One time I began rattling well after dawn, and perhaps 10 minutes later I saw a buck get up from his bed on a nearby ridge. I was trying to get a buck in for a hunter who was with me. I kept on, sometimes just raking gravel a little or tickling the antlers lightly. We were hidden in a small draw and every few minutes we could glimpse a part of the deer moving a step or two along the ridge. I fiddled with that deer for a whole hour. I was just about to leave in disgust when the buck, unable to figure out what was going on, walked down off the ridge and into the open and kept walking slowly and stiffly toward us. I

Climbing the ladder to a tower blind can be awkward if a hunter is encumbered with a rifle. It's easier and safer to tie a rope to the gun, as this man has done, and pull it up after getting into the blind. This tower is in the Texas Hill Country, in an exposed position with a wide view. Such towers become a permanent part of the landscape, so the structures don't spook the game. Towers are now used in a few Western and Southeastern places, but it wouldn't be quite accurate to say their use spread from Texas. They've been standard in Europe for centuries.

Bob Elman looks over a whitetail he killed in west-central Texas. He first spotted the animal from a scouting seat bolted to the bed of a pickup truck that had been converted into a hunting vehicle. The animal vanished into a long, narrow thicket, so Elman and two partners hunted along the thicket's edges and eventually pushed out two does and this buck.

didn't dare let him get too close, as alerted as he was. At possibly 45 yards my hunter dropped him.

Most Texas deer hunters do very little walking. One reason is that all but a negligible part of the hunting is on private ranch lands, and these have rough vehicle trails gridding them. Some hunters simply cruise around looking for deer, glassing, making a stalk when possible. The majority take a stand, either the high variety or on the ground. Stock-watering "tanks" (ponds) are numerous. Stands near these are invariably productive, and so are stands on ridges overlooking fairly open valleys. In some areas, winter wheat and oat patches draw deer by the dozens and are staked out by hunters.

The southern Brush Country gets virtually no walking hunters. There are sound reasons. A hunter can jump deer by gingerly prowling the brush but he will seldom get a shot. Even if he gets a running shot, in such cover they are not very effective and when he wounds a deer in this cover it is too often lost. Hunting in the Brush Country, when not from a tower, is all stand-hunting of one kind or another. This region has been sliced up with numerous bulldozed trails, many of them made originally by oil-exploration crews operating seismographs. These, of course, form open strips through the dense cover. A perfect stand on such trails is at an intersection that permits you to sit at trailside and watch in four directions by a little slow neck-craning. Another good one in rolling portions of this region is beside a trail at the top of a ridge, so you can see the small valleys on either side.

In moving, deer must cross these trails. Does may dally in them. Bucks seldom do. I've watched a trail intently for hours, then seen a buck barely poke his head and neck out. That's the time to shoot, if you have any target. When he crosses, it'll be—zip—and that's all.

By preseason scouting on leases or other large tracts, hunters occasionally get big bucks located. For example, I hunted for seven seasons on a lease of 9,000 acres near Laredo. The leaseowner was on the property every few days, bass-fishing the several tanks on it. Thus he knew pretty well the general areas where the most deer were. When the season opened we took stands, most of the time just below the brow of a hill so we could watch a small valley where good bucks had been seen. By being above them we could see well down into the dense cover. Hunting, no matter how you do it in the Brush Country, is difficult; it's challenging because you know there are real trophy whitetails somewhere in the tangle.

In eastern Oklahoma there is much forest land, and hunting methods are just about the same as anywhere east of the Mississippi. Some hunters love to prowl the woods, some select a stand and stay with it. I own a small ranch in the Hill Country of Texas that is exceptionally rugged and scenic. My boys and I have still-hunted the ridges and the brushy canyons there many times, moving very slowly and trying to come up on bucks unaware. This, too, is interesting hunting because it is difficult. The same basic technique is used by most hunters in New Mexico and Arizona after Coues deer. They glass a lot, and pussyfoot around the slopes and the canyons. They also throw rocks. That may sound silly, but sometimes it works. The Coues is a wily little character, and a buck often lies tight and will not move unless you all but step on him. Pitching rocks into draws often gets them out.

John Finegan, owner of Dolan Creek Ranch, makes a regular routine of hurling rocks with a big leather sling. His country is awesomely rugged, with large canyons. Hurling a few rocks from a rim to go clattering down the canyon soon moves deer. The only problem with the technique is that it produces running shots.

If I were a nonresident planning to visit the Southwest, I'd first select the state by success ratio and what deer I wanted. Texas is far and away highest in success. As I have said, a visitor taking a package hunt has a 100 percent expectation, unless he is trophy hunting. If I were after Coues deer, although southwestern New Mexico is rather neglected and has a good number, I'd go to southeastern Arizona. The record book tells why. Of heads listed in the latest edition, almost all came from Arizona.

To fill yourself in on public lands, the best way in both Arizona and New Mexico is to obtain Forest Service maps showing the national forests. But for Coues, by all means hire a guide if possible. Both state game departments may furnish a list (although, of course, no recommendations). In Oklahoma it is possible to get from the game department a listing of state and federal public lands. Many of the state tracts are called public hunting areas. A Forest Service map showing the grasslands and the Ouachita National Forest also would help.

Because the system in Texas is as it is, you won't get far by writing to the game department with a lot of questions. The department keeps no lease lists, day-hunt lists, or package-hunt lists. A Forest Service map will show you the national forests and national grasslands, but these areas won't offer you the best hunting. The route for a visitor is the package hunt. As I mentioned, chambers of commerce are often able to point you toward ranches that offer these. Also, watch the outdoor magazines for ads. Prices vary widely.

So far as hunting permission is concerned, in New Mexico and Arizona you don't need to worry much since there are ample public lands. In Texas, unless you're a real smooth talker with faith to spare, don't waste valuable time trying to get free access. Deer are a paying crop here. In Oklahoma there are enough public spots, and a few private landowners may succumb to a request.

What rifle do you need for the Southwest? I happen to be of the school that thinks it is pure malarkey to believe one caliber is suitable only in the East and another in the West. Certainly some do better than others. By and large, the same calibers are used in the Southwest that are used elsewhere. There are years when it's legal to take four Texas whitetails in a season, and I've done that several years in a row using a .243 with a 100-grain load. I've shot numerous Southwestern deer with the .308. The .30-06, the .270, and comparable calibers are much used. I personally wouldn't hunt without a scope, and my favorite is a 3×-9× variable of top quality. I use one in the live oak and cedar of the Hill Country, and down in the brush, and out in the western mountains for the small whitetails.

Having lived in Texas for over two decades now, and having hunted the other states under discussion here as well as from Maine to the Great Lakes to the Deep South, it seems to me that some of the most intriguing whitetail hunting on the continent is located here. For example, every deer hunter should eventually make a try for a good Coues buck. This is one of the wariest and smartest of the whitetail tribe. The diminutive Carmen Mountains deer is equally challenging, but not many hunters can get an opportunity to try for it. The first one I took, a young forkhorn, weighed just 45 pounds field-dressed. The last one was an adult, an 8-pointer, and he weighed 76 pounds field-dressed.

As hunter numbers grow and competition for leases in Texas becomes more severe, hunting the mahogany-horned busters of the Brush Country—which I consider the most challenging of all whitetail hunting—will not be possible for very many sportsmen. But for those who arrange a fee hunt elsewhere in Texas, the deer are certainly present in abundance. In Oklahoma, where deer were exceedingly scarce some years ago, the herd has been steadily expanding and the hunting steadily growing better. Hunting whitetails of the Southwest is an experience quite different from hunting them in other regions, and for my money it rivals the hunting anywhere.

CHAPTER

20

WHITETAILS OF THE WEST

by Jim Zumbo

There's a curious enigma in the West. Of all the deer in North America, whitetails are by far the most popular, but not in the Western States. The big-racked mule deer gets all the attention, while whitetails are ignored or lightly hunted by westerners.

Take Montana, for example, where deer habitat ranges from brushy creek bottoms to grassy ponderosa pine forests to horrid high-county evergreen thickets jammed with blowdowns and dense stands of spruce and fir. Whitetails and mule deer share many of these environments, but whitetails always come out second in popularity. Montanans and nonresidents alike would rather chase muleys.

Why is this so, especially since whitetails have captured the fancy of hunters throughout the rest of the country? I think the reason is the mule deer's traditional popularity among hunters in the West. This attitude seems to hold true wherever mule deer and whitetails occupy the same regions. Nonresidents commonly view Western deer hunting as a pursuit of muleys—big-eared, huge-antlered bucks not available anywhere but the West.

Broadly speaking (and not counting the whitetail in Texas, which is ably covered elsewhere in this book by Byron Dalrymple), there are two huntable whitetail subspecies in the West: the animal that lives in the northern latitudes including the states of Washington, Idaho, Montana, Wyoming, and Colorado; and the Coues whitetail that dwells in Arizona and New Mexico. It should be mentioned that there is a small population of Columbian whitetails in Oregon and Washington, but they're too few to be recognized as important quarry.

Let's look at the northern whitetail first.

This deer is at home in a wide variety of places, and, true to its reputation in the East, is remarkably adaptable. Biologists know this subspecies as the Northwest whitetail, *Odocoileus virginianus ochrourus*. Another subspecies, the Dakota whitetail, *Odocoileus virginianus Dakota*, ranges chiefly east of the Rockies but is commonly lumped together with the whitetails of the West, *O.v. ochrourus*.

Both of these deer will take almost anything nature can dish out. They thrive in practically every environment. In Colorado, for example, you'll find whitetails along brushy riverbottoms such as the South Platte, or in weedy creekbeds near the Kansas border where there's enough cover to hide in. In Wyoming, whitetails are fond of ponderosa pine forests, such as the Black Hills National Forest in the northeastern region. In Idaho, I've hunted whitetails in terrible blowdowns, deep in conifer thickets that seemed habitable only by elk. I've seen whitetails in Montana in rugged brakes of the Missouri River, as well as in ravines and canyons in the midst of extensive grassland prairies.

Despite this wide range of Western whitetail habitat, a good share of the deer are associated with agricultural areas. They bed in thick vegetation along streams and rivers, and feed at night in farm fields. In this situation, hunting techniques are fairly standard. You find a well-used trail in the brush, wait alongside it in a tree stand or ground blind, and hope a deer will wander by when you're ready for it. Obviously, you'll need to scout the area thoroughly to determine where deer are living, and you'll need to select the proper trail or trails to watch. I like to be near the junction of two or more trails so I'll have a better chance of seeing a moving deer.

In areas where they aren't hunted hard (meaning much of the West), whitetails leave cover in late afternoon and start feeding when there's plenty of shooting light left. If you can spot deer without their seeing you, you can make a careful stalk and try to get within shooting range. You'll have your work cut out for you, however, because whitetails are nervous when they're in the open and it's daylight. A good plan is to leave the feeding deer undisturbed and return in the morning long before the first hint of dawn. Pay

Bob Good gets a close-up, satisfied look at an excellent Western whitetail he killed with one shot from his .44 Magnum Smith & Wesson Model 29 revolver. He has good reason to be satisfied, because the buck, taken during a drive, was felled while moving at a full run.

Editors Zumbo and Elman had trouble deciding whether to put this photo in this chapter on Western whitetails or the chapter on whitetails in the Southwest. A borderline case that might qualify for either category, it shows Byron Dalrymple bringing in a Carmen Mountains whitetail. He must have been in good shape for the hunt. The Carmen Mountains whitetail is a small, light subspecies, but a buck is still quite a load to carry any distance, and desert hunting is hot and rigorous. As usual, Byron has his binoculars with him; field glasses are as valuable for Western whitetail hunting as for hunting mule deer.

attention to the breeze, and work your way through cover toward the area where you saw the deer. You'll take the risk of spooking deer in the dark as you sneak, but they generally calm down quickly in the blackness.

I recall a hunt for whitetails a few years back in Montana. I'd located a small herd, including a respectable buck, feeding along a barley field late in the afternoon. There wasn't enough time to try a stalk then, so I left them feeding and came back early the next morning. I parked my vehicle a half-mile from where I figured the deer were, and eased into a patch of woods next to the field. By shooting light I couldn't see any deer, but a few minutes later I caught movement across the field. Several does and fawns were slipping into a creek bed. The buck wasn't there, but 15 minutes later I saw him moving in the brush along the creek. He was too far for a shot, and I never saw him again. My strategy might have worked if they hadn't moved across the barley field, but that's the way it usually goes when hunting whitetails. It's seldom an easy hunt—you have to earn every buck you take, whether you're in the West or East.

Whitetails are commonly hunted in ponderosa pine forests that are reasonably open and offer good visibility. Deer seldom bed in the midst of the open trees, but like to hide in blowdowns, ravines, and underbrush. The best time to catch them in the open is in late afternoon and early morning. If agricultural areas are close to the forest, deer are likely to travel out of the trees and into fields to feed. If you can locate a trail or two that they travel to reach feeding areas, you'll have a good chance of ambushing a buck.

Still-hunting is well-suited to ponderosa forests. If you spook deer, the openness of the country might allow a shot at a running animal. Whitetails will bed in the thickest cover they can find; any dense vegetation should be suspect. Move carefully, always looking for signs of deer such as a horizontal shape, the twitch of an ear or a tail, or a bit of sunlight glinting off an antler, and always move with the breeze in your face. If possible, get above the thicket, where you'll have a better view. If a likely spot consistently produces deer but you can't get a shot during your approach, try a different tactic and watch the area from an elevated stand early in the morning. Be in position before shooting light.

A few years ago I hunted turkeys during the spring season in Wyoming's Black Hills National Forest. Every day I saw whitetails in the same ravine, probably because the draw was extremely brushy and had plenty of cover. If I ever return to that area for a fall hunt, I know where I'll start first.

Some of the toughest hunting for whitetails in the West is in the brakes or badlands of various river drainages. The Missouri is probably the most notable, with the worst of it in Montana. Some parts of the Missouri brakes are as rugged as any landscape in the West. A good deal of this land is inaccessibly by vehicle, and the areas blessed with roads are traveled only by wary hunters who respect the region. Rainy weather quickly turns roads into muddy quagmires, trapping unsuspecting hunters for days.

Because of the remoteness of the area, deer are lightly hunted and consequently escape hunters for enough seasons to grow respectable antlers.

Badlands bucks are often highly visible

The late Pete Czura, eminent outdoor photographer and writer, makes himself comfortable aboard a hunting vehicle as he outlines tactics with guide Joe Martin. Scouting vehicles like this have become common in the West and Southwest. If the hunter spots something promising in the distance, he can signal the driver by tapping the cab roof or window. Then it's time to get down and walk, stalk, and earn a buck.

because of the vastness, the openness of the terrain, but remember that you have to get back in there to see them at all. If you're relying on a vehicle to hunt with, use a spotting scope to glass as much country as you can. Do it in the morning, when deer are moving from feeding to bedding areas. If you see a distant buck, it might take the best part of a day to make a stalk. Plan on plenty of hiking, and don't pass up any canyons that feed into major drainages. Get as far away from roads as you can. Put on a daypack and head for the most remote areas you can. That's where you'll find unsuspecting bucks that are seldom disturbed by hunters.

Remember that whitetails will be in brushy areas. A rugged break with trees and undergrowth in the bottom is a likely bailiwick for a herd of whitetails, or a big, lone buck.

If you hunt whitetails in northwestern Montana, the Idaho panhandle, or other spots in the same general region, you'll be faced with heavy timber. Dense stands of pine, fir, and spruce will hide deer, and you'll have to hunt them like elk to score. Trail hunting is important here, because you'll need to ambush a deer to make him yours. Still-hunting is tough, if not almost impossible in some places. Thick blowdowns make silent walking difficult. You'll be crawling over and under fallen logs, tiptoeing along busted treetops, and climbing across rotten snags. Even a squirrel couldn't move about silently in that kind of forest debris.

I remember a hunt in Idaho's panhandle a dozen years ago. It took me a half-hour to negotiate a 200-yard patch of terrible blowdown. I'm sure I sounded like an infantry patrol moving through the woods. At first I tried my best to be quiet, but after the second branch snapped loudly I gave

That dark, meandering line that wavers across the meadow to the stream and woods is a Montana bear trail. But bears are not the only game in this kind of terrain. Both whitetails and mule deer can be found by hunters who know where to look. During most of the day, whitetails will tend to stay in brushy thickets, in the woods, and along the edges. *(Courtesy of Montana Chamber of Commerce)*

up. All I wanted to do was escape the nightmare tangle, walk to the next drainage, and start all over again.

This is great country for a deer drive, though the vastness of many Western forests requires more time and energy than a small woodlot in the East. Deer will be scattered more in the West, and you'll need to work a much larger territory to get them to cooperate. It's wise to scout first to determine the extent of deer use, then put on a drive if you've determined that whitetails are regularly inhabiting the area. In these big woods I like the silent drive rather than the noisy type, because there's too much room for deer to slip away unnoticed when they've pinpointed your location. If you walk quietly, deer won't have you pegged as well, and might expose themselves carelessly.

The Coues whitetail, hunted chiefly in Arizona but also in New Mexico and Mexico, is a small deer well-known for its wariness. It was named for an eminent nineteenth-century naturalist, Elliott Coues. Folks in Arizona pronounce this deer's name like the word "cows," but others say it like "coos," and some just call it the Arizona whitetail. However you pronounce it, you'll have nothing but respect for this deer once you hunt it. I know some experienced, well-traveled hunters who rate the Coues at the top of the list for intelligence.

In Arizona, the prime region for Coues, this subspecies can be hunted in relatively open country or in rugged mountains that will test the mettle of any Rocky Mountain mule-deer hunter. Steep, rocky slopes combined with dense patches of brush and timber make this a formidable place.

The Coues is a sneaky critter, and would rather hide than run when a hunter approaches. It's not uncommon for a deer to sit tight to the point where a hunter almost steps on it. When that happens, it takes a bit of luck and skill to calm down quickly enough to fire a bullet with accuracy.

Ed Park, my good friend and well-known outdoor writer, finds the Coues deer fascinating and hunts it as often as he can. Ed uses a combination of stalking and still and hunting, depending on the terrain and vegetation. If he spots deer without their seeing him, he figures a route to get within shooting distance and makes a stalk. While doing so, he's constantly alert for other deer in the vicinity that are hidden or temporarily out of sight.

John Doyle, a Tucson taxidermist, hunts the Coues with more fervor than most hunters. His strategy is to walk to a vantage point on a slope so he can glass an adjacent slope to the west. By looking west, he has the sun behind him, and the target slope gets first light since it faces east. After spotting deer and selecting one he likes, he keeps observing it until it beds down. Then he pinpoints the location and makes a careful stalk, using the wind to his advantage and making best use of screening vegetation.

Once thought to be a distinct species, the Coues is still listed separately from other whitetails in the Boone and Crockett trophy records. The separate classification remains valid in terms of trophy standings, because this subspecies has a lighter rack than northern whitetails. It's a small deer, seldom weighing much more than 100 pounds dressed. It takes a big old buck to hit three digits on the scale, though some will reach 125 pounds and more.

The rifle you use on Western whitetails should be one that you're familiar with. No need to buy something special. A lightweight firearm is nice if you intend to do a lot of walking. A scope is practical, and is common everywhere, though some hunters who pursue whitetails in dense timber prefer an open-sighted carbine. If you're hunting in open country, a flat-shooting rifle will give your bullet enough velocity to reach out at long distances, but use a caliber that will deliver sufficient energy at those yardages.

When you're hunting Western whitetails, it's possible that you might see mule deer in the same places. If your mind is set on whitetails, be careful when you see those antlers. If you're an experienced hunter you'll be able to tell the difference between a muley and whitetail instantly, but if you're new to the West you might have a problem. Most states allow you to take either species, so you won't be in trouble with the game department if you take a muley by mistake.

On the other hand, it's possible that in a given locale the season for one species has been open for a week, while the season has not yet opened for the other species. You should be sure of your state's current regulations, and be sure you can tell muleys from whitetails quickly in the field. On a whitetail, the antler tines jut directly from a single main beam on each side. On a muley, the main beam forks—and forks again on a mature buck, forming 4 long, relatively straight points to a side, or 5 if there are brow tines. The mule deer's ears tend to be larger than a whitetail's, of course, and a muley's tail is roughly cylindrical, white with a black tip, whereas that of a whitetail is a wide, tapering pennant with an outer surface the same color as the deer's back and a white underside that shows conspicuously when the animal "flags," or raises it in alarm. In screening cover or dim light, you may not be able to tell a whitetail from a muley by the ears, the tail, or the animal's size, but a buck's antlers should enable you to differentiate.

A nice aspect of Western whitetail hunting is the public land available to roam on. You can hunt for days and never see a posted sign. In areas where there is private land, many ranchers will grant permission to hunt on their property. Some charge reasonable "trespass fees." National forests and BLM lands in every state offer millions of acres to pursue whitetails on. In some areas you won't have much company from other hunters because whitetails don't have a big following. In some places you won't hear a shot for days—a welcome change from crowded woods in the Eastern, Southern, and Pacific states.

If it's a Boone and Crockett trophy whitetail you seek, look to Montana for the buck of your dreams. According to the latest edition of the Boone and Crockett book, Montana produced 19 record-class bucks in the typical category—nine of them since 1970. Other states that produced record western whitetails are as follows: Washington, seven; Idaho and Colorado, two each; and Wyoming, one.

Eventually, Western whitetails will probably be hunted with the same zeal as muleys. But it's downright smart to try for a Western buck now, while they're still lightly hunted. He might just be the biggest of your life.

CHAPTER

21

ALL-AMERICAN WHITETAIL SUBSPECIES

by Leonard Lee Rue, III

Whitetails are not only more numerous and far more widely distributed than mule deer—they also exhibit a far greater number of variations in their form. That is, they are split into many subspecies. True, there are also some differing types of muleys. A small, pale desert muley of the deep Southwest is not quite the same as the big Rocky Mountain strain. But muleys don't arouse nearly the confusion caused by the variations on the whitetail theme, and the two mule-deer subspecies that differ most from what hunters across the country regard as the norm will be covered in separate chapters, one on the Columbian blacktail and one on the Sitka blacktail. Therefore I've been asked to contribute a chapter intended to unravel the maze of whitetail types.

I can't say that the information I'm about to offer will help you collect venison in your part of the country (although here and there, where I consider habitat differences significant, I'll mention the kind of pockets likely to hold game). What this information will do is to give you a better idea of the type and size of deer—and the type and size of antlers, the quality of trophies—you're apt to encounter in a given region. It will also settle a lot of the traditional deer-camp arguments about which subspecies is really being hunted and how it compares with those in other locales. The true hunter wants to learn all he can about his game, so here is a short course in the scientific (and sometimes not so scientific) classification of whitetails.

The whitetail deer is found in all of the contiguous 48 states and in eight provinces of Canada. The whitetail is a member of the *cervidae* family, a group that originated in Asia and migrated to this continent, via

Author-photographer Lennie Rue poses with a young buck he took during New Jersey's shotgun season. This subspecies is classified as the Northern Woodland Whitetail *(O. v. borealis)* but Rue stresses that there has been so much intergrading of subspecies in some regions that any deer is likely to be the descendant of hybrids. In states like New Jersey, which at one time imported and released deer from other regions to replenish native stock, additional interbreeding occurred. Geographic characteristics have become blurred in such areas. *(Photo by Leonard Lee Rue, III)*

the Bering Sea Land Bridge, eons ago. However, the species is a native of North America, having developed on this continent some 20 million years ago. There are 30 subspecies of this deer recognized today.

The classification of all living things is known as taxonomy, a most exacting science but one that is split into two warring camps. The rivals have been called the "lumpers" and the "splitters" and both seem to go to extremes in their zeal to

The unusually pale Virginia Whitetail *(O.v. virginianus)* pictured here is not a true albino but an almost all-white mutant fawn. Such deer lack natural camouflage, and their chance of survival is therefore reduced. *(Photo by Leonard Lee Rue, III)*

prove their point and to discredit that of their opponents. The lumpers are those biologists who want to simplify (and perhaps oversimplify) the divisions and the differences found within a single species. The splitters are those who seize upon the slightest (and perhaps insignificant or imagined) differences, who magnify those differences, and then do everything possible to justify their reasoning. Both groups tend to go overboard.

A good example is the overclassification of the grizzly brown bear, *Ursus arctos*. Fully 87 North American subspecies have been classified. One splitter claimed that there were several subspecies of the brown bear just on Kodiak Island, and that they did not even interbreed, but he forgot to tell that to the bears. (By the way, subspecies do frequently interbreed where their ranges overlap.) One lumper wants all of the brown bears, found throughout the world, to be classified as a single subspecies.

A species is an organism that is genetically linked (genotypic) so that its members are sexually compatible, making reproduction possible. Most members of most species are also *phenotypic*, all having similar, visible, external characteristics making them identifiable as such. The physiological characteristics that make such identification possible include size, proportion, dentition, epidermal structures and appendages, etc. (However, I must add that in some species size varies astonishingly from one subspecies to another.)

The divisions within a single species creating the subspecies are based on certain factors that are subject to natural rules or laws. Geographic variations are the best examples, for they have evolved changes in size, color, and other adaptations to light, heat, moisture, regional vegetation, and so on.

Most warm-blooded creatures tend to be larger the farther north or south they range from the equator. An accepted biological rule states that body size, in a geographically variable species, averages larger in the cooler parts of that species' range. The larger a body, the smaller is its relative surface and the more efficiently that surface can be heated. Conversely, the hotter the habitat's temperature, the smaller the body and the larger its relative surface, allowing for greater heat dissipation.

My point in explaining all this is that today there are 17 subspecies, or "races," of the whitetail deer in the United States and Canada. (And 13 additional subspecies occur farther to the south; the distribution map in Appendix I of this book shows the range of the species as a whole, and a glance at it will reveal that the whitetail is found all the way down into Central America.)

The original divisions of these subspecies were based on skull characteristics, body size, and geographical locations. The little Key deer of Florida, *Odocoileus virginianus clavium*, is the smallest deer in the United States, and no one would have difficulty in identifying this unique whitetail race. The largest whitetail deer on our continent, *O. v. borealis*, is found in the northeastern United States and Canada, and most people could not tell it from any of the other large subspecies.

The deer of my home state of New Jersey is classified as *O. v. borealis*, yet I defy any expert in taxonomy to prove this and I'll tell you why. Around 1890, the whitetail deer in New Jersey had been reduced to less than 200 individuals. In an effort to save the deer, hunting was prohibited, new and stronger game laws were passed—and they were more strictly enforced. These measures helped, but of equal importance was the importation of hundreds of deer from many different states. Deer were purchased by the State of New Jersey and by many private individuals from Virginia, Maine, Michigan, and Wisconsin. Those from Maine, Michigan, and Wisconsin were of the same subspecies as our original deer, but those from Virginia were not. There are no records of the actual numbers imported, or how many from what states. The imported deer bred with the remnants of the native deer. Since the original importation, many deer have been transplanted, on many different occasions, to many different locations within the state. yet the subspecies in New Jersey is still classified as *O. v. borealis*. Within the state there is a tremendous variation in the size of the deer, depending on their habitat and the amount, quality, and types of food available. To further complicate the issue, unless there are marked physical geographic differences dividing the ranges of subspecies, there is usually an overlapping or intergrading between them, making identification arbitrary.

In many other areas the divisions between whitetail races are similarly blurred, so any grouping by state or region has to be regarded as a generalization. With that qualification in mind, you can form some idea of which deer you're likely to be hunting in your region by reading the following geographical descriptions covering the 17 subspecies of the United States and Canada.

1. The Virginia whitetail, *O. v. virginianus*, is the prototype of all of our whitetail deer. Fossil remnants were found in a cave in Virginia and named by the naturalist Constantine Rafinesque in 1832. Its range includes Virginia, West Virginia, Kentucky, Tennessee, North Carolina, South Carolina, Georgia, Alabama, and Mississippi. This is a large deer with fairly heavy antlers. It is hunted in all of the states it inhabits, and each state has a good deer population. It has a widely diversified habitat, ranging from the coastal marshes,

Few Eastern hunters realize that whitetails are distributed clear to California. This guide is leading a packhorse loaded with a Northwest whitetail *(O. v. ochrourus)* on a trail, through national forest land in California. *(Courtesy of U.S. Forest Service)*

swamplands, and pinelands to the "balds" found on the top of the Smoky Mountains. In some of the states, the swamps have such dense vegetation and are so difficult to get through that only the use of dogs makes the hunting of these deer possible.

2. The Northern woodland whitetail, *O. v. borealis*, is generally the largest of all the subspecies. The heaviest recorded weight is one from Michigan that tipped the scales at 425 pounds live-weight. It also has the largest range, being found in Maryland, Delaware, New Jersey, Pennsylvania, Ohio, Indiana, Illinois, Minnesota, Wisconsin, Michigan, New York, Connecticut, Rhode Island, Massachusetts, New Hampshire, Vermont, Maine, and in the Canadian provinces of New Brunswick, Nova Scotia, Quebec, Ontario, and a portion of Manitoba. More whitetails of this subspecies are hunted than any other. This area also has produced a large percentage of the top record whitetail heads listed in the Boone and Crockett *Records of Big Game*. The world-record head, scoring 206⅛ points, was shot in Burnett County, Wisconsin, in 1914 by James Jordan. The beams were both exactly 30 inches long. The head had 10 points. Whitetails sometimes have more points, but the beams on this one—both of them over 6 inches in circumference at the smallest place between the burr and the first point—were awesomely massive. The winter coat of some of the deer of this subspecies is the darkest of any of our deer.

The range is expanding steadily northward. As the virgin spruce forests of Quebec and Ontario are being cut for paper pulp, the land is sprouting back with all types of second-growth bushes and trees, producing almost unlimited browse. The wolves that were common in the virgin forest have been pushed back by man's activities in the area. With increased food and decreased predation, this whitetail is expanding both its range and its numbers.

3. The Dakota whitetail, *O. v. dacotensis*, is also a very large deer, running about as heavy as the *borealis* in body weight. When it comes to trophy heads, this subspecies has produced 11 of the top 25 records. The range covers North Dakota, South Dakota, and parts of Nebraska, Kansas, Wyoming, Montana, and the Canadian provinces of Manitoba, Saskatchewan, and Alberta. In winter, this deer appears quite dark. The bucks have heavy, widespread antlers. This is a deer of the river brakes. The timbered coulees, gullies, draws, and valleys are its home.

4. The Northwest whitetail, *O. v. ochrourus*, is another large one. This deer is found in parts of Montana, Idaho, Washington, Oregon, California, British Columbia, and Alberta. The largest whitetail I ever saw was either of this subspecies or it could have been a Dakota. It was in Glacier National Park that I saw this huge whitetail, and the two subspecies intergrade where their ranges overlap. Not even the experts can agree on where the range of one ends and the other begins.

Although there are no Northwest whitetails in the top 25 heads, this subspecies does have very widespread antlers. In coloration, its winter coat is a relatively light cinnamon brown.

5. The range of the Columbian whitetail, *O. v. leucurus*, has been greatly reduced. It formerly ranged along the Pacific Coast in Washington and Oregon, spreading eastward until it intergraded with the Northwest whitetail. Oregon does

This Columbian whitetail *(O. v. leucurus)* doesn't have an abnormal antler formation. The rack looks strange because bits of velvet still cling to the tips and are peeling. The range of this Pacific Coast subspecies overlaps that of the Northwest Whitetail. *(Photo by Leonard Lee Rue, III)*

These Carmen Mountains whitetails *(O. v. carminis)*, a spike buck and a doe, were photographed above the Rio Grande, near the boundary of Big Bend National Park. *(Photo by Leonard Lee Rue, III)*

not give figures for the state population and allows no hunting of them. Washington has perhaps 500 and allows no hunting of them. This subspecies is endangered. It's a large deer with high but narrow-spreading antlers.

6. The Coues, or Arizona, whitetail, *O. v. couesi*, is a small deer. At one time it was thought to be a distinct species, but more recent research has relegated it to a subspecies of the whitetail. Although small in general size, it has very large ears, giving it a resemblance to the mule deer. It also has a very large tail, leading to its nickname of "fantail." This deer is found in the dry, desert regions of southeastern California, southern Arizona, southwestern New Mexico, and down into Mexico. (Desert habitat accounts for the oversized ears.) The fantail is apparently isolated from intergrading with the Texas whitetail but it probably does intergrade in the southern part of its range with several Mexican subspecies. Arizona estimates it has about 50,000 Coues deer. New Mexico has about 10,000.

7. The Texas whitetail, *O. v. texanus*, is found in western Texas, Oklahoma, Kansas, southeastern Colorado, eastern New Mexico, and the northern portion of Mexico. Everything about Texas is big, even its population of whitetail deer; it has over 3 million of them. Texas has four subspecies, but the greatest numbers are of the Texas whitetail. The body size of this subspecies is the largest of all the Southern forms. The antlers are slender but widespreading; there are several record heads among the top 25.

8. The Carmen Mountains whitetail, *O. v. carminis*, is a small deer found in the Big Bend region of Texas. The range is limited to just the Carmen Mountains on both sides of the Rio Grande. Not many of these deer are hunted because most of their range falls within the boundaries of Big Bend National Park, where hunting is prohibited. There apparently is no intergrading with the much larger Texas whitetail. A buffer strip of semidesert and mule deer separates the ranges of the two subspecies.

9. The range of the Avery Island whitetail, *O. v. mcilhennyi*, stretches along the Gulf Coast of Taxas and Louisiana. This is the deer of Texas' Big Thicket. It is a large deer, with a dark, brownish winter coat, and it intergrades on the west, north, and east with the whitetails found there. It is smaller than the Texas whitetail, with antlers that tend to curve sharply inward at the points.

10. The Kansas whitetail, *O. v. macrourus*, is the fourth subspecies occurring in Texas. This deer is found in eastern Texas, Oklahoma, Kansas, Nebraska, Iowa, Missouri, Arkansas, and Louisiana. It is a large deer with very heavy main beams and short tines. Several deer of this type are among the top 25 record heads.

11. The Bull's Island whitetail, *O. v. tourinsulae*, is an isolated and very limited race, found only on Bull's Island, South Carolina.

12. The Hunting Island whitetail, *O. v. venatorius*, is another of South Carolina's minor variations, found only on Hunting Island.

13. The Hilton Head Island whitetail, *O. v. hiltonensis*, is still another South Carolinian variation, limited to Hilton Head Island.

14. The Blackbeard Island whitetail, *O.*

This big, rangy doe is a Kansas whitetail *(O. v. macrourus)* that was found by Rue as she grazed on the Oklahoma grasslands. *(Photo by Leonard Lee Rue, III)*

v. nigribarbis, is found on both Blackbeard and Sapelo Islands of Georgia, and nowhere else.

All of those last four subspecies are medium-size deer with fairly small antlers that are heavily ridged or wrinkled at the base. The islands they inhabit are far enough out in the ocean to prevent intergrading with the subspecies on the mainland or with one another. So far as I can find, hunting is allowed on some, if not all, of these islands.

15. The Florida whitetail, *O. v. seminolus*, is a large deer sporting a good rack. Some of these deer that I photographed in Okefenokee Swamp in Georgia were as large as the New Jersey deer, and some had antlers as large but perhaps not as widespreading. This is the deer of the Everglades.

16. The Florida coastal whitetail, *O. v. osceola*, is found in the Florida panhandle, southern Alabama, and Mississippi. It is not as large as the Florida or the Virginia whitetail but it does intergrade with both.

Here, a Florida whitetail *(O. v. seminolus)* is seen in a Georgia clearing with a typically dense palmetto thicket in the background. Larger-bodied than the other two Florida subspecies, this race tends to develop excellent antlers. *(Photo by Leonard Lee Rue, III)*

17. The smallest of the native deer is the diminutive Florida Key whitetail, *O. v. clavium*. The adult buck Key deer stands about 24 to 26 inches high at the shoulder and weighs between 45 and 65 pounds. No hunting is allowed for this race. In the past, a combination of man's development of the islands, destroying the deer's habitat, plus fires, hurricanes, and lack of hunting control reduced the Key deer population by 1949 to 30 individuals. With better protection and the establishment of the Key Deer National Wildlife Refuge in 1953, this deer's population was brought back up to several hundred. Some of these deer are killed each year by automobiles on the highway that runs through the Keys. If the government would, or could, purchase more land on the Keys before the habitat is destroyed, this deer's future would be assured.

Deer are very adaptable creatures. Many types of wildlife could not withstand the onslaught of civilization; the deer have thrived on it. The whitetail deer is the number one big-game animal in the country, and when most people think of deer hunting they think of whitetails. The opening up of the virgin forests, the reduction of native predators, the planting of new foods that the deer could eat, and proper research, management, and law enforcement have all combined to skyrocket the whitetail population to all-time highs. In some local areas, the deer population will have to decline in the future as man continues to need more land for his own burgeoning population. However, the same factors that increased the deer population should maintain it at the highest levels possible for all time. The future of the whitetail is bright.

PART III

Hunting All-American Mule Deer

CHAPTER

22

HUNTING THE DESERT MULE DEER

by Sam Fadala

The school bus grumbled to a stop, a cloud of dust from the dirt road boiling up over the back of the vehicle. The bus constituted a tour. The teachers and new principal of the desert community's school district were riding the back roads as a familiarization of the students' home area. I was one of the teachers, and seated next to me was the high school's new principal. Something I said to the man had caused the bus to be brought to a stop.

All I had said was, "I'll bet there are some nice bucks hanging out in those shady sand washes." The statement was innocent enough, but the principal laughed.

"Sure, right out in that cactus patch, Sam," he chuckled. "And out there in the brush I suppose there are a few herds of jackalopes running, too, right?"

I retorted that there was no joke to it. I knew there were some big muley bucks right there in the dry flatlands. In fact, I was so sure we could find abundant evidence of deer that I bet the man I could turn up good sign in less than five minutes.

"Would you be convinced if I showed you a big track, maybe some droppings, too?" I asked. He leaned up to the driver and ordered him to stop the bus.

This patch of terrain was in Arizona, not too far from the Mexico border—brushy, sandy, dry. Once in a while, the tall "tree" of the desert, the saguaro, appeared, its arms stretched upward as if in supplication. And there was the sometimes annoying *cholla*, too, also known as jumping cactus. Had we looked closely, we might have found delicate greens growing on the desert floor, little filaree, appearing as emerald blades of grass flattened against the ground.

In most states these days, a stipulated expanse of safety-orange garb is required by regulation, yet there are areas where camouflage is a big help to a hunter on stand. Some hunters solve the problem by wearing the minimum amount of orange, others by wearing camouflage-patterned orange clothing, available from several manufacturers. This camo-suited Southwesterner is heading for a stand where desert muleys often pass. It's thorny habitat may look relatively barren, but such land often supports a higher game population per square mile than the woodlands. *(Photo by James Tallon)*

Long, sandy washes crisscrossed the desert floor like creases on the face of an ancient Navajo. Patches of creosote bush dotted the landscape. Typical of desert areas, life here would not be readily seen in midday. But almost as if to help me prove there was no shortage of wildlife in the desert, a jackrabbit skittered away in a zigzag course when the man and I stepped out of the bus, and a sentry quail greeted us with its plaintive *che-qui-ta*.

And sure as taxes, there on the ground, pressed into the soft damp sand of a wash, was a track, the telltale points of cloven hooves, large and deep, impressive and proving. The man did not say a word. He looked around at the parched ground, the many kinds of cacti, the cuts of dry washes that could fill with monsoon rains and flood their banks, and the many, many thorny green things that adorned the desert like untouchable vegetable jewelry.

I knew the tracks would be there. Though not seen readily and not hunted to any great degree, the big-eared deer are indigenous to that type of terrain. Depending on where a man has hunted, he may think of mule deer as creatures of the Rockies or perhaps the grasslands and grain fields of the Midwest or—if he has in mind the blacktail variety of muley—the forests of the upper Pacific Coast. But plenty of mule deer flourish in the deserts, too. Not only in the part of the Southwest but in many other desert places, these deer thrive. They may be found on high, cold deserts in Wyoming, or the flatlands of Oregon. Nevada's desert houses them, too, as do the deserts of Colorado, Utah, and Texas. They also range the deserts of New Mexico, Arizona, and Mexico, and even the dry areas in Canada's Alberta and Saskatchewan provinces.

In places men have changed the desert into green fields of crops, and the deer change with the terrain, enjoying their own part of the harvest. But they live, too, where it seldom rains and they have adapted to gaining their moisture from plant life, while retaining body fluids by staying out of the hot sun, inactive, brushed up along shady washes and in dark thickets. The most intriguing desert deer I have ever seen were right on the ocean's edge in Mexico's Baja California. Here the big-antlered bucks may come down to the beach at night to pick up seaweed. By day they live in the rugged cactus country, some of the barest terrain I have ever seen.

Given, then, that these deer are present in the desert, often within easy driving distance of hunters, and that they are big deer, sleek, good to harvest for the larder, then why aren't more hunters after them?

Part of the answer was quite clear in the reactions of that high school principal. The man had lived in the Northwest, had hunted his deer in tall pines or wet, brushy canyons. He could scarcely believe that mule deer did, indeed, live on the desert. Also, the deer have had a poor press. Commonly, they are thought to be punier than their mountain cousins. And since they are not easily seen, they have been considered in short supply.

As for size, the desert deer is not a puny runt. On the average, the animal is just about the same size as its Rocky Mountain counterpart. I recall a Yuma, Arizona, big-buck contest in which most of the entries were from the famous Kaibab, including a couple of brutes that dressed at over 200 pounds. Yet the winner turned out to be a buck from the desert, and not just any desert but the extremely dry and sterile-appearing Sahara-type terrain around Yuma. That magnificent animal weighed over 225 pounds clean-dressed, and his rack, four points to a side, was heavy and wide.

On a Western hunt with an outfitter, a good guide performs many valuable services. Here, the guide uses a spotting scope to determine whether a distant pair of antlers is worth a long, arduous stalk. Being familiar with the country, he knows where to search for game, and his hunting experience makes him a good judge of range as well as trophy quality.

This muley buck displays the swollen neck that characterizes the rutting period. He's probably courting the doe. At first glance, the terrain looks very open, but there's plenty of brush as high as a muley's shoulder and more deer may well be concealed by the vegetation in the background.

A hunter glasses slopes sprinkled with sage and dotted with clumps of tall conifers. In midafternoon, some fine buck mule deer are probably bedded on those slopes, but it will take thorough scanning with good binoculars to pick any of them out.

An obviously tired but happy guide rests with his client's fine mule deer. A good mountain pony waits behind him. Horses—including surefooted pack animals and riding mounts—are provided by outfitters in country where a 4-wheel-drive vehicle has to be left behind, and where even the horses sometimes have to be tied while the hunters continue a climb on foot.

As the snows deepen in high country, mule deer migrate to lower elevations, but the low country has plenty of slopes and the deer are likely to head uphill if they detect human intrusion. This one isn't spooked; he's just heading toward a bedding area.

Buck mule deer, like whitetails, rub their antlers against saplings and thrash the shrubs during the onset of the rut. On this sagebrush flat, a muley buck releases pent-up energy and hostility as he wins a mock battle against the nearest vegetation.

Jim Zumbo glows with success over an exceptionally fine muley buck. The rifle is his favorite, a Featherweight .30-06 Winchester Model 70, mounted with a 4× Weaver scope. He's also equipped with 10×50 binoculars for glassing very open terrain, though he feels that 7×35 glasses are right for the majority of hunters in many parts of the country.

This muley buck has bedded down on a slope where he can sun himself, is concealed by the sage, and can see or scent any intruders coming up his hill. Deer remain watchful even when bedded. To get this close without spooking a bedded buck requires patience and skillful stalking. To take one by surprise in this situation is a great coup for any hunter.

Texas outfitter Robert Rogers displays an excellent axis buck taken by Craig Boddington. Unlike our native deer, these animals retain their spots when mature, as do many fallow deer. Good antler formation on an axis buck includes very long, fairly massive main beams, high and curving, with sizable brow and back tines.

Here's an extremely fine fallow deer exemplifying the white color phase of the species. Brown fallow deer can be somewhat harder to hunt because of their natural camouflage, but many hunters favor white bucks for their handsome and unusual appearance. This one is of record-book quality, with long brow and secondary tines, an impressive spread, and widely palmated main beams with plenty of points jutting from the palms. *(Courtesy of Texas Hunting Services)*

About the only difference between that desert deer and the mountain bucks was color. Mountain bucks tend to be a rich brown, while this desert specimen was light gray. This was not an age difference. The deer of the desert areas in the Southwest seem to be paler in color, closer to gray than to brown.

Now what about abundance? I believe that the desert deer are, in some places at least, as abundant per square mile as the mountain deer. In fact, in some forested mountain areas where the trees have denied the forest floor sunlight, food for deer is often less prevalent than in certain desert locales—depending, of course, on rainfall in the desert. No rain, less food. The desert has a remarkable preserving ability for seed, however, and given any moisture these dormant seeds spring to life. In a rainy season in the Southwest one year, scientists were amazed to discover the growth of plants that had not been recorded in the area for 20 previous years. The seed was there all that time, at rest, waiting for the type of deep-penetrating moisture that would urge growth. Given moisture, then, food is there for the desert deer.

But why bother with desert muleys when there are fine bucks in the mountains? Well, on an autumn day I might opt for the mountains, too, I suppose. But in the dead of winter, I think I would just as soon be on the desert. There are advantages.

First, obviously, there is the good weather of a desert winter in the Southwest. While skies may be overcast and the atmosphere cold in the northern wastelands, and while snow may hamper travel in the mountains, the dryer low places can be most inviting. And there is often a big bonus by way of small-game hunting. A man camped in the desert, say in Arizona in December (and there are special mule-deer seasons at that time in that state as well as the archery deer season), can not only hunt his mule deer, but will also be allowed quail and cottontail, doves at certain times, and waterfowl.

Let's suppose our new arrival to the desert has with him a couple of canteens for water; he is wearing a large, comfortable hat to keep the sun off his head and out of his eyes so he can look for deer; he is shod in light birdhunter boots, and he is all ready to harvest some of that desert venison. But after finding tracks just about everywhere, he still hasn't caught sight of a single patch of buckskin. How come? Just what is this desert mule deer all about?

Are these bucks craftier than their high-country cousins? No not really. No one holds greater esteem for the big desert bucks than I, but the hunter who figures he is being outsmarted by them is short-changing himself badly. As for cunning, I still have to allow the whitetail, especially the little Coues whitetail buck, an edge over the muley. This is based upon experience with both. These deer don't outsmart us. They outinstinct us. And it isn't so much what they do, but rather what they don't do. They don't move around a lot and they don't stand out like sore thumbs. That light-colored buck dressed in gray is a neutral blend that would nearly out-camouflage camouflage. Put him in a sand wash in the shade and he all but disappears. And he won't be out gamboling about the hills all day. In fact, as with most desert-dwellers, he will feed off and on in the night, eating into early morning, brush

This desert muley is standing in a typical maze of cactus, thornbush, dry, crackly, scratchy brush, and rocks. The scene happens to be Southwestern, but desert mule deer are also found up in the Great Basin and other semi-arid regions. They don't generally attain gigantic proportions, but where they can get adequate browse and water they often rival Rocky Mountain mule deer as trophies. *(Photo by James Tallon)*

Here a hunter has taken a stand on a point overlooking a wide valley, through which seasonally migrating mule deer pass. He's holding a heavy-barreled .25-06 rifle with a 4 × scope, a good choice in this sparsely vegetated Western desert where the open vistas can demand shots at mule deer that are as long as shots at Eastern woodchucks. *(Photo by Norm Nelson)*

up in the shade for most of the day, and feed, perhaps heavily, late in the afternoon.

The hunter who knows this will be up early. And he won't be back in camp eating his dinner until after dark. In fact, carrying a flashlight is imperative for the dedicated desert hunter. He should be close enough to camp to make it in without getting lost, but the best place for the hunter to be at dusk is out in the hills looking for deer.

There are several methods of harvesting the desert buck, and each hunter will have to decide his most successful and enjoyable method for himself. But a few basic approaches can be discussed. The simplest, and perhaps not too terribly successful, is the "walk-the-washes" plan. Unfortunately, this means of locating the deer of the desert seems to be most popular. It constitutes a rambling about in a rather aimless way along the washes in the hope of jumping a buck from his bed.

The hunter goes along the edges of the washes, shuffling by each brush pocket that might contain a resting deer, sometimes tossing rocks into these places. Of course, now and then luck will bring the hunter right to the spot and that big buck will jump up, ascend the side of the wash, and perhaps pause long enough to make a sure target of himself.

Another popular method is walking the deer trails and hoping to come upon a feeding buck in early morning or late evening. This means of collecting venison is also chancy. Deer trails in the desert do not seem to be as firmly established as they are in some other habitats, though deer and cattle will often use the same path to a waterhole daily, the cattle drinking at will, the deer waiting until dark or nearly dark.

This desert mule deer was jumped from his bed at about 4 p.m. on a hot December day when the local rattler poplation had come out of hibernation. He was lying on the shaded side of a rather deep dry wash, staying cool. Hearing a hunter, he rose and trotted for the top of the gulley, but he never made it over the rim. Desert muleys are popularly supposed to be small, but this one dressed out at about 170 pounds, so his live weight was well over 200 pounds. The hat at left belongs to Guide Biddy Martin, that on the right to the hunter, Bob Elman, who seems to have relinquished his rifle (an old .264 Magnum) just to find out if Southwestern guides object to serving as gunbearers.

Waiting in ambush along these trails is particularly fruitless, or has been so far as I have been concerned. Again, these deer are not inclined to move that much, and they do not have to cover huge tracts of land between bedding and feeding grounds. Further, as suggested above, they are most likely to avail themselves of water under the cover of darkness.

Walking with a partner can be an improvement on the walk-'em-out method. One way to use this form of hunter cooperation is to have one fellow move quickly and quietly along the edge of a wash for maybe 300 to 500 yards. The man who has moved ahead then takes a stand and waits while his partner slowly works up the wash. It helps if the second man, now walking in the wash, has the wind at his back, allowing his scent to go up the wash ahead of him. I have seen bucks catch this scent and move along the belly of the wash. In that event, the deer will work right into the partner who has secreted himself upwash. And if the wind is coming in the direction of the buck and partner in the wash, then the man in ambush has the same wind in his face. If he doesn't move, the buck will not detect him and an easy shot could be the reward.

Buck mule deer tend to be more gregarious than whitetail bucks, so a hunter isn't surprised to see two or more pairs of antlers with a group of does during the rut. A lot of the forage on this desert seems to consist of prickly pear and Spanish bayonet, yet these deer are obviously thriving.

Some men hunt the desert on the back of a horse or mule. I have never enjoyed desert hunting this way, even though I have found it an interesting way of hunting in the mountains. The desert horseman essentially uses the same tactics as the hunter who walks at random in the hope of scaring something up. Of course, the rider has the advantage of being able to cover many times more territory than the

Here's another deer to squelch the notion that desert muleys are scrawny. Sometimes the two-man drag is the only practical way to get a deer back to the hunting vehicle. With luck, though, the dragging distance on the desert may be shorter than in other habitat, because there's no tall timber to block the way of a 4-wheel-drive vehicle. *(Photo by Russell Tinsley)*

person on foot. He also has the disadvantage of being on the back of an animal, and it's likely that a big buck will let that horse come right past him and not stir from his hidden bed in the shade, preferring to simply sit tight until man and horse have gone away.

A step upward in productivity is the vantage-point, binocular approach. Here our hunter locates a perch that will show him as much terrain as possible. Even on the flatlands there are high points, hills and rock formations, that will put a man above the plain. From these the man glasses. But there is more to this than simply peering and hoping to spot a buck cavorting about the land.

First, the glass-user must get steady. An unsteady glass will do little good. It only tires the hunter's eyes and can even give him a headache or make him dizzy. Sometimes I use a walking staff on the desert to help me get around. However, since this type of terrain is generally easy to negotiate, the staff is employed more often as a tool for glassing, and it is used in two ways. If I am trying to cover ground between glassing out-crops, I will simply stand and prop the binoculars on the padded top of the stick. The stick is made from the stalk of the agave cactus. It is light as balsa and oak-strong. With a rubber crutch bumper on the bottom to quiet its movement, plus a handle of deer hide, tanned and glued in place, and a nice soft top of foam rubber under more tanned hide, it is a highly useful outdoor tool.

If I am seated, I try to locate a good rock to support my back. Then I thrust the stick out in front—jammed into the ground or against another rock. I place the binoculars on the padded top of the stick again. There is no heartbeat in that stick to shake the picture. Rested there solidly, I can carefully glass in comfort.

But I do not look for a deer. Because of camouflage, I try to uncover these deer by seeing *parts* of them rather than whole deer. The rump patch, though somewhat less pronounced than that of the mountain mule deer, is still a telltale sign. So are the light-colored fringes on the ears. sometimes an eye will glitter. Less often, I have found a rack swaying up above the grasses and brush of a sand wash.

Of course, a combination of methods and a refinement of the hunter's favorite ways are best. For me, this means plenty of glassing, with high-quality full-size glasses such as 9×35 or 9×36 or even 10×50. Such glasses are great aids in deer-finding. Remember that the object is to try to find a camouflaged creature. This means definition, which is the quality in optics that allows the hunter to discern between the dead branch of a fallen tree and the bony curve of a big buck's rack. An indistinct image just won't do when you're trying to detect details. To define, that is what definition is all about, and it comes with top-quality glasses.

Between sessions of glassing, and while walking from one point to another, I try to remain alert and I wouldn't think of passing a brush pile without giving it a kick or tossing in a rock on the chance that a big buck might be taking his siesta in there. If I'm with a friend, we might team up and try to work the washes so that one of us might chase a buck to the other. And when I feel very ambitious I will even glass the sides of hills for bedded deer, as the big muleys sometimes rest on these open hillsides on pleasant winter days.

Where to glass? When I look out across the terrain I try to pick out places that appear to have the low browse type of plants so loved by the big bucks. In early morning and late afternoon my glass has often picked out the feeding deer. Without camouflage, these bucks would be actually quite easy to find as they often feed right out in the open. But they blend well, and even though there may be but a few low bushes, the animals can still be very hard to detect. It takes patience.

Outfitted with canteens for water, stout pants that will ward off the catclaw thorns, light boots, and a decent hat, plus that pair of good binoculars and maybe the walking stick, the hunter is ready to go after the deer of the desert. By combining several methods and by using those glasses, he begins to weave a pattern of success. There are desert hunters who come home year after year with their venison because they have worked up a method that is right for them. But how do they find the hot spots, those places that house the big ones?

Scouting is the way. By scouting, I mean looking for those bucks after first getting a lead from fellow hunters, ranchers, game officials, and any other source, using topo maps, and working out the country to find the deer before the season. Many a Sunday picnic has turned out to be a scouting trip when the man who is driving the family for a sunny visit to the outdoors comes across a likely place for desert deer. He checks for sign, then he comes back with topo map in hand and he looks the country over carefully. He may well have a place that will render a good harvest come the season.

As for a choice of arms, there is plenty of cracker-barrel philosophy to apply here and there is always the fun of argument when caliber choice is brought up, be it for Tanzania elephant or Ohio groundhogs.

Ironically, the basic problem is that there is no problem. We have so many good mule-deer calibers suitable for desert hunting that the choice is sometimes difficult, though it should not be. The best way to make your selection is to match the rifle or pistol to your circumstances and technique.

The standard—and excellent—guns and cartridges are discussed elsewhere in this book, and most readers will be happy with one or another of the recommendations. But some of us do have special problems or desires. I have a friend who harvests his desert venison as an incidental bonus while hunting Gambel's quail. He carries a drilling—one of those triple-barreled European creations featuring side-by-side smoothbores plus a rifled barrel. His model combines the 12-gauge with a 7×57mm rifle. Another acquaintance is a backpacker who shaves every possible ounce from the weight of his gear. His personal solution was a rifle made by Frank Wells of Tucson, a custom specialist who hand-built for him a 6mm/222 that feels like a powder puff when compared to some of the blunderbusses I've toted. With hot handloads, it fires an 80-grain bullet at about 2,950 fps. Is that enough for mule deer? Well, it develops energy about like the factory-loaded .250 Savage cartridge. This means it's effective at limited distances, though I've seen it perform impressively on game. I'd say it's a 150-yard killer for the hunter who stalks his deer and shoots accurately.

Another solution for the man who wants to go light is—obviously—a handgun.

Those of you who would prefer something really small—something that rides in a holster—should read Chapter 10 on sidearms for deer, and give Bob Good's suggestions very serious consideration. Also very popular, not just on the deserts but everywhere, is the muzzleloader, and those of you who want to try black powder (or Pyrodex) should read Chapter 11 by Bill Hughes. Incidentally, I have killed an assortment of game with my Numrich .58 modified under-hammer, and I wouldn't hesitate to take after the biggest mule deer in the land with a properly loaded muzzle gun.

And then there is archery. The mule-deer hunter who has selected the bow as his tool would be well advised to use the high-hill, glassing technique. Then the game will be spotted before it spots the hunter and a good stalk can be made. Waiting at waterholes can sometimes produce good shooting, too, but as mentioned above, the bucks may not come to drink until after shooting hours.

If archery is your choice, a good set of matched arrows is a must. I have my bow rigged with a cushion plunger, a device that stabilizes my arrow flight, and a hunting stabilizer to dampen the vibration of the outfit. I use a bowsight with four pins, and my arrows seem to find the mark every time if I do my part, sighted-in for 20, 30, 40, and 50 yards.

Desert mule-deer hunting will be around as long as man refrains from covering the desert with concrete and exercises some common sense in game management. Despite what seems at first glance to be the world's most hostile terrain, the desert does quite well in feeding and taking care of its own. If anything, it is a shame that more good venison is not brought to the pan by means of a swift harvest by either well-placed rifle, or pistol shot, or razor-sharp arrow.

Natural enemies of the mule deer on the desert are few (unless one includes occasional prolonged drought among natural enemies). However, coyotes do eat fawns. Contrary to some of the TV propaganda I've seen, the coyote does not live on discarded peanut-butter sandwiches and crumpets alone. As my family has witnessed, they will ambush deer at waterholes and kill them. This is not an indictment of coyotes but it is a call to deal with them rationally, where possible and necessary, through management (not eradication). A fawn crop in the desert will be thinned by the little howlers, and since hunter success is usually low on the desert, this can be good—certainly better than having the deer destroy their own range should their numbers mount too high for the habitat. Where hunters are using deer for harvest, and where they wish to retain and maintain that population, a modest coyote-control program may be in order.

The feline predators are no problem on the desert. The bobcat has never appeared to be in any great number nor has it caused the decline of deer herds. As for the larger deer eater, the puma, its range is normally in the mountains. Thus, we conclude that by leaving habitat for the desert deer, by hunting to promote a reasonable harvest, and by engaging in a mild coyote-control program when game officials find it wise, we should have mule deer on the desert for a long time.

CHAPTER

23

HIGH-COUNTRY MULEYS

by Norman Strung

Is mule-deer hunting in the northern Rockies all that it's cracked up to be? You bet it is, and more. Taking up the trail of a big muley is excitement enough, and that first step also leads to woodland parks dappled with wildflowers, into tumbledowns of crags and peaks, and through the wildest country in the nation. It's an unbeatable combination: raw beauty and the challenge of a magnificent animal, finely attuned to its environment. But such a dream hunt isn't without a few rude awakenings that you had better open your eyes to before heading west.

Licenses should be your first consideration. Years ago, a nonresident could walk into any crossroads general store in Idaho, Montana, or Wyoming, plunk down $20 to $50, and pick up his deer tag. Today, things have changed considerably.

Prices for both resident and nonresident licenses have risen astronomically in the Rocky Mountain states. In most of these states, over-the-counter sales have also been curtailed. Nonresidents have to apply directly to the game department to purchase their licenses, and only a limited number of out-of-state licenses are sold—by lottery drawing in some states, first come, first served in others.

Resident hunting patterns in Montana have been similarly altered. There are intricate regulations regarding hunting districts, the length of seasons, whether or not you can shoot antlerless deer, a potpourri of laws that would confuse a Philadelphia lawyer. And similar changes have taken place in Wyoming, Colorado and Idaho—almost every Western state.

I don't relish the red tape and restrictions, but let me point out that all these annoyances are designed to preserve the object of my affection—the quality of hunting in the West. The big muleys are still present in great number; the clear air still greets you every morning; the mountains haven't changed. What has changed is the kind of hunt you must plan. Gone are the days when four buddies got together on a Tuesday night and casually decided to fly to Idaho for a hunt the next week. Changed, too, is the resident's plan to shoot two deer on a Saturday morning, 15 minutes outside of town. Hunting today's West requires planning, and careful attention to detail. Arrange the fundamentals of your trip early. Get license fees in the mail well in advance of deadlines. Study regulations, limits, and area boundaries carefully. In short, know exactly what you're getting into.

With this change in emphasis from casual to careful, time becomes extremely important. You're making a large investment in licenses, perhaps guide fees, and time spent planning. This investment should be at least matched by the time you spend afield.

If you live so far from the Rockies as to make your hunt a one-trip affair, I'd say a week should be the minimum time you budget for your hunt. If you plan several trips, try to set aside at least four hunting days for each visit. Even residents who live close to good hunting are better off if they make their hunt at least an overnighter. You need the time not just to get into the good hunting country, but to analyze and learn the terrain and the habits of the native deer. Sure, you could stumble across

Deep snow is supposed to help trigger the seasonal migration, pushing mule deer down from the high country. But you can't always bet on it. After an early snow, you may still find plenty of big bucks hanging back, lingering at the higher elevations as in this photo. The buck at right is a nice trophy.

a Christmas tree of a rack your first day out, but there are long odds against it. Dame Chance is a notoriously fickle provider.

Conditioning is another investment you must make if you're going to take your muley hunt seriously. The physical condition (or lack of it) of the clients I guide has proved to be the most important factor contributing to their chance of success. More times than I can count, the stamina required to hike that extra mile, to climb another 300 vertical feet to a rock outcrop, or to sprint uphill for 50 yards to an overlook has meant the difference between success and failure.

A specific example of how conditioning can come into play happened to me while I was hunting in Montana's Bridger Mountains right after a 6-inch snow had blanketed the area. I was counting on the fresh snow to reveal the elevation where the big bucks were hanging out. I'd climbed steadily for two hours and had topped out on a ridge when I cut my first big track, no more than a half-hour old by the condition of the disturbed snow crystals.

Although tracking down a buck isn't the best way to get a shot, I was interested in learning what this fellow was up to, so I stayed with his prints. Not 300 yards ahead, the straight path he took began to meander; a sure sign he was looking for a place to lie down, and a good indication that I'd come too far. I quickly looked around and, sure enough, caught a flash of mouse-brown flickering through the timber. I cursed my luck and impetuousness, but decided to play a hunch because the buck was running downhill.

I knew of a small dip in the ridgeback perhaps a quarter-mile away, and by the direction that muley was headed, there was a good chance he'd use that saddle for an escape route to higher ground. Heels and snow flew as I struggled to reach the pass before the deer, and the uphill run, a few drifts, and 7,000 feet of elevation just about did me in. But when I got to the saddle there he was, bouncing along with the curious spring-loaded muley gait. I got a solid shooting rest to compensate for my heaving chest and dropped the 4-pointer with a spine shot.

Admittedly, outrunning a muley is seldom a successful technique, but there will be many times when comparable stamina will make the difference between meat in the pot and track soup.

What's the best means of conditioning? Jogging builds up your wind. That's half the battle, but you won't be in real shape until you can climb eight flights of stairs without discomfort. And remember, you'll be doing that kind of climbing in the rarified air of 4,000- to 8,000-foot elevations, with approximately 20 extra pounds of rifle, shells, boots, clothing, and sandwiches.

So much for the bad news. Now the good news. There are more and bigger muleys in the Rocky Mountains than ever before. From the standpoint of numbers and quality of their quarry, Western deer hunters have never had it so good. Each year finds more and more deer in the Rockies. It's a controlled "explosion" brought about by careful management, and the net result is maximum numbers of deer for the available food supply. These large populations are reflected in hunter-success figures. The "average" Western state posts a figure of around 75 percent

In the high country of the Rocky Mountain region—encompassing fine deer habitat in Wyoming, Idaho, Montana, and Colorado—a hunter can glass enormous expanses from alpine meadows and ridges. The difficulty comes when he spots a good buck, because the chances are he'll have to make a very long, difficult stalk to get within shooting distance.

The hunter who killed the buck at right couldn't get into the picture because he had to snap the shutter (a good reason why some sportsmen use timer devices to trip a camera's shutter). But he was probably very happy to snap a photo of the lady, her fine buck, and his. From her clothing, it's obvious that the weather is chilly, but the snows haven't come and the alpine meadows are covered with high, lush vegetation, so the mule deer have remained up there. *(Courtesy of Montana Department of Fish, Wildlife and Parks)*

success. In my native Montana, hunters score about 90 percent of the time, bagging close to 100,000 deer a year.

The success ratios, balanced against the total harvest, are good indicators of the kind of hunting you can expect in a particular area, and I'd suggest you read the data and tips in this book's All-State Directory—Appendix 4—as part of your preliminary plans. But no matter which state you choose for your hunt, there are some hard-and-fast rules about where you'll find deer in the Rockies.

The most animals will be concentrated in and around the band of forest where timberlands meet fertile bottomlands. The cover will be a mix of conifers and deciduous brush that melts into pasture, farmland, or cottonwood-and-aspen riverbottoms below. It's this type of terrain that affords a muley a mix of choice foods, escape cover, and shelter in the winter.

A winter landscape like this is common in the Maine woods, but this scene was photographed in the high Rockies. In either region, still-hunting through the quiet, snow-clad woods can be very productive, and so can a carefully planned drive.

However, while this kind of country supports the densest populations of deer, *resident* animals will invariably be does, young-of-the year, and forkhorn-to-4-point bucks. These animals make for excellent eating, and a few of those 4-pointers carry mount-worthy racks, but the real trophies will more often be found at much higher elevations.

Fully mature mule-deer bucks are solitary creatures. Their superb condition affords them the latitude to migrate yearly between summer and winter ranges—distances that often exceed 50 miles. If a wrist-thick rack is your idea of a hunt, look for these animals in the forests and parks that lie within a mile of timberline. They'll remain in this kind of country until they are driven down by severe storms and deep snow, or by the madness of the rut.

It might be worth pointing out something about hunting these trophy-class deer though: it's a demanding sport—demanding in the preparations you must make if you want to organize your own hunt, demanding in terms of cost if you hire a guide, demanding in the sheer energy required of you, and demanding in, for lack of a better word, concentration. When you hunt among the heavy populations of muleys at lower elevations, you're always seeing deer. Sure, the majority of them won't wear horns, but there's always an electric excitement that accompanies a glimpse of any deer, and when you see a dozen or more a day you're enjoying the hunt even if you never touch the trigger. In the sky-high sanctuary of trophy-class bucks, there are fewer animals per square mile. You hunt harder and see less, and as a result, your interest wanes. Any hunter who lacks a keen edge of anticipation, and the concentration it engenders, is in the woods with two strikes against him. And therein lies the reason why some hunters who specialize in big muleys score every year while many others don't. The "experts" know and satisfy the demands of concentration. They look harder, they hunt longer, they cover more ground, and they harvest the trophy bucks.

Whether you choose to hunt the butterbucks of lower elevations or the trophy muleys of the high country, the key to taking these deer lies in a thorough understanding of their habits. Muleys move about in the morning and evening, and these are the times to watch and wait. Find a rocky outcrop or an overlook with an unobstructed view, and use a combination of your naked eyes and a scope or binoculars to scan the terrain. Use your eyes to detect movement, and your optics to identify what you saw move. There's a good chance you'll get a shot from this kind of stand. If you see a deer with your name on it moving toward you, the cardinal rule is to avoid being "sky-lighted." Get in back of something, or get something in back of you to break up your outline. Muleys aren't quite as sharp-eyed as whitetails, but they're quick to perceive the outline of a man, and its implications.

There's an even better chance you'll spot a deer that isn't following a path that will take him close to your stand. Mark the route he takes—for here, too, muleys follow certain patterns. They go downhill to feed, they go uphill to bed, and generally they move in a straight line, breaking right or left only when they near the feeding or bedding area. When you see where a deer's headed, you've got a good clue to his future location, and a good chance for a successful stalk.

When stalking muleys, you must go high and come down on the deer. If you try to approach them from below, every protective mechanism at the animal's disposal is working for him and against you. He's still got quite a few tricks going for him when you come down from above, but at least you've canceled some of his life insurance; his habit of facing downhill, his dogged instinct to escape by running uphill, and the messages carried by the winds. In the daytime, breezes normally blow from canyon bottoms to mountaintops.

When working down on a deer it's extremely important to move slowly. Assume each step you take is the one that will reveal some great, bedded buck, and con-

Even on the very high plateaus, dragging a big mule deer out doesn't always have to be a day-long test of stamina. Roads now extend all the way up onto many of these plateaus, and a 4-wheel-drive vehicle can manage many of those roads even when there's snow on the ground. The two hunters pictured here probably won't have very far to walk. *(Courtesy of Montana Department of Fish, Wildlife and Parks)*

centrate on seeing him before he sees you. At this point of the hunt, your eyes become your most important asset, for when you see a muley before he sees you, you've got him if you can shoot straight.

In the event that you spook your quarry, you can again depend on most muleys to respond to habit. Their first move will be to run directly away from you, but you can bet your favorite hunting boots that they'll soon cut left or right, then double back uphill, usually sticking to the brush of a coulee or canyon. It's in this situation that a sprint occasionally pays off.

While I can talk about this notion of predictability with honest conviction, I must also point out that as the muley you set your sights on gets bigger, older, and wiser, he becomes less locked into "normal" patterns. In the course of becoming a trophy-class animal, he'll surely have a few brushes with hunters, and will develop some unique traits as a result. The classic example is the well-known last look back. When you spook a young animal, you can whistle, yell, even take a shot in the air, and the critter will stop and look back, usually just before he reaches cover. I've tried that trick or seen it tried on five trophy-class muleys to date, and it had no effect whatever.

Another example of the kind of odd savvy muleys get with age occurred when Eli Spannagel, Carroll Kaup, and I were hunting the thick breaks on Eli's huge Montana ranch. The country amounts to rough, brushy drainages that slough off a high plain, and the common hunting technique is to drive a pickup from canyon head to canyon head, then walk out the coulees.

We were heading for our chosen hunting spot, driving along a ranch road, when Eli slowed the pickup to a crawl and looked quizzically into some brush that marked the start of a small coulee.

"That's a funny-looking tree," he said.

Carroll followed the direction of Eli's gaze and screwed up his eyebrows. "That's not a tree, that's a set of horns!"

"No," replied Eli, "horns can't be that big."

At that instant, the tree stood up and was found to be attached to the biggest muley any of us had ever seen.

There was a mad scramble for guns. By the time cases were thrown off and shells jacked into chambers the deer was long gone, but Eli knew his ranch. He roared off, as fast as his short legs could carry him, heading for a point of rocks with a grand view of the country below. It would be a long shot, but that deer had to pass within range. A quarter of an hour later, the three of us had watched from that windy promontory until our eyes teared. We hadn't seen a sign of the super-buck.

"I can't understand it." Eli shook his head. "he had to pass at least within sight."

"Maybe he crawled into a prairie-dog hole," Carroll hypothesized.

It seemed more logical than what actually happened, for when we neared the pickup, Eli once more uttered an epithet of disbelief, raised his .270, and shot the biggest buck of his life. The animal was peering at us from the shade of a huge ponderosa pine not 20 yeards from the brush where we'd first spotted him. It's that kind of unpredictable behavior that often makes a big buck so tough to come by—and also makes him such a special prize.

While that buck's reaction was unusual, so was the fact that he was downed at such close range. As a rule, muley hunting is a long-shot proposition. If you're unfamiliar with targets at 200- and 300-yard distances, be sure to make rifle practice part of your preparations. One thing my clients have taught me is to impress this need on anyone who lives east of Minnesota. When otherwise capable hunters are confronted with a 300-yard shot from a prone position, 50 percent of them crumble under the strain, a strain that I might add is totally imagined.

Expect most shots to fall between 100 and 300 yards. While exceptions will occur, that kind of average distance is best handled by calibers in the neighborhood of the .25-06, the .270, and the .30-06. If you get much more powerful than a .30-06, you'll do gross damage to muley meat at 100-yard ranges, and rifles with loads lighter than the .25-06 don't pack the power to kill cleanly beyond 300 yards. I know I'm opening a can of worms with these statements—sure, a well-placed shot from virtually any centerfire rifle will kill a

Hunting writer and guide Norm Strung (right) and one of his successful clients drag out a buck. The oxygen is thin at high altitude, and the rigors of climbing can tax the lungs and legs. Strung therefore emphasizes the need for physical conditioning before going on this type of hunt.

muley at 300 yards—but long experience and many misses have proved these three to be the most able calibers in most situations. My personal favorite is the .270.

I'm similarly opinionated on the use of scopes. They are nearly as important as your rifle when you're after mule deer. Snap shots at muleys are rare, so open sights are of no advantage. The precision aiming provided by crosshairs is also welcome on long shots, and you'll use your scope's magnifying ability to examine a hundred things in the course of a day afield. When it comes to magnification, there are excellent arguments for both 2½× and 4×. I have never found a need for a fixed-power scope above 4× when hunting mule deer, and although variables can be handy I've had several unfortunate experiences when clients forgot to turn back to 3× or 4× after examining a coyote at 10, and completely blew a shot because they couldn't find the animal in the scope. If you're thoroughly accustomed to using a variable, by all means keep it on the rifle you intend to use. It can be an excellent choice for high-country mule deer. But if there's a chance you might get flustered at the crucial instant and forget to turn down the magnification, you'll be a lot better off with a fixed-power instrument. On a hard and perhaps expensive hunt, you don't want to settle for an alibi in lieu of a trophy.

For all the excellent and carefully chosen equipment at a hunter's disposal, the most powerful ally you'll ever have is savvy, and learning to take racks regularly from the high country is an education that requires many years of careful study. If I had to sum up the differences between hunting the lowland whitetail and the mountain muley, I'd say taking muleys in the Rockies is deer hunting on a grand scale. Distances are greater, the physical and mental demands are greater, but to my way of thinking so are the rewards.

CHAPTER

24

LOW-DOWN AND MIDDLE-COUNTRY MULEYS

by Jim Zumbo

Sportsmen unfamiliar with the West commonly assume that hunting mule deer means hunting in the high country. Muleys are, indeed, hunted in high places (as described so well by Norm Strung in another chapter), but the West has many other environments and mule deer live in all of them. A hunter is well advised to know about these varied habitats, and know how to adapt his hunting to them.

For the sake of clarity, I'm talking about the Rocky Mountain mule deer, the biggest and most popular subspecies of the clan, and the one that inhabits more acres in the West than any other subspecies.

Let's look at a typical Western state and examine the mosaic of environments in it. Colorado is a prime choice because it's one of the finest states for muleys and is the leader in the production of trophy-class bucks.

Unlike the mixed hardwood forests of the East, where assorted trees grow together, most Western forests are "pure" or made up of single species. These vegetative communities are often sharply defined, depending on the elevation at which they live, the slope they inhabit, and other factors. For example, the type of vegetation on a north-facing slope might be vastly different from the vegetation on a south-facing slope.

Here are some typical plant ecosystems the mule deer hunter can encounter in Colorado. At the lowest elevations, greasewood, saltbush, and plants that can live in arid areas are found. Higher up, junipers start to appear, and still higher, pinyón trees mix with junipers to form extensive lowland forests that stretch for hundreds of miles. Still progressing upward, you'll start to see large expanses of

A hunter expects desert muleys to be found in semi-arid, often flat habitat, but Rocky Mountain muleys like these also exploit such environments. In Colorado, for instance, they're seen amid greasewood, saltbush, and sparse forbs in relatively flat, open terrain. Since the deer travel to water at night, there's no use hunting waterholes—but the routes to waterholes may be productive at the right times.

sagebrush that give way to lovely patches of quaking aspen. Above that you'll be into the high country and evergreen timber, including alpine fir and spruce. Aspens are at the upper limits of the lowland forests and are actually classed as being an intermediate-elevational species. But for our purposes, we'll include them in this chapter because they're an extremely important forest for mule deer, and they happen to provide my favorite hunting.

For simplicity, I'll outline each low and vegetative type and suggest techniques to hunt them.

The desert environment, the one composed of brush, cactus, and low-growing shrubs, is often overlooked by mule deer hunters. Deer aren't particularly numerous in this landform, but some big bucks—big enough to warrant your attention—are known to live year-round in them.

It would seem that the best place to start looking for your buck is at waterholes because of the desert climate and typical scarcity of water. True, but don't look *at* the waterholes and expect to ambush a deer—look *around* them if you see fresh tracks in the vicinity. Desert deer normally water at night, and you'll waste time hoping to waylay one at water. Deer may travel two or three miles to water in the desert. If you find numerous tracks around water, use the waterhole as the hub of your attention and hunt in likely places within a mile or two that might harbor deer. In the desert, you should look wherever there's cover, rocky outcrops, brushy arroyos—or any landscape feature that looks like it might appeal to deer. Muleys like to bed high so they can see below them. If there's a ridge or rocky knoll, get up on it and walk just under the top. You might kick bedded bucks out just below you.

There are often plenty of roads in the desert. Big bucks don't want to be disturbed, and they'll seek places that are as remote as possible. Leave your vehicle behind and hike into areas as far from roads as you dare.

Don't underestimate Western deserts. They are commonly ignored by hunters, many of whom drive through deserts blissfully ignorant of the rewards to be found. The rewards wear big antlers.

Sagebrush country is a desert as well, though it's not as arid as lowland deserts. Sage grows at fairly high elevations, and probably does best in areas between 6,000 and 8,000 feet. The plant grows all over the West, but the sagebrush environment I want to discuss here is the vast expanse, where sage grows from one horizon to the other. This is mule deer country, but it's not as easy to hunt as it looks. Though deer are highly visible in sage—and therefore they use distance as an instinctive defense—there are ways to hunt it with a good chance of success. It's difficult to get close to deer, because the openness of the terrain makes them as wary as antelope on the prairie. In the "good old days" you could drive a pick-up within shooting range of a big buck. Those deer are gone forever, though young bucks and on rare occasions a mature buck will be a bit too trusting.

Deer may travel to sagebrush areas to feed and then return to shelter in the early morning to bed down for the day, or they might live in the sage permanently. If undisturbed, they'll bed down in sagebrush, but always in a place where there is little or no human traffic.

In most sagebrush communities, clumps of brush such as serviceberry, mahogany, or other shrubs provide patches of cover. Those are places to start looking for deer. One way is to get up on a high vantage point before dawn and glass for feeding deer as shooting light approaches. Another is to wait until mid-morning when deer are bedded, and walk slowly into the brush patches with the wind in your face. If you jump deer, they often provide a shot while they're skedaddling away.

If you try the stand option, use your

A lot of hunters think of aspens and associated vegetation as being part of the high country, but actually these brushy woods typify an intermediate zone. Once the leaves are gone from these trees, visibility may be excellent. Heavily used game trails let you walk quietly enough to still-hunt, or you can take a stand where you can watch a sufficiently open though brushy slope. *(Courtesy of Wyoming Game and Fish Department)*

Valleys—particularly riverbottoms—attract Rocky Mountain muleys to their lush vegetation, which provides excellent feed and plenty of cover. There's an old proverb that mule deer graze high and browse low, but this Utah buck is grazing in a riverbottom pasture bordered by woods. *(Courtesy of Utah Travel Council)*

binoculars to glass every nook and cranny. Move down from your stand if you're satisfied no deer are around, and get up on another. Move quickly but cautiously. Deer will be headed for bedding areas after dawn, so you'll want to utilize those early minutes to your advantage. As you approach a vantage point, ease up slowly and look around before getting comfortable. Deer might be close by. A sudden movement could spook them.

If you spot deer and see a buck you like, you have several options. The first, of course, is to shoot if the deer is within range. Another is to determine the route of the feeding animals, then maneuver carefully to ambush them as they move toward your position. Another is to watch the deer until they bed down, then make a stalk. Finally, you can watch them bed down, then leave and come back in late afternoon when they'll get up to feed and perhaps move close to your location.

My favorite technique is to don a daypack and wander around in the sage, investigating canyons, ravines, rock outcrops, and other spots that might harbor deer. In this manner I might travel a dozen miles in a day, and I'm always amazed at the number of deer I see out there in the sea of sage. You might be, too. Try it.

In much of the Southwest, enormous pinyon-juniper forests harbor plenty of mule deer. These forests are common in deer-rich Utah and Colorado, as well as many other Western states. In several

Sagebrush fares best at elevations of 6,000 to 8,000 feet, though it also does well at lower elevations—and grows all over the West. In most sagebrush communities, clumps of serviceberry, mahogany, or other shrubs provide virtually all the cover there is. Hunt around such cover and you have a good chance of surprising a buck like this as he sneaks down to the sage to feed.

states, such as Nevada, Arizona, and New Mexico, this forest is the only choice hunters have to hunt in some regions. In other states, though, hunters avoid the pinyon-juniper forest because they don't realize the superb potential in them or they don't like to hunt them. They prefer higher country.

Trees usually grow close together in the forest, forming a tight canopy. Visibility is extremely limited, and the forest floor is often composed of loose shale that makes silent walking almost impossible. Still-hunting in this forest is tough, though some hunters do it successfully.

A workable plan is to look for small openings where deer feed. Since a good deal of the forest lacks deer forage because of the infertile soil and heavy shade, the animals must seek browse elsewhere. If you find a small sagebrush meadow and there's evidence that deer feed in it, watch it closely in the late afternoon. Remain there as long as you can, at least until shooting hours are almost over. Deer may linger until the light wanes before leaving the forest for the opening.

Drives work well in these forests, especially when the trees grow on fairly steep terrain and you can use a bit of logic to figure a strategy. If the forest is dense and grows on flat or slightly rolling country, the drive will be more difficult to engineer because deer can run virtually anywhere. In mountainous terrain, you can often coax them in the direction you want, and visibility might be better.

Some pinyon-juniper forests are fairly open, allowing still-hunting possibilities. If you can, pick a breezy day so the wind can help muffle your movements. Since the branches on these trees grow down to ground level, spotting a bedded or standing deer will be all but impossible. I've done it a few times, but few enough that I can recall each instance vividly.

High brush grows at intermediate elevations, and muleys love to live in it because it offers concealment and feed. Scrub oak is the most common, and grows in much of Colorado's big buck country, among other places. This vegetative type is mean and miserable to hunt in. Travel is hindered, and deer are usually heard instead of being seen. Plenty of unkind words have been uttered by hunters who attempt to travel this jungle. If you can get into the brush at all, a drive is best, and sometimes the only option. You can follow deer trails to penetrate the brush and hope for the best once you're in there. Be prepared to suffer, but give it a good try. Some of the biggest bucks in the West hang out in oak brush. And why not? They have everything they need, especially a distinct lack of human beings.

Quaking aspen grows everywhere in the West. It is a delightful forest to hunt in, and you can use every technique you know to hunt deer in it. In the autumn, during mule deer season, the leaves are gone from aspens and trees are naked. Visibility is often excellent, whether you're still-hunting or watching an aspen-covered slope from an adjacent ridge.

There are usually well-established trails in the aspens, allowing you to walk quietly, though the woods can be noisy if the leaves have just fallen and haven't been moistened by rain, snow, or dew.

Still-hunting is my strategy in the aspens. I love to walk along on a trail at first shooting light, moving just a few feet a minute. If I've done my homework I know where deer are likely to be, so I'm plenty enthusiastic. My concentration is up, and I'm confident I'll see deer.

Another fine technique is to sit on a canyon slope or ridge across from an aspen stand. Because of the angle of the slope, you'll be able to see into the trees from the side you're sitting on. Be most observant before the sun hits the area you're looking at, because that's when big bucks are on the move. Find your vantage point early, and prepare to sit tight until late in the morning.

Aspens can be driven, but deer can't be moved where you want them. There are enough trails in most aspen stands to let muleys run where they want. As a general rule however, spooked deer will run uphill. Place your standers in saddles or on points where they have a good view.

Pinyon-juniper stands are among Jim Zumbo's favorite places to hunt mule deer—and remember, Zumbo's favorite method is still-hunting. Visibility is limited, and loose shale is likely to make silent walking difficult, but Zumbo works his way along the edges, seeking openings where deer feed and then taking a stand in late afternoon near any small sagebrush meadow. Such meadows often edge the junipers and pinyons. Zumbo is shown here with a buck he took in just that kind of edge habitat.

If the woods are extremely noisy, sit tight and wait for other hunters to work for you. Otherwise, move along slowly, even though it sounds like you're walking on potato chips. Deer moving toward you might not hear you if you travel at intervals.

No matter what Western environment you choose, you can find mule deer there. The lower elevations can be very productive. Give them a shake on your next hunt.

CHAPTER

25

THE GREAT GRAIN-BELT BUCKS

by Bert Popowski

The era of the intercontinental trophy hunger is waning due to the sheer cost of guided trips for high-ranking heads to grace spacious trophy rooms. The traditional trophy hunter, who traveled to far-distant lands in a quest for a wide assortment of species, has been replaced by sportsmen of modest means who have turned to hunting for mature specimens of only a few species. If these wear splendid headgear, that's fine. But as a rule the main targets of such hunters are animals of outstanding eating qualities, those that can be served with pride to friends who may never have feasted on any meat that didn't come from a supermarket. One of life's delights for me has been the conversion of prissy people, mostly urbanites, who shrank from tasting the produce of my generous arsenal of firearms.

The flavor of most meat varies enormously according to the factors existing at the time the animals were harvested. It doesn't depend only on whether the critters are skinny or fat, male or female, young or adult. In the final analysis, it depends on the kind of food your game tucked away for weeks before you collected it. Of course, if you're a slob in the postmortem care of your game, you can ruin grand eating through sheer ignorance. But that isn't the game's fault.

In the case of venison, the quality depends on the time of year when your buck was shot, the neatness with which he was dispatched, field-dressed, and cooled out, and the kind of food on which he had been living. A buck taken late in the rut (or after it) is seldom any great eating prize. I say "seldom" because an over-the-hill buck that had little or no interest in pursuing does frequently produce venison steaks

Hunters who think of mule deer as creatures exclusively of the Western mountains and deserts are missing an excellent hunting opportunity. Grain Belt muleys are abundant and large. The impressive buck in this photo stands in a typical farm field.

These plump Montana bucks typify the well-fed muleys found in abundance from that state east into the Dakotas. The author of this chapter, the late Bert Popowski, was renowned for his prowess in hunting deer and antelope. He pointed out that muley bucks are particularly gregarious before the onset of the rut, when seasons are open in many areas. This means you'll frequently have to choose between bucks like these. The better rack is at right, of course. *(Courtesy of U.S. Fish and Wildlife Service)*

you can cut with a fork. In comparison, a rut-gaunted muley provides stringy and often musky meat.

Similarly, a buck that has been crippled and chased hard until he is finished off provides poor venison. Injury or fright will pump adrenalin into his bloodstream and thence throughout his muscular fibers. This toughens the meat and gives it a rank taste.

Even if none of these detrimental factors applies to the buck you bag, there's the possibility that your game lived on foods that embittered his flesh or, in some cases, gave it a bland tastelessness. Year after year, certain areas produce venison of the highest quality and others don't.

For instance, regardless of deer species, I wouldn't give much for a buck that has been fattened strictly in cornfields, with no nourishing and mild-flavored browse or mast to enrich the venison's flavor. Corn merely lays on the tallow and does little to give the meat tastiness. But if a deer feeds on small grains and then has access to such legumes as clover or alfalfa, or hazel or oak browse and mast, then I'll sprain my running gear to put my tag on him. Such "finishing" foods put a flavor into venison that makes it equal, and sometimes superior, to beef that has been fattened in pens. Lucky are the hunters who can pursue their venison in such grain-belt areas, for their bucks are tops in taste.

Bert Popowski is seen here seated comfortably on a high lookout commanding a wide view. The so-called Grain Belt on the eastern side of the Rockies contains a great deal of rugged terrain like this, as well as the gently rolling prairies that most people think of as the "grasslands."

There's a wide stretch of the Midwest (and that part of the West just beyond it) where the deer are big, the meat excellent, and the muleys populous enough to provide excellent hunting for those who know how, when, and where to collect their venison, and what sort of rifle to rely on for long shots at deer in open country.

For some inexplicable reason, *Odocoileus hemionus* joined many other wild species in being abundant in the western United States but never crossed the Mississippi. Muleys come in various "races" or subspecies that range from southwestern Canada throughout the Rockies and into northern Mexico. The Rocky Mountain form is advertised as the largest but bucks from the Grain Belt of the Midwest are their match. The easternmost range of any significance being at the edge of the Corn Belt, where corn and soybeans displace small grains as the major cash crop. So the muleys of which I write seldom get east of a center line drawn through the twin Dakotas and the same longitude passing through the tier of states to their south.

This is a vast area of open country, large tracts of which have been designated as part of the National Grasslands. During the early 1930s, when the grasslands were abused by overgrazing, the Great Depression and the severe Dust Bowl droughts and dust-drifting winds forced many landowners into bankruptcy. A great deal of acreage was retired from private ownership and thrown into a pool of land devoted exclusively to holding the soil and grazing a limited number of cattle.

South Dakota, as only one of eleven Western states participating in the National Grasslands Act, has a total of 864, 268 acres in three plots in the grasslands program. It also has some 240,000 acres of public hunting lands administered by its game department. Much of the grasslands part of this open range is excellent muley range simply because it is lightly subjected to human use. All of South Dakota's grasslands are located west of the Missouri River in a semi-arid, lightly populated area. They form a choice hunting portion of that grain-belt muley range I mentioned.

Hunters acquainted only with the whitetail can do themselves a big favor by studying all they can find about muley habits before taking after these deer of the spacious West. Basically, the difference in performance is this. When jumped, whitetails dodge into the nearest cover, around a ridge point or down into a valley; muleys, even when wounded, usually go up because generations of them have found safety in elevations. If there's no height of land within reasonable reach, a muley will take off across country, substituting miles of distance for a few hundred feet of elevation.

When hunted hard, whitetails learn to hide better on their crowded home range, sometimes concealing themselves in bits of low brush scarcely adequate to hide a cottontail. But muleys, used to spacious country, seldom tolerate much hunting pressure. They just abandon disturbed areas for more isolated spots.

Finally, muleys are very gregarious, though they may be separated by sexes before the rut. Thus, if you see one buck, large or small, you can be almost positive you're close to others and they're probably watching you. When one goes, they all move out. One time, after hunting hard during most of a very windy day without

Popowski (at right) and hunting partner Don Baldwin examine a massively-antlered mule deer taken on a high, grassy flat near the Cheyenne River.

finding a hair of game, I came up a slight rise into the wind. As my eyes uncovered a small bench it exploded with bucks, nine in all. By the time I had sorted them out and chosen "my" buck, they were all out of sight. I didn't get off a shot.

In open country, such as the comparatively level terrain devoted to raising grain and forage crops, it often pays to lean heavily on binocular prospecting instead of exposing yourself excessively by extensive walking or driving. Any bit of rough country, regardless of its vegetation, should be carefully glassed. Muley bucks may bed in the shade of a lone sagebrush or a single bush on an otherwise barren slope, or behind a tiny wrinkle in the land where vegetation is too short to hide behind. Look for wee flats just large enough to provide bedding space for a deer, or a notch or dry wash that will provide level spots in the shade. An inexperienced hunter can miss dozens of such semi-exposed hideaways because he can't believe good bucks could hide so well. Thousands of muleys have lived long and undisturbed lives because such cover wasn't adequately investigated. A buck with towering antlers may stretch his neck, lay his chin on the ground, and become a part of an enormous drab landscape which surrounds him on every side.

When actually working up on a buck discovered in such open hideouts, a direct foot approach simply allows him to slip away along any of several escape routes. But two hunters working together can move game toward each other, provided one of them ambushes the right escape route and covers it well. And, of course, a good long-range rifleman may be able to nail his trophy by simply spanning a range of several hundred yards.

Two types of acreage often serve as incubators for splendid muley bucks. One is the lavish scattering of historic or commemorative areas set aside as national monuments or parks. A Minnesota friend, who regularly hunts in Montana, usually drives through both ways at night to reduce the traffic he encounters. His favorite route goes past the Theodore Roosevelt National Monument in North Dakota, which serves as a home for some magnificently antlered trophies. At dusk they leave this refuge to feed on surrounding croplands and are often sighted approaching their dining areas. The extensive Badlands National Monument of my home state of South Dakota is another producer of grand heads; so is Wind Cave, scarcely a dozen miles away from where this is being written. Wise hunters scout the surrounding areas, determine the travel routes used by their game, and try to intercept them at dusk or dawn.

Then there's the second category of promising acreage: Any prominent feature of the country that's rugged in its topography is bound to attract fine muley bucks. For instance, such landmarks as buttes and hills are magnets for assorted wildlife, including fine mule deer. After a week of open season, they won't be exactly in those landmarks but bedded out in such open spots as I've previously described. Such breaks of rough country, though they may be miles away from croplands, provide sanctuary for grain-belt bucks. Mule deer, unlike whitetails, think nothing of sauntering a dozen miles a night to feed.

Archers are exceptionally successful in grain-belt muley hunting because they can waylay their game along established travel routes or in the rougher bits of habitat. I've known of archers meeting their game literally head-on, with shots taken at around 10 yards. In one sharply eroded Badlands formation I once watched an archer and a buck, on opposite sides of a knife-edged ridge, trying to outwait each other while separated by a mere dozen feet. The bowman finally blew it by shuffling his feet and the buck made long tracks. Since archery seasons usually precede firearms season, many muleys become quite apprehensive of ambushes. Then they come out later in the dusk hours and get back to safe sanctuaries before dawn breaks on the rifle hunters.

The connoisseur of choice venison will do his deer hunting as early as the opening of the season permits. He will also field-dress his buck as rapidly as possible, protect it against insects, birds, and beasts, and haul it in to some means of controlled cooling and ageing for at least a week at a constant temperature of around 40 degrees. Skinning should be delayed to avoid dehydrating the meat unless the weather is so hot that skinning in the field is mandatory to help get rid of the critter's body heat. If the temperature is right, just a bit above freezing, ageing goes on equally well with pelt on or off.

Since muleys are often killed in out-of-the-way places, some gentle means of getting the field-dressed carcass out to terminal transportation is advisable. If you just knock over your venison, gut it, and then immediately drag it roughly over rocks, stumps, and other obstacles, you'll bruise the meat. Severely bruised spots will become blood-shot. So the carcass should be allowed to cool enough to firm up, stiffening somewhat before being dragged. Even then, choose the smoothest drag route. It's a shame to batter choice meat.

Muleys lay on considerable tallow in preparation for the lean months. This conditioning weight is rapidly shed by the bucks during the rut, indicating the value of making early-season hunts to harvest the best venison. Does do not shed their conditioning tallow during the rut, though they do gradually pay it out during the long months of winter pregnancy. That's why our forefathers used to prefer to take does for winter meat. Though smaller in total weight, they were in better condition than post-rut bucks and so yielded tastier venison.

Another facet of bringing home fine venison is using a rifle that will kill cleanly if the buck is well hit. Although muleys are big deer, outsized cannons aren't needed to knock them down. After all, they're only deer, and a rifle suitable for whitetails will do a good job on muleys at similar distances. The main difference is that most muleys are taken at somewhat longer than usual whitetail distances so the hunter should be prepared—by practice, attitude, and rifle—to take his game at moderate antelope ranges. which is to say his rifle should be zeroed-in to hit on point-of-aim at 200 yards and he should memorize its trajectory at 300. In open country, shots at those ranges might be the best that muleys will offer.

Where to hit muleys is debatable. It depends largely on the pose your buck assumes at critical moments. Considering the probable ranges, I'd suggest that a novice study pictured poses of deer in all possible positions. The main thing is to get that bullet through the vitals without shooting up any significant amount of eating meat. Make it a rule to take the solidest possible shooting position, never shoot offhand if you can kneel or sit or even take a rest which approximates the solidity of the prone position. At long range you can't afford wobbles in your shooting iron. It's foolish to try for pinpoint hits if you can hold for the biggest fatal target of all, the lung area, but care shouldn't stop there. You should try to place your bullet in the center of that lung area, thus allowing for some error in judging range and wind deflection.

What rifle should you use? I know of no modern-day caliber that far surpasses the venerable .270 for plains hunting. The man with an accurate .270 needn't take a back seat to anyone toting a .308, .30-06, 7×57mm, or any other calibers below the 7mm Magnum or .300 Magnum. In the hands of a good shot and a capable hunter, the .243 Winchester or 6mm Remington may be rifle enough, but I prefer something spitting heavier than 100-grain bullets, both to hold up in velocity and to buck wind over normal muley-hunting ranges.

This magnificently-antlered non-typical mule deer will never be displaced from the record book. It's a grain-fed deer from Alberta, a province that has produced a number of record trophies.
(Photo by Bert Popowski)

The deer cartridges I would *not* choose for this open country are those of looping trajectory, such as the .44 Magnum, the .444, and even the revived .47-70.

Having mentioned antelope in connection with range, I should add that the hunter of grain-belt muleys has a sporting bonus: a wide variety of game that's fattening up to survive winter or to fuel migrations. Early deer seasons range from late September to late October, the very same months when all other wildlife is conditioning itself for the lean cold months to come. Nonresident nimrods frequently encounter bonanzas of such early migrants as mourning doves and teal. These are trailed by the larger waterfowl, plus local crops of upland game, including the historic prairie chickens and burly sage grouse. I've guided some visiting hunters who lived off lesser game they harvested as windfalls of muley scouting trips before the deer seasons opened. Some of them even became acquainted with my favorite of all Western game, the speedy pronghorn antelope.

Where to hunt grain-belt muleys depends on which areas are cropped with small grains and legumes or are devoted to raising livestock. Many parts of some Western states were naturally arid but have been salvaged by a checkerboarding of impounded waters for irrigation and a jigsawing of diverted runoff to fill livestock dams or reservoirs. Where these make the soil bloom, they are natural magnets for muleys and other wildlife. But the crop-growing season is short. Thus western North Dakota, with the potential of tapping the Missouri River impoundments, will steadily improve its grain-belt muley production.

Kansas has mule deer but confines its deer hunting to resident hunters. Nebraska and South Dakota have good

Oglala Sioux Rangers Sammy Cook (at left) and Johnny Swallow show off one of Bert Popowski's mule deer. They guided him to this buck on the Pine Ridge Reservation, one of his favorite grain-belt hunting places. *(Photo by Bert Popowski)*

herds on their western prairie lands. About 70 percent of their resident and visiting hunters fill their licenses.

The next tier of Western states, beginning with Montana and running through Wyoming and Colorado, are lavish muley producers. No clear-cut segregation can be made in the location of grain-belt and mountain muleys, though obviously the former are more easterly in the three states. Locally, it depends on where natural flatlands occur to allow farming and irrigation. Some of those croplands extend clear to the immense wheatlands of eastern Oregon and Washington, with occasional patches in south-central Idaho. Wherever they exist, muleys fatten on them.

It should be noted that many Western states have extensive Indian reservations on which human disturbance is about as light as on national grasslands and national forests. Some reservation lands are leased for cropping and running livestock, but this doesn't void hunting rights. These remain under tribal ownership and require the payment of trespass and/or hunting fees to the Tribal Council. Many reservations also require the use of Indian guides for visiting hunters.

All in all, hunting grain-belt muleys calls for more initiative than most other forms of deer hunting because so many variables can change from spot to spot according to the time of day, the quality of habitat, the kind of terrain, and the amount of human harassment. All deer are supposed to be nocturnal. But if considerable distances separate muley bedding grounds from feeding areas, muleys will be late getting home in the morning and will also head back toward feeding areas earlier than you might expect—starting out during daylight to feed throughout the night. Conversely, if their habitat provides food and shelter close together, muleys may bed down within a few hundred yards of where they fill their paunches. If the vegetation suits them and is undisturbed, they may lie up within neck's length of grub. So—whether on or off a reservation—a guide may be a big help to someone who isn't acquainted with the habits of the deer in a particular grain-belt muley haven.

CHAPTER

26

THE WEST COAST'S BLACKTAIL BONANZA

by Norm Nelson

Remember Cinderella? Her problem wasn't lack of beauty and grace and charm—it was just that no one on the home front appreciated her.

This is much the case with the Columbian blacktail, that dark brown wraith of the Pacific Coast forest country. Three Western states, Washington, Oregon, and California, have high populations of them. But in a good part of his range, the blacktail tends to be under-appreciated and under-hunted.

Take my home state of Washington. Better than two-thirds of the state's three million people live west of the Cascade crest, which is where the blacktails live, too. But every year, tens of thousands of western Washington hunters hie themselves over the mountain passes to hunt mule deer in the arid western uplands, while lots of prime blacktail hunting goes begging closer to home.

The reason, of course, is that muleys in open pine forests or range country are much easier to hunt. But the difficulty of taking your deer is one part of the blacktail's appeal. A good blacktail buck rates as a real trophy, antler size notwithstanding, in terms of hunter achievement.

Until recent times, the blacktail was classified as a distinct species. The biological pundits have demoted the blacktail to just a subspecies of the closely related mule deer, but to the hunter the Columbian blacktail is a far different deer, unique unto himself. His habits and habitat are just as different from a mule deer's as the blacktail's substantial tail brush is different from the muley's tiny posterior rope. Conventional mule-deer tactics aren't relevant to hunting blacktails.

The blacktail is not a daily long-distance commuter as many muleys are. A mule deer may feed in a valley bottom at night and bed in daytime one to three miles distant, up in high, rocky country offering the cover he craves. By contrast, the blacktail often has his bedroom and dining room in the same piece of forest. And in the rainier portions of his coastal range, he need not travel far to find water.

Chew on that information a bit. Get the point? Forest blacktails don't have to move about very much in their day-to-day life-support activities. And any deer that doesn't have to expose himself moving around is a lot tougher to hunt. His vulnerability to the sharp-eyed, listening hunter, who may be prowling or standing at a deer trail junction, is drastically reduced. That's only part of the problem. When the blacktail does start moving, he's likely to be traveling through the damnedest jungles you'll find this side of equatorial regions. I grew up hunting whitetails in the thick brush and post-fire, second-growth forests of northern Minnesota and thought I knew what thick cover was—until I moved to the Pacific Northwest. Here, typical blacktail habitat is likely to be incredibly thick young evergreens, close-spaced red alder, clumps of devil's club and sprawling vine maple, myrtle, or ferns that grow 6 feet high. A blacktail slinking through that cover is almost invisible much of the time.

Hot weather prevails during California's early blacktail season, so this hunter wears lightweight camo clothing. Some of the habitat, especially to the north, is extremely dense, but here he has found an excellent stand overlooking a slope of brush and scrub where visibility is good and where deer feed. *(Courtesy of Petersen Publishing Company)*

Late one fall afternoon, I picked a good stump with a view of deer trails in the 387,000-acre Clemons Tree Farm of the Weyerhaeuser Company in western Washington. In the last 30 minutes of shooting time, I heard the light shuffle of a deer wading fetlock deep through the stiff-leaved salal and cascara. Unfortunately, it didn't take quite the right trail and missed me by 20 feet, about the distance of a good living room's span, or close enough to take him with a fast bayonet charge, right? No dice. The deer was so thoroughly screened in doghair-thick baby hemlock that I never saw him, although I found droppings still at body temperature minutes later.

Thus, the blacktail is a very hard quarry to hang on a gambrel stick. That's not because he's super-smart, as Eastern white-tails have become after two centuries of white man's hunting. It's because the blacktail's coastal forest habitat gives him a big advantage over the hunter.

Even so, the cause is not hopeless. Tens of thousands of blacktails are taken annually in California, Oregon, and Washington (not to mention British Columbia and up in the Alaskan panhandle, home of the smaller Sitka blacktail). It helps to know more about the blacktail's ecology. Like his forest-dwelling peer, the whitetail, the Columbian blacktail does best in a "disturbed environment." Ancient virgin forests, untouched by man or natural catastrophe, have little or no food for the blacktail, and you'll rarely find him there.

A naturalist at the turn of the century, D. G. Elliot, spent five weeks in Washington's Olympic Mountains, virgin wilderness then and now, to take museum specimens. "Although we hunted continually," Elliot reported, "no elk were seen while we remained at this camp, and deer, the true blacktail, the only species found in these mountains, were very scarce, and we only succeeded in obtaining a doe and a fawn. ... I do not think I was ever before in a country that was apparently so devoid of animal life."

The problem is that thick forest shuts off sunlight from the forest floor. This drastically reduces the amount of brush and other browse. In turn, this means no game. However, blacktails historically could be found in places where major fires swept away an old-growth forest. This was one reason why coastal Indians did some primitive game management in the form of semi-controlled burning. Some of the "natural" prairies that settlers found in western Washington resulted form repeated burning by the Indians to provide clearings in which the camas lily, a staple food of theirs, was able to grow. These clearings also provided brush, low plants, and grasses to attract and maintain elk and deer populations.

Standing on a ridge in a Pacific Northwest forest, a blacktail hunter scans a timbered draw with his binoculars. Like Rocky Mountain mule deer, blacktails often move along the crest or upper part of a slope. But whereas a Rocky Mountain muley usually runs uphill when spooked, an alarmed blacktail is more likely to lunge downhill and into the thickest brush or timber he sees. *(Photo by Norm Nelson)*

This hunter is scouting a promising area. He's in a clear-cut that's blanketed with trailing blackberry between new sprouts of Douglas fir. Trailing blackberry is a prime blacktail food, and here it's close to excellent cover. *(Photo by Norm Nelson)*

Like the whitetail, the blacktail, where he could be found, was decimated by uncontrolled settler meat hunting. But better days were coming. Careless settlers' forest fires and the start of logging in the Northwest began to provide blacktail habitat that simply didn't exist in the untouched forest. The dominant Douglas fir here is best harvested by clear-cutting in blocks, since fir seedlings for the next forest generation need full sunlight. For several years after harvest, these clear-cuts provide a food-supply paradise for blacktails (plus elk, grouse, and band-tailed pigeons).

In a clear-cut, sunlight is available to quickly cover the logged-off area with trailing blackberry, huckleberry, young vine maple, and other low plants on which blacktails can thrive the year around. Of course, as the clear-cut is restocked with seedling trees, either by man or nature, it eventually grows back into a forest dense enough once more to shut off that sunlight-generated food supply. But that will take a few years, even with today's speeded-up planting by the forest industry. And by the time a former clear-cut becomes too overgrown with young timber to supply much deer food any longer, there will be other rotational harvest areas in the same neighborhood to supply new browse.

So, the overall picture for the blacktail is a bright one. Although effective fire suppression today means that nature no longer is doing much clear-cutting for the benefit of deer and other wildlife, perpetual-yield logging harvests are providing the same benefit without fire's wildlife casualties and possible loss of soil fertility in severe burns.

For the blacktail hunter, the obvious lesson is: go not to an old-growth, Walt Disney forest, but find an area that has had repeated logging activity in various spots during recent years.

Washington Game Department researchers list four stages of forest succession. These are clues to good deer hunting. Stage 1 involves recently logged or burned areas where existing vegetation is presently grasses and forbs (nonshrub, low-growing plants). Deer frequent these areas in late summer and early fall, particularly if there is a good stand of fireweed. However, in Stage 1 there are not enough of the browse shrub species available yet to provide late-fall and winter forage. Don't expect deer to be in one of these relatively new clear-cuts or burns in October simply because you saw blacktails there in August.

In Stage 2, the prominent vegetation has become shrubs. As the Washington Game Department's excellent book on blacktail research put it, "These [Stage 2] areas are approaching the peak productivity of deer forage and the forage produced is of high quality."

Later, in Stage 3, dominant vegetation has become second-growth coniferous or deciduous tree species, overshadowing the shrubs to some extent. Finally, in Stage 4 the timber species have grown big enough to allow only a few shade-tolerant shrub species, ferns, and a few forbs to exist. This is poor foraging for deer, but animals will use such an area for bedding or escape cover.

Therefore, a blacktail hunter does well if he starts by looking for country *with a combination of Stage 2, Stage 3, and Stage 4 areas*. Weed-overgrown clearings of Stage 2 provide plenty of food for blacktails. But except at the beginning of the season, a hunter may not catch deer well out in such open terrain. They often browse after dark.

Stage 3 sites have both the groceries for blacktails and somewhat better cover. During daylight hours, deer are likeliest to be either in the best cover features of Stage 3 land or in Stage 4 forests immediately adjoining Stage 2 and Stage 3 areas. Anywhere you find this diversity of sites in blacktail country, you are practically certain to find deer or at least deer sign.

A logical scheme for hunting under these conditions would be to start before daybreak by taking a stand at a downwind vantage point overlooking a clear-cut several years old—that is, either Stage 2 or Stage 3 land. Good binoculars are vital here. At shooting light, watch carefully along the edges of a clear-cut or old burn for deer drifting slowly back into the adjoining thicker forest cover.

If there is a lot of forest debris in the form of discarded limbs, tree tops, or burn snags, it can be tough to see the dark brown forms of blacktails threading their way through this slash. It can be even more difficult to make out antlers, which is why binoculars are strongly recommended.

The blacktail has some quirks of his own. Like the mule deer, the blacktail often travels along the face or crest of a ridge, something that whitetails are not too keen to do. But while a frightened muley often runs uphill to even higher ground, a startled blacktail will usually dive through the timber downhill. His aim is to get into the densest creek-bottom cover. In the rainy Cascades and Olympics, every valley has some kind of water course at the bottom. Along the creeks, thick stands of alder, vine maple, and some red cedar

Squatting in a big, brushy, weedy clearing, a hunter watches a blacktail through his scope. Fields like this, as well as old burns and clear-cuts with low second growth, are favorite feeding spots for these deer. As with whitetails, a hunter should scan the edges where deer may lurk in the fringes of cover.

provide better cover than the more open timber on the hillsides. Blacktails know this very well.

If a drive is planned using standers and drivers, care must be taken to cover both the creek bottom and the hillsides. There is no guarantee which route a blacktail will use, moving out ahead of the drivers. If he's not too spooked and figures he has the situation well in hand, he may stay on the face of a ridge working a hundred yards or more ahead of the drivers. If badly worried, he'll be sneaking through the thickest cover he can find down in the creek bottom. Of course, like other deer, he'll be traveling upwind.

Blacktails are as surefooted as Rocky Mountain mule deer and can negotiate steep hillsides. Since they live in heavy cover a good part of the time, they are not averse to traveling through the densest kind of thickets that even the cover-loving whitetail would tend to detour.

Obviously a blacktail hunter has problems in flat country due to the lack of visibility typical of the coastal forest. For this reason, chances are better when hunting on ridges. My preference is for country that is not too steep. This allows me to spend more time looking for deer either ahead on my ridge or on the face of an adjoining parallel ridge. In really steep terrain, one must spend too much time watching his footing and picking a route, instead of concentraing on looking for deer.

I also prefer a country with small water courses. This means that the paralleling ridges on each side of such a creek will be fairly close with a better chance of an in-range shot at a deer on the opposite side of a draw or a canyon.

In contrasting three decades or more of whitetail-hunting experience with considerably more than a decade of blacktail hunting, it's my conviction that the black-

These blacktail does are feeding in an old clear-cut that provides plenty of low, succulent browse. California, Oregon, and Washington are dotted with places like this where blacktails come to feed. *(Photo by Norm Nelson)*

It isn't often that you catch a fine Columbian blacktail buck like this standing in tall, open timber. To get this picture, wildlife photographer Leonard Lee Rue, IV worked and sweated for days, tracking, still-hunting, and watching from a special blind in an area where he had found copious sign and had even seen deer bedded. As in hunting whitetails and Rocky Mountain mule deer, scouting the habitat is an enormous help. *(Photo by Leonard Lee Rue, IV)*

tail is not as predictable in bad weather as a whitetail. When it rains hard, a whitetail can be counted on to move into the best of available cover, such as dense evergreens. But the blacktail is used to rain and will not necessarily hole up. He would starve if he did, since it rains pretty steadily for five months of the year in the coastal Northwest. Therefore, the hunter is as likely to find blacktails in the more open forest as in heavy cover, even though it may be raining.

Although blacktails range high into the mountains during the summer and early fall, snow will drive them down to the valleys. A hunter in the right place can take advantage of this, working to intercept movements of deer immediately before or after a snow storm in the high country.

The gorgeous mountain country of the Northwest is certainly the most scenic area for blacktail hunting, but don't overlook lowland forests bordering agricultural country. Like whitetails, blacktails have thrived on man's agricultural practices. Woodlot hunting in Northwest lowland farm country produces some fine bucks, since these tend to be better-fed than their hardscrabble brethren up on the rocky mountainsides. Down in California, blacktails tend to become serious agricultural pests. Like mule deer wrecking young alfalfa, blacktails tend to graze in the manner of sheep, lipping off clover and trefoil so close to the ground that the plants never recover. They also raise hob with young nut trees, prune shoots, and grape tendrils in the Golden State. And like whitetails, blacktails can live in wooded suburban areas, alternating forest foods with goodies out of gardens. I've seen them dash across roadways at night in a city of 150,000 population.

From north to south, blacktail hunting techniques don't vary greatly. The California hunter jump-shooting deer in hillside patches of oak and brush is following the same approach as the Oregon or Washington hunter threading through hillside timber in the hope of spotting a running buck on the opposite ravine slope. While the Northwesterner may try stand-hunting a forest clear-cut at dawn, the Californian may be glassing an agricultural field at daybreak; the strategies are the same.

Hunting conditions vary a lot, however. Early-season blacktail hunting in California can be a 100-degree affair with heat mirage shimmering the chamiso and sage hills. Farther north, the blacktail hunter assumes he is going to hunt wet. There is no escaping it; he will soon be soaked in the rain-drenched autumn forest, just from wet foliage alone, even if the day dawns clear after a typical night's drizzle.

The hot-weather blacktail hunter's garb is simple—something cool like a tee shirt, jeans, and a wide-brimmed hat. The Northern forest hunter had best wear wool. In time, it will get wet on him, but even wet wool has some heat-retaining value in cool weather. And blacktail hunting can be cool in October and November in the Northwest. Light bird boots may be best for the warm-zone hunter, but in the Northwest timber, lug soles of stiff rubber can be essential to avoid bad falls on wet forest debris. One hunter I know who is also a logger wears his sharp-spiked logging boots when hunting a favorite area with lots of blowdown timber. With his "corks" (a corruption of "caulks"), he can often travel a hundred yards at a time, silent and sure-footed as a stalking cougar, atop fallen fir and hemlock, often 6 to 10 feet above the ground.

For a long time, author Norm Nelson used the 3×-9× variable scope seen here. It performed well enough to account for the buck in this picture and a number of others, but Nelson now has a 2×-7× variable on his blacktail rifle. A variable scope is recommended for blacktail hunting, though you'll want the ring turned to a low setting for most of your shooting. *(Photo by Norm Nelson)*

Blacktail rifles offer an interesting problem. On the face of it, a Northwest hunter would be best off with a fast-handling lever, pump, or autoloader of moderate power. The Eastern whitetail hunter's classic .30-30 lever gun would appear perfect. And for a lot of blacktail hunting, a rifle of that genre is great.

But blacktail country and blacktails are unpredictable. A flat-topped, dense forest ridge may open up into a series of draws and canyons that offer shooting out to 300 yards or more on farther slopes. A powerful, accurate bolt-action rifle would be the ticket here, if it wears at least 4× in scope magnification. But, believe me, such a "Long Ranger" is practically useless in dense forest and brush.

So a compromise is called for. My choice would be an autoloader, pump, or lever-action. Caliber choice would be .308 or .30-06 with the longer, cross-canyon shots in mind. The need for a cartridge with power for versatility rules out the guns available only for close or mid-range cartridges like the .30-30 or .35 Remington.

Only as a last resort do I want a bolt-action for *timber*. Shots here tend to be often at fast-running game. Trees and brush conceal the target part of the time, offering only snapshot opportunities in natural "holes" in the forest cover. The faster a shooter can reload his chamber with minimum distraction or movement of his rifle from the shoulder, the better he can concentrate on the lightning-reflex business of picking a clear spot for a snapshot at fleeing game. With this in mind, the autoloader is best, the pump action is almost as good, the lever gun less so, and the bolt-action the worst of the lot. While damnable heresy to today's bolt-action cult, that's just the way it is down in the timber and puckerbrush, like it or not!

I recommended the .30-calibers for blacktail hunting because of overlaps with elk seasons in Oregon and Washington, plus the chance of collecting a big bonus black bear in these states. Those factors rule out something like the .243 even though it is adequate on blacktails.

Sighting equipment calls for as much thoughtful choice as the rifle. Iron sights would be okay in the thickets but no good for the clear-cuts or the canyon shots. The logical choice is a variable-power scope, 2×-7× or even 1½×-4×. The lower settings offer plenty of wide field for timber work, while the higher settings do the business on long-shot opportunities. The modern tapered crosshairs, thick through most of their span but tapering at the junction, are probably the best compromise. Standard crosshairs can be too hard to pick up in dark timber, dot reticles are too small for close-range snapshooting, and post reticles can be too coarse for long-range chances.

I personally favor the Pachmayr Lo-Swing mounts and have these on three of my favorite rifles. Even waterproof scopes of high quality can develop air leaks, leading to fogging in the wet forests. The tough woods-walking can lead to bone-wrenching falls that leave you wondering if your scope is still sighted in. Under either of those conditions—and I have had them happen several times—it's nice to be able to flip the mount over, leaving a good set of iron sights open to the eye without obstruction. In chronically wet woods, I simply unscrew the mount's center hinge collar and put the scope in my daypack, using iron sights until things dry out. Even an unfogged scope can be rendered semi-useless by water smears on the optics, and smears of this sort simply can't be prevented in dripping brush cover.

A good compass plus some basic understanding of the area is essential for forest blacktail hunting in the Northwest. These are big woods where a man, once lost, might never show up again. A decent pack is good for carrying rain gear while stump-sitting (but it will be too hot and noisy to wear if you're continually on the move). Also, a pack is dandy for packing out a boned and quartered buck on the day when you shoot one a mile back in some appalling blowdown that prevents dragging out the buck in one piece.

Blacktails vary greatly in size, depending upon region. In California, a blacktail buck will weigh from 60 to not over 100 pounds, dressed. Farther north, the Columbian variety can run from 150 up to 200 pounds, although the latter would be uncommon. Still farther north, the Sitka subspecies again is a small deer.

Blacktail racks are disappointing if matched with the awesome spread of a Rocky Mountain mule deer or the heavy-beamed, forward sweep of a Northern whitetail buck. Spikes and forks are common on blacktails, and 3-pointers are considered very "skookum" indeed. Once in a while, a hunter clobbers a really big, prime Northwest blacktail with 4 or 5 points on a side. This may well be a trophy of a lifetime and should be caped and handled as such for good taxidermy work; you may never get one like it in your sights again.

Where to hunt? Picking a general area is the least of your problems. As mentioned earlier, blacktails tend to be underhunted in much of their range. In northern California, Oregon, and Washington, plenty of federal forests and timber-company lands are open to all comers who behave themselves.

As always, preseason scouting, if possible, greatly enhances your chances. Pioneering a new area, it's a good idea to look up the local wildlife agent or biologist for specific information. In some years, temporary blacktail scarcities existed after die-offs due to freakishly severe winter conditions. Blacktails are not as winter-hardy as Northern muleys and whitetails. However, herds have recovered in places where winter loss occurred a few years earlier. The blacktail's future is bright. Stepped-logging rotations in coastal forest country mean more good blacktail habitat in years to come. The main management problem with blacktails in many areas is overpopulation, paired with underharvest of the deer.

I've been lucky enough to have lived in a variety of fine deer country, ranging from the Lake States to the Pacific Northwest. I've hunted and taken whitetails, muleys, and blacktails. Each has its own charm and challenge. Nothing tests the hunter's woodcraft and alertness like a whitetail in his typical habitat. That magnificent mountaineer, the Rocky Mountain mule deer, requires strong legs, good lungs, and shooting ability from the hunter. The blacktail offers his share of all these challenges. Hunting him can combine the best demands of both whitetails and muleys. That's why a good blacktail buck is my choice of a most-wanted deer trophy.

CHAPTER

27

CALLING ALL SITKA BLACKTAILS

by Don McKnight

Although Alaska is better known for Dall sheep, moose, caribou, and big bears, its Sitka blacktail deer provide some of the finest hunting to be had anywhere on the North American continent. With five-month seasons and limits of four deer per year, it is a deer hunter's dream come true. Where else are 60 to 70 percent success rates common and where else do 15 to 20 percent of licensed hunters kill four deer per year?

This little deer can be distinguished from its cousin the Columbian blacktail by its smaller size and short-legged, chunky appearance. An occasional exceptionally large buck may dress out at 200 pounds, but over much of the range the average mature buck will rarely exceed 100 to 120 pounds, field-dressed.

Antlers are relatively small, few scoring 110 points under the Boone and Crockett system. Yearlings and two-year-olds often wear only unbranched spikes. Branched antlers occur by the third year. Fully developed antlers on a mature buck may have four or five points per side, including a long brow tine (eye-guard). More typically, however, mature bucks carry only a fork on each side.

The Sitka blacktail originally was limited in distribution to the coastal rain forests from the Queen Charlotte Islands off the British Columbia coast north through the islands and mainland comprising the southeastern Alaska Panhandle. The northern portion of the range includes the "ABC" (Admiralty, Baranof, and Chicagof) Islands, where this deer and the Alaskan brown bear are the only native big-game animals (goats were transplanted to Baranof Island in 1923). On islands farther south, wolves and black bears share blacktail habitat, and all four species plus mountain goats inhabit the mainland. Thus a sportsman can combine his pursuit of the blacktail with a hunt for other Alaskan species, and a "mixed-bag" expedition for big game can be a memorable experience.

From 1916 through 1923 Sitka blacktails were captured on southeastern Alaska islands and transported to several islands in Prince William Sound near Cordova. These transplants, and several later ones to Kodiak Island and the Yakutat area, were successful and the species now provides hunting in these areas as well.

Sitka blacktail numbers, like those of most herbivores (plant-eaters) at the northern fringe of their range, fluctuate greatly from year to year. During a severe winter, heavy snow accumulations for prolonged periods result in major losses through starvation, and herds may be depleted by 30 to 60 percent. Several successive severe winters (as occurred during the early 1970s) leave deer numbers at very low levels. These little deer are extremely prolific, however, as demonstrated by a yearling doe shot in the mid-70s by a friend of mind. She was accompanied by a nearly grown fawn at the time and was about to ovulate twin ova—in all likelihood she would have given birth to three fawns before reaching the age of two years. It is not hard to see how deer numbers can rebound quickly when coastal Alaska is blessed with several mild winters in a row.

Stands of old-growth spruce and hemlock along beaches are the key to winter survival for this species throughout its range. Even though temperatures along Alaska's coast are moderated by the influence of the Japanese Current, snow accumulations even at sea level can be substantial. Under the closed canopy of spruces and hemlocks, snow depths are

A pair of fat Sitka bucks and a doe were feeding near the edge of an alpine meadow when the photographer sneaked up. They're scurrying away because the breeze shifted and they caught his scent. On clear, hot days (which are uncommon during the season) Sitka blacktails are drawn to high meadows like this, near snow patches where they can stay cool and escape swarms of insects. *(Photo by Loyal Johnson)*

less than in the open and deer can find enough twigs (mostly from blueberry bushes) and forbs, augmented by summer-stored fat supplies, to ensure survival. It is when snows pile up 4 or 5 feet deep even under these trees that winter losses become extreme.

Each spring, as snows recede with warming temperatures, Sitka blacktails begin to drift up to higher elevations. With nearly limitless supplies of high-quality food on alpine ranges (mostly low-growing herbs), they wax fat by the end of summer.

This generalized scheme of things is complicated by several factors. Obviously snowfall and snow accumulation vary between portions of the Sitka blacktail's range. In southeastern Alaska, more southerly areas receive less snow than those farther north. Islands along the outer coast, because of the influence of ocean temperatures, receive less snow than islands farther east. Deer herds at Yakutat and on the islands of Prince William Sound are heavily impacted by deep snows.

On some islands and much of the southeast Alaska mainland, wolves are a major predator of deer. Herds in these areas seem to recover from population lows more slowly than those on islands where wolves are not found. In addition, clear-cut logging practices on national forest lands in southeastern Alaska have had a detrimental impact on the area's deer herds. Timber removal results in increased browse production, but during the critical winter months all food may be covered with snow. The dependence of these deer on old-growth, beach-fringe timber—which is attractive to the timber industry—is their biggest problem for the future.

Sitka blacktails are small by comparison with other mule deer. This one, taken on a warm, typically misty day, was light enough for an easy drag to the beach. But even a 100-pound buck like this will provide plenty of fine venison. *(Photo by Loyal Johnson)*

Although annual deer-hunting seasons and limits in Alaska vary somewhat because of fluctuations in deer numbers, generally speaking the hunter can expect open seasons somewhere in the state anytime between August 1 and December 31. Limits over much of its range are four deer per year, with both bucks and does legal after September 15.

During August and early September most large bucks are on their alpine summer ranges and the hunter must plan on at least an overnight trip, hiking to about timberline, setting up a hasty camp, then hunting the high, open slopes. Weather can limit the opportunities to enjoy an alpine hunt—rarely do late summer rains cease for the few days necessary. Timberline occurs at 1,000 to 2,500 feet in most deer country, and with few trails or roads through the dense undergrowth such a hunt is only for those in good physical condition. Many hunters dress their animal and bone out its meat on the spot to minimize the weight they must pack on the treacherous and tiring descent.

Rewards of such a hunt are many. Alpine scenery and the view of surrounding fiords and timbered islands are breathtaking and the hunter will generally see many deer and other forms of wildlife. Because of the open terrain, a flat-shooting rifle equipped with a good scope is recommended. (I'll have more to say in a few moments about appropriate blacktail rifles for the lowlands and in bear country.)

Alpine hunting, although an excellent way to enjoy the Sitka blacktail and his country, is not a very efficient method of meat-gathering, and most of the annual harvest occurs during the months of November and December. As the season's first frosts kill alpine vegetation and October snows force deer to lower elevations, local deer hunters start to think seriously of filling their larders. Beginning in early November, deer are concentrated at lower elevations, visibility is better because most shrubs and bushes have lost their leaves, and the rut makes the animals less wary and therefore more vulnerable to hunting. (To the bear-shy hunter, another advantage is that by this time of the year many brownies have denned up for the winter in the high country now covered by snow.)

The wise hunter wastes little time hunting areas near the beach. He knows that most Sitka blacktails will be concentrated at or slightly above the snowline, moving to lower elevations only as snows accumulate to depths exceeding their tolerances. With each new snowfall the deer will move downhill to elevations where warmer temperatures result in rain rather than snow. As the snow stops and warming temperatures melt accumulations at low levels, deer will push back uphill, always staying as high as possible. Some of the easiest hunting occurs on a morning following a night of heavy snow right down to the beachline. Deer, concentrated along the beach fringe, will not yet have begun moving back to higher elevations; they can be tracked successfully and are easier to distinguish against the white background.

It is also in November and December that the Sitka deer hunter's biggest "ace in the hole"—his deer call—can be used most effectively. Aside from the mostly Southwestern technique of antler-rattling, the notion of calling deer is probably strange to most hunters below the Canadian border. But for some unknown reason, Sitka blacktails of both sexes at times respond spectacularly to the loud bleats produced in calling. Some believe deer come to a call out of curiosity or that it resembles the distress cry of a fawn. I'm becoming more and more convinced, however, that these diminuitive deer use vocalizations as an additional means for getting bucks and does together during the rutting season. Regardless of why it works, calling is a very effective and often exciting means of putting venison in the freezer.

Although a few of my deer-hunting acquaintances successfully call deer using the old Tlingit Indian trick of blowing through a blade of grass placed over their clenched thumbs, most hunters prefer to use a commercially manufactured call or one they have made themselves. For quite a few years one sporting-goods dealer has been selling all of the commercial quail calls he can put on the shelf; these calls produce a high-pitched bleat which is seemingly irresistible to Sitka deer. Some commercial predator calls appear to be equally good. I make my own by placing a rubber band between two notched sticks, then wrapping their ends with friction tape.

The secret of successful calling can be summed up in one word—perseverance. A deer might rush right up to the hunter before he can return the call to his pocket, but it is much more likely to sneak toward the source of the call, taking 10 to 15 minutes to arrive. I'm convinced that calling will work only under the following circumstances: First, the deer has not scented the caller; and second, the deer is near enough to hear the call. The second certainly is obvious enough but therein lies the limitation to the successes achieved by the caller. These deer have an excellent sense of smell, and unless conditions are perfect they can scent you as quickly as they can hear you. Dripping rain and many burbling streams at this time of the year dampen sound, and even a loud bleat can be heard only a short distance in these conditions. I've found calls to be completely useless on windy days, perhaps because the wind wafts my scent to the deer more readily or perhaps because it is too noisy for them to hear the call.

For late-season hunting many, including myself, successfully combine still-hunting with calling to get their deer. By walking quietly with many stops and much looking, particularly at dawn and just before dusk, it is possible to spot deer that are moving to and from bedding areas. At other times of day, when deer are holed up in the brush in their beds, calling will produce when still-hunting is futile. Deer are found in scattered groups at this time of year, so walk until you find fresh sign. Then poke around slowly, with a sharp eye peeled (always walking into any breeze). If this doesn't produce, pick a place with unimpaired visibility in all or most directions, make yourself comfortable, and call. Some people use several loud bleats followed up in 10 minutes or so with a couple more. I use a series of three long and two short blasts. Remain quietly in place for at least 15 minutes, carefully scanning the surrounding area for an inquisitive eye or out-of-place leg or back. Bucks, particularly, will sneak up to the source of the call, figure out they've been hoodwinked, and sneak away without being seen. I've listened to deer work all the way around my location until they got my scent and departed without my ever being able to see them.

On the other hand, I've stood in the middle of an open muskeg, called, and had a deer dash out of the brush right up to me, stopping at 20 feet to eye this strange creature standing on its hind legs. Another time, I walked into an opening, seated myself comfortably on a stump, and called, ignoring the wood-edge through which I had walked on the assumption that no deer would respond from that direction. After about 10 minutes some instinct made me look over my shoulder—right into the eyes of an inquisitive buck standing head-down 30 feet away.

A word of warning to those hunting Sitka blacktails where brown bears are found: They, too, will respond to a deer call. I know of one southeastern Alaska hunter whose throat constricts involuntarily whenever he attempts to blow his

Meager winter browse and heavy snows can seriously reduce the deer herds in southeastern Alaska. As with other Northern deer, their numbers tend to fluctuate greatly from year to year. The three blacktails on this beach are severely winter-weakened, with little chance of survival. This is why management programs are so crucial. *(Photo by Loyal Johnson)*

deer call in bear country. It seems he once had a huge old brownie coming running to his call, and was lucky enough to kill it with one shot at approximately 10 yards. Several years ago another fellow, hunting deer, shot a wolverine that came to his call.

This leads us to a discussion of firearms for use on Sitka blacktails. These little deer are easy to kill, and my favorite rifle for them is a .222 weighing about 6½ pounds with its 1¾× scope. Like many Alaska hunters, however, I refuse to shoot at a running deer, preferring a head or neck shot at a motionless animal. This way very little meat is lost. Unfortunately, most of my hunting is done in areas where there is a possibility of confronting a hungry or angry brown bear. In such areas I forsake the little .222 for the security of a heavier caliber. Several of my hunting companions feel comfortable in bear country only when toting their favorite .375 or .458 Magnum, relying on loaded-down cartridges and head or neck shots to reduce destruction of choice deer meat. I originally did my bear-country deer hunting with a .300 H&H Magnum, the heaviest caliber in my arsenal, but when several years passed without bear problems I reverted to an old favorite .270. This rifle, equipped with a 4× scope and weighing nearly 10 pounds, is an old friend that has killed many head of big game, but its weight makes it anything but the ideal deer rifle in southeastern Alaska. Most shots are at stationary animals at ranges of less than 50 yards and any lightweight rifle of heavy enough caliber to stop a bear in an emergency would be adequate. Because of the constant problem of keeping a scope dry in the rain and wet brush, a receiver sight would be ideal. Those who must use a scope will find several waterproof scope covers on the market. For sportsmen who prefer bowhunting for deer, blacktails offer an obviously great opportunity.

Rainy weather and moderate temperatures prevail throughout the hunting season, and wool clothing, which retains warmth in spite of being wet, is worn by most Alaskan deer hunters. Conventional rubberized rain parkas and rain pants will keep you drier but most hunters prefer to sacrifice comfort for stealth and wear only a waterproof hat with their wool clothing. Footgear most commonly seen is a pair of "southeastern sandals"—knee-high, gum-rubber boots. For those who have trouble maintaining their bearings in cloudy or foggy weather, particularly in thick brush, a pocket compass is a necessary piece of equipment.

Deer are plentiful within easy boating or hiking distance of most communities in the blacktail range, and often a successful hunt requires only a short walk or boat trip. Nevertheless, many hunters prefer the solitude provided by the numerous bays and coves far from towns. Air charter operations, using float-equipped small planes, are found in most coastal towns and provide an excellent means for getting to and from such areas. It must be remembered, however, that in Alaska it is illegal to hunt the same day you have flown to your hunting area.

The Forest Service maintains many rustic but comfortable cabins throughout southeastern Alaska and there are available on a reservation basis for a small fee. Tents are also popular, but they should be double-walled or equipped with a rain fly to ensure dryness.

Perhaps the most enjoyable way to hunt, particularly late in the season, is to use a large boat as a base camp, traveling from bay to bay and hunting new country daily. A variation of this is available in many communities, where local charter-boat operators offer one-day hunts. They take out 15 to 20 hunters before daylight, scatter them along the beach of a secluded bay, then pick them up at dusk. For the modest fee charged, this is one of the best hunting

Though Sitka blacktails tend to be diminutive, hunters occasionally take very large bucks. This one, on Montague Island in Prince William Sound, is an exceptional specimen that weighed 186 pounds dressed. *(Photo by Loyal Johnson)*

The old method of carrying a small field-dressed deer out by lashing it to your back like a pack is a dangerous, even foolhardy, procedure in areas where other hunters may be present. Someone getting just a glimpse of the carcass moving through screening brush might mistake it for live game. In this instance, the hunter was in a remote area where he felt sure no one was in the woods except his partner. After dressing his blacktail buck, he removed the head to lighten the load, make it less awkward—and make it look less like a live deer. Then he headed for the beach and a waiting boat. *(Photo by Loyal Johnson)*

bargains available anywhere. It used to be fashionable to hunt from a boat, cruising beachlines and shooting deer as they were seen. This practice was considered to be less than sporting, however, and regulations were enacted which prohibit the shooting of any big-game animal except wolves from a boat in southeastern Alaska.

Visitors to Alaska wanting to hunt Sitka blacktails are not required to book a guide, but unless they are seasoned woodsmen a guide is advisable. Boat-equipped guides reside in most southeastern communities and many of them take out parties of hunters for a week-long deer hunt at reasonable rates. The multitude of commercial fishing boats at berth during the off-season provides another possibility for a hunt. Chambers of commerce in most small towns would be a good contact for the prospective out-of-state deer hunter. If the nonresident prefers to go it alone, a letter or phone call to any Alaska Department of Fish & Game office would provide information on good areas to hunt, and contact with a Forest Service office would reserve a cabin. Aircraft charters are avalable with little advance notice.

Throughout its range in Alaska, the Sitka blacktail deer is an important source of meat for local residents. Its venison has a fine texture and an unexcelled flavor. Whether taken in high, open country during the early fall or in rain-drenched lowlands later in the season, this little deer offers a unique and memorable hunt.

CHAPTER 28

GUIDES AND OUTFITTERS—DO YOU NEED THEM?

by Jim Zumbo

There are a few locales where visiting whitetail hunters can secure the services of local guides or guide-outfitters, but a hunt with an outfitter usually means a Western hunt—for mule deer rather than whitetails, or for muleys plus other game. Whether you plan a do-it-yourself hunt or hire an outfitter can depend on a couple of important factors. Some of the places where mule deer live are easy to get to, and some are not. If you want a hunt in the high country that's accessible only by horse, an outfitter may be a necessity. Or if you have no idea where to hunt and want the services of a local, an outfitter is the answer.

Each year plenty of hunters put together a Western mule-deer trip on their own. Let's look at the requirements if this option appeals to you.

A sturdy vehicle is the first need. A 4-wheel-drive is the preferred rig, although there are plenty of places you can hunt without one *if* the weather cooperates. A period of rain or a snowstorm can quickly turn nice backcountry roads into muddy quagmires. There are all-weather roads you can hunt from, but you never know when you'll need to penetrate the mountains a bit more to find deer. Much of the best deer country is in the high elevations that might be out of reach because of an inadequate vehicle. Still, you can hunt the lowlands in every Western state and camp in areas adjacent to paved roads. It's possible to rent 4-wheel-drives in the larger towns, but they'll be in demand during deer season and will be expensive.

Perhaps the most important aspect of a do-it-yourself hunt is finding a place to go. That's not as difficult as it sounds, because deer are everywhere. What you need to do is find a spot that's better than average. Let's say you're driving west with a couple of buddies and you want to hunt the White River National Forest in Colorado. You've read about the Forest in outdoor magazines and you know it offers good deer hunting. You've never been there before, and have no idea where to start. If you've done your homework you'll have a map of the Forest. From there it's a matter of looking over the map and determining where your vehicle can go.

In most national forests there are paved roads and numerous secondary roads that are graded and well-maintained. Before you enter the mountains you can talk to locals about tips on where to go. The grocery clerk, gas station attendant, or barber might not tell you his favorite spot, but he can suggest a general area where you can begin looking.

A concentration of hunters is a clue that you're in good deer country. It might be wise to camp near other hunters so you

A well-supplied camp operated by a good outfitter is a blessing in some of the more remote Western deer country. Here, a party of hunters enjoys a hearty pre-dawn breakfast at a table in the roomy, stove-warmed dining tent of an efficient base camp.

Where a string of trail horses and pack horses is needed, most hunters require the services of a guide-outfitter. A ride into the wilderness adds enormously to the enjoyment of the hunt, but it's wise to practice your horsemanship and get into good physical condition beforehand. *(Courtesy of Montana Department of Fish, Wildlife and Parks)*

can exchange information around an evening campfire.

There are dozens of national forests in mule deer country. All offer hunting opportunities, some better than others.

Recently I drew a deer tag in Nevada. I considered myself fortunate, because it's tough to draw a permit in the lottery. I was to hunt a unit with which I was unfamiliar, and I had no idea where to start. The first thing I did was send for a map of the national forest where I'd be hunting. When it arrived, I looked it over carefully and got a feel for the terrain and road systems. The hunt started on a Saturday. I left my home in eastern Utah on Wednesday, drove 600 miles to Nevada, and on Thursday stopped at a Division of Wildlife office for information. An affable game warden suggested two or three good areas.

At an outfitter's camp on Idaho's Upper Selway, the packstring is about ready to head out. Note that some of the horses are loaded with game. It would be possible for a hunter to camp alone in this region, but it could be very difficult unless he had a good riding horse and, preferably, a pack animal as well. *(Courtesy of Idaho Fish and Game Department)*

I drove to one of them, and on Thursday night had my travel trailer parked in a cozy glade. I spent all day Friday scouting, and on Saturday I knew just where I wanted to be.

Besides national forests, there are millions of acres of public land administered by the U.S. Bureau of Land Management. You can walk for miles, day after day, and never see a posted sign. Much of this land is extremely good deer country. All BLM districts can supply maps of their lands.

Setting up your own camp can be a problem you don't want to deal with. You can bring a camp unit with you, or rent one, or base your hunt out of a motel. In plenty of areas, it's possible to get into deer country each day from a motel.

Now then, how about an outfitter? What can he do for you? The most obvious

A hunter examines the rack of a good Montana muley he has just taken, while a partner looks on. If you roam around country like this without a guide, it's best to have a well supplied 4-wheel-drive vehicle, a backpack, maps and a compass, and some prior knowledge of places to be hunted. You can obtain information and tips from local residents, conservation officers, and state agencies.

advantage is his ability to put you into good deer country and guide you. He knows the territory, and he should be able to offer you a reasonably good chance of getting a shot at a buck, though there's never a guarantee. Besides transporting you to the hunting spot, he'll give you a place to sleep, feed you, and get your deer back to camp or wherever it needs to go.

A big question, if you decide to hire an outfitter, is which one to book a hunt with. The best deer states have hundreds of outfitters to choose from. Most are good, reliable people, but there are enough cheaters out there to make you wary. To start with, most outfitters offer references. Ask for a list, but don't write to the hunters. You'll get more information on the telephone.

You can look over outfitter ads in outdoor magazines, or you can contact the outfitter's association in each state. Home offices for these organizations change continually. For a current address, write to the game department. Some outfitter associations have brochures listing all the members.

If you're still confused, you can book a hunt with a hunting consultant or booking agent. There are several who will take care of your needs. All you do is contact the agent, tell him the type of hunt you have in mind, and he'll arrange a hunt for you with an outfitter who offers the kind of hunt you're looking for. I know of only two reliable ways to find a good booking agent. The first and easiest is simply to get lucky—that is, to hear about a good one from an acquaintance who has arranged a hunt this way. The second is to read the advertisements in the various hunting publications. Pick a few ads that offer what you're looking for, contact the agents, compare their services, prices, and hunting locales—and, again, check their references.

I work a great deal through Jack Atcheson of Butte, Montana, who is one of the biggest booking agents in the country. Atcheson handles all the details of the hunt, and sees to it that everything is in order. As a businessman he can't afford to work with marginal outfitters, so he screens them and selects the best. You don't pay extra to book through an agent, since the commission is built into the hunt and the price is the same if you deal directly with the outfitter.

How much to pay for a hunt? Nowadays, figure an average of $200 to $300 per day, though the cost could be higher or lower depending on the outfitter. Most deer hunts run five, seven, or 10 days.

If you book with an outfitter, be sure he knows what you have in mind. If you want one guide to yourself, make your wishes known before the hunt; otherwise you might find there is one guide for every two hunters. If you have any physical problems, tell the outfitter. The last thing you want is to have an ailment while you're in the boonies. Be sure to sign a contract when you book, so that all the details are spelled out. You'll probably be expected to pay a 30 to 50 percent deposit when you book the hunt, with the remainder payable when you arrive.

Some of the best outfitters are booked a year in advance, so don't delay when you've decided to make your dream hunt. Many hunters book for the next season as soon as they complete a hunt.

Obtaining a deer permit isn't always easy. Some states, such as Idaho and Montana, offer a quota on a first-come, first-served basis. Wyoming, Arizona, and Nevada conduct a lottery draw. Some states set early deadlines for applications. Wyoming, for example, has a March 15 application deadline for nonresidents. When you decide on your hunt, write to the game department immediately for information.

The decision to hunt on your own or with an outfitter depends on you. There are plenty of mule deer out there. You must choose the type of hunt you want and can afford.

Appendices

APPENDIX

1

DISTRIBUTION OF WHITETAIL DEER AND MULE DEER

by Robert Elman

More than 20 million deer—perhaps many more—inhabit the United States and Canada. Among the 17 whitetail subspecies described by Leonard Lee Rue in Chapter 21, there are a few that survive only in small numbers and have a severely limited geographic range; but most of the 17 races are showing dramatic increases in their populations and are also expanding their range, colonizing new habitat. The various subspecies of mule deer (7 races according to some biologists, 9 or 11 according to others) total more than 8 million animals. A very conservative estimate places whitetail populations at well over 11 million, so it's reasonable to assume a combined total of more than 20 million. Some authorities believe those figures are too low, especially with regard to the whitetails.

The estimates fluctuate from region to region and from year to year, of course, depending on such factors as the severity of winter, competition from other species for the available food and cover—even animals as small as the gray squirrel affect the availability of mast and browse—and the destruction or improvement and occasional expansion of habitat. Sharp or continuing increases in deer population are not always desirable, however. A population higher than the local habitat's carrying capacity eventually results in overbrowsing, excessive predation, crowding, malnutrition, birth defects, and so forth. Ultimately such a population may plummet disastrously, as in the famous case of the Kaibab mule deer many years ago. Or the deer may simply become

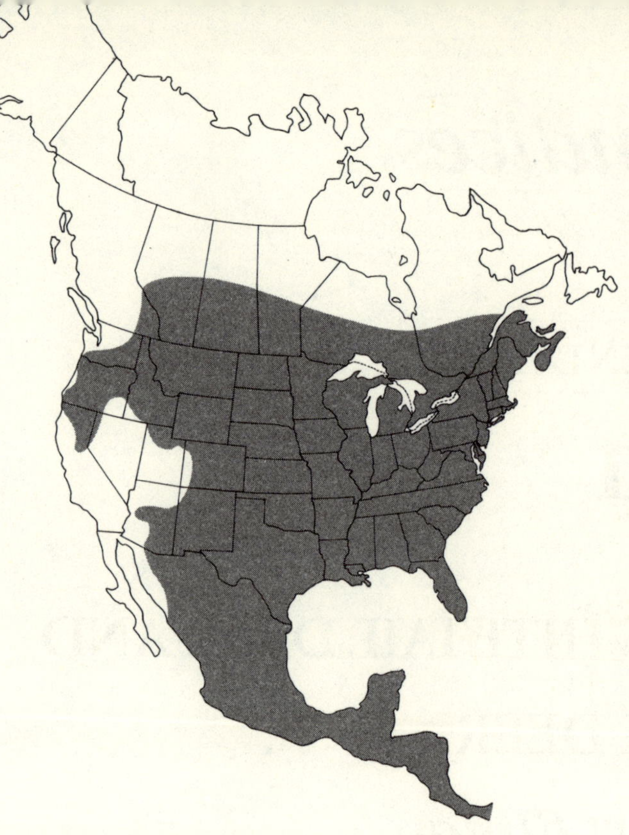

WHITETAIL DISTRIBUTION
(Odocoileus virginianus)
The shaded portion of the map shows the primary range of whitetail deer. Of 30 recognized subspecies distributed across the continent from central Canada to Panama, 17 inhabit Canada and the United States. There are some whitetails in every contiguous state. Even in the Western regions that appear barren on the map, the fringes of the whitetail range are expanding. All the same, these deer are scarce in Oregon, southwestern Idaho, and northern Arizona, and scarce or absent in large parts of Washington, California, Nevada, Utah, and Colorado. Elsewhere in the West, whitetail hunting can be excellent; for more information, see the chapter on Western whitetail hunting. In parts of the Southeast, the populations are so high that extended seasons and very liberal bag limits are the rule; in some upper Eastern states, recent years have seen the introduction of an unprecedented number of special seasons and/or extra-deer permits. See Appendix 4 for details concerning specific states.

stunted and unhealthy, a condition that can be seen now in some of the Northeastern whitetail herds.

It is also true that in several regions the deer—particularly muleys—suffered a serious decline in the mid-1970s. During this decline, seasons were shortened, doe seasons were severely reduced or eliminated in some areas, and some of the multiple bag limits were reduced to one deer perseason. Bits of the traditional deer range have been sacrificed to man's activities, including just about everything from livestock grazing to highway building. Yet even during the decline of the '70s, at least one subspecies, the Columbian blacktail (*Odocoileus hemionus columbianus*), increased its numbers and its range.

Happily, mule deer of other races are now showing dramatic increases in every state. Antlerless hunts have been reinstated in many areas to keep herds trimmed to the carrying capacity of their habitat, and annual harvests are at record levels.

The number and complexity of whitetail subspecies merited a separate chapter by Leonard Lee Rue (see Chapter 21). A few words should be added here concerning the seven generally accepted subspecies of mule deer.

The Rocky Mountain mule deer, most widespread and numerous of all the races, is the one found throughout most of the American West and a large portion of western Canada. The desert mule deer ranges from the deep Southwest down into Mexico. A small population on an island off Mexico's upper western coast is often classified separately, as Tiburon Island mule deer, but is sometimes grouped with desert mule deer. The California mule deer is found in lower California and perhaps parts of southwestern Nevada. Below that is the range of the Southern mule deer—in upper Baja California. Islanded mule deer off Baja's western coast are often classified separately, as Cedros Island mule deer, but sometimes grouped with Southern mule deer. Isolated from the upper Baja populations, at the lower end of Baja California, is a subspecies called the Peninsula mule deer. The two other subspecies about which biologists agree are the Columbian blacktail and the Sitka blacktail, each occurring in a long, narrow strip of coastal range. The Columbia blacktail is found from southern California northward into lower British Columbia. The Sitka blacktail's range begins almost halfway up the coast of British Columbia and extends through the southeastern Alaskan coast as well as some of the nearby Canadian and Alaskan islands.

Generally speaking, North America's deer populations are higher than they were when the land was first settled, and the fringes of distribution shown on the accompanying maps are slowly spreading, although some areas of concentrated human activity within those ranges have been rendered almost barren of habitat. Fortunately, game management has become sufficiently sophisticated so that the future of our deer now appears brighter than ever before. Whether the future remains bright will depend on whether enough of America's lands can be withheld from development and preserved in their present form so that they remain suitable as wildlife habitat.

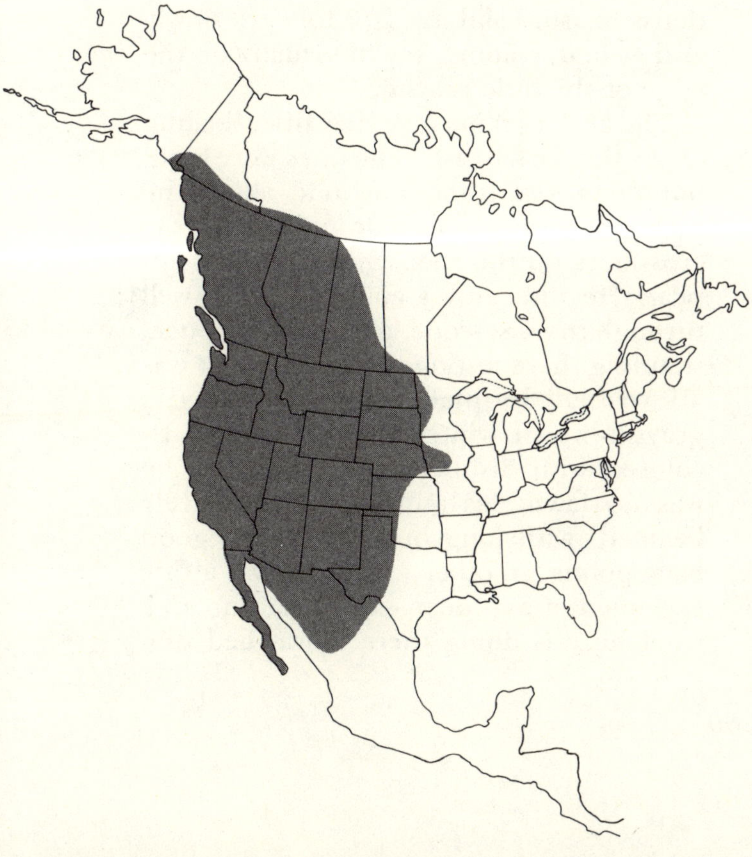

MULE DEER DISTRIBUTION
(Odocoileus hemionus)
The shaded portion of the map shows the primary distribution of mule deer. The muleys inhabiting the upper Northwest are the Sitka and Columbian blacktail subspecies. The Sitka blacktail *(O. h. sitkensis)* ranges from southeastern Alaska into upper British Columbia (see Chapter 27) and the Columbian blacktail *(O. h. columbianus)* ranges from British Columbia down into Washington, Oregon, and California (see Chapter 26). These two subspecies probably represent about 1.5 million of the more than 8 million mule deer. According to some taxonomists, there are nine other subspecies, or geographical races, but many biologists group them into fewer races since several subspecies tend to be very much alike. The various subspecies are of two main types, the Rocky Mountain mule deer and the paler, smaller desert mule deer of Mexico and the deep Southwest. The total mule deer range extends from southeastern Alaska and the lower Yukon down into northern Mexico, including the Mexican peninsula of Baja California, and from the Pacific Coast to the Plains States.

APPENDIX 2

HUNTING AMERICA'S EXOTIC DEER

By Craig Boddington

The shadows were lengthening and I turned up my collar against the increasing chill. I lay in good cover at the edge of a treeline. In front of me an open meadow stretched for 80 yards or so, and beyond that a brushy creek bottom. Most of the watercourse brush was too thick to see into, but directly in front of me it opened for a few yards. There were plenty of game trails in the creek bottom, and all of them crossed that little opening.

A few does and one spike buck had stepped boldly into the open, fed for a few minutes, and moved on. I felt certain a buck of some size would show just ahead of dark. The opening along the creek was getting harder to see as the twilight deepened. The evening breeze subsided and in the stillness I heard twigs cracking in the dense brush. I slid my .270 forward slowly and waited, training my binoculars on the edge of the little crossing.

The antlers came into view first, floating above the dark brush. The tines were high, but there was something odd about the rack. I brought up my rifle and trained the crosshairs on the spot where he must appear. He did, and I could see him well through the 4× scope. He was a fine buck, standing there testing the wind. But it was all wrong. In place of the whitetail's grayish-brown winter coat, he was buff-colored with distinct white spots. Yet he was no fawn; his antlers were massively beamed, with long brow tines and good back points. In other words, he was a fine specimen of axis deer—and I had no idea what he was doing there. I watched him

Craig Boddington measures the antlers of an axis deer. Most significant is the length of the main beams, and anything over 30 inches is considered quite good—anything over 32, exceptional. *(Courtesy of Petersen Publishing Company)*

until, just at dark, he drifted across the opening into the trees.

This was no game ranch, nor had the spotted axis deer of India ever been introduced there. Even so, the answer was quite simple. Texas Parks and Wildlife estimates that there are at least 10,000 free-ranging axis deer in that state today, perhaps twice that many. The first known U.S. release was on a Texas ranch in 1932; since then, axis deer (called chital in India) have been introduced to a number of ranches, with numbers believed to approach some 30,000 today. Like any wild animal, axis deer aren't easy to fence. Over the years, enough have escaped to develop free-ranging breeding populations in several Texas counties, including Bexar, Kerr, Kimble, Gillespie, Edwards, Kendall, and Llano.

The estimated 10,000 free-ranging axis deer make up only a third of the total population in the U.S. The remainder are on private ranches with game-proof fences. The axis deer are the most numerous of our non-native deer, and are considered by most hunters to be the most spectacular trophies. However, they aren't the only deer species introduced from foreign lands, nor the only one which has built up free-ranging populations. At this writing, the other "foreigners" found in

Texas Hill Country has become typical exotic-deer country. This is rolling terrain characterized by brushy patches interspersed with clearings and meadows. It's good terrain for glassing, and is loaded with logical spots for stand-hunting. *(Courtesy of Petersen Publishing Company)*

the U.S. are: fallow deer, sika deer, red deer, barasingha, and sambar. The latter two are found only on a couple of Texas ranches, with little or no hunting conducted. Both are natives of India and are of the *Cervus* genus (round-antlered deer, related to our elk). The barasingha is considered endangered, and the larger, elk-like sambar is definitely in trouble on its home range. Neither is likely to be plentiful enough in the U.S. to offer widespread hunting opportunities in the near future.

The rest of the non-native species, however, are reproducing rapidly and are being introduced into more areas all the time. The primary reason is demand by America's deer hunters. These deer offer good hunting, often at a time when native game seasons are closed. Their venison is excellent, and they are attractive, unusual trophies. We'll take a closer look at each of these deer later on, but first let's examine briefly the exotic-game ranching industry that has brought all of this about.

Unfortunately, the word "exotic" has developed negative connotations when used to describe foreign game species introduced into the United States. Due to questionable ethics, including hunting on very small acreage, on the part of a few unsportsmanlike game ranchers, "exotic deer" translates to many hunters as "fish in a barrel." For this reason, quite a few ranchers who raise these species prefer the

Toward evening and in the early morning axis deer often feed in the open unless hunting pressure has made them wary. These are herd animals; groups of 20 or so are common and aggregations of 100 or more not very unusual. *(Courtesy of Petersen Publishing Company)*

more accurate designation "non-indigenous" or "non-native" game.

Regardless of what name you prefer, we're talking about animals that evolution didn't put here—man did. The obvious question is, why? Hunting hasn't been the only motivation.

The exact time and place of the first releases is questionable with most exotic species. In some cases, several Texas ranches claim to be the site of the first release, and today it really doesn't matter. During the '30s, when fencing and labor were cheap, unusual species such as Indian blackbuck, Indian chital, and North African Barbary sheep (aoudad) were introduced on a few private ranches. The intention, strange as it sounds today, was purely ornamental. These animals were unusual, handsome, and seemed to adapt well to their new home. In other words, they were much like the peafowl and guinea hens that roam thousands of farmyards.

The ranchers who went to the expense of importing them were undoubtedly hunters, or at least very interested in wildlife—but hunting wasn't their object. Later, as the herds grew, breeding stock was sold to other ranches, and still more animals were imported. Visiting deer hunters began to comment that they'd sure like to have one of those axis deer, or blackbuck, or whatever, for their trophy room. When surplus males were available, such a request could be accommodated—usually for a fee.

The exotic hunting industry was born. One of the first, and still perhaps the best-known, of such operations was the famed Y.O. Ranch near Mountain Home, Texas. The Y.O. has remained active in both the game breeding and hunting industries, with breeding stock from there establishing herds all over Texas and other parts of the U.S.

Now, breeding stock, whether obtained from a ranch like the Y.O., from surplus zoo animals, or directly from its native land (a complex undertaking today), is expensive. For most ranchers who raise exotic species, the animals are a business—and hunting them is the harvest. That doesn't necessarily mean the hunting experience is inferior, but except in a few free-ranging situations, it means the hunting will be done for a fee.

It's nearly as expensive, over the long haul, to maintain a game-proof fence as it is to build it. In the half-century since axis deer were introduced, a lot of fences have been left unmended and a lot of deer have escaped to build the free-roaming populations mentioned earlier. To a lesser extent, the same is true of fallow and sika deer in Texas and elsewhere. There are free-ranging fallow deer in Kentucky, for example; and James Island, in British Columbia's Queen Charlotte chain, has a herd of free-ranging fallow deer classed as legal game. But by and large, fee hunting is a fact of life one must accept if one desires to hunt non-native deer.

Depending on the operation, this can take the form of a flat trophy fee payable when the animal is harvested, or it can be a daily guide fee that includes the taking of an animal. Prices vary tremendously from area to area, ranch to ranch, and depend on the species and its scarcity and/or desirability, trophy quality, and services provided.

Incidentally, the prospective hunter shouldn't plan on circumventing this business of fee hunting by planning to hunt some of Texas' free-ranging axis, fallow, or sika deer. About 98 percent of that huge state is private land, and thus virtually all of the free-ranging herds are on private land. Almost all game in Texas is managed as a cash crop, and to hunt the free-ranging exotics one must secure permission from the rancher whose land they're on. At the very least, you must expect to pay a "trespass fee" to hunt. Except in most unusual circumstances, the exotic deer will be hunted either on guided hunts or on private land where you will pay either a trophy fee or an access fee.

How do you find such a hunt, and will it be a good hunt? The latter question is a bit complex, but the former one is simple. You shop just as you would shop for any guided hunt. This includes word-of-mouth from friends who have been there, "Where-To-Go" sections in outdoor magazines, newsletters of the various hunters' organizations, and, most important, the information you'll get if you drop a note to the Exotic Wildlife Association, 1811-A Junction Highway, Kerrville, TX 78028. They have available directories of member hunting outfits and game-breeding ranches, and can provide quite a lot of useful information.

While the heart of exotic game ranching is in Texas, specifically in the Hill Country around Kerrville, those "foreigners"—and hunting opportunities for them—are widespread. In many states, the game department assumes jurisdiction over any deer species, and may prohibit importation of exotic deer. The reason is fear of competition with native deer. In such areas, exotic hunting is restricted to the sheep and goat species. However, exotic deer are found in such far-flung places as Florida, Pennsylvania, Michigan, Colorado, and Hawaii, to name just a few.

Will it be a good hunt? That depends on how well you do your homework, and also what you're looking for. Make no mistake, exotic deer are wild animals. On adequate acreage and in suitable habitat, they'll give you a run for your money—and they may elude you completely. Of course, the key words are "adequate acreage" and "suitable habitat." Put the brush-loving sika deer in a prairie or semi-desert enclosure of *any* size and you won't have much of a hunt. But put him in a relatively small pasture with plenty of dense cover where he can use his natural instincts, and you've got a hunt on your hands. I mentioned pastures and enclosures because, by and large, game-proof fences are a fact of life with exotic deer. These animals are valuable, and the man who owns them wants to keep them. Also, in most states game-proof fencing fulfills a legal requirement in order for the animals to be hunted. Whether that's a negative or positive factor depends on the cover, the terrain, and the size of the enclosure. And it also depends on you.

If you're the kind of hunter who needs an area the size of the Bob Marshall Wilderness to keep from feeling crowded, exotic hunting probably isn't for you. However, if you want a good hunt under fair-chase conditions, it's quite possible with exotic game.

The Exotic Wildlife Association defines fair chase as "hunting in an area, by any method, which provides the hunted animal with a reasonable chance and opportunity to avoid being found by the hunter or, having once been found by the hunter, to escape." There's no sensible way to define the acreage required to constitute fair chase. For example, under no circumstances could a hunt inside a 100-acre pen be considered fair chase. On the other hand, 500 acres of heavily wooded or brush terrain could give any of the exotic deer the chance to elude hunters indefinitely.

There are, of course, differences among all these deer in senses, wariness, and preference for cover. The sika deer, for example, is primarily a heavy-cover species and is shy and secretive. With any pressure at all, sika deer become practically nocturnal. Axis deer, on the other hand, prefer cover that's less dense, with openings and wooded glades. Since, to constitute fair chase, the animal should have the opportunity to use his natural instincts and habits to avoid the hunter, axis deer require a good deal more ground than sika.

It's a sad but true fact that some exotic "hunting" is conducted on very small acreage, and on some ranches exotic deer become quite tame from constant supplemental feeding. Perhaps there are a few collectors who simply want another trophy and don't much care. But to a *hunter*, these are the things that must be investigated before arranging an exotic deer hunt. Whether fenced or not, when the cover is natural and suited to the animal, and when the animal must fend for itself most of the time, and if it has established itself on that piece of ground and is part of a breeding population, then an exotic buck of *any* species will offer a challenging hunt.

When you plan an exotic deer hunt, you should check references before you make final arrangements. With antlered game, a key question is "what trophy quality is available?" You don't want to take an inferior animal, and since exotic deer will likely be unfamiliar to you, you will need to trust your guide's judgment or do lots of homework. But more important questions concern the quality of the *hunt* rather than the trophies—the type of terrain and size of the area, and the hunting methods employed. You want to feel challenged by the game, and you want to feel a sense of accomplishment if the hunt is successful. There are plenty of good ranches and good outfitters offering fair chase in the truest sense. But you do need to arrange such a hunt with some degree of care.

What are these exotic deer? What do they look like, what do they act like, why should one want to hunt them? The most common species, in descending order, are axis, fallow, sika, and red deer. Let's examine each of them.

AXIS DEER (*Axis axis*)

The axis deer, or chital, of India, Ceylon, and Nepal is by far our most numerous non-native deer, with good reason. This mid-sized deer is one of the world's most beautiful game animals, as stunning a trophy as any member of the deer family.

A fairly tropical animal, the axis deer thrives in Texas, where the bulk of the population is located. Other good herds are found on the Lightsey Ranch in Florida and on the Hawaiian islands of Lanai and Molokai. The axis deer is far and away the most popular exotic deer with trophy hunters, and in most areas a hunt for a trophy axis commands quite a price, generally something like $1,200 and up.

The axis is similar in size to our mule deer, although less blocky in the body and with somewhat longer legs. A buck will stand from about 36 to 38 inches at the shoulder and has a short face with smallish, rounded ears. Axis deer retain spots throughout life. The background color is buff, with a blanket of spots on the back and sides and a prominent white throat patch.

The bucks are quite spectacular. Typical antler-conformation is the main beam that curves out from the skull, then back, and pinches in somewhat for the last third so. There are normally ony two other points—a forward-and-upward-projecting brow tine, and a back point that comes off the rear of the main beam about two-thirds of the way up, then projects back and up.

The chief yardstick of trophy quality is the main beam, although the other points and the overall mass are also important. The world-record axis deer had main beams of some 40 inches, but serious trophy hunters consider anything over 32 inches splendid. Main beams of 28 inches and over, given good mass and good length on the other points, are definitely trophy quality. A good buck's brow tines will usually be some 10- to 15-inches long; the back points about 6 to 12 inches. Mass is also extremely important, if not to the trophy score, then to the overall beauty and impressiveness of the rack. Speaking of beauty, configuration is also important. The "bow" to the antlers—the curve that brings the main beams out and back in—is typical of the better bucks and considered desirable. Viewed from the front, this bend gives the antlers a beer-barrel shape.

Being tropical deer, axis bucks occasionally are found in hard antler throughout the year. However, the vast majority of the bucks seem to be in hard antler from about May through October. This varies a bit from area to area, and some ranchers report that the antler cycle is getting later, and may eventually conform to approximately that of the native whitetail deer. Whether that is true or not remains ques-

Craig Boddington felled this excellent axis buck with a .270 Winchester. The .270 is a good cartridge for exotic deer hunting. The antlers of an axis deer are judged on the basis of conformation, mass, length of main beams, and length of points—and this buck has it all. *(Courtesy of Petersen Publishing Company)*

tionable; in the meantime, axis deer offer an extremely pleasant off-season hunt when conventional deer hunting is not available.

Axis are "edge" animals, preferring neither the densest brush nor open country but semi-open terrain with brush and wooded glades to rest in and open areas to feed in. They will browse if necessary, but are primarily grazers. With regard to feeding, therefore, they compete little with native deer. Large herds of them can exist in areas with heavy concentrations of whitetails.

Since they are normally hunted in warm weather—often very hot weather—the primary hunting method is usually to glass clearings in the morning and evening. During midday they often bed down in the shade, and can be still-hunted in cover. However, since their spotted coat offers excellent camouflage in shade-dappled woods, catching them in the open offers a far better chance to evaluate trophy quality. If you have located axis deer in heavy cover, you're far better off to leave them undisturbed and be patient. Chances are, unless spooked, they'll venture into the open to feed just before dark.

Although axis deer are often found in large herds—sometimes up to 100—rutting bucks do not gather harems. Instead they wander alone, searching for receptive does. They do bellow at this time and form scrapes not unlike those of whitetail bucks. The rutting bellow, by the way, should not be confused with the high-pitched alarm screech or snort given by all axis deer just prior to taking flight.

During the rut, subordinate males form bachelor herds while the dominant males roam and breed. However, the herding instinct is quite strong; during most parts of the year bucks and does may be found in the same herd.

Axis deer are not particularly large, weighing around 175 to 200 pounds on the hoof. Since most are taken by glassing the edges of clearings and meadows, the shots can be long, calling for flat-shooting rifle, preferably scoped. The .243 is a good minimum caliber, with something on the order of a 7×57mm or .270 about ideal.

There are many good herds of axis deer in Texas, and large herds on the two Hawaiian Islands mentioned. Many of the

Texas herds are on very large acreage, where the animals are totally free-ranging, whether fenced or not.

A typical example—and perhaps the nation's best herd of axis deer—is Jeff and Fernne Hunt's Greenwood Valley Ranch, near Mountain Home, Texas. The ranch is fenced, if you can call one fence around some 11,000 acres "fenced-in." The terrain varies from rough and rocky to gently rolling to open pastures, with plenty of heavy brush. It definitely doesn't add up to a pushover hunt. The wife of a friend of mine badly wanted a *good* axis buck, and was hunting the Greenwood with outfitter Finn Aagaard. She turned down several acceptable bucks, and it took her four hunts—about 14 hunting days—before she found the one she wanted.

I made a delightful turkey/axis deer combination hunt a couple of years ago with outfitter Robert Rogers of Texas Hunting Services in Corpus Christi. We hunted the deer on a lovely ranch southwest of Corpus. It was in late spring, when the meadows were turning green and everything was in full bloom. We stalked the deer in delightfully cool, open oak woods, and took a very fine buck. But the time of year was so perfect and the country so pretty that success didn't matter much. It was a great hunt, and being some six months removed from normal deer seasons made it all the better!

FALLOW DEER (*Dama dama*)

Second most numerous exotic is the fallow deer, a European species. George Washington imported some for his Mount Vernon estate, and a few have been found here and there ever since. Their exact original range isn't known for certain, as they have been "park" deer in some parts of Europe for centuries—not really domesticated, but kept as ornamentation on many estates. This is probably why the fallow deer has a reputation for being unwary. Any wild animal that is fed, pampered, and not hunted will become trusting and appear less than wild. However, outfitters have observed that "hunter-educated" fallow deer become very smart and hard to hunt. I've personally seen a few free-ranging fallow deer that gave absolutely no impression of being dumb!

The fallow buck generally weighs a bit less than an axis, but is blockier and gives the appearance of rather short legs. These deer are found in three color phases—pure white, brown, and spotted. They are the same species regardless of color, with the same antler characteristics. White fallow deer are perhaps a bit more prized by many hunters, probably because they are so unusual-looking. However, the white color phase is a great deal easier to spot and therefore to hunt.

No two sets of fallow deer antlers are exactly alike, so it's difficult to describe what constitutes a "typical" set. However, in general terms, the main beam comes up, back, and then curves forward. There usually is a forward-jutting brow tine, and another tine or two coming forward about a third to half-way up. The top half of the main beam is distinctly palmated like a moose antler, with points usually coming off the back and top of the palm. This palmation is the single most typical feature of a good fallow rack, and therefore the first thing trophy hunters look for.

The very best fallow bucks will have

Fallow deer occur in a brown (frequently spotted) color phase and a white color phase. This one is an exceptional buck of the brown variety. The high, palmated antlers are characteristic of fallow deer. *(Courtesy of Texas Hunting Services)*

main beams some 23 to 28 inches long, with palms about 4 to 6 inches wide, and plenty of points.

Their antler cycle is quite similar to that of our native deer; they're in hard antler generally from September to early March, with the rut usually coming in October and November. The bucks fight fiercely, and often during this time, commonly damaging their antlers. The best time to hunt them is usually prior to the rut for just this reason; after the rut many of the better bucks have broken-off antlers.

They are normally hunted in much the same manner as axis deer, and seem to spend even more of their time in the open. However, when hunted heavily, they become brush-dwellers.

Though far less numerous than axis deer, they are far more widespread. That is partly due to their long history in this country and also partly due to their adaptability. They seem to thrive equally well in Texas and on British Columbia's James Island. Most of them are in private herds, but there are lots of private herds from coast to coast, and there must be quite a few here and there that have escaped and must be considered free-ranging. For years they've inhabited the Land Between the Lakes area, jointly administered by Kentucky and Tennessee.

I have seen them in Texas where none were supposed to be, and have heard about a small herd in northern California that nobody seems to claim. Most are on private ranches, with plenty of hunting opportunities readily available.

Many good bucks are taken in Texas, and some very fine ones have also come out of Pennsylvania recently. Wherever you choose to hunt, don't consider them "fish in a barrel" until you've been there. In a small enclosure, or where they have been kept as pets, sure they'll be easy. But they can be mighty difficult trophies on properly managed hunting land with good cover and plenty of ground for them to roam. A friend of mine recently had a delightful fallow deer hunt on Wild Hill Preserve in Vermont. This is heavy timber country with moderately large acreage—and he got skunked! Yes, they can be easy, but they don't have to be!

SIKA DEER (*Cervus nippon*)

Although the least common, and physically perhaps the least impressive of the three deer discussed so far, the secretive sika deer may be the most interesting and challenging to hunt. A round-antlered species that is rather closely related to our elk, the sika is very shy and loves thick cover. When hunted heavily, the sika becomes almost totally nocturnal. When pushed, this animal will hold to the closest cover in true whitetail fashion. Normally, though, it will venture into the open in early morning and late afternoon. A sika buck is a tough customer to bag.

Three subspecies are found in the U.S., but they interbreed freely, and probably very little pure stock of any subspecies remains. The chief difference between them is size—in both body and antler. Antlers are shaped somewhat like a miniature elk's, normally with three forward-jutting points off the main beam for a total of four points per side.

Native to Japan, Formosa, and China, the sika deer is now found in several American locales, including Texas and Pennsylvania. It's an adaptable species. This buck was photographed on a snowy day in a Pennsylvania preserve. Some authorities believe that, in addition to preserve herds, free-ranging sika deer are becoming more numerous, at least in Texas. During the rut the males bellow, or bugle. Fights are frequent, and many of the better males break off antler tines during these bouts. *(Photo by L. E. Robinson)*

The smallest subspecies is the Japanese race, weighing only about 125 pounds for a large buck, and with main beams measuring only some 18 inches on an exceptional head. The little Japanese sika is nearly pure black and is a very attractive animal.

Formosan sika are a step up in size, with bucks weighing up to 175 pounds. Coloration is quite different, typically reddish-brown with spots in the summer and more tan in the winter when the spots tend to fade out a bit. It has a white rear end with long powder-puff hair, and antlers somewhat longer than the Japenese variety.

The giants are the Chinese, or Dybowski's sika deer. These are much larger, with a buck weighing as much as 275 pounds and main beams running clear up to 30 inches. A superlative Chinese sika buck will typically add a fifth point per side. Coloration is similar to the Formosan sika deer, but without the long hair on the rear end. Chinese sikas are rare in the U.S., with pure breeding stock quite valuable. However, the interbreeding of these much larger deer with the smaller varieties will eventually increase the antler-growing potential.

Sika are not typically herd animals; usually one finds them in groups of about two

Noted outdoor writer Jon Sundra took this fine sika buck at the Y.O. Ranch in Texas. The length of the main beams is excellent, and the antler configuration—four points to a side—is typical of mature bucks. *(Courtesy of Jon Sundra)*

to four except during the rut. Bucks are usually in hard antler from about September through March, with the rut coming in October and November. Here the relationship to our elk becomes obvious. Sika bugle, and the sound is very similar to that made by the American elk, although perhaps without the degree of resonance that the elk's huge chest cavity gives the sound. Presumably, sika could be bugled in, although I don't know anyone who has tried it. During the rut, the males wallow in mudholes, urinate all over themselves, collect fairly large harems, and fight furiously. During the rut the wallow is an important key to finding sika; a buck will almost surely return to his own mudhole. Sika tend to break their points rather badly during the rut, so just before and during the first part of the mating season is probably the best time for a trophy hunt.

Hunting sika is not dissimilar to hunting the first two species discussed, but generally must be done both earlier and later in the day, more slowly, and with greater caution. Because the sika is more of a close-cover species, the shots will probably be at somewhat shorter range, and certainly the gun chosen should be fast-handling. However, I would still select a scoped rifle with the potential to reach out if required.

Sika deer aren't very numerous in the U.S. Most of them are in Texas, with very few private herds elsewhere. There is, in Texas, a fairly large free-ranging population. Outfitter Finn Aagaard of Wildlife Safaris in Llano, Texas, believes there are a great many more free-ranging sika deer than anyone realizes. Finn should know; his hunts emphasize fair chase, and are mostly on foot. In his company I've encountered quite a few sika deer—some of them on ranches with no known history of sika releases. In addition, several thousand wild sika deer inhabit Maryland, chiefly in Dorchester County, where they are legal game with an annual harvest of about 500.

Even though the sika population is undoubtedly growing, these miniature elk will probably always play third fiddle to axis and fallow deer. That's too bad; they are superb game animals, and are underrated by most American hunters.

RED DEER (*Cervus elaphus*)

The red stag has always been one of the most popular European game animals, and has been successfully introduced in New Zealand and South America as well as the U.S. Like the sika, red deer are of the *Cervus* clan, being round-antlered deer of the same genus as our elk. In fact, they are more than just closely related to elk; they are so similar that the untrained eye cannot easily tell them apart, and they will readily interbreed with elk.

Red deer are relatively rare in the U.S. and are valuable animals. Even so, the similarity to our elk and the interbreeding problem would seem to preclude free-ranging herds from ever being established. Time will tell, but for now there are several very good private herds of red deer.

Similar though they are to elk, there are some subtle differences. Red deer are slightly smaller, with bulls normally weighing around 450 to 500 pounds, live weight. The coat is more reddish brown and there is no rump patch. There is also a significant difference in antler conformation, although it isn't noticeable until a bull becomes mature and grows a fairly good rack. A typical trophy red deer will have a crown of three or more points clustered at the end of the main beam. Typical points may also extend in any direction off the main beam, whereas an elk's points almost always come forward.

In habits, red deer are very much like American elk, with a similar antler cycle. They bugle during the September rut, although most Europeans refer to this as roaring. Hunting may normally be done by glassing and stalking. Red deer are rare enough in the U.S. that a rancher fortunate enough to have a herd probably knows exactly what he has, and any hunting opportunities can be expected to be tightly controlled. Even so, the red deer's sheer size would indicate about a .270 as a minimum caliber.

The European red stag, slightly smaller and often paler than our elk, has been introduced in several American locales. Trophy quality doesn't usually match the trophies found in the better European hunting areas, but American herds are rapidly improving. The stag shown here is outstanding—one of the best yet recorded in the U.S. The hunter is Andy Kranik, and he took the stag in Pennsylvania with outfitter Les Robinson. *(Courtesy of L. E. Robinson)*

There are several small but healthy herds in Texas, plus a small herd on Bill Cox's Eagle Rock Ranch in Colorado. One of the nation's best red deer herds is in Pennsylvania; this herd has been developed by wildlife manager Les Robinson's Ponderosa Hunts, out of Mountbatten, Pennsylvania. This may well be the only place in the country where one can hunt red stag that match the quality available in Europe.

That seems odd, because almost all other exotics do well in this country—often better than in their native lands. Perhaps with time, the red deer will become more numerous. At this point, though, their chief attraction is for the devoted trophy collector. Most hunters will probably have a greater interest in axis, fallow, or sika deer. But whatever species appeals to you, the hunting can be excellent, the venison is superb, and the antlers are impressive and unusual.

APPENDIX

3

FAVORITE VENISON RECIPES

by Lois Zumbo

A hunter's wife is likely to have several problems. Probably the most common complaint is that her husband is away too much during hunting season, always on days when he ought to be raking the leaves, cleaning out the garage, minding the kids, or taking the long-suffering wife to the best restaurant in town. When I get the chance, I hunt with Jim, so maybe I'm luckier than some. But when I'm successful, that can just compound other problems because I have all the more deer in the freezer. In our case, we sometimes have an awful lot of one kind of meat on hand. And come to think of it, the resulting cook's dilemma is one that faces bachelor hunters, as well as the spouses of the married ones.

The most obvious problem is to come up with lots of different ways to prepare that meat. Sure, venison is delicious if the deer has been dressed, hung, transported, butchered, and stored properly. But *any* single kind of food, no matter how tasty, can become monotonous and boring if you have it often and know only a few ways to cook it.

A second problem is what to do with leftovers. And a third is how to fix a really good dinner on a busy day when dozens of other chores interfere.

For a number of years, I've been collecting and concocting recipes. Gather enough of them—and sufficiently different ones—and you can vary the menu so nicely that deer for dinner is never a repetitious bore. While some of those recipes are for roasts, steaks, and the like, others (meatloaf, chili, casserole, and so on) can turn leftovers into a treat. And some will be fast and easy—ideal for busy days.

I'm going to share nearly two dozen home-tested recipes here; dishes that have won the praise of family and friends. You probably have quite a few of your own, but you can never have too many.

BUSY DAY VENISON

3-pound venison roast
½ medium onion, sliced
½ cup ketchup
⅓ cup concentrated lemon juice
¼ teaspoon salt
¼ teaspoon garlic salt or garlic powder to taste
pepper to taste

Place roast in crock pot. Add all ingredients and simmer at low setting 6 to 8 hours, or until done. Serves 4.

CAMPFIRE VENISON

6 venison steaks
1 packet onion soup mix
¼ teaspoon seasoned salt
1 packet tomato soup mix
½ teaspoon garlic salt or garlic powder to taste
3 tablespoons butter
aluminum foil

Dot aluminum foil with half the butter. Place venison steaks on individual sheets of foil. Mix soups, salt, and garlic powder or garlic salt. Sprinkle half of mixture on meat. Turn meat over and sprinkle remaining mixture. Dot with remaining butter, wrap tightly in foil, and cook over open fire until done, or bake 1 hour at 350°. Serves 6.

VENISON SOUP

2 pounds ground venison
4 tablespoons salad oil
1 clove garlic, minced
¾ cup onion, diced
1½ cup potatoes, diced
1 cup carrots, diced
¼ cup barley
1 cup beef bouillon
½ teaspoon thyme
2 bay leaves
1 teaspoon salt (or to taste)
⅛ teaspoon pepper
1½ to 2 quarts water
1 #2 can whole tomatoes

Brown meat, garlic, and onion in oil in large pot. Add potatoes and carrots. Bring to a boil and add barley. Add remaining ingredients. Cover and simmer for 1½ to 2 hours. Add more water if necessary. Skim off fat just before serving. Serves 6.

DEER SOUP

4 pounds ground venison
3 medium onions
2 tablespoons salad oil
1 cup beef bouillon
1 tablespoon salt
1 to 2 tablespoons curry powder
5 tablespoons tomato sauce
1 tablespoon Worcestershire sauce
1 tablespoon lemon juice
¼ teaspoon turmeric
8 stalks celery, diced
¼ cup margarine
1 4-ounce can sliced mushrooms
2 quarts water

Sauté onions and celery in oil in heavy, deep pot. Add bouillon and simmer 10 minutes. Add other ingredients except for meat and mushrooms. Bring to boil. Add meat and mushrooms and simmer 2 hours or until meat is tender. Add more water if necessary. Serves 6.

VENISON POT ROAST

3½- to 4-pound venison roast
1 medium onion, sliced
3 tablespoons shortening
2 bay leaves
½ teaspoon leaf oregano
¼ teaspoon pepper
½ teaspoon salt
4 cups dry red wine

Mix onion, bay leaf, oregano, pepper, salt, and red wine together. Marinate meat in this mixture for 3 hours, turning frequently. Remove meat and pat dry. Brown meat in shortening in large Dutch oven. Roast in slow oven (300°) for 4 hours or until well done. Baste with marinade every 15 to 20 minutes. Serves 4 to 6.

HASH BROWNED VENISON

2 pounds ground venison
½ teaspoon onion salt or onion powder to taste
salt to taste
¼ teaspoon celery salt
dash pepper
1 pound frozen hash browned potatoes
1 tablespoon instant beef bouillon
⅔ cup water
2 tablespoons Parmesan cheese

Brown venison in skillet with salts, onion powder or onion salt, and pepper. Add hash browns. Add bouillon, and water, and simmer 20 minutes. Top with Parmesan cheese and serve immediately. Serves 5 to 6.

VENISON PEPPER STEAKS, ORIENTAL STYLE

1 pound venison steaks, thinly sliced
3 tablespoons olive oil
½ teaspoon garlic salt
1 teaspoon ginger root, mashed (optional)
3 tablespoons soy sauce
1 teaspoon sugar
3 tablespoons cornstarch
¼ cup sherry, vermouth, or water (your choice)
3 scallions, thinly sliced
1 can bean sprouts
2 tomatoes, peeled and sliced
2 green peppers, thinly sliced
pinch salt and pepper

Brown steaks in oil, garlic salt, and ginger root over moderate heat for 10 minutes. Add green peppers and tomatoes. Cover and cook over low heat for 5 minutes. Add bean sprouts, cover and simmer a few minutes longer. Mix cornstarch with wine and pour over mixture in the skillet. Season with salt, pepper, and soy sauce. The pepper steak is done when cornstarch has thickened. Add the scallions 1 minute before serving. Serves 3.

EASY-DO VENISON

2 pounds venison, cubed
1 10½-ounce can concentrated cream-of-celery soup
1 packet dry onion soup mix
2 tablespoons instant beef bouillon
1 cup canned whole tomatoes

Place meat in casserole dish. Add soups, bouillon, and tomatoes. Bake in preheated 325° oven for 2 hours or until done. Serves 4.

WOODLAND CASSEROLE

2 pounds venison cut into 1-inch cubes
flour
¼ to ½ teaspoon salt
⅛ teaspoon pepper
1 cube margarine
1¾ cup beef bouillon
1 cup dry red wine
2 bay leaves
½ teaspoon dried rosemary
¼ teaspoon leaf oregano
2 tablespoon parsley flakes
24 button mushrooms
1 medium onion, chopped
2 packages frozen peas, thawed
3 cups whipped potatoes
1 egg yolk, beaten
1 tablespoon water

Dredge venison in flour and sprinkle with salt and pepper. Melt butter in Dutch oven and quickly brown meat. Add bouillon and wine. Heat until mixture boils. Lower heat and add bay leaves, rosemary, oregano, and parsley flakes. Cover and simmer for 2 hours. Add mushrooms and onion; cook until tender. Add peas and cook until tender. Remove from heat. Stir in 2 tablespoons potatoes. Cover top of meat-vegetable mixture with thick layer of potatoes. Swirl top and brush lightly with egg yolk thinned with 1 tablespoon water. Bake at 400° until potatoes are golden brown. Serves 6.

VENISON STROGANOFF

1½ pounds venison round steak
½ cup oil
1 cup mushrooms, sliced
½ teaspoon onion salt
½ teaspoon garlic salt or garlic powder to taste
flour
pepper
2 cups beef bouillon
½ cup dry red wine
1 cup sour cream

Slice steak into thin strips. Mix flour, garlic powder or garlic salt, onion salt, and pepper. Roll meat in flour mixture, then brown in oil. Add mushrooms. When all is browned, stir in bouillon and wine. Cover and simmer for 1 hour or until tender. Stir in sour cream and heat through. Serve over hot noodles. Serves 3 to 4.

WESTERN CHILI

2 pounds ground venison
½ cup bacon grease
¾ cup onions, chopped
1 clove garlic, minced
3 tablespoons chili powder
2 cups cooked kidney beans
3½ cups whole tomatoes
1 cup tomato sauce
1 cup water
½ teaspoon salt
2 tablespoons flour mixed with 4 tablespoons water

Brown ground venison in oil in heavy skillet. Add onions and garlic, then brown for 5 more minutes. Add chili powder, tomatoes, tomato sauce, water, and salt. Simmer for 2 hours. Add flour-and-water paste and cook until mixture thickens. Add kidney beans and cook another 5 minutes. Serve hot, with French bread or hot biscuits. Serves 6.

CASSEROLE À LA VENISON

1½ pounds ground venison
¼ pound ground pork sausage
8 ounces egg noodles
1 tablespoon green pepper, chopped
1 small onion, chopped
1 cup fresh mushrooms, chopped
1 can condensed tomato soup
1 can whole-kernel corn
¼ teaspoon garlic powder
¼ teaspoon ground oregano
salt and pepper to taste

Boil noodles until tender in salted water. Drain. Brown sausage and ground venison. Add green pepper, onions, and mushrooms. Cook another 5 minutes. Add other ingredients. Place noodles in casserole and pour meat mixture over them. Bake 35 to 40 minutes at 325°. Serves 4.

HAWAIIAN VENISON

1 pound venison steaks
¼ cup flour
¼ cup margarine
½ cup boiling water
¼ teaspoon basil
¼ teaspoon rosemary
1 teaspoon pepper
2 to 3 pounds green peppers, diced
¾ cup pineapple chunks

SAUCE

½ cup pineapple juice
4 tablespoons lemon juice
¼ cup vinegar
½ cup sugar
2 teaspoons soy sauce

Cut steaks into cubes. Dredge in flour and brown in margarine. Add water, salt, pepper, basil, and rosemary, and simmer until tender. Add green pepper and pineapple chunks and simmer 5 minutes. Mix sauce (below) and pour into mixture. Simmer 5 minutes and serve over Chinese noodles or cooked rice. Serves 4 to 6.

VENISON AND BEANS

2 pounds cubed venison steaks
salt and pepper to taste
2 tablespoons flour
5 tablespoons margarine
1 cup hot water
1 4-ounce can mushrooms
1 medium onion, sliced
1 8-ounce can kidney beans
3 medium carrots, diced
1½ cups whole tomatoes
½ teaspoon dried oregano

Salt and pepper meat and dredge in flour. Brown in margarine. Add vegetables, water, and oregano. Cover and simmer slowly for 2 hours or until meat is tender. Serves 4.

SOUTH-OF-THE-BORDER CASSEROLE

1½ pounds ground venison
1 tablespoon salad oil
¼ teaspoon garlic salt
½ teaspoon onion salt or onion powder to taste
1½ pounds cheddar cheese, (grated)
1 cup black olives, chopped
1 small package frozen corn tortillas
½ cup taco sauce
½ cup ketchup
½ cup water

Brown ground venison in oil. Season with garlic salt and onion powder or onion salt. Cook until meat is done. Mix taco sauce and ketchup together (add more taco sauce if you wish). In a greased casserole, layer meat, taco sauce/ketchup mixture, tortillas, cheese, and black olives until everything is in the dish. Add water for extra moisture. Cover and bake at 350° for 30 to 45 minutes. Serves 4 to 6.

SPICY ROAST

5-pound venison roast
¼ cup wine vinegar
¼ cup dry red wine
½ cup chili sauce
1½ tablespoons flour
1 teaspoon Worcestershire sauce
1 teaspoon dry mustard
½ teaspoon chili powder
1½ teaspoons honey
2 teaspoons salt
¼ teaspoon pepper
4 strips bacon
½ cup margarine
2 cups hot water
flour

Dry meat well with paper towel. Mix together vinegar, chili sauce, flour, Worcestershire sauce, mustard, chili powder, salt, pepper, wine, and honey. Rub into meat. Place roast on rack in roasting pan. Lay bacon strips on meat. Dot with margarine and pour water in pan (not over meat). Brown in 450° oven, basting frequently with drippings. After about 1 hour, when meat is well browned, reduce heat to 350° and roast 4 hours longer if the animal was young. Add 1 hour if animal was old. Add more water as required. Thicken drippings and juice with flour for gravy. Serves 6.

STRIP STEAK

1 pound steak
½ teaspoon seasoned salt
½ teaspoon leaf oregano
2 tablespoons cornstarch
½ teaspoon parsley flakes
3 tablespoons sherry
salt (optional)
4 to 6 big onions, sliced
2 tablespoons salad oil

Cut meat into strips ¼-inch wide and 3 to 5 inches long. Place strips in bowl, add seasoned salt, oregano, parsley, cornstarch, and sherry. Sprinkle with salt if desired. Mix and let stand at least 15 minutes. Separate onion slices into rings and fry in salad oil in a heavy skillet for 2 to 4 minutes, stirring constantly. Onions should still be somewhat crisp. Remove to heated platter. Place steak strips in skillet, stirring constantly for 2 to 4 minutes. Add more oil if needed. Put onions back into skillet and mix with meat. Serve at once. Serves 3.

VENISON AND DUMPLINGS

3- to 4-pound venison roast
2 tablespoons salad oil
1 large can whole tomatoes, undrained
¼ cup wine vinegar
¾ teaspoon salt
½ teaspoon rosemary
½ teaspoon sugar
¼ teaspoon pepper
¼ teaspoon garlic salt or garlic powder to taste

1 cup flour
2 tablespoons fresh parsley
2 teaspoons baking powder
½ teaspoon salt

1 egg
¼ cup milk
2 tablespoons melted margarine

2 tablespoons cornstarch
¼ teaspooon garlic salt
¼ teaspoon onion salt

Brown meat quickly in oil. Add undrained tomatoes, vinegar, salt, sugar, rosemary, pepper, and garlic salt or garlic powder. Cover and simmer until meat is tender, adding more water if necessary.

To make dumplings, mix flour, parsley, baking powder, and salt together. Combine egg, milk and melted margarine. Add to flour mixture, stirring just until blended. Drop by spoonfuls into cooking meat mixture. Return to boiling and reduce heat. Cover and simmer until dumplings are cooked (12 to 15 minutes). Remove meat and dumplings to platter, leaving juices in pan. Add water to make 2¼ cups. Blend ¼ cup water and cornstarch. Stir into juices. Add garlic and onion salt. Cook until thick and bubbly. Serve with meat and dumplings. Serves 5 to 6.

MEATLOAF WITH SAUSAGE

2 pounds ground venison
¾ pound pork sausage
½ teaspoon parsley flakes
1 stalk celery, finely diced
½ teaspoon rosemary
1 cup dried bread crumbs
1 cup whole tomatoes, drained
1 egg
½ teaspoon salt
1 cup ketchup
2 teaspoons barbeque sauce

Place all ingredients except barbeque sauce in a bowl. Mix well. Turn into buttered baking dish. Pour barbeque sauce over top. Bake at 350° for 1 hour or until cooked through but moist. Serves 6.

MILK-MILD ROAST

2- to 3-pound venison roast
1 cup milk
3 tablespoons shortening
¼ teaspoon garlic salt
¼ teaspoon onion salt
salt and pepper (to taste)
1 can condensed cream-of-chicken soup
1 soup can water
¼ cup dry red wine

Soak venison in milk for at least 1 hour. Rinse well. Sprinkle with salt and pepper. Brown meat in shortening over high heat. Mix soup, water and wine. Pour over browned meat. Cover and bake at 350° for 2 hours or until tender. Serves 4.

CASSEROLE PATTIES

2 pounds ground venison
2 large carrots, grated
2 large potatoes, grated
1 small onion, grated
2 eggs
4 tablespoons flour
½ teaspoon salt
1 can condensed cream of chicken soup
1 soup can of milk

Mix meat, carrots, onion, egg, flour, salt, pepper, and potatoes in a large mixing bowl. Shape into patties. Fry in a skillet with enough cooking oil to prevent sticking. When patties are well browned and cooked through, place them in a greased casserole dish. Pour chicken soup diluted with milk over meat. Bake in covered casserole dish at 350° for 35 to 40 minutes. Serves 4.

TEA ROAST

3- to 4-pound venison roast
½ teaspoon seasoned salt
½ teaspoon garlic salt or garlic powder to taste
¼ teaspoon onion salt
3 tablespoons shortening.
2 cups strong black tea

Sprinkle seasonings on meat. Sear in shortening over high heat. Pour tea over roast. Cover and roast at 350° for 3 hours or until well cooked, adding more tea if necessary. Serves 4.

APPENDIX

4

DEER HUNTER'S ALL-STATE DIRECTORY

ALABAMA

Wildlife biologists figure there are about 1.2 million whitetails in Alabama, with an annual harvest of about 140,000 deer.

There is good hunting on state wildlife management areas, but competition is often fierce on the best areas. Some of the top spots are the Barbour, Butler, Hollins, and T.R. Miller WMA's, but hunting pressure is very heavy. The Tuskegee, Talladega, Bankhead, and Conecuh National Forests are also good, but crowds will be vying there as well.

Some places are better than others for trophy deer. Try these counties for big bucks: Macon, Barbour, Chambers, and Montgomery.

The best hunting in Alabama is usually on private land, and permission is difficult to obtain. You must have written permission from the landowner, and some of the best places are tied up in hunting leases. If you're an avid hunter, your best option is to arrange a lease agreement.

An excellent place for a day lease is Westervelt Lodge, Box 2362, Tuscaloosa, AL 35403 (205/553-6200). They have plenty of deer, including some big bucks.

Deer hunting with dogs is legal throughout much of Alabama, but some counties allow still-hunting only. They are DeKalb, Houston, Jackson, Lauderdale, Limestone, Madison, Marshall, and Morgan.

For information, contact the Alabama Department of conservation and Natural Resources, 64 North Union St., Montgomery, AL 36130 (205/832-6361).

ALASKA

About 150,000 Sitka blacktail deer live in Alaska, mostly in the coastal regions of the southeast. Kodiak Island has thriving populations, with good numbers of deer throughout.

This mule deer subspecies was originally limited to several islands off the British Columbia coast as well as parts of the panhandle of southeastern Alaska, but their range has increased somewhat and now extends to Admiralty, Baranof, and Chichagof islands.

The season on Sitka blacktails is long, with liberal limits. It's possible to take several deer, depending on the unit. There is plenty of public hunting land, and hunter pressure is light in much of the area. Most of the hunting is done by residents.

For information, contact the Alaska Department of Fish and Game, P.O. Box 3-2000, Juneau, AK 99802 (907/465-4265).

ARIZONA

Two subspecies of mule deer and whitetails inhabit this state. The Rocky Mountain mule deer and desert mule deer dwell in Arizona, with the bigger Rocky Mountain mule deer and the most numerous and popular among hunters. Generally, they live in the region north of the Mogollon Rim. Desert mule deer live south of the rim, while the most whitetails are in the southern mountain ranges, particularly in the Tucson area.

Wildlife officials estimate there are 200,000 mule deer and 50,000 whitetails in the state. Annual harvests average about 15,000 deer, with 23 percent hunter success.

Deer permits are issued by lottery, but each year several thousand whitetail permits are left over and are sold on a first-come, first-served basis.

The Kaibab region in the north is popular among hunters who want a big Rocky Mountain mule deer. Because deer populations are increasing, permit quotas have been increased, but permits are nonetheless tough to draw.

Arizona has several national forests and plenty of public land in BLM acreage to satisfy any hunter. Some of the best hunting is on public land.

Hunters looking for the Coues whitetail should try Arizona. This state produces the most Coues, as well as the biggest trophy bucks.

For information, contact the Arizona Game and Fish Department, 2222 West Greenway Rd., Phoenix, AZ 85023 (602/942-3000)

ARKANSAS

Hunters take about 40,000 deer each year in Arkansas, with a success ratio of about 17 percent for hunters who use firearms. Biologists estimate there are about 425,0000 whitetails in this state.

Some of the best counties in Arkansas are Arkansas, Ashley, Bradley, Calhoun, Cleveland, Dallas, Desha, Drew, Nevada, Ouachita, and Union. Dallas is often tops. Each of these counties can produce an annual kill of 1,500 deer. Some of the best hunting is on leased land, but there's good public hunting on several state wildlife management areas. Some of them are the White Rock, Poison Springs, Muddy Creek, Fort Chaffee, and Gulf Mountain WMA's.

For trophy bucks, try the Sylamore and Dagmar WMA's or the White River National Wildlife Refuge. There are also big bucks along the riverbottoms in Chicot and Desha counties.

Hunting with dogs is allowed during special seasons. Check regulations before hunting.

For information contact the Arkansas Game and Fish Commission, #2 Natural Resources Drive, Little Rock, AR 72205 (501/223-6300).

CALIFORNIA

Our most populous state has a sizable deer herd—with several subspecies represented. Blacktails are the most heavily hunted, but there are Rocky Mountain mule deer and other mule deer subspecies.

Almost 400,000 hunters pursue California's deer, but success is very low: around 10 percent. This is the lowest ratio of all the Western states. A primary reason is a traditional buck-only law. As a result, bucks are tough to locate in many hunting areas, especially on public lands where hunting pressure is heavy.

The state has several units that require a lottery draw for a permit. Those units have much higher hunter success rates, some of them 50 percent or better.

Though there are many national forests and other public lands in California, some of the best hunting is on private lands. Permission is extremely difficult to obtain, since most good properties are tied up by hunting clubs.

Nonetheless, there is good hunting to be had on the national forests if the hunter will walk in and beat the crowds.

Rocky Mountain mule deer are hunted in the extreme northeast, in Modoc and Lassen counties. Blacktails range from the coast to the high country of the Sierras.

California offers some very early deer seasons. Zone A normally has a starting date in August. Other zones have varying opening dates.

For information contact the California Department of Fish and Game, 1416 Ninth St., Sacramento, CA 95814 (916/445-3531).

COLORADO

This is the prime state for a trophy Rocky Mountain mule deer. Colorado is by far the top producer of Boone and Crockett bucks, including the world record mule deer, killed in 1972.

Deer are increasing rapidly after a slump in the mid-1970s. Antlerless permits are being offered in areas where deer herds were at record lows just a few years ago.

There are whitetails in the eastern region, chiefly along the South Platte riverbottoms near Sterling and in brushy creekbottoms near the Kansas border. Whitetail permits must be obtained in a lottery drawing, but mule deer permits are unlimited to residents and nonresidents provided they're purchased prior to midnight before opening day.

Where to go for a trophy mule deer in Colorado? Biologists figure big bucks are rather evenly distributed, but a few counties offer a better chance. They are Dolores, San Miguel, Grand, Eagle, and Summit.

There are several national forests that offer plenty of public hunting. The Uncompahgre and San Juan are good choices for a hunter seeking a trophy. Be aware, however, that the forests are crowded in Colorado, so you'll need to do some hiking to get away from other hunters.

For information, contact the Colorado Division of Wildlife, 6060 Broadway, Denver, CO 80216 (303/825-1192).

CONNECTICUT

About 40,000 whitetails inhabit this heavily populated state. Herds have been increasing nicely—in the mid-1950s there were only about 8,000 deer in Connecticut.

Multiple permits are available, with up to four per hunter. Special permits are offered for muzzleloader, bow, shotgun, and state and private lands.

On state lands, the only legal firearms are shotguns with rifled slugs. However, private landowners may allow hunters to use a rifle; the caliber must be larger than 6mm. There are 131,000 acres of state lands for deer hunting, but permits must be obtained in a lottery. The law allows each hunter to apply for four state areas—there are 23 in all. Top areas are the Housatonic, Pachaug, Meshomasic, and Salmon River State Forests.

Big bucks are taken throughout the state, but the northwest region is generally considered the best. This region includes part of the Berkshire Mountain range. Litchfield County is tops. Another good area is in the northeast-central region bordering Massachusetts.

For information, contact the Connecticut Department of Environmental Protection, State Office Building, 165 Capitol Ave., Hartford, CT 06115 (203/566-4683).

DELAWARE

Delaware has about 8,000 whitetails on some 1,000 square miles of deer habitat. About 2,000 deer are killed annually, most of them less than two years old. Whitetails have excellent feed and grow large; an average yearling buck is a 6-pointer and weighs 125 pounds.

Deer are distributed pretty evenly throughout the state, although the heaviest harvest is along the Maryland/Delaware border where hunting is most popular. Marshes in the east hold deer, but access is difficult because of the wet terrain. The central region is intensely cultivated, with little deer cover.

About 50,000 acres of public land are open to deer hunting. The Little Creek, Norman G. Wilder, and Blackiston Wildlife Management Areas allow unrestricted deer hunting. The Woodland Beach Wildlife Area and Logan land tract at Little Creek require daily drawings for access.

The lightest hunting pressure is in Sussex County, which has a good whitetail population.

For more information, contact the Delaware Division of Fish and Wildlife, Tatnall Building, Box 1401, Dover, DE 19901 (302/736-4431).

FLORIDA

Wildlife officials in Florida figure there are about 650,000 whitetails in the state. Each fall, hunters take about 65,000 deer, scoring a success ratio of about 30 percent.

Deer are often on the small side because of poor habitat conditions. A 100-pound deer is about average.

There is good hunting on private land, but permission is not easy to obtain. Many hunters look to the state wildlife management areas that offer public hunting. On the best WMA's you need the luck of the draw, because a lottery determines who gets a permit. Although competition is keen for the best areas, the less popular areas offer a good chance of getting a permit.

A top WMA is Joe Budd in Gadsden County. Wildlife officials figure this WMA has an amazing rate of one deer per 10 acres. Other WMA's with good reputations are Bull Creek, Green Swamp, and Camp Blanding.

The biggest bucks come from the northern region, in the counties of Leon, Jefferson, and Jackson. Public areas that offer a chance at a dandy buck are Apalachee, St. Regis, and La Floresta Perdida WMA's.

The Ocala National Forest has slipped a bit in terms of deer harvest, and new regulations have been enacted. These include dog hunting restrictions and special quotas.

For information, contact the Florida Game and Fresh Water Fish Commission, 620 South Meridian St., Tallahassee, FL 32301 (904/488-1960).

GEORGIA

With a population of more than 750,000 whitetails, Georgia is a prime deer hunting state. Hunters take a consistent harvest of about 120,000 deer annually. Good forage is responsible for the healthy deer herd.

The coastal preserves at Ossabaw and Sapelo Islands have high densities of deer. Hunting by permit only is often outstanding, with hunter success as high as 70 percent recently. Other superb areas are Jasper, Greene, Oglethorpe, Talbot, and Wilkes counties. For good public hunting, try the B.F. Grant, Cedar Creek, Clark Hill, Ocmulgee, and Rum Creek areas.

If you want a shot at a big buck, give the western Piedmont region a go. You won't find as many deer, but they'll be bigger. The counties of Troup, Heard, Meriwether, Spalding, Coweta, Pike, and Upson are all good. In the northern region, try the Chattahoochee National Forest for a big buck.

Hunting with dogs is allowed, but there are restrictions.

For information, contact the Georgia Department of Natural Resources, 270 Washington Street Southwest, Atlanta, GA 30334 (404/656-3530).

IDAHO

This state offers very good hunting for Rocky Mountain mule deer and whitetails. Biologists estimate there are about 250,000 deer in the state. Whitetails dwell in the long, slender region known as the Panhandle, while mule deer inhabit most of the state.

Average hunter harvests run around 50,000 deer annually, with mule deer, the more popular species, comprising most of the harvest.

Most mule deer hunting occurs south of the Salmon River, which runs from east to west across the state. There is good hunting in the Salmon River drainage itself, as well as in the Snake River and its drainages.

For trophy hunting, the area near Soda

Springs in the southeast is best. The Caribou, Wasatch, and Sawtooth National Forests have long been known for big bucks.

There are 10 national forests to hunt in Idaho, as well as large tracts of public land managed by the Bureau of Land Management. In some backcountry units there are early September hunts. These are good opportunities for big bucks.

Resident deer permits are unlimited in Idaho, but nonresidents must buy tags on a first-come, first-served basis. The state reserves a quota of 10,500.

For information, contact the Idaho Fish and Game Department, 600 South Walnut, Box 25, Boise, ID 83707 (208/334-3700).

ILLINOIS

During a normal year, some 80,000 Illinois hunters kill about 20,000 whitetails, for a success ratio of about 25 percent. Hunting seasons are short—generally consisting of two three-day periods.

The best hunting occurs on the Shawnee National Forest in the south. In the same area there are four state forests and several conservation areas that offer good hunting opportunities.

Top counties in terms of harvest are Adams, Hancock, Jackson, Jo Daviess, Johnson, Pike, Pope, Union, and Williamson. Broadly speaking, the Illinois and Mississippi River valleys are popular among deer hunters. In the northwest, Ogle, Whiteside, and Winnebago counties are good.

A quota system is used to determine the number of hunters in each county in order to regulate the harvest closely. These counties typically have the highest quotas: Adams, Bureau, Carroll, Hancock, Jackson, Jo Daviess, Johnson, Pike, Pope, Union, and Williamson.

Nonresidents buy a license on a reciprocal arrangement, whereby they pay the same fee that their state charges for nonresidents. The minimum fee is $50.

For information, contact the Illinois Department of Conservation, Deer Permit Office, Room 210, Lincoln Tower Plaza, 524 South Second St., Springfield, IL 62706 (217/782-6302).

INDIANA

This state attracts plenty of interest from bow and muzzleloading hunters, as well as shotgun hunters. During a recent season, about 90,000 shotgunners, 40,000 bowhunters, and 23,000 muzzleloaders tried for a deer in Indiana. They killed a total of 18,000 whitetails. Interestingly, hunters who used muzzleloaders had slightly higher success ratio than those who used shotguns. What's more, the primitive hunters are taking their deer in half the time it took them a few years back.

Indiana deer regions consist of zones. The best is Zone 6, which recently produced about 35 percent of the state's total harvest. Zone 2 was next, which gave up about 16 percent of the whitetails taken. Next came Zone 1, followed by Zones 7, 5, 4, and 3.

The southern part of Indiana provides the most deer, and is very popular among hunters. Some of the biggest bucks are in the south as well, largely because winter die-offs and nutritional deficits aren't problems. Most trophy bucks come from riverbottoms and brushy stream areas. Counties that have produced trophy racks are Pike, Jefferson, Perry, Spencer, and Sullivan, all in the south.

For information, contact the Indiana Division of Fish and Wildlife, 608 State Office Building, Indianapolis, IN 46204 (317/232-4087).

IOWA

Deer are present in every Iowa county, with most of them in the southeastern and northeastern regions. In this state, deer do best in forested habitat, so the large timbered areas have the biggest concentrations of whitetails. The most deer annually come from Zones 4, 5, and 6, yet the best hunter success ratios are often in Zones 1, 2, and 7.

Forested areas attract plenty of hunters, and pressure is hard. Many hunters overlook small patches of cover where wary bucks hide when they're pushed around.

During a recent season, some 80,000 hunters using firearms killed 20,000 deer. Hunters after bucks only scored a 30 percent success ratio, while shotgunners with either-sex tags scored 55 percent. Bowhunters had an amazingly high 26 percent success ratio. Only residents may hunt deer in Iowa.

For information, contact the Iowa State Conservation Commission, Wallace State Office Building, Des Moines, IA 50319 (515/281-5145).

KANSAS

Both mule deer and whitetails inhabit Kansas, but whitetails are more numerous. Muleys inhabit the north-central and western counties. Hunter success ratios in those regions are generally high.

Nonresidents cannot hunt in this state, and residents must apply for a permit in a lottery. Competition for permits is extremely keen in areas that have the highest deer populations.

Bowhunters almost equal the number of firearms hunters in Kansas. During a recent season there were 14,000 gunners and 12,000 bowhunters. Hunter success was 50 and 27 percent, respectively, which makes Kansas the top state in the Midwest for bowhunting success. Bowhunters do even better than the statewide average in Chautaqua, Decatur, Elk, Haskell, Jackson, Nemaha, and Stevens counties. About 1,000 muzzleloaders take to the Kansas woods as well.

Brushy, forested cover is best, with some of the finest country situated along the hills above the Kansas and Missouri Rivers, in the Cross-Timbers area of the southeast, and in the oak-hickory forests of the eastern uplands.

Deer live in a very small portion of Kansas—about 5 percent of the state's total area. Most of the habitat is adjacent to rivers and streams. Trophy hunters fare best in McPherson and Marshall counties.

For information, contact the Kansas Fish and Game Commission, Box 54A, RR2, Pratt, KS 67124 (316/672-5911).

KENTUCKY

Whitetails in Kentucky are on the increase, with dramatic rises continuing in many areas. The statewide population of about 160,000 deer isn't very large, but the herds are growing rapidly. In some counties the harvest has doubled over the last few years. Some 20,000 deer were killed during a recent season, with a hunter success ratio of 15 to 20 percent.

The western farm counties have the most deer. Fort Campbell, next to the Tennessee border, has a very large herd of whitetails. The installation has a primitive-weapons, bow, and gun season. For information write the Outdoor Recreation Branch, Hunting and Fishing Unit, Fort Campbell, KY 42223 (502/798-2175).

For big bucks, look to the region between Lexington and Louisville and Cincinnati, Ohio. Some big racks come out of the Land Between the Lakes area each year as well.

For information, contact the Kentucky Department of Fish and Wildlife Resources, Arnold L. Mitchell Building, #1 Game Farm Rd., Frankfort, KY 40601 (502/564-3400).

LOUISIANA

Whitetail hunting is excellent in Louisiana, and should remain that way. Biologists say there are more than 400,000 deer in the state. Each fall, hunters take 100,000 of them, and the success ratio is very good—a respectable 55 percent.

For public hunting, the following parishes are recommended: Bienville, Claiborne, De Soto, Natchitoches, Red River, Vernon, Winn, and the southern parts of La Salle and Catahoula. If you ask permission, you can hunt some of the private lands in these parishes.

Some of the best hunting is locked up in leases. Nice bucks come from leased areas on the East Feliciana, West Feliciana, and St. Landry parishes.

For sheer numbers of deer, the private leaseholds in Concordia, East Carroll, Iberville, Madison, Pointe Coupee, St. Martin, Tensas, and West Feliciana parishes are best. The sportsman who is strange to the area and is looking for a place to hunt should try these parishes: Allen, Beauregard, Bienville, Claiborne, De Soto, Grant, Jackson, Natchitoches, Rapides, Red River, Sabine, Union, Vernon, Winn, and the western part of Caldwell. Also, the Cities Service, Sabine, Thistlewhite, and Union Wildlife Management Areas are good, as well as the Kisatchie National Forest.

For information, contact the Louisiana Department of Wildlife and Fisheries, 400 Royal St., New Orleans, LA 70130 (504/568-5667).

MAINE

The annual deer harvest in this state runs from 30,000 to 40,000, with some enormous whitetail bucks killed each year. An organization called the Biggest Bucks in Maine Club awards jacket patches to hunters who kill bucks bigger than 200 pounds. More than 500 patches are given each year.

Maine has 17 million acres of woodlands. Generally, the biggest bucks come from the northern region, which is lightly hunted. The southern region gets most of the pressure and the highest harvest. Much of the state is owned by large timber companies, and their lands can often be hunted if permission is requested.

Waldo County usually has the highest deer kill, but permission is difficult to obtain on much of its private lands. Other good counties are Kennebec, Knox, Lincoln, Sagadahoc, and Somerset. These are farmland regions of rolling hills and second-growth woodlots. The northern region is heavily timbered with evergreens, and much of it is unroaded.

Opening day each year is a Saturday, but only residents may hunt on that day. Sunday hunting is prohibited, so nonresidents must wait until Monday to hunt.

For information contact the Maine Department of Inland Fisheries and Wildlife, 284 State Street, Station #41, Augusta, ME 04333 (207/289-2766).

MARYLAND

Maryland is home to about 85,000 whitetails. Hunters take about 15,000 annually, the biggest bucks coming from the Eastern Shore region, where an average yearling weighs about 120 pounds. In addition to whitetails, there are about 3,000 wild sika deer, most of them in Dorchester County and a few on Assateague Island. Whitetails are increasing rapidly in Maryland, and are showing up in urban areas including Annapolis and the outskirts of Washington, D.C.

Private land is heavily posted, but 200,000 acres of public land are open to hunting.

Dorchester County is usually tops in harvest, yielding upwards of 1,500 whitetails and about 500 sikas each year. Allegany county in the west is next, followed by Worchester, Garrett, Kent, Washington, and Charles counties.

About 100,000 hunters, most of them residents, try for Maryland deer. About half the harvest is taken on opening day.

For information, contact the Department of Natural Resources, Wildlife Administration, Tawes State Office Building, Annapolis, MD 21401 (301/269-3195).

MASSACHUSETTS

Whitetails are making a dramatic increase in Massachusetts, with upwards of 50,000 deer in the state. Each year about 65,000 shotgun hunters, 13,000 bowhunters, and 7,000 muzzleloading hunters take to the woods. Rifles are prohibited.

Bucks only are allowed on a regular license, but about 5,000 either-sex permits are issued annually. The odds of drawing a permit are about one in seven. In case you're lucky enough to draw, the hunter success ratio is about 15 percent. Obviously, it isn't easy to take a deer in Massachusetts.

The region west of the Connecticut River is best, with the Berkshire Mountains especially good. Berkshire, Franklin, Hampshire, and Hampden counties are tops, providing almost half of the total harvest in the state.

For information, contact the Massachusetts Division of Fisheries and Wildlife, State Office Building, Government Center, 100 Cambridge St., Boston, MA 02202 (617/727-3151).

MICHIGAN

During a good year, Michigan hunters harvest more than 150,000 whitetails. More than 750,000 firearms hunters take to the woods each year for a chance at a whitetail.

The highest buck kill often comes from these counties: Alcona, Clare, Gladwin,

Mecosta, Missaukee, Ogemaw, Osceola, and Roscommon, in the central part of the Lower Peninsula. In the Upper Peninsula, Delta, Mackinac, Marquette, the Menominee have the highest harvest.

The southern part of the Lower Peninsula continues to produce plenty of deer. Over the last decade, the kill in this region increased from 14,000 to 45,000 deer annually. Prime counties here are Ionia, Montcalm, and Tuscola.

In the Upper Peninsula, trophy bucks traditionally come from Alger, Baraga, Dickinson, Iron, Marquette, and Schoolcraft counties.

If you want to encounter fewer hunters, try Cheboygan and Emmet counties, south of the Mackinaw Bridge.

Michigan has an estimated 1.2 million whitetails. In addition to hunters using modern firearms, almost a quarter of a million bow and blackpowder hunters took to the woods and killed 30,000 deer during a recent season.

For information, contact the Michigan Department of Natural Resources, Mason Building, Box 30028, Lansing, MI 48909 (517/373-1220).

MINNESOTA

Wildlife officials estimate that Minnesota has more than 700,000 whitetails, sought by more than 350,000 gunners each year.

Antlerless permits are issued on a quota basis, while buck-only licenses are unlimited. Harvest figures have been rising—and topped 100,000 deer in a recent season.

The biggest harvest comes from the agricultural regions. The next area for high harvest is in the southeast, where there are extensive hardwood forests.

Deer Management Zones 4 and 5 in the southeastern part of the state have the highest hunter-success ratio, usually better than 40 percent. During a recent season, hunter success throughout the state was about 28 percent. The poorest hunter success was in Zones 1 and 2 in the northeastern and north-central region. Though success figures are highest in the southeast, most of the deer country there is private and permission is often difficult to obtain. There is more public land in the north—and fewer hunters. Hunter success there usually averages 20 percent.

For more information, contact the Minnesota Department of Natural Resources, Division of Fish and Wildlife, 300 Centennial Building, 658 Cedar St., St. Paul, MN 55155 (612/296-3344).

MISSISSIPPI

About a million whitetails inhabit Mississippi, and an annual kill of about 200,000 is reported. Hunter success averages a comfortable 50 percent.

Private lands offer very good hunting, and there are plenty of public areas as well. If you're looking for a big buck, try along the riverbottoms in Adams, Claiborne, Wilkinson, and Jefferson counties. You'll have to ask permission to hunt on much of this land. For public hunting, the Homochitto National Forest in this area, near Natchez, is very good.

The southern counties ordinarily produce the most deer but not the biggest. Try the Leaf River, Homochitto, Copiah, Red Creek, Pascagoula, and Wolf River Wildlife Management areas, as well as nearby national forests.

Hunting with dogs is restricted by season and region. Many muzzleloader, bow, and special hunts are held. The limit on deer is one adult buck per day, but antlerless deer are available in accordance with various regulations.

For information, contact the Department of Wildlife Conservation, Southport Mall, Box 451, Jackson, MS 39205 (601/961-5300).

MISSOURI

Whitetails in the Show-Me State are in good shape, numbering about 400,000. During a recent season, hunters with firearms killed 50,000 deer. Bowhunters took an additional 3,500 whitetails. Hunter-success ratios were 19 percent for gun hunters, 8 percent for bowhunters.

Missouri's deer have rapidly increased their range. In three decades, they spread from their original concentration in the Ozarks to areas throughout the state. In a recent year, a dozen counties each gave up more than 1,000 whitetails.

The county with the highest harvest was Gasconade, with almost 2,000 deer. Other consistent producers include Osage, followed by Franklin and Texas counties. Also good are Adair, Benton, Callaway, Knox, Macon, Ozark, St. Genevieve, and Warren counties.

The top deer management unit is often Unit 10, which has accounted for almost 7,000 deer annually. Units 20 and 5 often yield more than 5,000 deer each, followed closely by Unit 4. Unit 12 is also good.

Certain wildlife areas have special hunts. They include Caney Mountain, Drury, Peck Ranch, Howell Island, Mincy, Swan Lake, Weldon Spring, and Rebel's Cove Wildlife Areas.

For information, contact the Missouri Department of Conservation, Wildlife Division, Box 1748, Jefferson City, MO 65102 (314/751-4115).

MONTANA

This state has an increasing deer population, with good herds of both Rocky Mountain mule deer and whitetails. Mule deer are most popular and are found statewide, though a good share of the hunting occurs in the southwestern region. Whitetails are well distributed and are hunted all around the state.

Resident deer tags are unlimited, but nonresidents must either buy a limited-quota combination tag (which is good for elk, deer, black bear, fishing, and small game) or they must apply for a special A or B tag in a lottery. However, a number of left-over tags are often available after the drawing. The state authorizes 17,000 combination tags which usually sell out by May.

Whitetails are a "sleeper" species in Montana. Few hunters seem to recognize the potential here for big bucks. Consider this fact: According to the Boone and Crockett record book, 36 whitetails have come from Montana—19 typical and 17 non-typical bucks. This makes Montana a top state for trophy whitetails. Big bucks come from scattered locations, although the northwestern, north-central, and southeastern regions seem to be best.

There is plenty of public land to hunt in Montana, especially in the western region.

In the east, some of the best hunting is on private land, but ranchers often give permission to hunters who ask.

For information, contact the Montana Department of Fish, Wildlife, and Parks, 1420 East Sixth, Helena, MT 59601 (406/449-2535).

NEBRASKA

Both whitetails and mule deer inhabit Nebraska. For the most part, muleys are in the western region known as the Panhandle.

Hunter success is excellent, with statewide figures as high as 65 percent. About 30,000 deer licenses are offered each year. During a recent season, about 6,500 muleys and 11,000 whitetails were taken. About 80 percent of the whitetails were bucks, and some 75 percent of the mule deer were bucks.

The top mule deer unit is usually the Pine Ridge Management Unit, but the Frenchman and Sandhills units are also very good.

Holt County is often best for whitetails, with an annual harvest better than 600 deer. Other good counties are Sheridan, Knox, Keya Paha, Cherry, and Antelope.

The best whitetail management unit is the Blue Unit, which can yield 1,500 whitetails in a season. The Missouri Unit and Elkhorn Unit generally produce more than 1,000 each, and Wahoo Unit is another respectable spot to hunt.

For information, contact the Nebraska Game and Parks Commission, 2200 North 33rd St., Box 30370, Lincoln, NE 68503 (402/464-0641).

NEVADA

Most people who don't know Nevada view this state as a barren, arid region with mediocre hunting opportunities. The truth is that Nevada has superb mule deer hunting, with extremely high success ratios. During a typical year, hunter success statewide is above 60 percent. In some units it's as high as 80 percent. Better yet, a big part of the harvest is made up of mature 4-point bucks. (That's "Western count," 4 points to a side—an 8-pointer in Eastern terminology.) In most Western states, by contrast, yearling bucks are in the majority.

About 10,000 deer are killed each year, and the figure is higher in years when weather is good during the season.

Deer permits must be obtained in a drawing. Both residents and nonresidents must apply for a tag. The prime spot for a deer is the region surrounding Elko, but tags for that region are hard to draw because of the demand for them. Each year it's possible to put in for five areas. Of course, the computer might draw one of your least favorite choices, which means you'll have to hunt an unfamiliar area or one you don't know as well as you'd like. You must be prepared to scout prior to the season.

Only Rocky Mountain mule deer inhabit Nevada. Biologists figure about 125,000 to 150,000 adult deer live in the state.

For information, contact the Nevada Department of Wildlife, Box 10678, Reno, NV 89520 (702/784-6214).

NEW HAMPSHIRE

This New England state produces very big bucks. Each year, deer weighing more than 200 pounds are recorded, and they come from every region. About 40,000 whitetails live in New Hampshire, their numbers fluctuating in accordance with the severity of the winter.

The annual harvest is around 5,000 to 6,000 deer, including bucks and does. An either-sex law is in effect, though wildlife officials have been experimenting with a bucks-only hunt in the west-central region.

Finding a place to hunt is not a problem in this state. Many landowners give permission to hunt, and all state parks are open to hunting. The White Mountain National Forest offers plenty of public hunting as well.

The best deer counties are Belknap, Carroll, and Grafton.

While the heaviest hunting pressure occurs on the first day of the season, most deer are taken after a good snowfall. Astute hunters wait for snow conditions before hunting seriously.

For information, contact the New Hampshire Fish and Game Department, 34 Bridge St., Concord, NH 03301 (603/271-3421).

NEW JERSEY

Though New Jersey is considered to be a heavily populated state with much industry and urban sprawl, about 125,000 whitetails are estimated to live there. About that same number of hunters take to the woods annually for a deer.

More than 22,000 whitetails are harvested each year. Hunters take about 10,000 during the regular firearms (shotgun only) season, another 5,000 during the special permit season, another 5,000 during the bow season, and about 1,000 during the muzzleloader season. By taking advantage of the various seasons and permits, it's theoretically possible to kill seven deer each year. You can get two during the regular firearms buck season, two during the fall bow season, two if you draw a Great Swamp National Refuge hunt permit, and one during the winter bow season. If you don't apply for a Great Swamp permit, you can try for an either-sex shotgun or muzzleloader permit. You can apply for one or the other, not both. The limit is one deer in these special seasons.

The best hunting is in the north-central counties of Hunterdon, Warren, and Salem. Hunterdon is usually tops, with an average harvest of five bucks per square mile. Trophy hunters fare best in Mercer County, particularly along the Delaware River. Sussex County, in the north, is also excellent.

New Jersey has about 3 million acres of deer country, but some top areas are posted, There are, however, thousands of acres of public land in the wildlife management areas, state forests, and federal land in the Delaware Water Gap National Recreation Area.

For information, contact the New Jersey Division of Fish, Game, and Wildlife, CN400, Trenton, NJ 08625 (609/292-2965).

NEW MEXICO

Four subspecies of deer live in New Mexico: Rocky Mountain mule deer, desert mule deer, Coues whitetails, and Texas whitetails. Wildlife officials estimate there are about 260,000 mule deer, 10,000 Coues deer, and 8,000 Texas whitetails. Rocky Mountain muleys generally live in the northern half of the state, desert mule deer in the southern regions, Coues whitetails in the central and southwestern areas, and Texas whitetails in the south. The Rocky Mountain mule deer is the most popular, as it is in every state where it's found.

New Mexico hunters take about 20,000 deer each year and have a 20 percent success ratio.

Trophy hunters who want a crack at a big buck should try the Pecos Wilderness area of the Santa Fe National Forest or remote parts of the Carson National Forest.

Besides several national forests and more than 12 million acres of BLM lands, a number of Indian reservations offer deer hunting. They include the Jicarilla Apache Tribe, Box 147, Dulce, NM, the Mescalero Apache Tribe, Mescalero, NM 88340; and the Zuni Tribe, Box 338, Zuni, NM 87327. It's a good idea to write to a tribe long in advance of the season for details regarding fees, guides, bookings, and regulations. In addition, there is the Vermejo Ranch, long known for excellent deer hunting. For information about fees, guides, accommodations, and so on, write Vermejo Ranch, Drawer E, Raton, NM 87740.

For general information, contact the New Mexico Game and Fish Department, Villagra Building, Santa Fe, NM 87503 (505/827-2923).

NEW YORK

The deer population in New York has never been as high as it is in the 1980s. Record harvests have been recorded recently—above 160,000 whitetails annually. Wildlife officials expect that the harvest will be stabilized at 120,000 deer each year. To cope with large deer herds, antlerless permits have been liberal—up to 200,000 during a recent fall season. The buck take is excellent, more than 75,000 annually.

For a big buck, the Adirondack Mountains in the north are best, but hunting is difficult in the heavily timbered forests. Success is not high, and only skillful, experienced hunters score consistently. The heaviest hunting pressure is in the southeast, especially in the Catskill Mountain region. There is also heavy pressure in the western region near Syracuse, Rochester, and Buffalo.

In the Adirondack Region, St. Lawrence County is usually tops. Other good counties are Herkimer, Washington, Hamilton, and Oneida. In the southeast region, Delaware County is best, with a harvest that recently approached 15,000 deer. Other counties with large deer harvests are Sullivan, Otsego, Columbia, Greene, and Dutchess. The central-western region has three top-producing counties—Cattaraugus, Steuben, and Allegany. Chautauqua county is also a good spot.

There are plenty of state wildlife areas, as well as the sprawling Adirondack region and Catskill region that offer public hunting.

For information, contact the New York State Department of Environmental Conservation, Division of Fish and Wildlife, 50 Wolf Road, Albany, NY 12233 (518/457-5690).

NORTH CAROLINA

Healthy herds of some 300,000 whitetails live in North Carolina. Hunters recently took a record high of 35,000 deer in a season, indicating that whitetails are in good shape. An either-sex hunting program, initiated a few years ago, is believed to be responsible for the improvement of the herds.

The Piedmont area is considered tops for big bucks. Alamance, Chatham, Durham, and Guilford counties have traditionally produced most of North Carolina's trophy bucks. Another good spot is along the Neuse River in Wayne County. A serious trophy hunter should try this spot. Northampton County has also yielded some dandy bucks in the past, though they're harder to find there. The Nantahala and Pisgah Wildlife Management Areas offer good public hunting.

If you just want to tag a deer, try Bertie, Bladen, Halifax and Pender counties. Good public wildlife management areas are Croatan, Thurmond Chatham, and Sand Hills.

For information contact the North Carolina Wildlife Resources Commission, Archdale Building, 512 North Salisbury Street, Raleigh, NC 27611 (919/733-7291).

NORTH DAKOTA

Hunting is good in North Dakota, but permits are issued in a drawing and even residents don't get to hunt when the luck of the draw goes against them. Typically, more than 60,000 hunters apply for 45,000 permits.

Each year, some 25,000 whitetails and 2,500 mule deer are killed. The statewide hunter success figure is a very respectable 61 percent for firearms hunters. Bowhunters killed 1,200 deer during a recent season, for a 15 percent success ratio.

The best whitetail hunting is usually along the Missouri River and in the southern portion of the Coteau Hills. Some good counties in the state are Wells, Foster, Stutsman, Bottineau, Ward, and Benson.

Most hunters try for deer permits in the eastern part of the state, where competition is keenest. Bear in mind that there are some management units in the west where all the permits are not issued.

McKenzie County in the far west is one of the best in the state in terms of hunter success—often 70 percent or better. Mercer and Oliver counties, also in the west, are good as well. East of the Missouri River you can expect good hunting in Burleigh, Logan, Emmons, La Moure, McIntosh, Dickey, and McLean.

For information, contact the North Dakota Game and Fish Department, 2121 Lovett Ave., Bismarck, ND 58505 (701/224-2180).

OHIO

About 120,000 whitetails dwell in Ohio. Each year, hunters take about 40,000. The hunter-success ratio in Ohio is about 20 percent, and most of those deer come from the eastern parts of the state.

About 75 percent of the deer herd is concentrated in the southeastern and east-central regions. Counties in this area are in Zone 4, which is by far the best place in terms of hunter success. Next come Zones 1 and 3. (Zone 2 has the lowest hunter success.)

In Zone 4, seven counties are best every year. They are Muskingum, Ashtabula, Coshocton, Guernsey, Harrison, Meigs, and Washington. Usually they produce at least 600 deer each.

Forested regions are always best in Ohio, often supporting substantially more deer than other areas. Unfortunately, some of the choice places are posted, and it's hard to obtain permission to hunt them. However, Ohio has good public hunting, much of it in rugged country. The southeastern part of the state, which has the best hunting, also has the sparsest human population.

For information, contact the Ohio Department of Natural Resources, Division of Wildlife, District 1, 1500 Dublin Rd., Columbus, OH 43215 (614/265-7038).

OKLAHOMA

About 150,000 whitetails inhabit Oklahoma, and some 15,000 are taken by hunters each year. Hunter success runs around 10 percent.

For big deer, Osage County and other counties in the northeast are good, as well as Pittsburg and Pushmataha counties in the southeast. In Osage County, there is good public hunting on the Hulah and Osage Wildlife Management Areas. In Pittsburg, the Bolen Hollow Wildlife Management Area is good.

McAllister Military Depot is the best bet for a deer, though they aren't as large as in other places. To hunt McAllister you must draw a permit.

The Ouachita National Forest is a good public hunting area, and the Weyerhauser Corporation allows hunting on its timber lands. Write to Weyerhauser at Wright City, OK 74766.

For general information, contact the Oklahoma Department of Wildlife Conservation, 1801 Lincoln Blvd., Oklahoma City, OK 73152 (405/521-3851).

OREGON

Hunters pursue blacktail deer and Rocky Mountain muleys in Oregon. There are few whitetails, but not enough to warrant a hunt. Wildlife officials figure there are about 300,000 Rocky Mountain mule deer and 450,000 blacktails. Though the latter are more numerous, most hunters favor the bigger Rocky Mountain mule deer.

Blacktails live in the western region, where they thrive in exceedingly dense rain forests. Many hunters look for them in old burned-over areas or in logged areas.

Oregon's deer harvest is high, often the highest of all the western states. Hunters traditionally kill 100,000 or more deer annually. The bulk of the harvest comes from the eastern region where the bigger and more popular Rocky Mountain mule deer live. The hunter-success ratio is highest in the east, running around 30 percent. Blacktail hunters usually score 25 percent or so.

There are 13 national forests and plenty of BLM public lands in Oregon. For blacktails, popular spots are the Siskiyou and Siuslaw National Forests along the coast and the Umpqua, Rogue River, Willamette, and Mount Hood National Forests in the Cascade mountains. In the east, Deschutes, Fremont, and Winema are top choices.

Oregon deer permits are unlimited, though there are special units that have a quota and require a lottery draw.

For information, contact the Oregon Department of Fish and Wildlife, Box 3503, Portland, OR 97208 (503/229-5551).

PENNSYLVANIA

This is an excellent deer state, with annual whitetail harvests as high as 150,000. Population estimates place the deer herd at an amazing 750,000 animals.

Whitetails are well distributed on 17 million acres. Few places aren't hunted; even heavily urbanized areas are available to bowhunters. Muzzleloading has become exceedingly popular, with about 150,000 hunters harvesting nearly 10,000 deer annually.

The southwestern region has had increasing numbers of deer because agricultural areas are sprouting woodlots that offer shelter and forage for whitetails. The mountainous north-central counties have had more stabilized populations.

Potter County has traditionally been the favorite among Pennsylvania hunters. Deer numbers are high and hunter pressure is heavy. Much of the county is public land, consisting of state forest or state game lands. Elsewhere there are 5 million acres of farmlands under cooperative agreements with the State Game Commission.

Hunters looking for big bucks usually focus their efforts in the area between the Delaware and Susquehanna rivers in the southeastern region.

Posting isn't a big problem in the state, though it's difficult to obtain permission to hunt near urban areas. It's wise to make hunting arrangements long before the season starts.

For information, contact the Pennsylvania Game Commission, Box 1567, Harrisburg, PA 17120 (717/787-6286).

RHODE ISLAND

Our smallest state also has the smallest deer population—about 2,500 whitetails. The annual harvest amounts to about 250 deer.

Shotgun hunters account for the most deer, but bowhunters take a substantial number, and a few are killed by muzzleloaders.

The town of Exeter is tops for deer. Other towns that provide whitetails are West Greenwich, Hopkinton, Charlestown, Burrillville, Glocester, Coventry, Foster, Richmond, South Kingstown, North Kingstown, and Scituate. The Arcadia Game Management Area usually produces the biggest buck harvest. Big River GMA is also good, and a few deer are taken from George Washington, Burlingame, Indian Cedar Swamp, Buck Hill, and Great Swamp GMA's.

There are 32,000 acres of public hunting available on a first-come, first-served basis within the GMA system. Private lands are difficult to hunt because permission is tough to obtain, and landowners must sign your license every day you hunt.

For information, contact the Rhode Island Division of Fish and Wildlife, Tower Hill Rd., Washington County Government Center, Wakefield, RI 02879 (401/789-3094).

SOUTH CAROLINA

An increasing whitetail herd is providing excellent hunting in South Carolina. About 250,000 deer live in the state, and hunters recently have been taking 40,000 deer each autumn.

The highest deer populations are in the coastal lowlands, including Florence, Marion, Sumter, and Williamsburg counties. The Francis Marion National Forest offers the bulk of the public hunting in the area. Most hunters use dogs when they hunt this region.

Big deer traditionally come from the central and western Piedmont counties. These are good bets: Abbeville, Cherokee, Edgefield, Fairfield, Greenwood, Laurens, McCormick, Saluda, Spartanburg, and Union counties. In the northwest, look for a big buck in the Mountain Hunt Unit.

Limits and antlerless permits vary widely with the season and locale. Extra fees are required for hunting on Game Management Areas.

For information, contact the South Carolina Wildlife and Marine Resources Department, Rembert C. Dennis Building, Box 167, Columbia SC 29202 (803/758-0007).

SOUTH DAKOTA

Both mule deer and whitetails live in South Dakota. Hunter success averages an impressive 60 percent for gun hunters and 20 percent for bowhunters.

The state is divided into three major regions: East River, West River, and the Black Hills. The East River includes all the counties east of the Missouri River, which flows through the state from north to south. The West River includes all counties west of the Missouri, except for the Black Hills which is designated as a separate unit.

A lottery system is used to issue deer licenses, and it's tough to draw in all but the Black Hills region. Nonresidents have their best luck in the Black Hills because available tags are seldom sold out.

There is plenty of public land in the Black Hills, and hunters willing to walk away from roads often find much of the forest to themselves. Both mule deer and whitetails live in the forest. If you draw a tag on the East or West River units and don't have a spot lined up, it's best to start early because permission is difficult to obtain in some of the choice areas.

For information, contact the South Dakota Department of Game, Fish, and Parks, Sigurd Anderson Building, Pierre, SD 57501 (605/773-3485).

TENNESSEE

A healthy herd of whitetails dwell in this state, with populations estimated at about 350,000. Each year hunters take about 30,000 animals, with a hunter-success ratio of about 15 percent.

For big bucks, try the Catoosa Wildlife Management Area, the Cherokee National Forest, and the bottomlands in western Tennessee. These counties are best: Benton, Henry, Fayette, and Stewart.

If you want a deer and aren't concerned about size, try the counties along the Tennessee River, such as Carroll, Hardeman, Humphreys, and Chester. The area known as Land Between the Lakes, and nearby

Fort Campbell Military Reservation are both good, but a permit is required.

Though there is plenty of public land in Tennessee, some of the best hunting is on private land. Fortunately, many landowners will give permission to hunt.

For information contact the Tennessee Wildlife Resource Agency, Box 40747, Nashville, TN 37204 (615/741-1512).

TEXAS

This state has about 3 million whitetails, far more than any other state. Each year, hunters kill about 300,000, which is also a higher figure than in any other state.

The catch is access to hunting land. Texans must pay for their hunting, since less than 2 percent or the land is public. Each year, the average hunter pays anywhere from $500 to $1,000 or more for a lease.

Most leases are tied up solidly, but you can buy a day lease or a multiple-day lease in some areas. The best way to find one is to contact a chamber of commerce or a regional state wildlife office. You can also hunt for a fee on one of the large private ranches such as the Y.O., near Kerrville.

A great deal of Texas whitetail hunting is done from elevated stands because of the dense brush. In some areas, very little hunting is done from ground level.

The biggest bucks are in South Texas, but hunting is most expensive there and leases are almost impossible to buy into. Some of the best leases have a waiting list of hunters who want to buy in.

There is also a sizable mule deer herd in the state, chiefly in the mountain country west of the Pecos River. Biologists figure there are about 150,000 muleys. Hunters take about 5,000 annually. The success ratio for both whitetails and muleys runs about 45 percent.

For information, contact the Texas Parks and Wildlife Department, 4200 Smith School Rd., Austin, TX 78744 (512/479-4800).

UTAH

This is exclusively a Rocky Mountain mule deer state. Wildlife officials figure there are a half-million or more of these animals in Utah, with herds scattered throughout the state.

During good years, hunters harvest some 65,000 or more bucks, with hunter success running 40 percent or better.

Most deer live in the northern half of the state, but there are large herds in other regions as well. The southern and eastern regions are recovering from a severe mule deer decline in the mid-1970s, and are producing nice bucks. The Manti Mountains in central Utah are popular, as is the foothill country of the Uinta Mountains in the northeast.

Good spots for trophy bucks are hard to predict for a given year because fine racks have been taken from various places. All the same, some prime areas are in the mountains around Morgan and Richfield and in the Wasatch Mountains east of Salt Lake City and Ogden.

The Book Cliffs Mountains in the northeast were once renowned for deer hunting, and they're currently making a slow comeback. The Deseret Land and Livestock Ranch near Morgan has outstanding deer hunting for big muleys, but the chances of obtaining a permit there are slim.

Utah's deer tags are unlimited for residents and nonresidents and can be purchased during the season.

For information contact the Utah Division of Wildlife Resources, 1596 West North Temple, Salt Lake City, UT 84116 (801/533-9333).

VERMONT

This state supports almost 150,000 whitetails. Hunters kill 20,000 or more annually, at least half of those being antlerless deer.

Top counties include Rutland, Windsor, Windham, Bennington, Orange, and Washington. Other good bets are Caledonia, Addison, Lamoille, Orleans, Essex, Chittenden, and Franklin counties.

There are about 5.2 million acres of public land in Vermont, and private lands are not heavily posted. Big bucks weigh more than 200 pounds and come from every part of the state.

While a substantial number of deer are taken on opening day, some of the biggest bucks are killed after a heavy snowfall. Trophy hunters wait until late in the season before trying to claim a buck, since the rut begins in late November when the season closes.

For more information, contact the Vermont Agency of Environmental Conservation, Fish and Game Department, Montpelier, VT 05602 (802/828-3371).

VIRGINIA

During good years, Virginia hunters take 70,000 or more whitetails. The statewide herd numbers about 400,000 and is doing well.

Public land abounds, with more than 2 million acres open to hunters. There are many good wildlife management areas, especially around the Jefferson and George Washington National Forests.

In the western part of the state, Rockinham, Shenandoah, Highland, and Rockbridge counties are tops for a trophy buck. In the east, try Southampton, Sussex, or Surry for a big buck.

There is good private-land hunting in Virginia. The Continental Can Company, Box 340, Hopewell, VA 23860, has 300,000 acres in top deer country. A modest fee is required for a permit.

For sheer numbers of deer, try public lands in Brunswick, Prince Edward, Buckinham, Appomattox, and Amelia counties.

For information contact the Virginia Commission of Game and Inland Fisheries, Box 11104, Richmond, VA 23230 (804/257-1000).

WASHINGTON

Rocky Mountain mule deer, whitetails, and blacktails all live in Washington, offering deer hunters a variety of hunting opportunities.

Wildlife biologists estimate there are about 250,000 blacktails along the Coastal Range. Hunting takes place from the beaches to the mountains. Some of the best counties include Lewis, Grays Harbor, and Cowlitz. Several national forests offer top deer hunting in the region, and there also is very good hunting on lands owned by large timber companies, many of which allow deer hunting.

Rocky Mountain mule deer are in excellent condition and they number about 200,000. The best place to hunt them is huge Okanogan County in the north-central region. The Okanogan National Forest is a good spot, offering plenty of public land.

Some 60,000 whitetails live in the state, and they are hunted in the northeastern region. Pend Oreille and Stevens counties are tops.

About 50,000 deer are harvested annually, Rocky Mountain mule deer being the most popular. The blacktails may be underharvested in many areas. Hunters seem to avoid them because of the thick cover they live in. Deer permits are unlimited for both residents and nonresidents.

For information contact the Washington Department of Game, 600 North Capitol Way, Olympia, WA 98504 (206/753-5700).

WEST VIRGINIA

A quarter of a million hunters try for a whitetail each year in Virginia. The woods are crowded throughout the state on the opener, with about 70 percent of the harvest taken on that day. The state yields a respectable harvest of about 75,000 deer during a good year.

Public hunting is good, especially on the 1.5 million acres of national forests. Lands near large metropolitan areas such as Washington and Baltimore are tough to hunt unless you're in a hunting club. Posting in the eastern panhandle is a problem as well.

Good hunting opportunities are available north of Highway 60. Top-producing counties are Ritchie and Tyler in the west, Hampshire and Hardy in the east, and Lewis and Upshur in the central region. For a big buck, Tyler is probably best. You can expect the most hunter crowding in Ritchie, Tyler, Tucker, Hardy, Hampshire, and Pendleton counties.

A unique situation prevails in Tucker and Grant counties in the northeast. Some 40,000 acres of good deer country is owned by the Western Maryland Railroad. Local volunteer fire departments sell permits for these lands and use the revenue to help support their fire companies.

For information, contact the West Virginia Department of Natural Resources, Division of Wildlife, 1800 Washington St. East, Charleston, WV 25305 (304/348-2771).

WISCONSIN

A large herd of whitetails thrives in Wisconsin. The animals number at least 850,000. Generally speaking, the top counties are in the central part of the state. During past seasons, almost 200,000 deer have been killed annually by gun and bowhunters. Hunter success runs 25 percent or so for firearms and 18 percent for the bow. The archers have taken upwards of 30,000 deer in a single season. About 160,000 people hunt with a bow in Wisconsin each year.

The top counties for deer harvests are Jackson, Marinette, Sauk, Waupaca, Marathon, Adams, Iowa, Shawano, Waushara, and Wood. Whitetail harvests in each of these counties run from 4,500 to 8,000 deer during good years. Most, however, are composed of private lands, and hunting permission is difficult to obtain in some places.

There are good public hunting areas in Jackson, Marinette, and Wood counties, but hunter competition is heavy. For uncrowded woods, there's plenty of public hunting in the northern part of Wisconsin, which also offers the best chance for a trophy buck. These counties are tops for a big racks: Bayfield, Sawyer, Vilas, Rusk, and Price.

For more information contact the Wisconsin Bureau of Wildlife Management, Department of Natural Resources, Box 7921, Madison, WI 53707 (608/266-1877).

WYOMING

Wyoming has the distinction of having a higher hunter-success ratio than any other Western state—usually around 65 percent. There are about 350,000 mule deer and 50,000 whitetails in the state, mule deer being by far the more popular quarry.

Whitetails inhabit the north-central and northeastern regions, and biologists say they are spreading westward. The Black Hills National Forest offers good public hunting, but some of the best whitetail hunting is on private land. Ranchers often give permission, though some ask for a modest trespass fee.

The biggest mule deer dwell in the Bridger-Teton National Forest and other areas in the western half of the state. The Salt River and Greys River drainages are prime places for a big buck. Other good spots are in the mountains around Jackson and in the region between Cody and Yellowstone Park.

The deer season traditionally opens in mid-October, but some units open in early September. These are backcountry units, fine spots for a big buck. Some require that a buck have at least four points on one side to be legal game.

Nonresidents must apply for deer permits in a lottery, and tags are hard to obtain in the most popular regions. Each year, however, tags are available for some good regions after the drawing on a first-come, first-served basis.

For information, contact the Wyoming Game and Fish Department, Cheyenne, WY 82002 (307/777-7631).

APPENDIX

5

WHO'S WHO AMONG OUR AUTHORS

by Robert Elman

There are so many deer hunters in America that it's probably safe to assume they include a considerable number who are new to hunting, new to this country, or new to the reading of hunting literature. (Or, for all I know, there may be a few who are just plain new to reading.) I have therefore been asked to add a few brief notes concerning the credentials of our all-star cast of authors. Since it really *is* an all-star cast, I can't give anyone top billing. Jim Zumbo, who is abnormally modest for an outdoor writer, has suggested that I tell who's who in alphabetical order. This will be the first time I've taken his advice since the day in Wyoming when he told me to pass up anything less than a good 4-point buck.

L. James Bashline is an Associate Editor of *Field & Stream*, a publication in which his articles appear regularly, and he writes a popular column entitled "A Seat by the Window" for *Pennsylvania Sportsman* magazine. In addition, he writes for a number of major outdoor publications and has hosted several TV specials concerned with outdoor recreation and wildlife. He also compiled and edited one of the finest anthologies of hunting and fishing literature I've ever read. Entitled *America's Great Outdoors*, it was sponsored by the Outdoor Writers Association of America. This volume, now in great demand by collectors, is a celebration of 200 years of great outdoor journalism. Readers know Jim as an expert hunter and angler. I know him as a friend. My only criticism is that when we hunt upland birds or waterfowl together, he too often wipes my eye. Some people are better shots than they need to be.

Erwin A. Bauer (who has never revealed to me why I and most of his other friends are asked to call him "Joe") is Editor-at-Large for *Outdoor Life*, a world-renowned nature photographer, a writer whose works have appeared in all the major outdoor magazines, an avid hunter, a keen and observant naturalist, and a hell of a nice guy. He's also the author of almost a dozen books, one of his fairly recent ones being a marvelous volume entitled *Photographing the West*. Joe often hunts, fishes, and camps with his wife Peggy, and together they've written a couple of excellent camping books. I can no longer remember how long I've known Joe Bauer, but I can tell you he's an extraordinary woodsman. His close-up (not telephoto) pictures of whitetails and mule deer certainly prove he knows how to get close to game.

Craig Boddington, who used to be editor of the *Guns & Ammo* Specialty Publications for Petersen's Publishing Company, is now Editor of *Petersen's Hunting* magazine. A well-known big-game hunter, Craig has hunted extensively in Canada, Mexico, Africa, Alaska, and all over the lower 48 states. Not long ago, he completed a "grand slam" on native American deer by taking a whitetail, Coues whitetail, blacktail, and mule deer in a single season. His knowledge of exotic deer in America is obvious from the information he provides in this book—as well as the photos of his trophies. I got to know Craig through Jim Zumbo, who turned out to be a master of understatement when he said, "That guy Boddington is a rugged hunter."

Tom Brakefield is another outdoorsman who can legitimately be called rugged. He's the kind who never has to breathe hard when he strides up and down mountains carrying a hundredweight of sophisticated photographic gear. One of our first wildlife photographers, he's contributed magnificent pictures to just about every magazine you can think of. Sometimes these pictures illustrate his own articles, for he's also a well-known writer. Tom has hunted all kinds of game, large and small, from Florida to Alaska, and has written a number of books, including *Sportsman's Complete Book of Trophy and Meat Care, Big Game Hunter's Digest*, and *Hunting Big-Game Trophies*. Although he lives up here among us damnyankees, he grew up in the Deep South, and his chapters on Southern deer-hunting methods are based on plenty of experience.

Jim Carmichel is another son of Dixie, and for about 20 years I've been a number-one fan of the Man from Tennessee. Jim has lived in the West as well as the South, but right now I'm not sure he stays in any one place long enough to call it home. Seems as if he's always off on safari somewhere. As most hunting readers know, he's Shooting Editor of *Outdoor Life*, a noted big-game hunter, and a winner of high honors in competitive shooting with both rifle and shotgun. He's also adept with a handgun, by the way. Long ago, when he was working with the Tennessee Game and Fish Commission, I was one of the first editors to recognize his great talent. He told me that if I hadn't bought one of his early stories he might have quit writing and become a wealthy businessman. I therefore claim that I saved Jim Carmichel from a miserable fate. Jim writes books as well as articles, of course, and he's author of an excellent Winchester Press book, *The Modern Rifle*.

Byron W. Dalrymple is a hunter, fisherman, camper, photographer, and writer whose pictures and articles have been welcomed by millions of readers for more than three decades. He's also written a good many books about hunting. I guess he must have begun writing when he was hardly more than a boy, because I remember learning from his articles when I was a kid probing the mysteries of squirrel hunting—and he doesn't look any older than I am. With regard to deer, Byron ought to be awarded a Doctorate of Hunting Knowledge. He was the first man ever to write in any detail about the Carmen Mountains whitetails of the Big Bend Country. He's extremely adept at rattling up Texas whitetail bucks, a technique he describes in this book, and he's no slouch at putting the scope on mule deer, either.

Robert Elman is yours truly, and I'm not all that thrilled about having to write a paragraph on the topic of what a splendid fellow I am. The truth is, I'm the kind of hunter who can tell you in valuable detail what not to do because I've done it. Over the years, I've fallen down slopes, stepped in beaver holes, fallen asleep on stand, forgotten my knife, and gone on a one-shot deer and antelope hunt because I left my rifle's clip at home. Well, it did turn out to be a successful one-shot hunt, and I've harvested a bit of venison on a number of other occasions as well, so I qualify as a deer-hunting writer and editor. Having convinced myself I'm qualified, I've written more than a dozen books and edited others, most of them on hunting, fishing, or other subjects related to nature and outdoor recreation. I also happen to know all these other deer-hunting writers, which was somewhat helpful in compiling this book. It's no bad thing to bask in their glory.

Sam Fadala has something in common with Teddy Roosevelt. Like Roosevelt, Sam was a more or less urban Easterner with a boyhood illness that required an outdoor cure. Born in Albany, New York, he moved out to Tucson, where the clean, dry air and desert sun remedied his chronic asthma. For years he was a teacher, which probably means he's overeducated for an outdoor writer, but he's been eminently successful all the same. His work has appeared in *Sports Afield, Outdoor Life, Field & Stream, The American Rifleman, The American Hunter*, and I don't know how many other magazines. He's also the author of several books, including *Blackpowder Hunting* and *The Complete Black Powder Handbook.* He and his wife Nancy and their children spend so much time camping and hunting that it's hard to understand how he manages to do all that writing.

Steve Ferber tells more and funnier stories than any other guest I've had at Shirttail Deer Camp. Also worth mentioning, I suppose, is the fact that he's been listed in the *Who's Who of Sports* and *New York Times Record Book of Sports* because he's won over a thousand trophies in rifle, pistol, and shotgun competitions, established 16 national shooting records, and (when he was a member and coach of the U.S. Navy Shooting Team) was awarded the Distinguished Pistol Shooter's Badge by the Secretary of the Navy. Even as this is being written, the number of his trophies and awards has probably climbed, because he's been doing a lot of trapshooting lately. His articles about shooting and hunting have appeared in many outdoor periodicals, but he no longer does as much writing as he used to because he's kept too busy as publisher and president of Aqua-Field Publications, an innovative company that produces high-quality magazines about all sorts of outdoor recreation.

Bob Good is Board Chairman of the American Sportsman's Club and publisher of *Sporting World* magazine. I first met him at a conference of outdoor writers, where he was introduced to me as a hunting authority and outstanding handgunner. I've since learned for myself that he is both. He's also a first-rate game cook, as Jim Zumbo and I learned when we were his guests at a Colorado hunting camp. Bob has hunted almost everywhere in the United States, as well as Canada, Mexico, Central America, Germany, and several African countries—yet whitetail deer are still his favorite quarry and he never misses a season. For a number of years, he has hunted almost exclusively with handguns. He's a Field Editor for *Sixgunner* magazine, and his work also appears in a number of other outdoor publications.

B.R. Hughes was, I believe, a simple free-lance writer when I first became acquainted with his work years ago. He's still a free-lance writer—and a busy one—but he's also editor of *The Muzzleloader*, a magazine to which I've had the pleasure of contributing articles on historic firearms. Like the rest of us, he's harvested whitetails and mule deer with conventional rifles; like not quite so many of us, he's also taken those and many other kinds of game, large and small, with muzzleloading arms. He and Sam Fadala have much in common, since both of them are muzzleloading authorities, both are avid hunters, and both have been professional educators. Bill has taught college courses in journalism. I tend to think of him in connection with *The Muzzleloader* and *Gun Week* because he's done so much work for those publications, but actually he's been published in a great many other periodicals, including most of the leading magazines dealing with guns, hunting, and target shooting.

John Madson has taken me bird shooting in Illinois, thereby joining Jim Bashline and the ranks of others who have wiped my eye. I bear him no malice, though. He's a friend, a considerate sportsman, a genuine authority on nature, and one of our finest hunting writers. Several years ago, he retired as Assistant Director of Conservation for Winchester-Western, but—fortunately—he will never retire as a writer. He has written a number of information-packed books on various game species, and his work has appeared in many magazines, ranging from the standard outdoor publications to *Audubon* and *National Geographic*. He has earned a great array of honors, including the Jade of Chiefs Award, the highest honor bestowed by the Outdoor Writers Association of America.

Don McKnight was Research Chief with Alaska's Division of Game when I first contacted him, back in 1975. In a recent letter, he told me he's switched to another job in that agency. "Now," he said, "I'm the Regional Supervisor for Southeastern Alaska (all the better to hunt deer and work at ensuring maintenance of deer populations for future generations of hunters)." Although Dan isn't a professional writer, his chapter on the Sitka blacktail certainly proves he's a natural-born writer. One of the more perplexing problems in compiling this book was to find someone who was qualified to give advice, based on long experience, about hunting this subspecies of mule deer. The Sitka blacktail is so limited in distribution, and inhabits an area so far from the contiguous states where most deer hunting is done, that few professional writers have had sufficient experience hunting the animal. At about the time when chapters were being assigned to various authors, Tom Brakefield had just returned from Alaska and he mentioned that he had met a real expert on Sitka blacktails. As a result, I phoned Don up in Alaska, followed the call with a letter, and in due course obtained the most informative piece of writing I'd ever seen on Alaska's deer.

Norm Nelson knows a great deal about both Midwestern and Far Western deer. For many years he was a Minnesota newspaper editor, but he has now lived in the State of Washington for well over a decade. After moving to the Pacific Coast, he became Resource Information Manager for the Weyerhaeuser Company, and to do that job effectively he had to make himself extremely knowledgeable about West Coast hunting. He's an expert at hunting not only blacktails, but Rocky Mountain mule deer and whitetails, as well. In fact, he's the author of a fine book entitled *Hunting the Whitetail Deer*. When I last talked to Norm, he'd written hundreds of articles for *Field & Stream, Outdoor Life, Sports Afield, Gun Digest, The American Rifleman, The American Hunter, Petersen's Hunting*, and others. He'd also contributed to several anthologies. I can't keep score anymore.

David Petzal is Editor of *Mechanix Illustrated* and Associate Shooting Editor of *Field & Stream*. He has also edited such fine sporting anthologies as *The Expert's Book of the Shooting Sports* and *The Expert's Book of Upland Game and Waterfowl Hunting*. In addition, he's a hell of a shot with both rifle and shotgun. Dave's an old friend whose wry, quirky wit has lightened my burden in publishing offices and enhanced my enjoyment on hunts. When I first knew Dave, he was an outstanding target rifleman and decimator of chucks at extraordinary ranges, but only a casual shotgunner. Several other friends and I took him bird hunting, got him interested in shotgunning, and watched in dismay as he quickly became better with a shotgun than most of us ever will be. Similarly, when I first knew him he put more store in chucks than big game, but with his woodsmanship and marksmanship it was inevitable that he became an outstanding big-game hunter. He has now collected assorted trophies both on this continent and in Africa. He has also taken more deer than I have, for which I grudgingly forgive him because it's a delight to be with him in the field or in print.

Bert Popowski died in 1982. I had known him, admired his vast hunting knowledge, and bought his stories for years. Yet I'd never met him until 1981, for all of our dealings had been by phone and letter. I'll always be thankful that in the last year of his life I visited with him in the cabin he had built almost 50 years before in South Dakota's Custer State Park. He had been ill for a long time and he suspected that the end wasn't far off, but he was as jovial as ever, as full of jokes, good stories, and an eagerness to swap hunting and nature lore as any man could be. It was a great privilege to know him. During a career that spanned half a century, he wrote more than 2,300 articles and nine major books. His first feature story appeared in *Outdoor Life* in 1931, and shortly before his death he completed his last work, a Winchester Press book entitled *The Hunter's Book of the Pronghorn Antelope*, written in collaboration with a Canadian colleague, Wilf Pyle. In 1980, his beloved state had presented him with a special award as Dean of South Dakota Outdoor Writers. It was well earned. Bert was a champion crow caller, a pronghorn expert, a marvelous pheasant and waterfowl hunter, a superb deer hunter, an astute naturalist, a delightful writer, and a warm, gentle friend.

Leonard Lee Rue has probably taught me more about wildlife and the outdoors in general than any other man. Not that he was attempting to clear my mind of cobwebs or that I was searching for a guru of the hunt. It was just that no one could hunt with Len—or even just walk through the woods and fields with him—and not learn something. He's the most observant hunter I've ever been with. Not even a nibbled twig seems to escape his eye, the eye of a masterful wildlife photographer and naturalist. And his consistent hunting success (as well as his success at photographing wild creatures that are notoriously camera-shy) proves he knows how to read sign. His pictures appear regularly in *Audubon* and *National Wildlife*, as well as many other magazines. He contributes a monthly feature on various game species to *The American Hunter*. And he has written a great many excellent books, including *The Deer of North America, The World of the Ruffed Grouse, Complete Guide to Game Animals*, and (with his friend Josef Fischl) *After Your Deer is Down*.

Norman Strung is an outdoor writer's outdoor writer, yet he doesn't do it full-time because he insists on devoting much of his time and energy to being a licensed Montana hunting and fishing guide—another profession at which he's enormously successful. Norm doesn't need my help in providing potential hunting clients with references but, if my memory is accurate, Dave Petzal has taken more than one fine buck on trips with Norm, and he plans to make repeat visits. Norm could just write for a living, but he prefers to put up with a few more dudes and a few less editors. Deer are by no means the only game in Norm Strung's repertoire of hunting skills. He's the author of one of my favorite books—*Misty Mornings and Moonless Nights: A Waterfowler's Guide*. He writes for *Field & Stream, Sports Afield, Outdoor Life, Gray's Sporting Journal, Boy's Life, Exploring*, and others. Sorry Norm, but I'm getting tired of listing all these magazines.

Russell Tinsley is a very fine all-around hunter. Thinking about his career and his exploits, it seems to me almost inevitable that he'd be an expert archer. Long, long ago, he became an exceptionally skillful varmint caller, and anyone who can bring raccoons, coyotes, foxes, and bobcats within rock-tossing range is going to be tempted to try bowhunting. He not only tried it but became unusually adept and eventually wrote a highly-praised book entitled *Bow Hunter's Guide*. A Texan with a Texas-size grin, Russ is outdoor columnist for the Austin *American Statesman*. He's also the author of countless magazine articles (no, I'm not going to list all those magazines again) and eight books on hunting, fishing, and other outdoor activities. Which reminds me, he and his good friend Murry Burnham have written a book, *Murry Burnham's Hunting Secrets*, published by Winchester Press. Most readers know Murry as a famous hunter and maker of fine game calls and other hunting equipment. Russ says he's learned a tremendous amount from Murry, and Murry claims he's learned a great deal from Russ. Maybe that attitude is what makes them both such fine hunters.

Leonard M. Wright, Jr., is a problem writer. He's had a long, successful career as a promotion executive, doesn't have to write for a living, and doesn't like to write at all unless he feels he has something new or very useful to say. To make an editor's life yet more frustrating, he insists he's an angler first and hunter second—or maybe third. Only rarely does he write about hunting. His highly acclaimed books have included a ponderously titled but brilliant how-to manual, *Fishing the Dry Fly as a Living Insect*, and a couple with somewhat less daunting titles—*Fly-Fishing Heresies* and the *Winchester Press Fish-Finding Guide*. He has also written articles for a wide assortment of publications, including *Esquire*, *The New York Times*, and some of the aforementioned sporting magazines. But he doesn't usually write about one of his most polished skills: deer hunting. I talked him into it. I'm glad.

Jim Zumbo is Editor-at-Large for *Outdoor Life*. His hunting and fishing articles have also appeared in a many other outdoor magazines, and he's the author of an outstanding Winchester Press book, *Hunting America's Mule Deer*. Having said too much about him in the Introduction, I don't have much to add here. Perhaps just a couple of brief details. When I'm out with him, I always feel confident that at least one of us will kill a deer. He's been hunting practically all his life, and I don't know anyone who's better at it. What's more, when the day is done he smokes my cigars and I drink his whisky and neither of us keeps score. If you're looking for a hunting partner, that's the kind you want.

Lois Zumbo is Jim's wife. She hunts very well (but lets him do most of it); she fishes very well (but lets him do most of it); she even writes well (but lets him do most of it). She also cooks game exceptionally well, and once in a while she lets him do that, too, but more often she boots him out of the kitchen. If you're looking for a spouse, that's the kind you want.

Two more people—**Joy Flora** and **Rick Methot**—deserve a special acknowledgment here. For their extremely valuable editorial help in shaping this book, the word "thanks" is inadequate.

Index

Aagaard, Finn, 288
Access fee, 284
Adrenalin of deer, effect of, on taste of meat, 245
Aging deer meat, 140
Aiming rifles, 179, 249
Aimpoint sights, 96
Alabama, deer hunting in, 73-80, 163-166, 167, 168, **306-307**
Alaska, deer hunting in, 263-270, **306-307**
Alberta, Canada, 250
All-State Directory, Deer Hunter's, **306-327**
Antlerless hunts, 278
Antlers; *see also* Trophy buck
  rattling, in Southwestern states, 185-188
  symmetry of, 121-123
Appalachian Mountains, 150-161
Apple scent, 111
Archery; *see* Bowhunting
Arizona, deer hunting in, 180, 181, 183, 189, 190, 192, 198, 212-223, 240, 276, **307**
Arizona whitetail deer; *see* Coues whitetail deer
Arkansas, deer hunting in, 99, **307-308**
Arms, gear, and methods for hunting deer, 1-148
Arrows, 111, 112, 114, 223; *see also* Bowhunting
Aspen forests, hunting mule deer in, 238, 241
Atcheson, Jack, 276
Autoloaders, 5-6, 13, 95
Avery Island whitetail deer (*Odocoileus virginianus meilhennyi*), 207
Axis deer (*Axis axis*), 280-281, 284, 285, 286-288

Backpack for still-hunting, 41-42
Backtracking in snow, 37
Badlands National Monument, 248
Baker, Lew, 170, 172, 176
Baldwin, Don, 247
Barasingha, 282
Bashline, L. James, 151, 153, 155, 328
Bauer, Erwin A., 328-329
Bear, Fred, 108
Bedding site, scouting, 24-25
Big Bend National Park, 206, 207
Binoculars, 14-21, 221-223, 247
Black Hills National Forest, 193, 195
Blackbeard Island whitetail deer (*Odocoileus virginianus nigribarbis*), 207-209
Blackbuck, Indian, 283
Blackhawk, Ruger, 93
Blacktail deer, 11-13, 253-262
  alarm reaction of, 255, 257-258
  clothing for hunting, 260
  Columbian; *see* Columbian blacktail deer
  driving, 258
  rifles for, 11-13, 260-261
  scouting for, 262
  Sitka; *see* Sitka blacktail deer
  tracks of, 27, 28
  trophy buck, 122, 130-131
Blind, high, 183-184, 185, 187, 188; *see also* Stand-hunting with deer stand
Blowflies and deer meat, 138-139
Bobcat, 223
Boddington, Craig, 287, 329
Bolt-action rifle, 6, 9-10, 179
Booking agent, 275
Boone and Crockett Club, 118, 120-123, 205
Bow, 112, 224; *see also* Bowhunting
  compound, 113
  longbow, 117
  recurve, 109
  silencer for, 109
  stabilizer for, 224
Bowhunting, 108-117
  arrows for, 111, 112, 114, 223
  bow for; *see* Bow
  camouflage for, 109, 110, 117
  for desert mule deer, 223
  equipment for, 112
  for grain-belt mule deer, 248
  "jumping the string" in, 109, 111-112
  for mule deer, 110-111
  range of, 110
  scents for, 111
  for Sitka blacktail deer, 268
  stand for, 111
  for whitetail deer, 110-111
Bowsight, 224
Box Elder Country, Utah, 120
Brakefield, Tom, 60, 329
Bridger Mountains, 226
Brush, hunting mule deer in, 240-241
Brush Country, Texas, 180-182, 183-184, 189, 191
Brush rifle, 178-179
Brush-busting, 160, 168
Buck, trophy; *see* Trophy buck
Buck rub, 26-30, 41, 54, 174-175
Buckshot, 8, 78-79, 166-167
Buckskins, 140-143
Bullets; *see* Cartridges
Bull's Island whitetail deer (*Odocoileus virginianus tourinsulae*), 207
Burnett County, Wisconsin, 124
Burnham, Murry, 333-334
Burris, Doug, Jr., 125

"Cactus horns," 121-122
Caliber of rifle for deer hunting, 11
  for blacktail deer, 261
  in Eastern states, 160
  for mule deer, 100-101, 104, 222, 232-233
  for West Coast blacktail deer, 261
California, deer hunting in, 204, 253-262, 289, **308**
California mule deer, distribution of, 279
Calling Sitka blacktail deer, 266-267
Camouflage, 50-51, 56, 109, 110, 117, 213
Camp, outfitter's, 272, 274
Camp care, 138-139; *see also* Field-dressing
Canada, 72-73, 78, 175, 250
Canoe float trip, scouting by, 175
Caping; *see* Taxidermy
Carbines, 5, 6
Carmen Mountains whitetail deer (*Odocoileus virginianus carminis*), 182, 190, 194, 206, 207
Carmichel, Jim, 58, 329
Cartier, John, 175-176
Cartridge
  "deer," 4-5
  for handguns, 87, 88, 89-90
  for mule deer, 9
  for whitetail deer, 4-5, 7
Cedar scent, 111
Cedros Island mule deer, distribution of, 279
Chinese sika deer, 290
Chital, Indian, 281, 283, 286; *see also* Axis deer
Clear-cuts and West Coast blacktail deer, 256, 257
Clemons Tree Farm, 254
Clothing for deer hunting
  in desert, 215, 222
  for still-hunting, 39-41, 46
  for blacktail deer, 260
  woolen, 143, 269

Colorado, deer hunting in, 125, 192, 193, 199, 235-236, 239-240, 252, 272, 292, **308-309**
Colt Python, 93
Columbian blacktail deer (*Odocoileus hemionus columbianus*), 253-262
  distribution of, 278, 279
  Sitka blacktail deer distinguished from, 263
Columbian whitetail deer (*Odocoileus virginianus leucurus*), 192, 205-207
Compass, 33, 34, 261
Connecticut, deer hunting in, **309**
Cook, Sammy, 251
Cooling, hanging deer for, 139, 141, 142, 146-147
Coues, Elliott, 198
Coues whitetail deer (*Odocoileus virginianus couesi*), 183, 189, 190, 198-199, 207
  trophy buck, 122, 128-129
Cox, Bill, 292
Coyotes and desert mule deer, 223
Crosshairs, 18, 20, 42
Czura, Pete, 196

Dakota whitetail deer (*Odocoileus virginianus Dakota*), 193, 205
Dalrymple, Byron W., 185, 194, 329-330
Dan Wesson .44 Magnum, 94
Darner, Kirt, 23, 119, 123
Day-pack for still-hunting, 41-42
De Voto, Bernard, 143
Deer
  arms, gear, and methods for, 1-148
  axis, 280-281, 284, 285, 286-288
  blacktail; *see* Blacktail deer
  driving; *see* Driving deer
  exotic, 280-292
  hanging for cooling, 139, 141, 142, 146-147
  hauling out, 134-136
  mule; *see* Mule deer
  quartering, 138, 141
  rifles and shotguns for, 3-13
  skinning, 135-136
  spotting before they see you, 45
  weight of, 147-148
  whitetail; *see* Whitetail deer
Deer bed, scouting, 25
Deer dogs, 71-80, 166-167
Deer Hunter's All-State Directory, 306-327
  in Alabama, 73-80, 163-166, 167, 168, **306-307**
  in Alaska, 263-270, **306-307**
  in Arizona, 180, 181, 183, 189, 190, 192, 198, 212-223, 240, 276, **307**
  in Arkansas, 99, **307-308**
  in Canada, 72-73, 78, 175, 250
  in California, 204, 253-262, 289, **308**
  in Colorado, 125, 192, 193, 199, 235-236, 239-240, 252, 272, 292, **308-309**
  in Connecticut, **309**
  in Delaware, **309**
  in Eastern states; *see* Eastern states, deer hunting in, 150-161
  fee, 182, 190, 284
  in Florida, 73-80, 163, 168, 203, 209, **309-310**
  in Georgia, 73-80, 150, 166-167, 168, 208-209, **310**
  in Hawaiian Islands, 286, 287
  in Idaho, 192, 193, 199, 274, 276, **310-311**
  in Illinois, **311**
  in Indiana, **311-312**
  in Iowa, **312**
  in Kansas, 251-252, **312**
  in Kentucky, 167, 168, 170, 177, 289, **312-313**
  leased, 163-167, 182
  in Louisiana, **313**
  in Maine, 150, 151, 153, 159, **313-314**
  in Maryland, 159, **314**
  in Massachusetts, **314**
  in Mexico, 198
  in Michigan, 176, **314-315**
  Midwestern; *see* Midwestern deer hunting
  in Minnesota, 170, 172, 178, **315**
  in Mississippi, 73-80, 166-167, **315-316**
  in Missouri, 121, 176, **316**
  in Montana, 192, 193, 195, 196-198, 199, 224, 226, 228, 244, 252, 275, 276, **316-317**
  in Nebraska, 251-252, **317**
  in Nevada, 240, 273-274, 276, **317**
  in New Hampshire, **318**
  in New Jersey, 59-62, 150, 153, 154, 201, 203-204, **318**
  in New Mexico, 121, 180, 181, 183, 189, 190, 192, 198, 240, **319**
  in New York, 150, 159, **319**
  in North Carolina, 168, **320**
  in North Dakota, 248, 251, **320**
  in Ohio, 159, 170, **320-321**
  in Oklahoma, 180, 181, 189, 190, 191, **321**
  in Oregon, 253-262, **321-322**
  in Pennsylvania, 150, 152, 154, 157, 159-160, 289, 290, 292, **322**
  in Rhode Island, **322**
  in Rocky Mountain states, 224-234
  in Saskatchewan, 121
  in South Carolina, 207, **323**
  in South Dakota, 246, 248, 251-252, **323**
  in Southeastern states, 73-74, 162-169
  in Southern states; *see* Southern states, deer hunting in
  in Southwestern states; *see* Southwestern states, deer hunting in
  in Tennessee, 67, 167, 168, 177, 289, **323-324**
  in Texas, 123, 146, 163, 180-191, 207, 282-292, **324**
  in Utah, 106, 120, 239-240, **324-325**
  in Vermont, 150, 289, **325**
  in Virginia, 168, 169, **325**
  in Washington, 192, 199, 253-262, **325-326**
  in West Virginia, **326**
  in Wisconsin, 124, **326-327**
  in Wyoming, 192, 193, 195, 252, 276, **327**
Deer jacking, 175
Deer meat; *see* Venison
Deer rub, 26-30, 41, 54, 174-175
Deer stand; *see* Stand-hunting
Deerskin, 138, 140-143
Delaware, deer hunting in, **309**
Desert mule deer; *see* Mule deer, desert
Dog-hunting, 71-80, 166-167
Dolan Creek Ranch, 182, 189
Dolores County, Colorado, 125
Dot reticle, 18-19, 20, 42
Doyle, John, 198
Dragging deer, 136
Driving deer, 58-70
  artificial noisemakers and, 60
  backstops in, 61-62
  blacktail deer, 258
  in early morning, 68-69
  in Eastern states, 154, 155-156
  horses in, 67
  midday, 69
  in Midwest, 175
  mule deer, 64, 66-68
  pebble-tossing in, 69
  in snow, 65
  strategic stands in, 66
  Western whitetail deer, 198
Droppings, scouting, 25
Dry leaves, still-hunting in, 45-46
Dual-thickness crosshair reticle, 7-8, 10, 18, 20-21, 42
Dybowski's sika deer, 290

Eagle Rock Ranch, 292
Eastern states, deer hunting in, 150-161
  brush-busting and, 160

driving in, 154, 155-156
hunting pressure in, 152
permission for, 153-155
private land in, 153-155
public land in, 153
rifles for, 160
stand-hunting in, 151, 152
still-hunting in, 151, 152, 156-160
stump hunter and, 155, 156-157
success ratio of, 152
tracking in, 157-159
watch-and-wait method of, 155
Edwards Plateau, Texas, 181
Elevated deer stand, 49-51, 53, 111; *see also* Stand-hunting with deer stand
Elliot, D. G., 255
Elman, Ellen, 110
Elman, Robert, 47, 52-53, 134, 154, 188, 218, 330
Exotic deer, 280-292
Exotic hunting industry, 283-284
Exotic Wildlife Association, 284, 285
Extended eye relief (EER) scope, 96

Fadala, Sam, 330
Fair chase, definition of, 285
Fallow deer (*Dama dama*), 282, 284, 288-289
Fantail; *see* Coues whitetail deer
Fee hunting, 182, 190, 284
Ferber, Steve, 330
Field-dressing, 134-143, 144-148
bleeding deer, 134-135
blowflies and, 138-139
and camp care, venison, and buckskins, 134-143
"fisting" hide, 138
hanging deer for cooling, 139, 141, 142, 146-147
hauling deer out, 134-136
skinning and quartering deer, 135-136
sticking knives, 134-135, 144
transporting meat home, 139
trophies, 138
weight of deer, 147-148
Finegan, John, 189
Flintlock; *see* Muzzleloaders
Float trip, canoe, scouting by, 175
Florida, deer hunting in, 73-80, 163, 168, 203, 209, **309-310**
Florida coastal whitetail deer (*Odocoileus virginianus osceola*), 209
Florida whitetail deer (*Odocoileus virginianus seminolus*), 208-209
Forest
aspen, 238, 241
pinyon-juniper, 239-240, 241
succession stages of, 256-257
Formosan sika deer, 290
Four-wheel drive vehicle, 271-272
French River, Ontario, 78

Game bags, 138
Game-proof fence, 284, 285
Gardner, Dan, 106
Gear, arms, and methods for all-American deer, 1-148
Georgia, deer hunting in, 73-80, 150, 166-167, 168, 208-209, **310**
Good, Bob, 10, 87, 90, 94, 193, 331
Good, Robert, 92
Greenwood Valley Ranch, 288
Guides, 271-276

Handguns and handgun hunting, 81-88, 89-98, 222-223
aimpoint sights, 96
attitude of animal, 84
automatics, 95
barrel lengths, 94
bullets, 88
cartridges, 89-90
competitive, 83
ear protectors, 95-96
electronic aiming devices, 96
grips, 95
handloading cartridges, 87
holster, 86, 96-98
open sights, 83
powder, 87-88
practicing, 81-82
range, 84
running shots, 84
scents for hunting, 98
scope sights, 87, 96
shooting rest, 82-83, 85
sight alignment, 82
single-shot pistols, 92
steady hold, 82-83
trigger pull, 95
two-handed hold, 82-83, 85
venting, 95
Hanging deer for cooling, 139, 141, 142, 146-147
Harrison, George, 157
Hauling deer, 134-136
Hawaiian Islands, 286, 287
Herrett, Steve, 92
.30 Herrett, 92
.357 Herrett, 92
"High sits," 183-184
Hill Country, Texas, 181-182, 187, 282, 284
Hilton Head Island whitetail deer (*Odocoileus virginianus hiltonensis*), 207
Hogue, Lorry, 39
Holster for handgun, 86, 96-98
Horses, 67, 136, 219-221, 273
Hughes, Bill R., 101, 331
Hunsacker, Alton, 120
Hunt, Fernne, 288
Hunt, Jeff, 288
Hunting clubs in Southern states, 163-167, 169
Hunting consultant, 275
Hunting Island whitetail deer (*Odocoileus virginianus venatorius*), 207

Idaho, deer hunting in, 192, 193, 199, 274, 276, **310-311**
Illinois, deer hunting in, **311**
Indian blackbuck, 283
Indian chital, 281, 283, 286; *see also* Axis deer
Indian reservations, hunting deer on, 84, 121, 252
Indiana, deer hunting in, **311-312**
Iowa, deer hunting in, **312**
Iron sights, 7, 83, 105, 261
Isbell, Tex, 98

Japanese sika deer, 290
Jones, J. D., 90, 92
Jordan, James, 124, 205

Kaibab mule deer, 277
Kansas, deer hunting in, 251-252, **312**
Kansas whitetail deer (*Odocoileus virginianus macrourus*), 207, 208
Kaup, Carroll, 232
Kelly, Larry, 90
Kentucky, deer hunting in, 167, 168, 170, 177, 289, **312-313**
Kentucky Lake, 177
Key Deer National Wildlife Refuge, 209
Key whitetail deer (*Odocoileus virginianus clavium*), 203, 209
Koller, Larry, 52
Kranik, Andy, 292

La Pile Creek, Arkansas, 99
Lake Barkley, 177
Lanai, 286, 287
Land Between the Lakes, 177, 289
Leased hunting, 163-167, 182
Lever-action rifles, 5, 179
Lightsey Ranch, 286
Lincoln National Forest, 183
Long eye relief (LER) scope, 96
Longbow, 117
Long-range rifles, 178-179

Lost, how to avoid becoming, 31-37
Louisiana, deer hunting in, **313**
Lubricants for muzzleloaders, 101

Madson, John, 138, 144, 147, 331
Maine, deer hunting in, 150, 151, 153, 159, **313-314**
Mannlicher-stocked carbines, 5, 6
Maps, 33-34, 153
Marking trail, 37
Martin, Biddy, 218
Martin, Joe, 196
Maryland, deer hunting in, 159, **314**
Massachusetts, deer hunting in, **314**
Maxi-Ball, 101
Maxi-Lube, 101
McAllister Military Depot, Oklahoma, 181
McFall, Waddy F., 147
McKnight, Don, 331-332
Metatarsal glands, removal of, 135, 139, 146
Mexico, 198
Michigan, deer hunting in, 176, **314-315**
Midwestern deer hunting, 170-179
  canoe float trip, scouting by, 175
  driving in, 175
  preseason scouting, 174-175
  rifles for, 178-179
  stalking in, 175
  stand-hunting in, 175-176, 177-178
  still-hunting in, 175
  Milek, Bob, 90, 92
Minie ball, 101, 106
Minnesota, deer hunting in, 170, 172, 178, **315**
Mississippi, deer hunting in, 73-80, 166-167, **315-316**
Missouri, deer hunting in, 121, 176, **316**
Molokai, 286, 287
Montana, deer hunting in, 192, 193, 195, 196-198, 199, 224, 226, 228, 244, 252, 275, 276, **316-317**
Morgan Canyon, New Mexico, 84-86
Mountain Home, Texas, 288
Mountbatten, Pennsylvania, 292
Mule deer (*Odocoileus hemionus*), 8-11, 211-276
  alarm reaction of, 64, 66, 241, 255, 257
  bowhunting, 110-111, 223
  California, distribution of, 278-279
  Cedros Island, distribution of, 279
  desert, 212-223, 237
    binoculars and, 221-223
    bowhunting, 223
    clothing for hunting, 215, 222
    distribution of, 278-279
    handguns for, 222-223
    hunting on horseback, 219-221
    rifles for, 222
    scouting for, 222
    stand-hunting of, 217
    walking deer trails for, 217, 218, 221
  distinguishing Western whitetail deer from, 199
  distribution of, 277-279
  driving, 64, 66-68
  grain-belt, 242-252
    bowhunting, 248
    rifles for, 249-250
  high-country, 224-234
    hunter-success figures for, 226-228
    physical condition of hunter, 226
    rifles for, 232-234
    "sky-lighted" hunter and, 230
    snow and, 225
    stalking, 230-231
    stand-hunting of, 230
  Kaibab, 277
  low-down and middle-country, 235-241
    in aspen forests, 238, 241
    in desert environment, 237
    in high brush, 240-241
    in pinyon-juniper forests, 239-240, 241
    in sagebrush country, 237-239, 240
    waterholes and, 236, 237
  Peninsula, distribution of, 279
  rifles for, 9-13, 42
  Rocky Mountain, distribution of, 278, 279
  Southern, distribution of, 279
  Tiburon Island, distribution of, 278-279
  trophy buck, 119, 122
    nontypical, 120, 122, 132-133, 250
    typical, 122, 125, 130-131
Muzzleloaders, 99-107
  caliber of, 100-101, 104
  Civil War replicas 103
  cleaning, 106
  fouling barrel, 104
  loads for, 104
  lubricants for, 101
  Maxi-Ball for, 101
  Minie-Ball for, 101, 106
  patch lubricant for, 101
  patch material for, 104
  percussion caps for, 104
  powder for, 104, 106
  round balls for, 101, 104, 106
  scope for, 105
  sights for, 104-105
National Grasslands, 246
National monuments and parks, hunting mule deer in, 248
National Shooting Sports Foundation, 99
Nebraska, deer hunting in, 251-252, **317**
Nelson, Norm, 260, 332
Nevada, deer hunting in, 240, 273-274, 276, **317**
New Hampshire, deer hunting in, **318**
New Jersey, deer hunting in, 59-62, 150, 153, 154, 201, 203-204, **318**
New Mexico, deer hunting in, 121, 180, 181, 183, 189, 190, 192, 198, 240, **319**
New York, deer hunting in, 150, 159, **319**
Nontypical bucks; *see* Trophy buck
North Carolina, deer hunting in, 168, **320**
North Dakota, deer hunting in, 248, 251, **320**
North Star as guide, 36
Northern whitetail deer, 192-198
Northern woodland whitetail deer (*Odocoileus virginianus borealis*), 201, 203-204, 205
Northwest whitetail deer (*Odocoileus virginianus ochrourus*), 193, 204, 205

O'Connor, Jack, 178
Ohio, deer hunting in, 159, 170, **320-321**
Oklahoma, deer hunting in, 180, 181, 189, 190, 191, **321**
Olympic Mountains, 255
Open sights, 13, 83
Optics for hunting deer, 14-21
Oregon, deer hunting in, 253-262, **321-322**
Ouachita National Forest, 181, 190
Outfitters, 274-276

Page, Warren, 59-60
Park, Ed, 198
Parks, national, hunting mule deer in, 248
Pawlak, Dan, 104
Peninsula mule deer, distribution of, 279
Pennsylvania, deer hunting in, 150, 152, 154, 157, 159-160, 289, 290, 292, **322**
Pennsylvania Gamelands, 63-63
Percussion rifle, 102-103, 106; *see also* Muzzleloaders

Petzal, David, 332
Physical condition of hunter, 123-124, 226
Pine Ridge Reservation, 251
Pinyon-juniper forests, 68, 239-240, 241
Pistol, single-shot, 92
Ponderosa Hunts, 292
Popowski, Bert, 332-333
Porro prism binoculars, 15-16
Portable deer stand, 49-50, 53; *see also* Stand-hunting
Post reticle, 18, 20, 42
Preseason scouting, 22-30, 54-56, 174-175, 189, 262
Private land, 153-155, 182
Public land, 153, 182
Pump-action rifles, 179
Pyle, Wilf, 332

Quail call, calling Sitka blacktail deer with, 267
Quartering deer, 138, 141

Rack of trophy buck, 118-133
Rattling antlers, 185-188
Recipes for venison, 293-305
Records of North American Big Game, 120-123
Recurve bow, 109
Red deer (*Cervus elaphus*), 282, 291-292
Redhawk, Ruger, 93
Revolvers, 88
Rhode Island, deer hunting in, **322**
Rhodes, Raymond, 103
Reticle, 7-8, 17-19, 20, 42, 261
  crosshairs, 18, 20, 42, 261
  dot, 18-19, 20, 42, 261
  dual-thickness crosshairs, 18, 20-21, 42, 261
  Duplex, 10
  post, 18, 20, 42, 261
Rifled slugs, 8-9, 166-167
Rifles, 3-13, 178-179
  aiming, 179
  bolt-action, 6, 9-10, 179
  for blacktail deer, 11-13, 260-261
  in brush, 178-179
  caliber of, 11
  for desert mule deer, 222
  in Eastern states, 160
  for grain-belt mule deer, 249-250
  for high-country mule deer, 232-233
  lever-action, 179
  long-range, 178-179
  in Midwest, 178-179
  for mule deer, 10-13, 42
  pump-action, 179
  semi-automatic, 179
  for Sitka blacktail deer, 266, 268
  in Southern states, 163, 167, 168
  in Southwestern states, 190
  for still-hunting, 5, 42
  for whitetail deer, 42, 199
Robinson, Les, 292
Rocky Mountain mule deer, distribution of, 278, 279
Rocky Mountain states, 224-234
Rogers, Robert, 288
Roof prism binoculars, 15-16
Rub; *see* Buck rub
Rue, Leonard Lee, 50, 100, 201, 208, 259, 277, 278, 333
Ruger Blackhawk, 93
Ruger Redhawk, 93
Ruger Super Blackhawk, 93

Sambar, 282
Saskatchewan, Province of, 121
Scents, 53-54, 98, 111
  apple, 111
  cedar, 111
  skunk, 98, 111
Scope, 168
  binoculars and, 16, 18-21
  for blacktail deer, 13, 260, 261
  for handguns, 96
  for mule deer, 10, 233-234
  for muzzleloaders, 105
  power of, 20
  see-through mounts for, 13, 21
  silhouette, 96
  spotting, 19, 21
  for still-hunting, 42
  swing-away, 13, 21, 261
  variable, 20, 260, 261
  waterproof, 21
  for whitetail deer, 7, 199
Scope caps, 13, 21
Scoring charts for trophy bucks
  nontypical mule deer, 132-133
  nontypical whitetail and Coues deer, 128-129
  typical mule and blacktail deer, 130-131
  typical whitetail and Coues deer, 126-127
Scouting, 22-30
  bedding site, 24-25
  buck vs. doe tracks, 24
  buck rub, 26-30, 41, 54, 174-175
  in desert, 222
  droppings, 25
  preseason, 22-30, 54-56, 174-175, 189, 262
  scrapes, 30, 54
  sign of recent browsing, 25-26
  snow, 23-24
  tracks, 23-24
  vehicles for, 196
Self-climbing deer platform, 49-50
Semi-automatic rifles, 179
Shooting rest for handgun hunting, 82-83, 85
Shotguns for deer, 3-13, 160
Sight
  aimpoint, 96
  alignment of, in handgun hunting, 82
  for blacktail deer, 13, 261
  iron, 7, 83, 105, 261
  for mule deer, 104-105
  open, 13
  for whitetail deer, 7, 8
Sign, checking for, 171
Sika deer (*Cervus nippon*), 282, 284, 285, 289-291
Sitka blacktail deer (*Odocoileus hemionus sitkensis*), 263-270
  in alpine summer ranges, 265-266
  bowhunting, 268
  calling, 266-267
  clothing for hunting, 269
  distinguished from Columbian blacktail deer, 263
  distribution of, 279
  rifles for, 266, 268
  still-hunting and calling, 266-267
Skinning deer, 135-136, 138, 141
Slugs, rifled, 8-9, 166-167
Smith & Wesson Model 57, 90-91, 93, 95
Snow
  backtracking in, 37
  driving deer in, 65
  and hunting high-country mule deer, 225
  scouting in, 23-24
  still-hunting in, 45, 46
Snyder, Howard, 159-160
South Carolina, deer hunting in, 207, **323**
South Dakota, deer hunting in, 246, 248, 251-252, **323**
Southeastern states, deer hunting in, 73-74, 162-169
Southern mule deer, distribution of, 279
Southern states, deer hunting in, 71-80, 162-169
  brush-busting and, 168
  hunting clubs in, 163-167, 169
  leased hunting in, 163-167
  rifles in, 163, 166-167, 168
Southwestern states, deer hunting in, 180-191
  day hunting in, 182
  fee hunting in, 182, 190

leased hunting in, 182
package hunts in, 182, 189-190
private land in, 182
public land in, 182
rattling antlers in, 185-188
rifles for, 190
stand-hunting in, 183-184, 185, 187, 188-189
walking in, 188-189
Spannagel, Eli, 232
Spotting scope, 19, 21
Stalking, 49, 175, 230-231
Stand-hunting
with deer stand, 48-57
for bowhunting, 111
camouflage for, 50-51
elevated , 49-51, 53
ground-level, 51, 111
natural, 52-53
portable, 49-50, 53
scent in, 53-54
self-climbing platform, 49-50
stump as, 52-53
of desert mule deer, 217
in Eastern states, 151, 152
of high-country mule deer, 230
in Midwest, 175-176, 177-178
in sagebrush country, 237-239
in Southwestern states, 183-184, 185, 187, 188-189
of Western whitetail deer, 193
Still-hunting, 38-47, 65
above major rise or ledge, 46-47
binoculars for, 18
in dry leaves, 45-46
in Eastern states, 151, 152, 156-160
equipment for, 39-44
footwear for, 39-40, 46
location for, 44-45
in Midwest, 175
rifles for, 5, 42
for Sitka blacktail deer, 267
in snow, 45, 46
speed of, 45
Strung, Norman, 10, 233, 332
"Stump-sitters," 52-53, 155, 156-157
Sun as guide, 36
Sundra, Jon, 291
Swallow, Johnny, 251

Tallow, 249
Tanning buckskins, 143
Taxidermy, 144-148
Tennessee, deer hunting in, 67, 167, 168, 177, 289, **323-324**
Texas, deer hunting in, 123, 146, 163, 180-191, 207, 282-292, **324**
Texas Hunting Services, 288
Texas whitetail deer (*Odocoileus virginianus texanus*), 207
Theodore Roosevelt National Monument, 248
Thompson/Center Contender, 90, 91, 92, 96-97
Tracking, New England method of, 157-158
Tiburn Island mule deer, distribution of, 278-279
Tinsley, Russell, 109, 116, 333-334
Towers in Southwestern States, 183-184, 185, 187, 188; *see also* Stand-hunting
Tracks, scouting for, 23-24, 27, 28, 157-159, 174, 175
Trespass fee, 284
Trophy fee, 284
Trophy buck, 118-133, 205
blacktail deer, 122
Coues whitetail deer, 122
mule deer, 119, 120, 122, 125, 250
rack of, 118-133
scoring charts for; *see* Scoring charts for trophy bucks
symmetry of antlers of, 121-123
whitetail, 118-119, 121-122, 124, 155

Utah, deer hunting in, 106, 120, 239-240, **324-325**

Vehicle for hunting deer, 196, 271-272
Venison, 138, 139-140
aging at home, 140
flavor of, 242-245
grain-belt, quality of, 242-245
preventing hair from getting on, 135, 144-146
recipes for, 293-305
trading at locker plant, 140
transporting home, 139
Venting of handgun, 95
Vermont, deer hunting in, 150, 289, **325**
Virginia, deer hunting in, 168, 169, **325**
Virginia whitetail deer (*Odocoileus virginianus virginianus*), 202, 204-205

Walking deer trails, 188-189, 217-218, 221, 237-239
Walking staff, 221
"Walk-the-washes" plan for hunting desert mule deer, 217-218, 221
Washington, deer hunting in, 192, 199, 253-262, **325-326**
Watch-and-wait hunting in Eastern states, 155
Waterholes, mule deer near, 236, 237
Waterproof scope, 21
Wenmohs, Jerry, 115-117
West Virginia, deer hunting in, **326**
Western whitetail deer; *see* Whitetail deer, Western
White River National Forest, 272
Whitetail deer (*Odocoileus virginianus*), 149-209
Arizona; *see* Coues whitetail deer
Avery Island, 207
Blackbeard Island, 207-209
bowhunting, 110-111
Bull's Island, 207
Carmen Mountains, 190, 194, 206, 207
Columbian, 192, 205-207
Coues, 126-127, 189, 190, 198-199, 207
Dakota, 193, 205
distribution of, 277-279
Florida, 208-209
Florida coastal, 209
Hilton Head Island, 207
Hunting Island, 207
Kansas, 207, 208
Key, 203, 209
Northern woodland, 201, 203-204, 205
Northwestern, 193, 204, 205
rifles for, 3-9, 42
subspecies of, 200-209
Texas, 207
trophy bucks, 118-119
nontypical, 121, 122, 128-129, 155
typical, 121-122, 124, 126-127
Virginia, 202, 204-205
Western, 192-199
Coues; *see* Coues whitetail deer
distinguishing from mule deer, 199
driving, 198
northern, 192-198
rifles for, 199
stand-hunting of, 193
still-hunting of, 195
Wild Hill Preserve, 289
Winchester Model 70 Rifle, 4, 12
Winchester .30-.30, 94
Winchester 196 powder for handguns, 88
Wind Cave, 248
Wisconsin, deer hunting in, 124, **326-327**
Woolen clothing, 143, 269
Wright, Leonard M., Jr., 58, 334
Wyoming, deer hunting in, 192, 193, 195, 252, 276, **327**

Y. O. Ranch, 62, 182, 283-284, 291

Zumbo, Jim, 10-11, 12, 66, 158-159, 241, 334
Zumbo, Lois, 334